JOHN BURROUGHS
AN AMERICAN NATURALIST

JOHN BURROUGHS

AN AMERICAN NATURALIST

Edward J. Renehan, Jr.

BLACK·DOME

Black Dome Press Corp.
RR 1, Box 422
Hensonville, New York 12439

Published by
Black Dome Press Corp.
RR1, Box 422
Hensonville, New York 12439
Tel: (518) 734-6357
Fax: (518) 734-5802

Originally published by Chelsea Green Publishing Company,
Post Mills, Vermont
Copyright © 1992 by Edward J. Renehan, Jr.

First Paperback Edition 1998

ISBN 1-883789-16-8

Library of Congress Cataloging-in-Publication Data

Renehan, Edward, 1956-
    John Burroughs: an American naturalist/by Edward J.
Renehan, Jr. — 1st paperback ed.
    p. cm.
    Includes bibliographical references (p.   ) and index.
    ISBN 1-883789-16-8
    1. Burroughs, John, 1837-1921 — Biography. 2. Authors,
American — 19th century — Biography. 3. Naturalists — United
States — Biography. I. Title.
    [PS1226.R46 1998]
    508.73'092 — dc21
    [B}   98-15903
                                                    CIP

Printed in the USA

Dedicated to my parents,
with love and thanks.

— E. J. R.

ACKNOWLEDGMENTS

AT THE END OF any project such as this, one is left with many debts for wise counsel and generous help along the way. Here I am pleased to acknowledge these debts with gratitude.

First and foremost, I must thank Elizabeth Burroughs Kelley and Ursula Burroughs Love, granddaughters of John Burroughs, who have shown me every kindness during the more than twelve years that I have involved myself in the study of Burroughs and his era. These women spent their childhoods in West Park, New York, close to their grandfather's busy presence. They were young women at the time of his death. They knew him well, and generously shared their wealth of recollections with me. Elizabeth Kelley is herself a fine writer and the author of an intimate portrait of her grandfather. Entitled *John Burroughs, Naturalist* and first published in 1959, the book is an essential resource for any serious student of Burroughs. Another Burroughs family member who has helped through the years with both information and friendship is Joan Chamberlin, a great-great-granddaughter.

Professors Alfred H. Marks and H. R. Stoneback of the State University of New York at New Paltz, and Professor Frank Bergon of Vassar, have performed important ground-breaking scholarship on Burroughs and his era, scholarship without which this book would certainly have been the less. Professors Marks and Stoneback read and commented on early drafts of this manuscript. The late Robert Penn Warren read a few very early drafts of sections of this book when first composed as essays and articles more than a decade ago.

Winthrop Aldrich, devoted champion of all things related to Hudson Valley history and culture, petitioned for this book in a conversation more than twelve years ago and thus sparked my first serious research. Kingdon Gould, Jr., great-grandson of Burroughs's boyhood friend Jay Gould, provided generous assistance, as did Professor Maury Klein of the University of Rhode Island, author of the most definitive biography of Gould to date. The late Lewis Mumford and his wife Sophia took time to help me get acquainted with their neighborhood of Amenia Junction, Leedsville, New York, where Burroughs's friend Myron Benton spent most of his life.

I could not have written this book without drawing on the resources of the Vassar College Library (Special Collections), The New York Public Library (Henry and Albert Berg Collection), and the Clifton Waller Barrett Library at the University of Virginia, which are the three principal repositories for Burroughs materials. Also of tremendous value have been the Bienicke Collection at the Yale University Library, the Manuscript Division of The Library of Congress (chief repository for Whitman material, including the Feinberg Collection), and the special collections of the Houghton and Widener Libraries at Harvard University, the Henry Huntington Library, the New York Historical Society, and the Pierpont Morgan Library.

For encouragement and continuous faith I thank my publishers, Ian and Margo Baldwin of Chelsea Green. The book was made better by deft editorial suggestions from Helen Whybrow and Jim Schley, both of Chelsea Green. Ann Aspell is responsible for the book's superb interior design. I am indebted to my friend Christopher Bentley who read parts of this manuscript and accompanied me on successive climbs of Burroughs's two favorite mountains: Slide and Wittenberg, in the Catskills. My brother, James Renehan, joined me on an exploration of the Burroughs homestead farm and Burroughs's "home" mountain—Old Clump—at Roxbury, New York. H. R. Stoneback came along on a two-day hike tracing the course of Black Creek, one of Burroughs's favorite trout streams, from its source in Clintondale, New York, to its junction with the Hudson due north of Burroughs's West Park farm. An acknowledgment here also for my nephew, Jamison Ruby, who has helped inspire me to many things, just one of them being the completion of this book.

Last, but certainly not least, my gratitude and love go to my wife Christa, son William, and daughter Katherine, who allowed the ghost of John Burroughs to haunt our home and who tolerated the distraction the wily old spook often caused in me.

E. J. R.
Lynbrook, New York
July 14, 1992

CONTENTS

PROLOGUE:
JOHN THE BAPTIST

*Nature love . . . does not come to a man or woman who is wholly absorbed
in selfish or worldly or material ends. Except ye become in a measure as little
children, ye cannot enter the kingdom of Nature—as Audubon entered it, as
Thoreau entered it, as Bryant and Amiel entered it, and as all those enter it
who make it a resource in their lives and an instrument of their culture.*

— *"The Gospel of Nature," in the 1912 book*
Time and Change

BEGINNING NOT LONG AFTER the end of the Civil War and continuing through the first decade of the twentieth century, it was much
the fashion of the American upper and middle classes to hike, watch
birds, and in other ways seek out and enjoy wild nature. The same
affluent Easterners who purchased books and read literary magazines such as *Scribner's* and the *Atlantic Monthly* also set great store
in country houses, gardens, and annual vacations that included
hiking in the Catskills or the Berkshires. As the American industrial
state expanded in the years after the Civil War, it created a new
middle class with the wherewithal and leisure to pursue picturesque
rural nature. At the same time it spawned the growth of sprawling
urban landscapes, adding further incentive for citizens of the new
middle class to seek nature. Through his more than two dozen
popular books of nature essays, the first of which was published in
1871, John Burroughs provided a steady stream of encouragement,
instruction, and inspiration for men and women of the educated
classes who chose to take up hiking and nature study as an antidote
to a society increasingly mortgaged to the advance of technology and
the rise of cities.

As Lewis Mumford has suggested, the golden day of America's

promising rural agrarian civilization was cut short by the Civil War and subsequently undermined as manufacturing interests drew men away from the country to growing metropolitan centers. This deterioration of local country life during the brown decades of industrialization that followed the Civil War was accompanied by a general devastation of the natural environment.[1] John Burroughs gently suggested in his writings that he thought it better for one to live in the country, on a farm, than in the city. He quietly let it be known that industrial pursuits were probably not very healthy for either mind or body. He occasionally proposed that only local, agricultural economies could be counted on to forge a way of life that honestly tended toward the good of all and did not, as Burroughs's acquaintance Henry Demarest Lloyd put it, pit "wealth against commonwealth." But Burroughs never made it his mission to sing this message too loudly; he never made it his business to drive the point home in unequivocal terms. Only at the end of his last unhappy decade, at the start of the 1920s and the dawn of the Jazz Age, would the aged and sickly Burroughs scan with sad eloquence the modern American horizon of smokestacks and slums—what he came to call "the devil's laboratory"—and publicly mourn the fate of the world as industrial science began to outpace humankind's capacity to use its results wisely.[2]

John Burroughs was the immediate contemporary of the robber barons who fathered the brownstone and cast-iron urbanization of the post-Civil War expansion. He had been born in the same decade as virtually all the tycoons who rose to define the values, mores, and industrial pace of the era. Burroughs was born in 1837. One year before him, in the same Catskill village, Jay Gould first saw the light of the world. Andrew Carnegie was born in 1835, J. P. Morgan in 1837, and John D. Rockefeller in 1839. Two other contemporaries, Mark Twain and Charles Dudley Warner, supplied a name for the epoch these moguls came to define in the title of their 1873 book, *The Gilded Age.* Twain and Warner saw the decades that these men shaped as being characterized by money lust, hardness, and cynicism. It was a time, in Twain's words, "of incredible rottenness."[3] Burroughs's close friend Walt Whitman expressed a similar emotion in *Democratic Vistas,* where he wrote, "The depravity of the business classes of our country is not less than has been supposed, but infinitely greater." [4]

In his most perceptive moments, Burroughs cited a direct link between the frantic urge for money getting and the alienation of man from nature. The chief business of America in the latter half of the nineteenth century was the taming and plundering of the wild landscape. The great fortunes were all based on either harvesting the natural wealth of the country in oil, coal, and lumber, or on building the industrial infrastructure of the railroads and cities that was so quickly displacing forest and meadow. Burroughs wrote in a letter to his friend, the farmer and poet Myron Benton, that he believed the removal of populations from the country to the city was "nothing short of a spiritual catastrophe." The migration from rural districts to urban neighborhoods and pursuits signaled for Burroughs the loss of a sense of place—the all-important umbilical between man and land with which he believed the soul thrived and without which it withered. [5]

Burroughs often used the metaphor of the steam locomotive to represent the monolithic machine that was all things industrial and urban. The steam train sliced through the virgin forests like a knife and put riders in a false relationship with the reality of the natural world. "We are removed from nature and life by the whole distance of our wealth and refinement," he wrote in his journal on January 17, 1866. "The earth is overlaid with inventions and improvements . . . A man may live now and travel without hardly coming in contact with the earth or air. He can go around the world in a parlor. Life is intensely artificial . . . The ambition now is to get wealth and die a Christian—become rats if necessary to achieve these ends." [6]

These words were penned early in life. The mature, less idealistic Burroughs was no muckraker. Quite to the contrary, he generally respected wealth and those who possessed it. Although he had reservations about the way in which "the greed of the capital" (as he called it in one uncharacteristic magazine article) dictated the course of the nation's progress, he generally did not use the pulpit of publication to lobby against the status quo. [7] Burroughs counted among his personal friends many of the fathers of the American industrial state, including Jay Gould, Andrew Carnegie, E. H. Harriman, Henry Ford, and Thomas Edison. By and large, Burroughs's essays encouraged a garden-style nature appreciation that was not threatening to these barons of mechanization. Jay Gould, who made his first small fortune destroying the forests of the Catskills in the tannery business and then made a far larger fortune speculating in railroad stocks and bonds, was a devoted reader of the essays written by his old friend of boyhood, John Burroughs. Ford and Edison fancied themselves amateur ornithologists, and made pilgrimages to the Catskills to spot birds with Burroughs.

In 1913 Henry Ford joined Burroughs in petitioning Congress to support the Weakes-McLean bill for the protection of endangered species. At the same time that he lobbied in Washington for passage of the new law, Ford was in the midst of planning a major industrial complex which would require the destruction of over one thousand acres of wild marshland beside Detroit's Rouge River. Andrew Carnegie, who had turned the skyline of Pittsburgh into a dark palisade of smokestacks, donated money to the New York City school system to purchase volumes of Burroughs's nature essays for inner-city youths. The railroad magnate E. H. Harriman brought Burroughs along as one of several naturalists-in-residence for his expedition to Alaska in 1899—a trip concerned with identifying the natural resources of the territory with an eye toward development and exploitation rather than preservation.

Despite the fact that he was generally mute with regard to the industrial excesses of his era, there is one important thing that redeems Burroughs. In essay after essay, he tried to instill a new, modern element of faith into the faithless decades of the Gilded Age. In their novel, *The Gilded Age*, Twain and Warner proposed that the country as a whole had entered into a malaise defined entirely by the worship and pursuit of money. Twain suggested that like the heroes of another civilization, America's multi-millionaires were being made into pharaohs. Their pyramids were the iron rail lines they laid, the steel suspension bridges they built, and the factories where many labored for the aggrandizement of the few. The agnostic Twain went so far as to suggest that cold cash was the closest thing to a God that modern man possessed—the one great common denominator. "Who is God, the one only and true?" Twain asked readers of the *New*

York Tribune in the fall of 1871. "Money is God. Gold and Greenbacks and Stock—father, son, and the ghost of same—three persons in one; these are the true and only God, mighty and supreme." [8] The cynical Twain may have correctly isolated the poison that was invading America's soul, but he recommended no antidote. Burroughs did.

Burroughs's great hero, Ralph Waldo Emerson, had written, "The day does not seem wholly profane in which we have given heed to some natural object." [9] Burroughs in turn suggested that a love of nature possessed "a distinctly religious value." [10] The Bible said, "In Him we live, and move, and have our being." In this instance Burroughs, who had rejected his own fundamentalist Baptist roots along with all other traditional notions of a personal God, urged his readers to take the Bible literally. "How childish this talk is, that we can be nearer God, nearer heaven, in some other world, than we are here!" wrote Burroughs in 1883. "What irreligion and atheism it is! The child in its mother's womb is no nearer its mother than you and I and all men are at all times near God." [11] Burroughs recommended to his readers that they go to the woods to develop a personal relationship with nature that did not "vulgarize it and rob it of its divinity." Confronted with Darwin's revelations on the origin of species, Burroughs believed that thoughtful individuals of modern times required a tabernacle of worship different from that where their superstitious fathers had prostrated themselves. [12] In the final analysis, he believed the experience of wild nature to be the embodiment of the best and most real form of prayer. "Saints and devotees have gone into the wilderness to find God," he wrote. "Of course, they took God with them, and the silence and detachment enabled them to hear the still, small voice of their own souls." [13]

For Burroughs, the Christian tenet of sin followed by redemption found its analogy in the citizens of cities who returned to seek the pleasure and solitude of the wooded countryside. As in the stories of St. Paul and Thomas Aquinas, knowledge of God was all the sweeter and all the more profound following salvation after a fall from Grace. Burroughs suggested that the idea of the city was born of fear and sin. Rude and barbarous people needed cities. The necessity of defense had built the first cities—Ur, Babylon, and Carthage. The weaker the law, the stronger the city. "After Cain slew Abel he went out and built a city," wrote Burroughs. And he suggested that it was calculated greed and a crude lack of faith that had laid the foundation for every city since. Hence, Burroughs argued that the city was "older" than the country. "Truly, man made the city," Burroughs wrote, "and after he became sufficiently civilized, not afraid of solitude, and knew on what terms to live with nature, God promoted him to life in the country." [14] It was only after his abdication of the forest to industrialization that man could realize the true sanctity of nature. It was only after seeing the hell of the urban that he could realize the heaven of the rural. Only after sin could he find redemption.

Burroughs's third book of nature essays, published in 1879, was titled *Locusts and Wild Honey*. In his preface, Burroughs hinted that the title of the book was an allegory. Burroughs's allusion was to another John, John the Baptist, "the voice crying in the wilderness" who "fed on locusts and wild honey." The modern prophet Burroughs proselytized for a new church of the woodlands. The new and most necessary baptism was a baptism in nature. Amid the trees, by forest streams, he believed one could find a cure for the vanity and vexation of spirit that the growing American industrial colossus doled out in such generous portions. In days of increasing urbanization and "scientific barbarism," wrote Burroughs, the woods could set one free. [15]

PEPACTON

. . . the time we have lived and mellowed, and that has been hallowed by the presence of friends, or parents, or by great events, is forever gone; this we keep only in memory . . . We can keep the old—all except the old time. The old house, the old fields, and, in a measure, the old friends; but the atmosphere that bathed it all—the past days—these we cannot keep.

— Journal Entry, April 14, 1886

THE DATE WAS APRIL 3, 1912. The place was the palatial Bird Hall of the American Museum of Natural History in New York City. At the front of the Hall sat a tall, elderly man with a long white beard that made him look very much like Santa Claus. His chair was propped against the wall and elevated on a box, as though it were a throne. Before him stood six hundred school children who had come to pay homage. The children stared at the old man in silence. Their teachers had told them he was a great writer of books about something called "nature," and that he lived in a cabin far away amid the splendid freedom of the wild woods. The children were instructed to be on their absolutely best behavior, for this was a very special occasion for the man who looked like Santa Claus. John Burroughs was turning seventy-five years old today.

The teachers had explained to the boys and girls that Burroughs claimed friendship with many notable figures of his day: men who were successful not in the arts or sciences, but in the accumulation of wealth and power. One is sure they mentioned that Burroughs was on the closest terms with Theodore Roosevelt, E. H. Harriman, Andrew Carnegie, Thomas Edison, and Henry Ford. It is doubtful, however, that the children learned that Burroughs had been an intimate of Walt Whitman for nearly thirty years, and had written two books about the poet. Whitman's *Leaves of Grass* was not yet accepted as the great work that Burroughs and a few other disciples believed it was. In most polite circles, Whitman's poems were considered obscene. *Leaves of Grass* was not likely to be mentioned in schools. In fact, the book was banned in several states.

The naturalist Henry Fairfield Osborn, who was present at the American Museum on the occasion of the birthday celebration, recalled later how "twelve bright girls and boys, each representing a volume of the edition of his [Burroughs's] collected works and wearing the name of the volume suspended in front, came forward to recite passages from his books." The nature essays of John Burroughs had for more than twenty years been packaged by his publisher, Houghton Mifflin, into special editions as children's reading primers. By 1912, these were used in almost every school district in the country—and were just one of the reasons why Burroughs was a very famous man. [1]

The children who now paraded before the elderly Burroughs were almost all impoverished immigrants from inner city schools— Czechs, Hungarians, Poles, and Slavs. Their lives summed up the city environment at its worst. They lived in cramped slums on crowded streets where vice was never far away. They ate unfresh food imported at exorbitant prices from an unseen hinterland. And their parents were chained to long work days in dark, unventilated sweatshops. Many of these boys and girls were destined for a similar fate in the very near future. For now, however, they were reprieved; and their teachers marshaled them to show this famous old man how much they loved his writings.

". . . we go to nature for solitude and communion with our own souls," recited a little girl in an inexpensive but neatly pressed linen dress. "Nature attunes us to a higher and finer mood. This love springs from our religious needs and instincts." Next a boy stood up—a boy who had never seen an open field. "One's own landscape comes in time to be a sort of outlying part of himself," he quoted. ". . . cut those trees, and he bleeds; mar those hills, he suffers." Thus was Burroughs's singing prose of the free woods reduced to a drill which pupils of city schools were made to learn by rote. Every boy and girl in turn uttered descriptions of a world that, despite all of Burroughs's eloquence, they could not possibly understand. The children seemed awestruck—but not by Burroughs. Coming from crowded tenements as they did, more likely they were in awe of the grand enormity of this museum built by wealthy men as a home for dead animals. One guesses they were less impressed with the benign old man before them who, it was said, was the maker of the words they'd been made to spend the week memorizing. No matter how heartfelt or beautifully written, the fact was that Burroughs's essays could only send to nature those who were free to go.

Burroughs himself felt the situation to be awkward. The irony of traveling to Manhattan to hear these children of the city recite to him his own nature essays was not lost on him. As Burroughs rose to speak, he tried his best to impart something of genuine value to the boys and girls lined up in five straight columns before him. He took both their teachers and the museum staff by surprise when he used his remarks to condemn both the institution in which he found himself standing and also the institution that he sensed his own prose had become.

He told the children that natural history museums were a sham, and that one was no more likely to find nature in the American Museum than in one of his own "little green books." He said the millions of dollars that had been poured into the construction of this particular museum could have been much better spent upon the endowment of "lands to be left pristine and safe from the incursion of factory and tenement." He pointed to the stuffed birds that lined the walls of the great hall and informed the children that this was not nature. "A bird shot and stuffed and botanized is no bird at all," he told them. "And a bird described by another in cold print is something less than you deserve. Do not go to museums to find Nature. Do not rely on schoolbooks. Have your mothers and fathers take you to the park or the seashore. Watch the sparrows circle over you, hear the gulls screech, follow the squirrel to his nest in the hollow of the old oak. Nature is nothing at all when it is twice removed. It is only real when you reach out and touch it with your hands." Echoing a sentiment he had expressed in the 1880s essay, "Science and Literature," Burroughs said that he seldom went into a natural history museum without feeling as if he were attending a funeral. ". . . the birds and animals lie stark and stiff, or else, what is worse, stand up in ghastly mockery of life, and the people pass along and gaze at them through the glass with the same cold and unprofitable curiosity that they gaze upon the face of their dead neighbor in his coffin." He urged the boys and girls not to mistake the "dead, dissected nature" of the museum for the real thing.[2]

The children stared at him in silence. Nature dead or nature alive—it was a moot point for them. No trees grew in the asphalt courtyards between the tenements. No birds but ill-tempered city pigeons, picking through garbage, offered themselves for observation. No trout beckoned from the East River, where raw sewage floated on the tide. And even if the boys could find a trout hole somewhere within walking distance of the slums, the ambition would not have been to catch and eat the fish but to catch and sell it. These were hard times, in the early days of 1912. Money was tight, wages low, jobs scarce.

Seventy-five years earlier John Burroughs had been born into a similar economic situation, though not a similar social one. The Panic of 1837 had led to a severe depression that persisted well into the 1840s. It was in this troubled economy that the young John Burroughs was raised. But he was lucky in the respect that, though he did have to endure hardship, he endured it in the country on a farm.

One of John Burroughs's best friends growing up in the Catskills had been Jay Gould, who went on to become the most legendary of Gilded Age robber barons. Like Gould in his way, Burroughs had reached for fame and success. But instead of building a golden tabernacle of stocks and bonds Burroughs tried to weave a web of words that might help redeem the modern world from a long industrial night. In his books and essays Burroughs sang the praises of such simple things as the sweet light of day, the tree it fell on, the creek that flowed by the tree, and the life that mingled in that singularly mystical place that was the wild. His ambition was simple: to assure that the mystical place did not become a mythical one, and that it remain a thing of genuine, perceived value to his contemporaries.

❧

Whenever Walt Whitman talked about his boyhood home of Long Island, he called the place by its aboriginal name: Paumanok. Perhaps imitating the poet who was his friend, mentor, and hero, John Burroughs usually referred to his native stream, the East Branch of the Delaware, by the name local Indians had given it: Pepacton. The Pepacton is a gentle current in those upper portions beside which Burroughs spent his childhood. The river drains what Burroughs described as "a high pastoral country lifted into long, round-backed hills and rugged, wooded ranges by the subsiding impulse of the Catskill range." [3]

John Burroughs was born in the watershed of the Pepacton on April 3, 1837, during the same year Victoria ascended to the throne of England. Charles Darwin's voyage on the *Beagle* had ended six months earlier. The battle of the Alamo occurred just a few months before Burroughs's birth. Martin Van Buren, the eighth president of the United States and a native of New York, had been in office since January after succeeding Andrew Jackson. Walt Whitman was a young schoolteacher at Smithtown, Long Island. Ralph Waldo Emerson was about to deliver his "American Scholar" address, which Oliver Wendell Holmes would call America's "intellectual declaration of independence." It was the year that the abolitionist editor Elijah Lovejoy was murdered by a proslavery mob in Alton, Illinois. Nathaniel Hawthorne had just published *The Snow-Image, and Other Twice-told Tales*. Herman Melville, eighteen years old, was clerking in a New York bank and contemplating the idea of going to sea. John James Audubon had several months of work left on his massive study, *The Birds of America*. The twenty-year-old Frederick Douglass had one more year to endure before he would be able to flee his life of slavery in Maryland.

Whenever the nostalgic Burroughs wrote or spoke about the "home farm" where he was born and raised just outside Roxbury, Delaware County, New York, he painted a quaint, Currier & Ives–style picture of his life there. He spoke of his good luck in having been born on a farm in humble circumstances. He likewise said he considered it a good omen to have been born in the spring, when all of nature was new. According to Burroughs's romantic portrait of the scene as painted in the memoir *My Boyhood*, his father Chauncey had probably tapped the sugarbush just a few weeks before John's first loud cries. With florid prose he described how the bluebird, robin, and song sparrow may well have appeared at the homestead that very day. It was a season when dwindling drifts of snow showed the stain of dirt along the hillside, when the stone walls that crossed and recrossed the checkerboard fields were seen again for the first time since November.[4]

In fact, the checkerboard fields were less picturesque than they were unforgiving. The pastures covered an uncompromising foundation of Devonian rock and shale. Inhospitable to the plow, most of the red soil was useless for growing anything but grass. Looking at his youth with a romantic longing, the mature Burroughs would call the country "ideal for pasture" when, in reality, it was simply no good for anything else. Every third or fourth acre might be tillable enough to yield rye, oats, buckwheat, or yellow corn, but hay was the primary and (according to Burroughs) "most natural" crop.

The Burroughs family had endured the severe geography and climate of the rural Catskill Mountains for three generations before John was born—but the line of the Burroughs family in the United States goes back much further than that. The earliest lineal ancestor of John Burroughs of which we have record is Burroughs's great-grandfather's great-grandfather, another John Burroughs. This John came from the West Indies to settle in Stratford, Connecticut, in 1690. He married Patience Hinman in 1694. The eldest of their ten children was Stephen, who was born in 1695 and married Ruth Nichols in 1719. Stephen and Ruth's third child, born in 1729, was Stephen Burroughs, Jr., who became a noted shipbuilder, astronomer, and mathematician and was the inventor of the federal monetary system adopted by Congress in 1790. Stephen's younger brother Ephraim, born in 1740, was the great-grandfather of John Burroughs.

Ephraim moved to the Catskill Mountain town of Stamford, New York, at about the time of the Revolution with a group of settlers from Bridgeport, Connecticut. At Stamford, Ephraim ran a moderately successful dairy farm and reared a large family. When he died in 1818, he was buried in an unmarked grave in a field between

Hobart and Stamford that during Burroughs's boyhood was under cultivation. The great-grandson often expressed regret that he did not know the exact spot where the old man's body lay. One of Ephraim's seven sons was John Burroughs's grandfather, Eden. Eden married Rachel Avery in 1795 and moved over the mountain to a homestead in the village of Roxbury. He cut his own road through the woods, over which he carried his wife and all their goods on a sled drawn by a yoke of oxen. It was Eden who settled the land that John was to grow up on, the homestead to which he would always return—indeed, the place at which he would establish his summer home for the last ten years of his life. Eden built a house of birch and maple logs with a black-ash bark roof, a great stone chimney, and a floor of hewn logs. A few years later he put up a frame house.

When in his seventies, John Burroughs would trap woodchucks in the ruins of his grandfather's frame house. He would bring his son Julian, then in his thirties, and they would stand on the remaining joists to survey the open, rotting floor timbers that had collapsed to mingle with weeds and bushes sprouting up from the old root cellar beneath. Burroughs waved his walking stick and pointed out to Julian the location of the various rooms. Here had stood the chamber where Julian's grandfather was born, there the room in which his great-grandmother died. Then Burroughs showed Julian where the path had led to the now-vanished barn, and mused aloud about the lives of his forebears on this site just a few dozen rods away from the house of his own boyhood. His parents spent the first few years of their married life here before purchasing the adjacent house and farm and moving there in 1826.

Burroughs admired Thomas Carlyle who, like Thoreau and Wordsworth, seemed to be a man of the strongest local attachments. "The hill I first saw the sun rise over," Carlyle had written, "when the Sun and I and all things were yet in their auroral hour—who can divorce me from it. Mystic, deep as the world's center, are the roots I have struck into my Native Soil; no tree that grows is rooted so." Like Carlyle, Burroughs also had a deep psychic connection not only to the geography of his home region, but also to his kin who lingered there both above and below ground. Burroughs would return to Roxbury as an old man in a vain attempt to reclaim all these ghosts of his past. "How sacred is memory," he wrote Whitman in an 1890 letter. "As one grows old, how much he lives in the past, how trivial and cheap seems the present." [5]

He spoke to a friend of the strange psychological "disease" with which he was afflicted. The problem was a "homesickness which home cannot cure." When away from the place of his boyhood, he yearned to return, as though he could find his youthful contentment and satisfaction there in the circle of the hills. "But I know I should not," he said. "The soul's thirst can never be slaked. My hunger is the hunger of the imagination. Bring all my dead back again, and place me amid them in the old home, and a vague longing and regret would still possess me." At age eighty he wrote in his journal that as time passed, the world became to him more and more a Golgotha— a place of graves. "The days do not merely pass, we bury them; they are of us, like us, and in them we bury our own image, a real part of ourselves." [6]

His nostalgia was a consuming one, and it included in no small way a deep yearning for a certain preindustrial pastoral innocence that perhaps had never actually existed in a pure form, but which nevertheless seemed, when viewed through the colored glass of memory, to have been quite real in the days of his boyhood. This nostalgia was the reason why so much of his writing was devoted to forging a peace between the landscape and a people whose lives were increasingly based on mechanization. He mourned the loss of the way of life he had known in his boyhood—his father and mother's America—just as much as he mourned the loss of the people themselves. And he also mourned his personal loss of the simple, straightforward, Testament-based faith by which his parents and grandparents had gladly governed their lives. The old man's nostalgia was for a green world of ever-productive farms, pure waters, and good, simple people upon which an all-powerful God looked down. His craving was insatiable, his melancholy profound.

JOHN BURROUGHS WAS THE SEVENTH of the ten children of Chauncey and Amy Kelly Burroughs, and their fifth son. Of all his brothers and sisters, only John was to pursue anything beyond the most rudimentary of educations; only John was to leave the Catskills and make a name for himself in the world. Hiram, the eldest of the Burroughs children, was born in 1827. Olly Ann was about two years younger than Hiram. The next in line were Wilson, Curtis, Edmund (who died in infancy), and Jane. Born in 1837, John was followed in 1839 by Eden and in 1840 by Evaline who was to die when she was twelve. All the brothers save for John grew to become full-time farmers and hunters. All the sisters married local men who followed similar pursuits. (In 1912, while being interviewed about his famous brother for the *New York Times,* Eden Burroughs confided to the correspondent that one of his winter hunting adventures had yielded the material Burroughs used in the popular essay, "A White Day and A Red Fox." Eden sighed, shook his head, and looked at the reporter. "I shot the fox and got five dollars for it," said Eden. "John wrote a piece about it, and got seventy-five.")[7]

John Burroughs's mother, Amy Kelly Burroughs, had been born in Rensselaer County, near Albany, in 1808. Shortly thereafter her parents relocated to Delaware County. She was eighteen when she married Chauncey Burroughs in February, 1824. Amy had little schooling; she could read a bit, but could not write or cipher. She was short and stout, and had brown hair and blue eyes. Described by Burroughs as a woman with "great emotional capacity, who felt more than she thought," she was devoutly religious. Looking back on his mother many years after her death at the age of seventy-two in 1880, Burroughs was to say that he saw himself in her "perpetually." He wrote that whatever was most valuable in his books came from her—"the background of feeling, of pity, of love." He said he owed to his mother his love of nature and his introspective habit of mind. "In her line were the dreamers and fishermen and hunters," recalled Burroughs. He wrote that his mother was not vivacious and did not have a sunny disposition. She was always "a little in shadow . . . given to brooding and to dwelling upon the more serious aspects of life." Decades of work and care left their mark in a perceptible taint of sadness that invaded all her other moods.[8]

Like that of other farm wives of the region, Amy's life was one long, intense round of washing, cooking, berry picking, sugar making, candle and soap making, sewing, knitting, and mending. Amy was up with the rest of the household at sunup in the summer and before sunup in the winter. The Burroughs farm shipped over two tons of butter annually. Amy oversaw every aspect of the butter-making process, from skimming the pans to packing the butter in tubs. She also sewed the children's clothes and wove her own cloth. Burroughs would recall his mother's loom pounding away hour after hour in the chamber of an outbuilding where she was weaving a carpet. As a small boy he would help do some of the quilling—running the yarn or linen thread on spools to be used in the shuttles of the loom. There was a small field of the farm that was devoted to growing flax from which Amy would spin thread that would later be woven into cloth for shirts, towels, and sheets.

Burroughs's father, Chauncey, had been born in Roxbury on December 20, 1803. "He received a fair schooling for those times—the three R's—and taught school one or two winters," wrote Burroughs. "His reading was the Bible and hymn-book, his weekly secular paper, and a monthly religious paper." Chauncey had red hair and freckles. He was to tell his sons that as a young man he'd been wicked, quarrelsome, and mean. He'd had a taste for betting on horses and cards, and was a drinker of whiskey. However, in early manhood Chauncey "experienced religion," as he put it in a letter to John, and joined the Baptist Church of which his parents were members. Then all his bad habits were discarded. "He stopped swearing and Sabbath-breaking," wrote his son twenty-five years after the man was dead, "and other forms of wickedness, and be-came an exemplary member of the community. He was a man of un-impeachable veracity: bigoted and intolerant in his religious and political views, but a good neighbor, a kind father, a worthy citizen, a fond husband, and a consistent member of his church. He im-proved his farm, paid his debts, and kept his faith." [9]

His father was not a refined man. Burroughs would recall that he had, in fact, very boorish habits. His behavior at the table was based on "a kind of selfishness, but it was like that of children—thoughtless and uncalculating." He always dove in immediately and picked for the best trout, the biggest potato, the largest cob of corn. "It never occurred to him to decline a thing on the score of manners. Mother used to say it was 'hoggishness,' and he would not gainsay her. I doubt if he ever said 'Thank you' to any person in his life." Chauncey was also somewhat ill-mannered in that he made "a great deal of noise" about the farm. Chauncey had a strong voice, and could send it over the hills a mile away. He was always hallooing to the cows, the sheep, the boys. "He never went away from home, while I was a boy on the farm, without stopping out on the 'big hill,' and calling back to us some command, or renewal of some order, generally entirely superfluous, always to the annoyance of Mother, if she was beside him—his voice was so loud and harsh. Often he would call twice before he got out of sight."

Chauncey's religion was the first and most basic element of his life and thought. He said he was sometimes so carried away by the sermons of a local Baptist preacher, Elder Jim Mead, as not to know whether he was "in the body or out of the body"—so strong was the hand of the Lord upon him. Once, in young John's presence, the man suddenly fell down to his knees to pray in the middle of the hog pen. "It was a time of unusual religious excitement with him, no doubt," Burroughs recalled. "I heard, and ran away, knowing it was not for me to hear." Burroughs was to remember how his Baptist father and Jerry Bouton, a Methodist neighbor, would argue tenets of predestination and salvation for hours over whittle-sticks. Each man launched into text after text defending his own particular Protestant ethic. Burroughs recalled that Chauncey was appalled by the Methodist's "cheap and easy terms of salvation." The elder Burroughs's God was that of Jonathan Edwards, an angry Calvinist Lord with no mercy to spare on men who were sinners one and all— and certainly none to spare on those who, like Bouton, seemed to Chauncey more concerned with justifying sin than condemning it.[10]

ONE OF BURROUGHS'S FIRST memories was of his father joining in with other men of the neighborhood on a nighttime march to support the candidacy of Harrison for president and Tyler for vice-president. The year was 1839. Burroughs was two years old. When an old man he would still vividly remember the sight of Chauncey and the others rolling by the house in a lumber wagon after sun-down. All the men waved torches. A coon—the campaign em-blem—was hoisted high on a pole. Another early memory was of the hired girl throwing his cap down the steps. As he stood crying, he looked up on the sidehill and saw his father with a bag slung across his shoulders, striding across the furrows sowing grain. "It was a warm spring day, and as I looked hillward wistfully, I wished Father would come down and punish the girl for throwing my cap down the stairs," he wrote. "Little insignificant things, but how they stick."

What other impressions survived in the mind of the old man from those distant days before articulation and independence, before the assertion of self and the transformation of the insular toddler into a social youth? He recalled lying on the hearth in the evening to catch the big, light-colored, long-legged house crickets. He remembered running away from home and getting as far as the turn in the road by the Deacon Woods, a few rods from the house, before he looked back and, seeing how far away he was from home, ran back crying. "I have seen a young robin do the very same thing on its first journey from the nest," he wrote in 1913. He also remembered sitting in the kitchen of the old home in winter, during the time of cornshelling. The great splint basket had a long frying-pan handle thrust through its two handles. Two of his older brothers sat in straight-backed chairs on either side of the basket and scraped the ears of corn clean against the iron of the handle. He heard the kernels rattle, the shower of them falling in the basket. With the cobs that lay in a pile beside the basket, little John built towers, placing the cobs one upon the other until they toppled or until one of the shellers succumbed to the temptation to kick the tower over. His mother sat nearby sewing. Her tallow dip hung on the back of her chair.

The child matures; the memories change. Recollections of relationships now, of friendships, adventures, and betrayals. He remembered the local bully—"the meanest boy I ever knew, and he became the meanest man"—who found him sulking under a tree in the corner of the schoolyard. "He bribed me with a slate pencil into confessing what I was crying about, but as soon as I had told him, he ran away with the pencil, shouting my secret to the other boys." There was another item on the dark side of his childhood memories. He would never be able to forget a string of unhappy Christmases in the home of his fundamentalist parents who always treated the occasion as strictly a holy day. There was never any gift giving at Christmas, never a party. One year, after he'd learned from a friend at school that if he hung up his stocking by the fireplace on Christmas Eve, Santa Claus would leave him something, young John defied his parents and went ahead and did so. The response from Chauncey was needlessly cruel. All John found in the stocking the next morning was a frozen piece of horse manure.

The boy who told Burroughs of Santa Claus was Jay Gould. The Goulds had come to Delaware County in the same migration of settlers that had brought the Burroughs family from Connecticut in the 1770s. Burroughs's great-grandfather and Gould's great-grandfather had been pioneers together. The families had been friends and neighbors for generations. The two boys' chief schoolyard occupation was wrestling in a circle drawn in the dirt with a stick. Though Gould was slight of build, he "was very plucky and hard to beat," Burroughs recalled. When in a match, the small Gould suddenly seemed to be "made of steel and rubber." As Maury Klein tells us in his excellent biography of Gould, Burroughs and Gould could not have been more dissimilar. Gould was ambitious, precise, studied, and quick-witted. In contrast, the young Burroughs possessed a strong but as yet unfocused intelligence, was undisciplined in his schoolwork, and maintained his person in a slovenly manner. Yet the two were very close.

Once Burroughs and Gould grew to be teenagers, they left the Catskills to fulfill their individual destinies. They fell completely and permanently out of touch, although there is no record of there having been any argument or bitterness between them. Each was most certainly aware of the other's successes through the years. A well-thumbed set of the works of John Burroughs sits to this day in the library of Lyndhurst, Jay Gould's old mansion at Tarrytown, New York. Late in Burroughs's life, two decades after Jay Gould's death in 1892, Gould's daughter Helen became a friend and benefactress of the naturalist. During a 1911 journey to California, Burroughs went fifty miles out of his way during a busy lecture tour to stop at Pasadena and visit Gould's sister, Annie Gould Hough, an elderly woman whom Burroughs remembered as a childhood playmate of his sisters. As Klein has pointed out, Burroughs would never be able to shake the memory of Gould. "It is a curious psychological fact that the two men outside my own family of whom I have oftenest dreamed in my sleep are Emerson and Jay Gould," he wrote, "one to whom I owe so much, the other to whom I owe nothing; one whose name I revere, the other whose name I associate, as does the world, with the dark way of speculative finance." [11]

Memories of Gould were probably accompanied for Burroughs by memories of his maternal grandfather, "Granther" Kelly, who used to take both boys on trouting expeditions up Rose's Brook, Hardscrabble Creek, Meeker's Hollow, and Furlow Lake. "Early in the morning he would dig worms for bait," wrote Burroughs, "and we would go fishing over in West Settlement, or in Montgomery Hollow. I went with him when he was past eighty. He would steal along the streams and 'snake' out the trout, walking as briskly as I." The old man instilled a lifelong love of trouting in John. He would write nostalgically that trout streams were plentiful in the valley of his boyhood. He crossed them, and was often lured and detained by them, on his way to and from school. "We bathed in them during the long summer noons and felt for trout under their banks," he wrote in a book that ended up being a favorite of Gould's, *Locusts and Wild Honey*. "When but a few hours could be had, gained perhaps by doing some piece of work about the farm or garden in half the allotted time, the little creek that headed in the paternal domain was handy; when half a day was at one's disposal there were the hemlocks, less than a mile distant, with their loitering, meditative, log impeded stream and their dusky, fragrant depths." [12]

Trouting provided a vital link to the rural paradise of his boyhood memory. It also provided a link to the people who had shared with him that sweet green landscape of his youth. In a journal entry made shortly after the death of his father in the 1880s, Burroughs commented that he'd had a glimpse of his father in a dream. "We were at the table, and a plate of trout was being passed around, and I saw Father pick out the big one, as I have so often seen him do." In the dream of the mourning Burroughs, the trout became a metaphor by which to achieve communion with the past. In "Speckled Trout," one of several trouting-related essays in *Locusts and Wild Honey*, Burroughs spoke of the fierce appetite developed by the search for the trout—an appetite that could only properly be assuaged by the fish itself. Burroughs's hunger was not just physical, but also spiritual and sentimental. Just as his craving for his boyhood was insatiable, so too was his taste for trout. Thus, on his annual fishing expeditions to the Catskills, he was voracious. He always took and ate as many trout as he possibly could. He chronicled the numbers in his journal. "We have eaten trout by the hundred," he wrote from the banks of a Catskill stream in the summer of 1869. In the summer of 1878, he commented in his journal that he had caught "10 lbs. of beautiful trout—103 in all" at Meeker's Hollow. In 1883, at Rose's Brook with his brother Curtis: "Took 32 trout in the stream of my boyhood." In 1894, at Snyder Hollow with his son, Julian: "Took and ate about 90 trout from 5 to 10 inches . . . A delicious time. Never had better." At age eighty-one, he waded the deep swift waters of the Neversink while friends watched anxiously, and took eighteen trout out of the Catskill stream. The diminished number was due less to his advanced age than it was to the fact that by this time, after the end of World War I, most Catskill waters were overfished.

In his seventies, when asked to provide an autobiographical summing up, he used fishing as the central metaphor for his life. "I have gone a-fishing while others were struggling and groaning and losing their souls in the great social or political or business maelstrom," he wrote. "I know, too I have gone a-fishing while others have labored in slums and given their lives for the betterment of their fellows. But I have been a good fisherman, and I should have been a poor missionary, or reformer." [13]

The high priest of Burroughs's cult of the trout, his devoutly religious grandfather, Granther Kelly, was born in 1767. As a teenager, Kelly was a soldier in Washington's army at Valley Forge, "doing justice to his country and honor to himself," as the young Jay Gould wrote in his *A History of Delaware County*. The old man often dressed in his old blue military coat with brass buttons. Gould tells us that Kelly once met Lafayette during the Revolution, and that he had adopted Lafayette's hatred of slavery. He and his wife allowed their house nearby to the Burroughs homestead to be used as a stop of the Underground Railroad. "I was there one morning when they entertained a colored minister overnight, probably a fugitive slave," recalled Burroughs. "He prayed—how lustily he prayed!" The minister told the fascinated boy of his life on a South Carolina rice plantation: of long summer days spent harvesting rice in bug-ridden swamps, of malaria, of his family being sold away from him, and the whip. "I remember him leaving in a wagon that would take him to another 'safe' house near Albany. He stood up on the hay at the back of the wagon shouting blessings down on Grandma and Granther and me."

Kelly's involvement with the abolition movement was a direct result not just of his hero-worship of Lafayette, but also of his involvement with his church. Kelly's already strong faith had been renewed during the wave of Protestant revivals known as the Second Great Awakening. When this evangelical enthusiasm swept New England and upstate New York in the late 1840s, it carried with it a healthy strain of political radicalism. Devotees were prompted to take an active role in rectifying a variety of social problems. The most important movement to gain from this divinely inspired activism was abolitionism. For one of God's children to enslave another was a violation of God's higher law, even if it might not be a violation of the law of the land. The brother who most needed help in this world was the black brother. In helping the black man be redeemed from immoral servitude, Kelly hoped to redeem himself, and the world, from sin.

In addition to faith in God, Granther Kelly also had faith in spooks and hobgoblins. He would tell the boy old tales of cold terrors as the two sunk their lines into lonesome mountain streams. As a result, Burroughs suffered from an acute aversion to darkness until he was well into his teens. The world was, at heart, a frightening place. He did not like to clean the stables of the big barn because of the great black hole beneath. "I was tortured with the thought of what might lurk there in the black abyss." He also did not care to walk past the burying ground on the hillside at night. If he found this to be necessary, he walked very slowly and quietly. He was afraid to run lest he wake the ghosts of the dead with his commotion and have them fast at his heels. There were other fearful experiences. As an old man he would still remember the day in his youth when terror had accompanied the sight of a great hawk circling above, then swooping to earth as if aimed right at him. Burroughs hid behind a stone wall until the hawk disappeared.

On June 9, 1913, John Burroughs was the halfhearted guest of honor for the unveiling of a bird fountain at Fair Lane, the home of Henry Ford in Dearborn, Michigan. The absurd monument, which Burroughs told his son looked "like what might have happened if Father had tried to build a Roman fountain in the south field," was made from stone gathered on the old Burroughs homestead. This was stone that John helped his bothers collect for a wall in his youth. Burroughs had been annoyed several months earlier when he happened upon several of Henry Ford's men collecting the rocks from a distant section of the farm. Even after it was explained that the remnants of the stone wall were being taken for use as part of a special surprise being prepared for Burroughs by his friend Ford, Burroughs still hadn't liked the idea of parting with these relics of his childhood. But he acquiesced. Burroughs almost always wound up acquiescing when it came to Ford. "He's paid a great deal more for that wall than I would have," the disgruntled Burroughs told the amused workers. "So let him have it, then." Then he sat down on the grass and watched them go on with their task.

It had been little more than a year before that Ford, an enthusiastic amateur ornithologist, sought out Burroughs. In December of 1912 Ford wrote Burroughs a fan letter saying that as thanks for the pleasure Burroughs's books had brought him, Ford would like to give Burroughs a Model T. The offer of the car to the famous writer was at once a sincere gesture from a genuine admirer and a brilliant publicity gimmick. Burroughs had recently published some essays on the negative impact of industrialization and its products on the American woodlands. Burroughs had gone so far as to propose that the automobile was a demon on wheels with the ability to "seek out even the most secluded nook or corner of the forest and befoul it with noise and smoke." Ford hoped that snapshots of Burroughs behind the wheel of a Model T would diffuse the impact of the old man's published remarks.

Gift giving on the part of Ford was to characterize the relationship of the two men. In 1913, Ford would have an even more substantial present to give—the very same homestead where Burroughs had been raised. Over the previous thirty years, since the death of his parents, Burroughs had labored mightily to keep the place in the family. He had cosigned more than one bank mortgage in order that first his brother Hiram and then, in turn, his brother Curtis might hold on to the land, which was always only marginally profitable. Keeping the property in the family was a constant struggle. The current owner was Curtis Burroughs's son John C. Burroughs. John C. was heavily mortgaged, his uncle being the nervous guarantor of a good many of the notes. Ford came to the rescue by making a substantial offer to John C. for outright sale of the property. He then turned the deed over to Burroughs. John C. was kept on to run the dairy business for his uncle. He remained with his family in the main farmhouse. The elder John Burroughs reserved only a small adjacent dwelling for himself. It was one which he'd rented from John C. for several summers and had named "Woodchuck Lodge," in honor of the local population of furry pests that routinely raided the nearby trash pile.

Ford had been raised on a farm himself. He had read with a great sense of nostalgia Burroughs's many accounts of his boyhood on these 320 acres of rock-strewn meadows. Ford's own fondest childhood memories were all rural in character. His earliest recollection was of going out to the fields with his father to see four sparrow eggs in a nest beneath a fallen oak tree. Ford often referred to Fair Lane, his home in Dearborn, as a farm. Once a year, limousines were dispatched about the Detroit area to gather Ford's relatives and bring them to one of the hundreds of acres of working hayfields the automaker owned just outside the city limits. The chauffeurs would recommend that the Ford uncles, aunts, and cousins put on work clothes. Then they would drive to a place in the fields that Mr. Ford had designated. There Ford would be waiting; and there all would commence to work together mowing hay. This ancient rite of harvest was one that Ford professed to find more personally fulfilling than any other act he engaged in the whole year long. There was not a single Fordson tractor in sight. The only tool was the traditional scythe.

Ford shared Burroughs's sentimental longing for the American past of simple faith and rural innocence. He did not care to think of himself as the creator of an industrial monolith that worked against the healthy continuation of an agrarian way of life. He much preferred to believe that his automobile and the factory that produced it could thrive in harmony with rural environments and economies. In lean times the personnel department of the Ford Motor Company was instructed to schedule layoffs to coincide with the harvest season, so that men with nothing better to do could at least go back to their family farms and be of use there. Ford built dozens of small plants and factories on streams and rivers throughout the rural countryside of southeast Michigan. The idea was that these village industries should bring town and country together in the best and most healthy way possible. Picturesque watermills housed clean, well-lit, human-sized workshops where local villagers could produce components and accessories for Ford cars in winter and then have jobs held for them while they went to the fields from April through October.

After reading John Burroughs, Ford had in turn gone to the works of Burroughs's great influence, Ralph Waldo Emerson, for inspiration, guidance, and spiritual renewal. Ford had always questioned in the back of his mind whether the smokestacks he'd made to dominate the Detroit skyline were a blessing or a curse. In the writings of Emerson, he found words of solace. As early as the 1850s, Emerson had written that "machinery and transcendentalism agree well." Embracing the "technological sublime," the philosopher had written that machines were "new and necessary facts" that, when designed correctly and employed toward positive ends, were essentially in harmony with nature. Emerson wrote that the sharply engineered lines of the frontiersman's axe, the technology of the steam locomotive, and the aerodynamic billowing of the scientifically designed clipper ship's sails were all examples of mechanization that had brought Americans into closer and deeper contact with the natural mysteries of their own continent. Burroughs, who had always been fascinated and easily seduced by men of wealth and power, wrote Ford that "were Emerson alive today, he certainly would add the Model T to that list." Now that he counted Ford as a friend, Burroughs completely revised his opinion of Ford's machine. It was no longer a demon on wheels.

Unlike other of the moguls Burroughs had known, Ford unwit-

tingly aided Burroughs in taming, if not solving, a major philosophical dilemma that had plagued him for years. Burroughs had
read Henry Demarest Lloyd's radical treatise *Wealth Against Commonwealth* with great sympathy in the 1890s. After reading Lloyd,
Burroughs had been left with the annoying, inconvenient, lingering
notion that there were terrible inequities in the United States. Yet
Burroughs also subscribed to the popular Gilded Age notion that
laissez-faire capitalism should be viewed in a Darwinian context.
Burroughs devoutly believed, along with other social Darwinists,
that free market competition spurred innovation and served to make
sure that the most intelligent and able of men—the natural elite—
gained and maintained authority and became what Thomas Wentworth Higginson would call a "natural aristocracy of the dollar." In
the final analysis, Burroughs saw the great fortunes and the men
who made them as crucial engines without which the country would
be doomed.

He held in more awe than disdain the many millionaires—such
as the steel magnate Andrew Carnegie—that he'd come to know.
Carnegie was the endower of universities and the builder of libraries.
He had been a major supporter of Walt Whitman during the poet's
old age. Yet Carnegie was also the man responsible for unleashing
brute force on the Homestead strikers. And he was the chief architect of the city of Pittsburgh, which Burroughs described in his
journal as "a rank industrial Hell, the evil face of a concrete future."
Now came Ford, the industrial titan who was the father of the
benevolent "five dollar day" and also an appreciator of all things
rural and picturesque. This was the same Ford whom the journalist
John Reed, one of the founders of the American Communist party,
would idealize as a "miracle worker" and "a friend to labor" in a
1916 article. (And yet it was also the same Ford who later, in 1937,
would order company detectives to savagely beat Walter Reuther
and other UAW strikers on a picket line outside a Ford plant in
Detroit.) Ford seemed to Burroughs to be a natural aristocrat who
tempered his power with concern for the common good. It seemed
that Ford's wealth did not work against, but rather for, the commonwealth. Unlike his other acquaintances among the nation's
ruling class, Ford helped Burroughs believe that the cycle of capital-
ist social Darwinism actually could, in the end, work to benefit all.

No sooner had Ford purchased the home farm for Burroughs than he came like an anxious boy to visit the acres of which he'd read so often in Burroughs's books. Burroughs sat in the shade of the porch and watched as a parade of cars moved past the house and into the orchard, where ten of Ford's personal aides began erecting tents and setting up a field kitchen. By the time Ford arrived half an hour later, the camp was almost entirely prepared. Burroughs treated the carmaker to a glass of raw milk—fresh from the udder that morning, just as Ford always insisted on having it at home. Then Burroughs took Ford on a walking tour of the farm. Slowly, methodically, they visited all the spots of the homestead that had figured in Burroughs's writings. First Ford asked to see the spring, then the old hay barn where as a boy Burroughs had been sure that spooks and goblins lurked in dark recesses. Then they went to the nearby trout stream.

At one point, as the two men tramped across an open field where Burroughs as a boy had tended the cows, Ford wondered aloud whether a small Ford plant—another one of his village industry factories—might make sense for Roxbury. Nothing was to come of the notion, but Burroughs told Ford he thought the idea an excellent one. He knew lots of local farmboys who would jump at the chance to work for Ford. Not a few of them were his own nephews and grandnephews. Visiting Detroit in the spring of 1913, Burroughs penned a journal description of the Ford automobile factory in which he unconsciously described it as though it were a farm, citing the size of the spread, what grew on it, and in what quantity. "The Ford plant covers over 49 acres. The cars grow before your eyes, and every day a thousand of them issue." [14]

MANY IN ROXBURY EXPECTED great things of young Jay Gould, who was always so punctilious in dress and impressive in academic performance. Few, however, would have forecast that Gould's friend, the inarticulate and unkempt John Burroughs, would end his days as the intimate of presidents and the friend of captains of industry. While Jay Gould had thrived in the structured atmosphere of rigorous classroom work, his friend Burroughs was undisciplined and generally not inspired to any concentrated effort, whether in the classroom or in the field. "Hoeing corn, weeding in the garden, and picking stone was a drudgery . . ." he wrote. "I always wanted some element of play in my work; buckling down to any sort of routine always galled me." A onetime neighbor, Martin Caswell, recalled that he had worked often in the hayfields with Burroughs. "He'd walk along and carry the rake on his shoulder, and his father would call out, 'John, why don't you rake?' and John would say, 'There ain't enough there yet.' But Chauncey would shout, 'By Phagus! you rake what is there!'" [15]

It was a great temptation to leave the tedium of field chores for the adventures of exploring the woods. And this was a temptation to which Burroughs yielded whenever possible. He fast became intrigued with the chaos of forest that surrounded Roxbury. Like most boys of the neighborhood, Burroughs was an avid hunter. Fox, pigeon, and other game were plentiful. And, of course, the trout beckoned with a force that was not to be denied. Long hikes through the woods in search of meat for the family table, or in quest of the perfect fishing hole, helped John learn the book of nature without ever formally studying it. As an old man, he'd recollect that he knew well the ways of the wild things when he was still small. He was acquainted with the different bumblebees, and had made a collection of their combs and honey before he had entered his teens. He'd watched the tree frogs and had captured them and held them till they piped sitting in his hand. And he had watched the leaf cutters and followed them to their nests in an old rail, or under a stone.

His daily routine to age seventeen included bringing the cows to and from pasture in summer and cleaning the stables in winter. He would write that he had a sort of "filial regard" for the cow, a "rural divinity" that had commanded the vast majority of his youthful worship and service. Every Sunday morning the cows were salted. Burroughs took a pail with three or four quarts of coarse salt and, followed by the eager herd, went to the field where he laid the salt in handfuls on smooth stones and clear places of turf. Then the cows would quickly move in for their feast. "If you want to know how good salt is," wrote Burroughs, "see a cow eat it. She gives the true saline smack. How she dwells upon it, and gnaws the sward and licks the stones where it has been deposited." Looking back to his romantic vision of boyhood on the farm, Burroughs said it seemed to him that the cow was the most delightful feeder among animals. In the deep nostalgia of old age, even the eating habits of the brutish herd were to become something to be praised and cherished. He wrote that there was virtue in the cow, that a wholesome odor exhaled from her. The quality and aroma of miles of meadow and pasture lands were defined by her presence. He would rather, he said, be the guardian of cattle than the keeper of the great seal of the nation. Where the cow was, there were the lost days and places of his youth—there was Arcadia.[16]

As Burroughs grew older, every icon of the childhood that he idealized was eventually raised up, dusted off, and displayed as a treasured memory in his prose. He wrote that the water from the spring out back of the old farmhouse tasted in memory far finer than the sweetest of wines. And he even reminisced joyfully about the intense days of labor involved in nurturing the herd. Burroughs professed in later years to have found the hard work of the dairy farm invigorating, but contemporaries (including his brothers) say he made a regular habit of complaining loudly about having to do chores. As a young man just beginning to keep a notebook and write seriously, Burroughs would philosophize on the environment and work of the farm. "When he [man] makes the soil beautiful and productive he makes his mind beautiful and productive," wrote Burroughs in 1855. "He absorbs whatever he creates. His growth is commensurate with the work of his hands." When Burroughs wrote these words, he was employed as a schoolteacher and safely removed from the reality of the tough manual labor demanded to make the field beautiful. Yet he knew whereof he spoke.

The cattle demanded much hay. When the cattle were made to browse on weeds and other wild growths due to drought, the milk and butter they produced betrayed this. Tender grass, blossoming clover, and well-cured hay made the milk delicious and the butter sweet. To get the winter's hay harvested in good condition, before the grass got too ripe, was an arduous, backbreaking task. Burroughs was to characterize it as a "thirty or forty day war, in which the farmer and his 'hands' are pitted against the heat and the rain and the legions of timothy and clover." Of necessity, if not enthusiasm,

Burroughs became an expert mower when still young. Day after day, hour after hour, he stood up to the grass and struck level and sure with his scythe. Many years after his days of childhood labor in the hayfield, Burroughs's prowess with the scythe would serve him well when he agreed to a request of Henry Ford and took part in a reenactment of the old "hay war" there in the same field of the home farm.

Just as both Ford and Burroughs had mowed hay when young, so too had each of them harvested maple sugar. John and his brothers used a crude and wasteful manner of tapping the trees on the hillside, their tool being the old sap gouge instead of the latter-day auger. First, they cut a slanting gash in the tree about three inches long and half an inch deep. The gouge was driven in an inch below this. Then the spile—two inches wide and a foot or more in length—was attached. This process gave the tree a double and unnecessary wound. An insignificant cut from a half-inch bit could do the same job more efficiently, and was much less detrimental to the tree. The modern method was the one Ford and Burroughs adopted when they gathered and boiled sap together.

During Burroughs's boyhood, the sap had been carried to the boiling place by the aid of a neck yoke. Then it was boiled and steamed off in immense kettles set in huge stone arches custom-built for the purpose. Now Henry Ford's manservants did most of the heavy work. A Ford truck brought the pails of sap from the trees to the boil fire. Ford hovered over the boil fire with a youthful excitement that Burroughs could not quite bring himself to share. (Ford's entourage, Burroughs told his son, had turned the "pleasant task" of gathering the sugar into a "wild spectacle" and a "sham." One didn't need a staff of fifteen to gather and boil sap from seven maples.) Surrounded by assistants and secretaries in suits and ties, Ford slapped his hands together with delight and told the skeptical Burroughs that he felt as though he had just walked into a page from a much-loved book of youth.

There was one more boyhood chore that the mature Burroughs would recreate with Henry Ford. With his army of footmen being made to stand in for the toughest of the work, Ford insisted on helping Burroughs mend a section of the nearly ten miles of stone

walls on the homestead. Burroughs had written that the mainte-
nance of the walls was a seemingly eternal struggle passed on from
father to son. Burroughs's father usually counted on building forty
or fifty rods of stone wall each year. The work was traditionally
planned for spring and early summer. These stone walls were, as
Burroughs recalled, "the only lines of poetry and prose" his father
ever wrote. "They are still legible on the face of the landscape and
cannot be easily erased from it." The walls were a bit of order
gathered out of the chaos and confusion of nature. How wounded
and torn the meadow looked once the stones for the wall had been
ripped from it, "bleeding as it were, in a score of places" when the
job was finished. "But the further surgery of the plough and harrow,
followed by the healing touch of the seasons, soon made all whole
again." [17]

The mountainside that was left so wounded was that of Old
Clump, the high hill that held the homestead in its lap. This was the
mountain, wrote Burroughs, "out of whose loins I sprang." The first
deer's horn he ever found was discovered under a jutting rock when,
as a boy, he was on his way to the top. His trips to salt and count the
sheep often took him there, and his "boyhood thirst for the wild and
adventurous" took him there still oftener. "Old Clump used to lift
me up into the air three thousand feet," he wrote, "and make me
acquainted with the full-chested exhilaration that awaits one on
mountain tops." Ford does not seem to have been interested in a
hike to the summit of Old Clump. There was no road to the top,
only a trail. The car could not go up. Perhaps because of this, there is
no record of an ascent by the two men. Had Ford requested it,
Burroughs certainly would have made the hike. He was to be a
regular visitor to that summit, reached only by foot, until well into
his seventies.

2

STUDENT & TEACHER

Writing is the spoils of living; it is reporting what we saw after the vision has left us; or, more familiarly, it is catching the fish which the tide has left far up on our shores in the low and depressed places.

—Journal Entry, April 9, 1859

NO SMALL PART OF WHAT brought John Burroughs to the American Museum of Natural History on that day in 1912 was that he saw himself as having a special obligation to schoolchildren and teachers. He made his living as a master of rural schools for the first ten years of his professional life. The man he called his "spiritual" father, Emerson, had taught school when young, as had his natural father Chauncey. Burroughs's other great influence, Whitman, also listed schoolmastering among his many professions. Late in life, the busy celebrity author took time, of which he did not have much, to serve on the board of trustees for the little one-room schoolhouse where the children of his neighbors attended. When teachers in distant classrooms wrote him to ask that he address a few words to their students he invariably took the time to do so. "Let me hope also that when you have reached my age you will be as well and as young as I am," he wrote in a characteristic letter to one such class when he was seventy-three. "I am still a boy at heart, and enjoy almost everything that boys do, except making a racket." [1]

Burroughs had a firm, and probably correct, belief that he could trace his personal success back to one great, inspired teacher he would always remember and honor. As a youth John had never been a strong student. He was routinely indifferent to his studies. He was regularly outshone by his friend, the precocious Jay Gould. In early 1849 an outstanding teacher by the name of James Oliver arrived at Roxbury and helped the twelve-year-old Burroughs discover a previously unknown thirst for knowledge. Oliver was fresh out of the State Normal School at Albany. Young and energetic, he possessed a powerful combination of enthusiasm, intelligence, and inspiration and brought a messianic sense of urgency to what he did. Burroughs thrived with the dynamic Oliver as tutor. Suddenly his algebra and his grammar were not painful studies, but invigorating exercises. "We all got a real start in that school," Burroughs was to write many years later, "for under Mr. Oliver we acquired a genuine love of learning." Elsewhere Burroughs wrote that he was not one of Oliver's favorite scholars. "I was eclipsed by Jay Gould." Nevertheless, wrote Burroughs, "Mr. Oliver was the best teacher my youth knew." Both Burroughs and Gould tell us in diary notes written in later years that James Oliver was an exceptional individual. Both men were to look back decades later and leave a large amount of the credit for their successes at Oliver's door.

Oliver eventually became engaged to Gould's sister, Polly, shortly before her sudden death from consumption in 1853. ("Polly Gould," wrote Burroughs, who as a schoolboy had nourished a crush on her, "was the flower of the family—a very sweet girl.") [2] Not long after this tragedy, a disheartened Oliver quit teaching and moved to the Kansas territory—but he left behind more than one student inspired to greatness. Out of seven boys in Oliver's class who had experienced his teaching from about age twelve to age sixteen, four were to move on to lead vital lives. There were Burroughs and Gould; there was also John Champlin, who was to go into law, follow Oliver in the migration west, and end his days as Chief Justice of the Kansas State Supreme Court; and there was Rice Bouton, who went on to become a Methodist minister and rector of the famous Five Points Mission in Manhattan.

Like most schoolmasters of the day, Oliver "boarded round" with his students' families on a rotating basis. One winter night when staying at the Burroughs farm, he hiked up to the snowy top of Old Clump and came back with the skull of a fox, about which he promptly wrote a poem. The event and the poem are minor, but both had a major impact on Burroughs. "Up until then I thought poems were always only to be about olden days, distant palaces, and strange lands," he wrote in a letter to Oliver many decades later. "It seems so simple a thing—but to the rude, naive boy full of pretensions, complacencies, and foolish assumptions, the notion that something—anything—on my home mountain could inspire a real poem—actual literature—was a revelation." It was a lesson he would forget at least once before learning it anew from Whitman and retaining it forever after: literature was made from life, and life was where and how one found it.

AFTER GRADUATING FROM THE little country school at Roxbury, the sixteen-year-old Burroughs spent the autumn of 1853 removing boulders from the sidehill lot of the homestead farm, preparing it for the spring planting of rye and buckwheat. After months of pleading, he'd exacted a grudging promise from his father that were he diligent in this task, he might spend the winter attending nearby Harpersfield Seminary, a college preparatory school. Day after day, he sweated and strained at his work in the fields. Night after night he read borrowed books—Shakespeare, Johnson, and Swift—in order to lay the foundation for successful study at Harpersfield. When the lot was cleared of stone, however, and the winter winds blew hard against the windows of the little house at the corner of the large field, Chauncey backed down on his word. Harpersfield was an expensive proposition. None of the other boys had demanded so luxurious an education. The little West Settlement school had been good enough for them. It would have to be good enough for John as well, unless he cared to go out and earn the Harpersfield tuition money for himself. Chauncey's sudden change of heart devastated John. He had set his hopes on a full semester at Harpersfield Seminary where he could test his intellectual mettle and get a feel for the way he would make in the world. The promise had been betrayed; all of John's great expectations had come to nothing.

He decided that he would earn the tuition money himself. Early in the spring of 1854, his traveling bag packed with his few possessions and only a dollar or two in his pocket, John Burroughs set out by foot to cross over the mountain and begin life in the world as an adult. He walked eight miles in a snow squall to an uncle's house, and then was driven the next morning to a tavern on the turnpike. From there he took a coach to Olive, in northern Ulster County. In geographical distance this was a place not thirty miles from home, but the psychological distance was surely far greater. He was not yet seventeen years old and had never lived without the circle of his family surrounding him. Now he would have to learn to do so.

At Olive he met with Dr. Abram Hull, an acquaintance of his parents who had promised to drive him about the surrounding country in search of a school that might be willing to allow the callow youth to call himself a teacher. They found an opening in the village of Tongore (Olive Township). Wages were eleven dollars per month. Burroughs would board around with the families of his students. "It was natural that any boy in Delaware County who was ambitious should go down to Ulster County and teach school," Burroughs was to recall. "It had been the custom for years. The Ulster trustees looked to the Delaware boys to apply. It was the obvious way to earn money, if you did not want to stay on the farm."

What sort of figure did he cut, this boy John Burroughs who went out to make his way in the world as a man? Jay Gould's sister, Anna, recalled that the teenage Burroughs was extremely bashful, had no social aptitude, and was likely to stammer. He often gave the impression of being anxious or embarrassed. He was a creature of moods. On the whole, recalled Anna, he seemed ruminative, withdrawn, and unsure of himself. John Champlin would remember that the young John Burroughs was generally shy and tentative, his manner nervous and awkward, his voice hesitant. His statements usually ended with a rising pitch that implied inquiry. His tone and habit of speaking suggested that he wanted his listeners to reassure him by giving some sign of affirmation for what he was saying. Most girls found him attractive, perhaps in part because of his shyness but also because of his trim, muscular, six-foot frame, his clean-shaven face, and his temperate habits. Unlike many other young men of the region, Burroughs hardly ever took a drink. And when he did, it was never to excess. This would be the case throughout his life. He did not seem to notice the girls much, however, no matter how much they tried to get his attention—Anna Gould among them.

Full of self-doubt, trying to understand and fulfill myriad vague aspirations, Burroughs began his teaching career on Monday morning, April 11, 1854. He had approximately twenty-five pupils aged six to thirteen. To this assemblage he taught the rudimentary branches of the tree of knowledge: reading, writing, and arithmetic. Although hardly older than his students, Burroughs proved a good teacher. He had a talent for explaining things in an interesting manner, and was not a strict disciplinarian. What saved him was a knack for gaining the good will of the students, and governing with that. He kept as his model the memory of the tolerant, inspired teaching he had experienced at the hand of James Oliver. His ambition, he wrote his mother, was to be as good a teacher as Oliver. He would settle for nothing less.

Several of the boys in this first class of John Burroughs were to become Union soldiers in the Civil War; two would die in the battle of Gettysburg. One who survived the same battle that killed so many other Ulster County "Blues" lived into the 1930s. As an old man, he wrote down his memories of the days when the famous bearded naturalist John Burroughs was, as a beardless teenager, the master of a one-room school. "Mr. Burroughs did not pace around much. Our previous teacher had liked to walk circles around the room, always holding the switch in his hand. He liked to come up behind you and catch you by surprise doodling, or napping, or staring out the window. Then the switch would come down. Mr. Burroughs had no stick." He was soft spoken. He often put his hands in his pants pockets as he patiently stood before them, addressing the subject of his lecture. He sometimes spent much of the day reading to the class from whatever book had currently caught his attention. After the end of class, it was not unknown for him to go along with some of the older boys so that they might show him the better fishing holes of Olive.

As James Oliver had done, Burroughs took to reading to his

class from stories that appeared in the weekly newspaper. He allowed half an hour every day for a discussion of current events and modern literature. That May, a crowd of leading Boston citizens chose to protest the Fugitive Slave Law by attacking Boston's federal court house. With guns and knives in hand, they vainly attempted to rescue the captured runaway slave Anthony Burns before his deportation south. Almost simultaneous with this event, Congress passed the Kansas-Nebraska Act, which signaled the continued penetration of slavery into the new western territories. Far removed from the reign of slavery, a team from the American Naval Observatory concluded a program of transatlantic soundings that revealed a shallow underwater plateau running between Newfoundland and Ireland,—a plateau that seemed to have been placed there especially to accommodate a submarine telegraph line. Within weeks, Cyrus Field announced the formation of a company to lay an Atlantic cable. Meanwhile, a thirty-seven-year-old sometime surveyor by the name of Henry Thoreau published a book called *Walden.*

Burroughs's own reading, as recorded in a tattered journal, was an odd combination of quality and naive literature. It did not include *Walden.* He read instead Gibbon's *Decline and Fall of the Roman Empire* one week and then followed it up with a choice bit of popular nonsense: a handbook on phrenology published by the firm of Fowler & Wells. This was a book that young Burroughs regarded as being "highly scientific" because of its initial statement that "everything springs from the egg." He subsequently subscribed to a phrenological journal, and spent a dollar (of which he did not have many) to commission a chart of his head. When he began to try to write, experimenting with odd paragraphs in the little notebook that always rode in his hip pocket, the first topic he chose was a defense of phrenology as a science. "Partly my own, I suppose, and partly from the *Phrenological Journal,*" he recalled of the piece. "I must have been trying to string those sentences together—poor, high-flown stuff. I had no ideas, and was just playing with words, you see. I suppose that is the way many begin to write." [3]

Another book in his bag was *The Complete Letter Writer,* the examples in which he used as models for many awkward and stilted pieces of correspondence. When his grandfather Kelly died that summer, Burroughs wrote a note of condolence to his family modeled upon one in the book. A few weeks later, he wrote a letter to a Roxbury friend and perhaps would-be sweetheart, Mary Taft, the first sentence of which was: "Dear Madam, It was a question among the Stoics whether the whole of human life afforded more pleasure, or more pain." The girl wrote back in a similar tone a few weeks later: "I at last find myself in the attitude to address a few scattered thoughts to you through the medium of the pen." [4]

Burroughs was himself beginning to try to do a great deal by way of the medium of the pen. In the spare rooms and haylofts in which he found himself on his round of "guesting" at his students' homes, he spent the evening hours filling notebook after notebook. There are no memoirs of boyish frivolity here, no jokes, no mention of ball games played or fishing excursions with friends, no descriptions of the pretty older sisters of his students who made a point to comb their hair so carefully before they carried the young schoolmaster an unasked-for glass of milk after dinner. His notebooks from the period are instead crammed full of earnest paragraphs, mostly concerned with the construction of a sound philosophical foundation on which to build a learned and "good" life.

> For whatever else man was intended, it is evident he was destined to . . . contemplate and reflect as well as to move and exert. Physical and mental labor are the inevitable condition of his earthly existence. Physical labor is requisite to maintain him in the capacity of an organized being. It is the food of his body and the strength of his mind. Mental labor is indispensable to develop his powers of mind and expand and enlighten his understanding. The active powers of man necessarily follow the dictates of his understanding . . . [unless] the ignorance which naturally darken[s] his understanding be dissipated and his intellect directed in the pursuit of substantial knowledge he never can experience that health of body and happiness of mind of which his nature is susceptible. For the absence of one arises from the neglect of the other . . . Learn, therefore he must suffer. [5]

Teaching through October of 1854, he earned a little over fifty dollars. He decided to use the money to pay his way for five months at the Ashland Collegiate Institute in nearby Greene County for the winter term. There he had a room to himself and intensive classes in algebra, geometry, chemistry, French, logic, and composition. The institute, which was in its inaugural year, was a Methodist school. This made Chauncey Burroughs nervous. He told neighbors he wouldn't be surprised if his son returned at the end of term and announced a calling to preach the distasteful faith of John Wesley. Burroughs was a successful student in all his courses. He gained something of a reputation as a speaker when he won a heated debate over the Crimean War in which he took the side of England and France against Russia. He admitted to his son many years later that virtually all the arguments he'd used in the debate had been pilfered from an article on the war in *Harper's Magazine*.

When the term at Ashland ended in April of 1855, Burroughs was broke. He would need to find another teaching position to be able to continue with his studies. The Olive job had been taken by another when Burroughs enrolled at Ashland. He heard of several openings in the area of Plainfield, New Jersey, and he talked Chauncey into advancing him a few dollars to finance a job-hunting trip. The eighteen-year old had never before been more than thirty miles from home. He remained on deck for every moment of the ninety-mile steamboat journey down the Hudson from Kingston to Hoboken. As the boat passed Manhattan, Burroughs was awed by the sight of the vast metropolis of buildings, docks, people, and smokestacks. When the New Jersey job search proved unsuccessful, Burroughs made a point of stopping in Manhattan on his return.

He spent part of his day in New York idling outside the office of Fowler & Wells, publishers of the books and journals on phrenology that he so admired. (In just two months' time Fowler & Wells would publish the first edition of *Leaves of Grass*. The book was to change Burroughs's life; but he would not become aware of it for another five years.) After failing to muster the courage to go inside the print shop and introduce himself as a potential author, he wandered on to explore the rest of the city. He stopped at the famous Crystal Palace, an enormous octagon of glass and iron that stood on the present site of Bryant Park, between Fifth and Sixth avenues on Forty-second Street. The Palace sported the largest dome in the Western world—larger even than that of St. Paul's in London. The glass ceiling measured 123 feet high and 100 feet in diameter, and was supported by twenty-four iron columns. All of this housed nearly five acres of display and shop space.

Young Burroughs was both dazzled and disturbed by the spectacle. It seemed, he wrote a friend, that the whole village of Roxbury could fit under the gigantic enclosure. A guard told him that the Palace hosted over six thousand visitors per day—more than double the population of his home valley. "Put a farm under that transparent lid," he wrote in his notebook, "and grow anything you want all year round. The only thing lacking is moisture—but then a race that can invent a Crystal Palace must also be able to invent artificial rain. There is room enough in that huge, enclosed sky for a fair number of man-made clouds." He was impressed. Still, he wrote, there was something "chilling" and "unnatural" about the place. "Whether it is the grotesque size or the cold, unharmonious texture of metal and glass (as opposed to wood) construction, I do not know. But the idea that the future might be nothing but soaring glass and steel does make one ill-at-ease."

There were other things that gave pause as well. He crossed Forty-second Street and rode a steam elevator—one of the first in New York—to the top of the Latting Observatory, a popular tourist attraction that rose an astonishing 280 feet in the air. Using the bank of telescopes at the top, he surveyed the panorama of the great city as it rolled out across the island of Manhattan. He turned the telescope 360 degrees on its stand to take in the vast scene of factories, slums, and grime-choked streets surrounded by two rivers that already, in 1855, were brown with human and industrial waste. On the distant horizon, he could make out squares of idyllic green farmland in New Jersey and Long Island.

Aboard the train that carried him back to the Catskills, sitting beside a bag of used books he'd purchased at the stalls on William Street, he commented in his notebook that of all the people he'd seen in New York, he somehow got the feeling that none of them were really happy being there. "There is no 'hello' for the stranger," he wrote. "There is no feeling of fellowship, as one has up at home. Indeed, New York gives you quite the opposite notion. You feel you should clutch your wallet tightly. You sense a constant, undefined threat as you mingle in that vast, anonymous crowd. And you sense that if that threat becomes a real one, there are none about you to whom you might turn for aid. A certain element of faith and charity seems to be missing from the city. I must think further about this." [6]

He had spent so much of his traveling money on books that he had only enough cash to pay his fare to Griffin's Corners—twelve miles from Roxbury. He walked the rest of the way, across the side of Batavia Mountain, with a knapsack full of volumes that included Locke's *Essay on Human Understanding*, several of Dr. Johnson's works, and Saint-Pierre's *Studies of Nature*. "I reached home on the twentieth of May with an empty pocket and empty stomach, but with a bagful of books," he would recall. When he got home, he stayed home. He worked on the farm all that summer of 1855. In his spare time he devoured Locke, Johnson, and Saint-Pierre. When he was done with these, he sat down and mapped out seventy-nine additional works in a list that bore a disciplined headline: "Books I will read." The titles included Poe's poems and stories, Hume's essays, Bacon's works, *Don Quixote*, Webster's speeches, the writings of Hawthorne, and histories of the Crusades, the British Empire, and Greece. With big plans for expanding his intellectual horizons, that autumn found him once again back at Olive Township, in old Tongore, coaching his pupils of the year before.

DESPITE HIS RETURN TO the provincial insularity of the Catskills, Burroughs was experiencing a major personal change. While in New York he had seen, if not patronized, his first prostitutes. And the William Street bookstalls had sheltered their share of dealers in engraved erotica, which he had noticed carefully without actually investing in. Now, at Tongore, the eighteen-year-old Burroughs eyed the young ladies of the town with renewed interest.

One, in particular, seemed to be making fervid attempts to gain his attention. Attractive and strong-willed, with a trim, compact figure and dark, curly hair, Ursula North was thirteen months Burroughs's senior. Ursula was one of seven children. Her uncle was a trustee of the Tongore school. Her father, Uriah North, was one of the most prosperous farmers in the town of Olive, as his father had been before him. Her mother, Lydia, was a staunch Baptist who fasted every Sunday. Ursula herself was very devout, industrious, and thrifty. She worked long hours every day helping out around the farm. She had been away during Burroughs's first term at Tongore, living with relatives in Manhattan where she'd met and become engaged to a member of the Seventh Regiment. "But after she returned home [she] realized she did not love him well enough to marry him," recalled Ursula's sister Amanda in 1921, "so wrote and broke the engagement."

Little documentation of the courtship between John Burroughs and Ursula North exists. Burroughs's notebook was, at least at this time in his life, in no way a diary. The tattered pages serve as a guide to his intellectual development, but reveal little of his private life. We must piece together the early evolution of the romance from a few stray notes that survive, notes that primarily were sent by one party to the other to schedule or confirm a variety of contrived meetings and, later, formal dates at public events. Initially, Ursula seems to have been the pursuer to the extent that any respectable woman pursued any man in the 1850s. In mid-September, she sent a note to Burroughs saying that she intended to be present at a church supper with her parents, and that she hoped he might be planning to attend as well. She would "greatly appreciate" the opportunity to continue "the interesting but all too brief discussion" she'd enjoyed when meeting him a few weeks earlier at another social gathering. Two weeks later she wrote again, saying that if he did not mind she would have her father escort her to the school on an evening soon to watch a spelling bee "and see you administer the contest." A few days after the bee, she wrote to invite him to dinner with her family. In early November, comes the first note from Burroughs to Ursula, proposing that he escort her to a "donation party" for the school. Soon he was accompanying her to the Baptist church every Sunday.

By the close of term in April of 1856, after eight months of courtship, John Burroughs and Ursula North became engaged. There was an element of strain on what should have been a joyous event. The commitment from Burroughs seems to have been extorted. Ursula, growing weary of his silence with regard to the prospects for their future together, appears to have tried to spark his jealousy by flirting with another young man. In so small a town as Tongore, news of the flirtation was bound to get back to Burroughs. It did. He reacted. There was a spat. And there was the inevitable note from Ursula. "I think whoever it was that told you that yarn what you spoke of, must have a principle so small that you could blow it through a Hummingbird's quill into a little Red Ant's eye and they would only wink at it." She adamantly denied that the flirtation had taken place. However, she added, she could not be blamed for anything even were it true in the absence of any commitment from John. "A girl who wants a husband is likely to continue to look until she knows she has found one," she wrote. It was shortly after that John let Ursula know that she had indeed found one and should most definitely stop looking.

John wrote many letters about Ursula to his brother Curtis, who was living at home. Curtis was also pursuing a courtship. The two young men were both preoccupied with the sexual aspects of their relationships. In their frequent letters, they exchanged tales of their slow progress toward intimacy with their respective loves. John's descriptions of Ursula in his letters to Curtis always emphasized the physical. He did not discuss her personality or education, but rather the delicate smallness of her waist and hands, the soft whiteness of her skin, the piercing beauty of her eyes. He used the most florid prose when writing of his desires, cloaking naked thoughts in romantic language. He wrote Curtis of "vivid dreams of Ursula, dreams during which all of love's finest longings are fully requited." And he wrote of his frustration at Ursula's unwillingness to "favor" him with "her touch."

Up until his promise of marriage, all he seems to have taken away from the relationship in the way of the sensual gratification he craved was what he could get from the sedate holding of hands— this taking place only in broad daylight and only while sitting on the open front porch of her father's house. After the engagement, there were walks alone on country lanes. There were kisses and there were hands on hips, but nothing more. "Ursula gives me the slightest sample of the feast that is to come. She wets my taste and makes the saliva run," he wrote Curtis. "But she would have my soul before the main course is served. She would own it outright." [7]

BURROUGHS SAW HIMSELF IN print for the first time in May of 1856. The May 13 edition of a local paper near Roxbury, the *Bloomville Mirror,* carried an essay entitled "Vagaries viz. Spiritualism," signed with the nom de plume, "Philomath." The article attacked a previous one in a recent issue that argued for belief in the reality of all forms of metaphysical materializations. Burroughs's response is crammed full of big words. The machinery of the language is aimed less at doing the job of debunking the notion of ghosts than at showing off vocabulary. "And how consistent is it with every notion we ought to entertain of those celestial beings, to suppose they would leave the bright shores of immortality and descend to this obscure corner of creation," expounded Burroughs. "And why not make their visits in the light of day as well as under the cover of night? " [8]

Jay Gould had also been published in the *Bloomville Mirror.* In fact, it was he who introduced Burroughs to the owner of the little paper, Simon Champion, and encouraged Champion to publish some of Burroughs's writings. Champion had excerpted several sections of Gould's huge work-in-progress, *A History of Delaware County,* which the entrepreneurial Gould would publish himself in September of 1856. Gould had worked on his history for more than a year, while making a living as a surveyor. In a note to his friend Burroughs, Gould described the drudgery of his painstaking research into old deeds, diaries, and yellowed newspapers. (He had also interviewed many elder citizens of the community, including several of Burroughs's great aunts and uncles.) The prose of Gould's book is turgid at best. Nevertheless *A History of Delaware County* remains an important and reliable source of information on the region.

Although two years had passed without much contact between them, Gould and Burroughs were brought together once again, briefly, by a shared fascination with death, dying, and what, if anything, lay beyond the grave. This interest had been part of the impetus for Burroughs's "Vagaries viz. Spiritualism" paper. Now he and Gould, both of whom had experienced the death of a sibling during their adolescence, shared several discussions on the topic of immortality. One evening in the company of the master of the Roxbury Academy, J. W. McLany, Burroughs and Gould went to the home of a young man dying of consumption. Their intention was to watch with studious detachment as the man in the sickbed labored toward his final breath. "We watched with interest the changes of the body while the soul was departing," recalled McLany. "We yearned to behold with spiritual vision the immortal spirit as it passed away and to follow it in its flight within the portals of the spirit world." Burroughs stayed in the sickroom for only a few moments. He could not bear to witness the agony and delirium of the death struggle. After more than an hour, McLany and Gould emerged to announce with grave authority that the spirit had departed without being seen. That night, Gould was to write in his diary that "as regards the future world, except what the Bible reveals, I am unable to fathom its mysteries, but as to the present, I am determined to use all my best energies to accomplish this life's highest possibilities." [9]

Burroughs, like Gould, was in a period of intense religious confusion. He wanted desperately to be able to believe in the traditional Christian faith that was so important to his parents and to Ursula. Yet he had doubts—serious, and he feared, heretical doubts. Early in the spring of 1856, he went one night to a tent-meeting revival on the riverbank not far from Roxbury. Caught up in the excitement of the preacher's sermon and the chants and singing of the congregation, he stepped forward to be baptized and born again in the chilly waters of the Delaware. The river sparkled with the reflected light of the many torches that circled the tent. One after another those seeking baptism were seized, submerged, and held down while the preacher implored the Lord to cleanse away their sins and make them holy. One after another they emerged from the water praising Jesus, shouting that they had felt his power. When Burroughs's turn came, he allowed himself to be put down under the surface, and there he waited for the hand of God to touch him.

When he was brought back up, he shouted hallelujahs and praised the Lord Jesus as enthusiastically as had all the others, giving thanks for his salvation. Then he walked forlornly out of the water and up the road toward home. He wrote in his journal later that night of his exasperation at having felt "nothing" after asking the Lord to "take possession" of his soul. He wondered how many of the other proclamations of the "saved" were, like his, a fraud. He would have given anything to feel the spirit move within him. He would not at all have minded the safe, easy complacency that traditional belief would have yielded. "I look upon that man as lucky who feels a want the Church can supply," he would write. "We do not like to feel isolated and alone." He often expressed his admiration for the contentment his father felt when he sat in his pew at the old Roxbury meetinghouse every Sunday. "I would gladly have sat in the pew, too, if I could," he wrote. But he couldn't. The simple faith that required no reason would never be a part of him.

WHEN HE FINISHED TEACHING at Tongore in mid-April of 1856, Burroughs was left with enough money to enroll in Cooperstown Seminary, another college preparatory school, until the end of the summer term. It was at Cooperstown that he got the first hint of how he could find the warmth of faith in a universe that was, he suspected, devoid of a personal God. It was here that he first read the essays of Ralph Waldo Emerson, whose works had not made the seventy-nine-volume list of essential books that he had assembled the year before. Burroughs would recall that he read Emerson "in a sort of ecstasy." In Emerson, Burroughs found a philosophy of daring and inspiring affirmation: a revolutionary, natural theology that was the solvent of encrusted forms and traditions. Emerson's essay "Nature," composed the year before Burroughs was born, turned him toward finding the vital element of faith he had felt himself lacking.

In "Nature," Emerson proposed a religious emotion that was essentially pantheistic. He suggested a new theology that empha-sized the spiritual value of the physical world. "Standing on the bare ground," wrote Emerson, "my head bathed by the blithe air and uplifted into infinite space,—all mean egotism vanishes. I become a transparent eyeball; I am nothing; I see all; the currents of the

Universal Being circulate through me. I am part or parcel of God." Unifying all elements of natural creation equally was not, Emerson suggested, a personal God but rather an "Over-Soul" that contained the combined diverse phenomena of life in the universe. In his "Divinity School Address," Emerson attacked formal religion and championed intuitive, personal, spiritual experience. ". . . a man contains all that is needful to his government within himself," wrote Emerson. "As there is no screen or ceiling between our heads and the infinite heavens, so there is no bar or wall in the soul where man, the effect, ceases, and God, the cause, begins." Emerson emphasized the universality of moral law and the infinitude of the private man. He argued that the individual, in searching for a sound ethical base for his life, should turn not to God, nor to the state, nor to society, but to nature for the answer. In his address "The American Scholar," which Emerson delivered the August after Burroughs was born, he proposed that one's agenda should be to study nature and through that process come to know one's self.

Burroughs carried Emerson's *Essays* with him when he left Cooperstown in the autumn of 1856 and went to teach at Buffalo Grove, Illinois. The trip west was occasioned by several factors. A few of his friends from the seminary had found teaching posts in the region of Buffalo Grove and Polo, Illinois, and urged him to follow. Also, there seems to have been a momentary falling out with Ursula: an argument, a torrent of rash words from both of them, followed by a period of distance and relative coldness, although they remained engaged. It was a foreshadowing of what was to come, a scene that would be enacted again and again for more than fifty years. "Ursula speaks her mind always, no matter how many traps the truth sets off," he wrote Curtis. "The truth is not always a good thing. Yes, sometimes the truth is a very hurtful thing. In the long run, it can sometimes turn out not even to be the truth at all." To her sister, Ursula wrote, "John is a good man and I know it, but he needs someone to wake him up. He can't spend his whole life scribbling and expect to get anywhere. We will never have enough to marry on if he doesn't get his nose out of them books." [10]

Such was the state of their engagement when John left for Illinois. They each still told others that the relationship was solid, but both had doubts. They corresponded fairly regularly, swapping coldly polite pages filled with inquiries after family and friends. He did not tell her that he was cultivating a romance with a young lady of Polo. He told her instead that he was spending much time writing, which was also true. The theme of the one essay he wrote and rewrote endlessly during his months in Buffalo Grove, "Revolutions," was linked to the shift he was feeling in his emotions. Six months earlier, he would have sworn that he knew without any doubt that Ursula was the woman for him, that she was his destiny. Now, confronted with doubts, he sensed himself in the throes of nothing less than a personal revolution.

He viewed the upheaval as positive. "Revolutions," he wrote, "are the natural result [of the] progressive spirit, and the legitimate offspring of its vigorous and healthful growth. They are but shocks from the car of progress which, so far from indicating the slackening of its speed, are the sure evidence of its increasing velocity." As a part of his attempt at personal rebellion, he cultivated long, flowing, bohemian locks. On his way back to New York that spring, after having lost the Polo girl to another young man, he stopped in Chicago and had a photograph taken. The picture, the first we have of him, makes him look quite the young artist. But the affected hairstyle was to be short-lived. As soon as Ursula saw the hair, she explained that either the curls would come off or their wedding would be off. He was now resigned to the fact that she was the only woman prepared to have him for a husband; and he seems to have been intently interested in becoming one. So compromise was in order. Scissors were asked for, and the job done. All that was left of Burroughs's first brief fling at revolution was his little essay, which he would never publish.

In late July of 1857, the twenty-year-old Burroughs began teaching school at the village of High Falls, near Kingston, New York. On Saturday, September 12, he canceled class and walked the country road from Kingston to Olive in order to attend a wedding: his own. Ursula's mother had died just a few weeks before. The ceremony was short; the company small. None of Burroughs's relatives attended as his father did not believe he was mature enough to marry. The wedding was held in Ursula's home. The honeymoon took place in an upstairs bedroom while her father dozed down the hall. Burroughs left no account of the wedding night either in the form of a letter to Curtis or as a journal entry, save to tell of his annoyance when Ursula insisted on their getting down on their knees to pray before approaching the marital bed. "The old God of the Baptists is not a very useful bedroom accoutrement," he complained.

Ursula remained in her father's house after the ceremony while John returned to High Falls two days after the wedding. He was still boarding around. He had no place to move her into, and no prospect of one. If the frequency of his trips back to Olive is any indication, he soon overcame both Ursula's penchant for prayer and the inhibiting factor of her father sleeping only a few yards away from the conjugal bed. He made the long hike two and three times a week to be with her. He had given her his soul; now he would have her flesh. She told her sister Amanda that John was very affectionate, sometimes "overly so." It was to be more than a year before husband and wife would move in together. Burroughs continued to teach, first at High Falls, then at Rosendale (a little Ulster County town not far from Kingston on the Rondout Creek), and then in Newark, New Jersey. Finally, in February of 1859, the couple set up house in East Orange, New Jersey, where he was engaged to teach at a salary of fifty dollars per month, without board. During the next three years there would still be brief periods of economically imposed separation, but they were, as of 1859, seriously and truly together, for better or for worse.

3

MYRON BENTON &
TROUTBECK

*[When I first met Myron Benton] I had just begun to get hold of myself
with my pen; I was like a young bird just out of the nest. My flights were
short and rather awkward.*

— *from Burroughs's Introduction to
Charles Benton's pamphlet*
'Troutbeck, A Dutchess County
Homestead," 1916

BY LATE 1859, BURROUGHS was writing a periodic column for the
Saturday Press, a small New York literary journal that paid nothing,
or next to nothing, for contributions. His writing was still quite
affected, as is evidenced by the title of his occasional column:
"Fragments from the Table of an Intellectual Epicure." The pen
name under which he published was "All Souls." This All Souls was
a wordy spirit who specialized in strained analogies. "Every book
and every sermon ought to be a pair of magnetic slippers that shall
make us dance to a new tune, and feel as if we were walking on
thunderbolts," wrote All Souls in one typical column. "There is
nothing so healthy as a freshet in the soul. A man needs to be elated
and depressed; to be lifted up until he feels he could grab the big
dipper and . . . sunk down till one foot breaks through Hades."

He was describing his own character quite accurately: puffed up
and full of confidence one day, bitterly depressed and pessimistic the
next. He tried to ease his nervous insecurity about his talents, ambitions, and future by telling himself there was "nothing so healthy"
as these drastic mood swings. Every single one, he told himself, was
needed and helpful and improved his perspective on himself and the

world. There were more down days than up because, as Ursula kept reminding him, his prospects did not look good. She complained that there was not enough money in schoolteaching. He grew more and more depressed when he realized the only promise that schoolmastering held was a gypsylike migration every year or so, from one district to another, and the need for supplementary labor to make ends meet. Back in Olive, Ursula had grown up on one of the most profitable and best-run farms in the county. Her father had hired seasonal workers by the dozens to bring in the crops. Now she found herself accompanying her husband to hire out as a laborer to pick strawberries when school was not in session. No, she told him, schoolteaching would not do. Neither would writing. Small New York literary magazines such as the *Saturday Press* and the *Leader* loyally published a steady stream of papers from Burroughs on such Emerson-like subjects as "A Thought on Culture," "World Growth," "Theory and Practice," and "Some of the Ways of Power." But Ursula was unimpressed. She would applaud his writing when it brought in some cash, and not before.

Burroughs made several halfhearted stabs at other occupations. He got a job as an apprentice draftsman at a Newburgh carriage factory but was fired after a week when he demonstrated no aptitude at all. Later, while teaching at Orange, New Jersey, he and another young would-be writer, Elijah Allen, tried their hands at becoming lecture impresarios. They engaged the popular poet Bayard Taylor to speak, rented a hall in Newark, sold tickets, and made seventy-five cents apiece. Following his flirtation with lecture promotion, he returned to his old teaching position at Olive. In the evenings he read medicine with Dr. Hull, having decided that doctors made a good living. Like the draftsman job and the lecture trade, however, Burroughs's career as a medical student would also be short-lived. Other options, or illusions of options, came and went. He would take Ursula west and become a ticket agent for the railroads. He would move back to Newark and open a belt-buckle factory. He would get a mortgage and buy the old home from his parents, there to live peacefully among the cows. In the midst of these brief enthusiasms, he sat down and wrote a poem entitled "Waiting," the theme of which was complacency. His real instinct, as revealed in the poem, was to wait out circumstances. He was reactive rather than proactive. He would let his future find him rather than he it.

> I stay my haste. I make delays.
> For what awaits this eager pace?
> I stand amid eternal ways.
> And what is mine shall know my face.

Ursula was not happy with his complacency. With each passing enthusiasm, she became more uncertain of their future together. She knew what she wanted, and what she wanted was not much to ask for—a home, a predictable livelihood, security. Burroughs, on the other hand, was clearly without a focused ambition. The archer had his arrow, but no target was in sight. He loved books. He remained attracted to the romantic notion of being a writer while flirting with other potential careers. But he had yet to expend any real effort toward a life in literature. His writings were by and large nothing more than unanalytic, lazy imitations of the work of others. He reached far away from his own world for topics, and so wrote paper after paper on such subjects as "Revolutions" and "Cities" when what he knew about was trout fishing and farmlore. He'd forgotten James Oliver's poem about the skull of the fox. He'd forgotten that if one's own experience was not worthy of literature, then nothing was.

Ursula seems to have embarked upon some extreme programs to make him realize that he was wasting both their time. At Marlboro-on-Hudson, just above Newburgh, where Burroughs taught from the fall of 1860 to the spring of 1861, he and Ursula lived in a rented house not far from the school. Early in their tenure at Marlboro, Ursula forbade John to use their parlor for "scribbling." When he insisted, she locked the door. That made him angry, so he kicked the door till he broke the lock. Then, too upset to write, he took his gun and went to the woods. After that, when he wanted to write, he would go up to the attic and sit on the stairs. Using the top step for his desk, he got light from a little attic window. If he insisted on "masquerading" as a writer, she wrote her sister, "the fool" would have to do it where she did not have to watch. [1]

❧

EARLY IN THE AUTUMN of 1860, James Russell Lowell, the essayist and poet who was then serving as editor-at-large for the *Atlantic Monthly*, received an intriguing and perplexing submission for the magazine. The item was an essay entitled "Expression." It came from a young man who wrote in the accompanying note that he was employed as a schoolteacher in the Hudson River town of Marlboro, New York. He said that he had composed the essay that summer while working as a fieldhand for his parents on a dairy farm somewhere in the Catskill Mountains. Lowell had a vague recollection of having seen the name—John Burroughs—in print somewhere before, but beyond this he had no prior knowledge of the person who claimed to be the author of the piece. After reading the essay once, Lowell decided it was quite fine. After reading it twice, he decided it was plagiarized.

The paper had clearly been written by Emerson. There was no mistaking Emerson's style of presentation. Every paragraph bore the stamp of the philosopher of the moral sentiment. In "Nature" Emerson had suggested that nature was something completely undefinable that "leads us on and on, but arrives nowhere, keeps no faith with us. All promise outruns the performance. We live in a system of approximations. Every end is prospective of some other end, which is also temporary; a round and final success nowhere." The essay that Burroughs had sent in turn proposed that nature existed in the mind of man not as an absolute realization, but as a condition, as something that was constantly "becoming." And this was God's art of expression. "We can behold nothing pure; all that we see is compounded and mixed," wrote the author. "Nature stands related to us at a certain angle, and at a little remove either way—back toward its grosser side, or up towards its ideal tendency—would place it beyond our ken."

Lowell wanted to accept "Expression" for publication in the *Atlantic*. But before he did so, he checked through Emerson's published works in order to assure himself that the article had not appeared previously. He took the added precaution of writing to Emerson directly. Emerson responded that he was not the author of

"Expression," but that he could see why Lowell would be prompted to raise the question. This young Burroughs certainly had a style and point-of-view that were distinctly reminiscent of his own. [2]

In the *Atlantic Monthly* of the 1860s, contributions were always published anonymously. When "Expression" appeared in the issue of November 1860, many readers assumed it to be by Emerson, as was evidenced by letters to the editor that were printed in subsequent issues. For the next fifty years, both "Poole's Index" and "Hill's Rhetoric" would credit the essay to Emerson. Late in life, after a weighty accumulation of fame put Burroughs in a strong position to correct these errors of attribution, he would not bother to make the effort to do so. He would tell his son, Julian, that even though he was the author of "Expression," the essay was actually more Emerson's than his own. At the time that he wrote "Expression," he explained in a letter to Julian, he was "so much under the Emersonian spell so as not to have had a personality of my own." He told Julian that there was a degree of idolatry involved in his early experience of Emerson. "I was looking for heroes in those days. I was very young. I was very unsure of myself and my ambitions. And I did not understand Emerson at all. But youth always looks for some great man to model itself upon—and I was in no state of mind to hear my own hero's message which said that heroes were a dangerous thing to have, and that the only real greatness one's world had to offer resided within one's own self." [3]

The event of the publication of "Expression" in the November 1860 *Atlantic Monthly* was a watershed in Burroughs's development as an individual and a writer. In one sense Burroughs was flattered that something from his pen might be confused with the prose of his great hero; but in another sense he was horrified. "The essay had some merit, but it reeked with the Emersonian spirit and manner . . ." he wrote many years later. "I quickly saw that this kind of thing would not do for me." He had to get on ground of his own. He had to get the Emersonian musk out of his garments. To this end, he decided to bury his garments in the earth, as it were, and see what his native soil would do toward drawing out the scent. He began to write on all manner of rural themes—sugar making, cows, haying, stone walls. "I wrote about things of which I knew, and was, therefore, bound to be more sincere with myself than in writing on Emersonian themes." [4]

To make a guru of Emerson had been to deny the very heart of the Emersonian message, which said it was folly to have any master. "There is a time in every man's education," wrote Emerson, "when he arrives at the conviction that envy is ignorance, that imitation is suicide." Whitman would later confide to Burroughs that he too, as a young man, had gone through a similar confusion. Whitman found the cure in Emerson's own philosophy. "The best part of Emersonism," wrote Whitman to Burroughs, "is that it breeds the giant that destroys itself. 'Who wants to be any man's mere follower?' lurks behind every page." [5]

Now, trying earnestly to write from his own true experience, Burroughs retreated to the past that was really him, the country childhood and the simple things that had shaped his being. He found the personal revolution in thought and culture he'd sought in so many distant places when he turned his focus back on that rural farmstead where he'd had his beginning. By going home to find his themes, he also found a genuine voice and an inspired vision. The cup he filled now with sincere recollection, he had first emptied, he wrote, of "hollow, heartless rhetoric" on topics thrice-removed from his personal knowledge and deepest concerns. "We would do well to read in the woods and fields;" he wrote, speaking mostly of himself, "to muse in the barn and barnyard; to court familiarity with cows and sheep and swine and hens and haymows . . . that we may infuse something fresh and real into our culture and speech." [6]

IN THE SPRING OF 1862, Ursula decided the twenty-five-year-old Burroughs was "impure" in the way he made "unending demands" on her with regard to physical favors. She had consulted with her minister back home in Olive, and had been advised that Burroughs's constant attentions were "unhealthy" and "unclean." She used all these descriptive phrases in a note—yet another note—she gave him at the close of the spring term. It was time for them to shut down their rented Marlboro house and return to his parents' home in the

Catskills, as had been their custom for several summers. She had decided that this year she would go to visit relatives in Troy. She believed he should spend July and August by himself, so as to have an opportunity to learn chastity and self-control. "There should be more to a marriage than what you want to bring, or what you want me to give," she wrote in the candid letter. "Just as there is more than a bedroom to a house, there is more than the activity of a bedroom to a marriage. I would like to think that I share more than just that part of your life. I would like to think that our love can rise above the mere physical to a higher and more wholesome plane." [7]

Burroughs put up with the separation, but did not hide the fact that he did not like it. He tried to make her jealous in letters written from Roxbury, where he worked in his parents' fields all summer to earn seven or eight dollars that would not be payable until October. "Yesterday I put on my best 'bib and tucker,' and went down to the village to church," he wrote. "The girls looked charmingly at me, and I looked charmingly back again. So, so." [8] Of course he had not gone to church. He had reached a point where he genuinely detested the exercise of a church service. He could rarely be coaxed to church when his wife wanted to be accompanied, let alone when he had no partner pestering him to attend.

Ursula's attitude about sex was either that she did not find Burroughs very attractive over time, or that she was uncomfortable with the sexual act itself. Either attitude would have been much at variance with what Burroughs was encountering in the women he was beginning to meet through his growing circle of literary and bohemian friends.

Burroughs visited Pfaff's beer cellar, the hub of Manhattan's literary bohemia, in mid-April of 1862. (The bar was located under the Broadway pavement near Bleeker Street in Greenwich Village.) He was hoping to get a glimpse of Walt Whitman, whose poems had greatly interested him ever since he'd read "A Child's Reminiscence" (later entitled "Out of the Cradle Endlessly Rocking") in the Christmas 1859 issue of the *Saturday Press*. He was disappointed when he did not find the poet at the bar. Instead Burroughs met Henry Clapp, the former editor of the defunct *Saturday Press* who was now editor of the *Leader*.

Burroughs had corresponded with Clapp often and had contributed many articles to his publications. Clapp greeted him warmly and bought him a beer. The witty, alcoholic Clapp was, it soon became obvious to Burroughs, the king of the place. Clapp's queen, who sat by his side, was Ada Clare, an actress and writer who was notorious for having unapologetically borne a child out of wedlock by the composer and piano virtuoso Louis Moreau Gottschalk. ("Ada Clare is really beautiful," Burroughs was to write to a friend, "not a characterless beauty, but a singular, unique beauty.") Burroughs also met another writer and actress, Adah Isaacs Menken, who had been married four times (including one marriage to a heavyweight boxing champ known as the Benicia Boy). At the time Burroughs met her, she had the starring role in a Byronic melodrama *Mazeppa*, a part that called for her to wear just a G-string over flesh-tinted tights. The costume made her famous as the "naked lady . . . the most perfectly developed woman in the world."

At the bar, with Adah Menken hovering close by his arm and eyeing him up and down longingly, the nervous Burroughs sat for an hour or more and listened to Clapp's stories of literary personalities. The editor Horace Greeley, Clapp said, was "a self-made man who worships his creator." Clapp spoke at length about his literary assistant, Thomas Bailey Aldrich, who he said was headed for great things as a writer. (Thirty years later Mark Twain would call Aldrich "the wittiest man in seven centuries.") And he talked of Whitman, whom he considered the greatest poet yet produced by America. (Clapp was to die of cirrhosis of the liver in 1865, after a brief attempt to revive the *Saturday Press* during which he would be the first to publish Whitman's "O Captain! My Captain" and Twain's "The Celebrated Jumping Frog of Calaveras County.") A few days after his visit to Pfaff's, Burroughs wrote to Elijah Allen that Menken had tried to "keep" him for the night, but that he had passed up the opportunity. "Don't ask me why I did so, given Ursie's behavior of late," he wrote. "I suppose my intellect sanctions more freedom than do my emotions. Perhaps if I read a bit more of Whitman I shall end up less chaste." [9]

Being completely chaste that summer at the home farm, with his wife a hundred miles away, he had plenty of time to write. He composed (and then rewrote three times) a paper on the theme of "Analogy" that would be published in *Knickerbocker Magazine* the following December. Sitting at a table in his old bedroom at his parents' house, he filled the essay with language that was symptomatic of the era in which he found himself. The Civil War had begun not long before, and was much on his mind. His older brother Hiram was thinking of joining the Delaware militia that would soon be bound for the battlefields of Virginia. His father talked of little else than the news from the front. "Nature is no disunionist," Burroughs wrote in his essay, "but forever aims at wholeness and continuity, linking the smallest with the greatest, the lowest with the highest, the nearest with the remotest, and balancing the whole as one body. " Toward the end of the summer, he used the war to try to leverage Ursula into coming back to him. "I know not how the hearts of other people may be ossified," he wrote, "or turned to stone, but I know mine is flesh and blood, eminently so. The probabilities are that I shall enlist, and if you are not here before one week, you need not come, as by that time I shall (I hope) pass through Kingston as Lieutenant in the first Regm. of Delaware Blues." He added that if he should not return, it was arranged that she should feel no want, "except it be to want another husband, which want can be easily supplied. I pity him, however, if you leave him as you do me."[10]

He actually had no intention of joining the army, although he was downright enthusiastic about the outbreak of war. "Only guns will free the black man," he had written to James Oliver several years before, when the latter had unwittingly found himself in the middle of a civil war being fought in the Kansas territory between Free-Soil and proslavery settlers. Oliver had written to Burroughs with complaints about Captain John Brown, whose Free-Soil militia was making blood flow all over the territory in order to keep slavery out of Kansas. In May of 1856, Brown and his men kidnapped five unarmed pro-slavery settlers along Pottawatomie Creek, in Kansas, and split their heads with broadswords. Oliver, who was an abolitionist himself, had written Burroughs that he was nevertheless horrified by the murders. "Brown is right," Burroughs responded to Oliver. "It may be an inconvenient fact—but the fact is that it will take blood (lots of it) to wash away the stain of slavery." Of course, not all were as delighted as Burroughs with the advent of war. In a poem published in the *Leader*, Whitman voiced distress. "Schemes, politics fail—all is shaken—all gives way," he wrote. "Nothing is sure."

To a new friend, the poet and tobacco farmer Myron Benton of Amenia Junction, Leedsville, New York, Burroughs wrote in the fall of 1862 that the "war feeling" ran high with him, "but I have not enlisted and probably shall not." His tremendous sympathy for the cause of union and abolition was counterbalanced, he wrote, by the fact that he had lost all confidence in the generals who commanded the armies of the North, "not one of whom I would serve under without compulsion." McClellan, Halleck, and the others seemed to Burroughs to rely too much on precise tactical equations instead of on "dash and bravery and rapidity." The Army of the Potomac, he wrote Benton from the safety of his Catskill Mountains fireside, spent too much time planning attacks instead of launching them. [11]

Myron Benton, the correspondent with whom Burroughs shared these sentiments, was a young man of about Burroughs's age who he had not yet met. Benton's enormous farm—an inherited 800-acre spread the size of New York's Central Park—lay some miles east of Poughkeepsie. Benton was twenty-eight years old in 1862—three years older than Burroughs. He was a minor pastoral poet whose work had appeared regularly in the *Saturday Press*, the *Radical*, and other magazines. Benton is less well known today for his poems than for the fact that the last letter of the dying Thoreau, composed in March of 1862, was written to him. "If I were to live, I should have much to report on Natural History generally," Thoreau said to the young man whose letter of appreciation he'd recently received. "I suppose that I have not many months to live."

Benton was much in the habit of sending out notes to strangers whom he admired. This was how he first came in contact with Burroughs that summer after Thoreau's death. "I thought," wrote Benton, "as the expression of one obscure opinion, I would pen you a word thanking you for the pleasure your writings have given me. I have only seen them, to recognize them, in the *Leader* for the past three or four months." Benton was taken with a series of papers on rural themes that Burroughs had written under the general heading of "From the Back Country." Burroughs's writings, Benton told him, were full of "deep and excellent thought." [12]

Burroughs received Benton's unsolicited letter of praise just when he needed it most—when he was greatly ill at ease about himself and his prospects. "Your friendly greeting found me in a hayfield," Burroughs wrote in answer. "I am sincerely obliged to you for your kindly expression of interest. I did not suppose my scribblings in the *Leader* would attract attention in any quarter, much less call forth expressions like your own." [13]

Several letters were exchanged. It turned out that Burroughs and Benton had much in common. Both men had agrarian roots, and both were devotees of Emerson, Thoreau, and Whitman. Burroughs decided he wanted to meet this distant soul mate. "Do you ever come to Poughkeepsie?" he asked. "Perhaps we might meet there. Suggest any place between here and New York that you might have occasion to be at, and I could probably see you. " [14] A meeting was arranged for the autumn. Burroughs had reclaimed his wife (after a promise of less passion on his part) and returned to Olive to take up teaching at his old school. On a crisp Friday in October, Burroughs traveled to Poughkeepsie where he met Benton at a hotel on Main Street. The two went for a walk and wound up sitting on a rocky point just south of the dock for the Highland ferry on the Hudson River. "We sat there an hour or more and opened our minds to each other," wrote Burroughs. "Charles Benton, Myron's brother, had enlisted in the 150th Regiment, which was then in camp near Poughkeepsie. We saw him then—a fine farm boy, just out of his teens, and in the afternoon Myron drove me home with him to Leedsville, thirty miles away." [15]

Benton's farm, Troutbeck, lay on the Webatuck River (a branch of the Housatonic), not far from the New York-Connecticut border. The place was idyllic. A spring flowed twenty yards from the old farmhouse in which Benton and his brother had been raised. A long, gradual flight of stone steps led from the back porch down to the spring, which welled up through white sand and gravel and sometimes overflowed into the nearby river. "Trout come up from the Weebatook [*sic*] River and dwell there and become domesticated," Burroughs wrote, "and take lumps of butter from your hand, or rake the ends of your fingers if you tempt them." [16] A huge lawn encompassing ten acres circled the house and rolled down to the river. Visiting the spot in 1922, Sinclair Lewis would call it "not a lawn," but rather "a grass grown cathedral."

As they walked about the farm, Benton explained to Burroughs that the place had been bought by his grandfather, Caleb Benton, in 1793. In addition to the house in which Benton lived, built in 1765, there were several other homes on the farm. The Delamater House, in which George Washington spent a night during the Revolutionary War, had been built built by John Delamater in 1761. Century Lodge, the birthplace of Myron's cousin, the poet and essayist Joel Benton, had been built in 1794 by Joel's grandfather, another Joel Benton, who had been a member of the state legislature. Finally, there was also The Maples, originally built as part of a woolen mill about 1809, and later renovated by Myron Benton into a home for his brother Charles.

"The Benton farm came nearer being the ideal farm and country home than any farm I had ever seen," Burroughs would recall. The landscape in which Troutbeck found itself situated was one of repose, contentment, bounty.

> It sits there in a series of easy fertile river and glacier benches and gently rolling pasture lands, with the placid and picturesque Webatuck winding leisurely through it, walled in on the west and north by a high wooded ridge which gives one a comforting sense of protection and seclusion, running away to the east in a broad expanse of meadow land dotted with noble oaks and elms, suggesting a bounty of hay and grain on the easiest terms, lifted up in the southwest into low rounded hills and wooded slopes, then opening its arms to the south in many acres of tillable land to all the genial influences that one so readily associated with such an exposure. [17]

Burroughs brought with him to Troutbeck a copy of Whitman's *Leaves of Grass*. The book was a recent gift from Elijah Allen. Although Burroughs and Benton had seen Whitman's poems in the *Leader* and other magazines, this was the first chance either of them had to pour through the length and breadth of the *Leaves*. They hiked to a distant pasture of Benton's farm, through fields of cut tobacco plants, to a large boulder that Benton called "Mulberry Rock" because of the bushes that surrounded it. [18] With a bag of chestnuts to snack on, the two new friends spent several hours taking turns reading aloud to each other from Whitman's book. They also exchanged information about the poet, of which Burroughs seems to have had the most bountiful supply. When Burroughs had visited Pfaff's, Clapp told him that Whitman lived in Brooklyn, was unmarried, and earned about seven or eight dollars a week writing for the newspapers. Not long before, the poet had written a series of papers for the *Leader* on his experiences as a volunteer at New York Hospital, which had recently been taken over by the military to receive wounded from the fields of battle in Virginia and Pennsylvania. Both Burroughs and Benton had read Whitman's hospital sketches with great interest.

Two weeks before Burroughs's visit to Pfaff's, Whitman gave a reading at which he unveiled a poem that was soon published in the *Boston Evening Transcript*, the *Leader*, and *Harper's Weekly*. Burroughs brought the *Leader* with him to Benton's farm and read to Benton the new Whitman piece that had not yet made it into *Leaves*. It was a poem that Burroughs told Benton he did not like: a poem that by emphasizing the individual human tragedies of the war tended to discount the necessity of the fight. Burroughs believed the war against the Confederacy fulfilled a critical need for a "bloody rupture" in the country after which all might be made whole again, stronger and better for the pain of the violation. In the poem Whitman implied that he thought the bloodletting of civil war too great a misery to endure for the promised rewards of abolition and union.

> Beat! Beat! drums—blow! bugles! blow!
> Through the windows—through doors—burst like a
>   ruthless force,
> Into the solemn church, and scatter the congregation,
> Into the school where the scholar is studying;
> Leave not the bridegroom quiet—no happiness must he
>   have now with his bride,
> Nor the peaceful farmer any peace, ploughing his field or

gathering his grain,
So fierce you whirr and pound you drums—so shrill you
bugles blow . . .

"Your visit here will be retained in my memory . . . very long and
sweetly," wrote Benton to Burroughs shortly after the latter's stop at
Troutbeck. "My life has been somewhat destitute of friends of a
certain class. I mean those whose bias of mind is such that they can
call forth (of that kind which you can) sympathies in certain regions
which had before been shut off by a kind of impassable 'Northwest
Passage'—a frigid strait for voyaging undoubtedly, but there was a
warm open sea around the Pole within." Burroughs was equally
delighted with Benton, whom he would describe as "a poet and
philosopher, a farmer, and a reviewer, cultivating the alluvian of his
Webutuck [*sic*] Valley but turning up the deepest sub-soil with his
philosophical spade." [19]

Burroughs would write that it was the "tranquil, sane" spirit of
Troutbeck that begat Myron Benton. "Such a man," he wrote, "is
only the outcome of a family after it has dwelt long and lovingly in
one spot, and its soil of life has become rich, as it were." Benton's
poems were of his farm. And his days were spent nurturing his acres
with the same diligence and love he brought to his poems. "Benton
is a poet who writes his poetry in the landscape as well as in his
books," wrote Burroughs. "He is a beautifier of the land. One such
lover of nature in every neighborhood would soon change the aspect
of the whole country." Benton was "a planter of trees, a preserver of
old picturesque cottages, lover of paths and streams, and beautifier
of highways." He was a seeker and cultivator of all that gives flavor
to a place. He was therefore also "the practical poet of whom the
country everywhere needs more." [20] They would remain friends for
forty years.

In December Burroughs wrote Benton of a move he had just
made. He'd given up his post at Olive in favor of a more lucrative
teaching position. His new location was Highland Falls, on the
Hudson below Newburgh, close by the Military Academy at West

Point. "I am quite pleasantly located right in the midst of the [Hudson] Highlands," he wrote, "and Nature looks at me with a very stern and rugged face. West Point is only two miles away, the river one quarter of a mile, and Cozzen's famous hotel in our very midst." [21] Burroughs next wrote Benton in early January, inviting him down and sweetening the invitation with an image he thought the bachelor Benton would surely find appealing. "It strikes me [this place] would be a perfect paradise to a young unmarried man," wrote Burroughs, "as a certain element of the population which is much given to bonnets and blushes greatly predominates. Only a few hours ago I was whirling among a lot of the steel-shod beauties on the pond, and of course played the gallant in assisting them on and off with their skates. Think of that for a married man!" [22]

In the same letter, Burroughs told Benton that there was a "splendid" library at West Point, and that he felt like laying "forcible hands" on it. "I can go in and read for an hour or two, but cannot bring a book away with me." The collection was vast. It included an especially fine assortment of works on natural history which he found himself dipping into frequently. That spring, he went on several hikes with Professor Eddy, a botanist from the academy, and began an informal program of self-tutoring in the frequency and variety of wild-flowers in the Hudson Highlands. "I have taken an unusual interest in the flowers this spring," he wrote Benton in April of 1863. "The corydalis and hepatica grow here in great abundance; also the trailing arbutus, I am told, but I have not found it yet. I have been looking for the claytonia, but have not seen it yet, have you? Tell me the name of some very rare plant that you have found, and I will look for it here." [23] He kept a log of what plants he spotted, in what numbers, and in what terrain. He recorded dates of first blooms at various elevations.

In early July, while the three-day battle of Gettysburg raged and laid waste to 51,000 lives, the war hawk Burroughs hiked the quiet woods on the south side of Stormking Mountain, near Highland Falls, and recorded twelve varieties of flowers in his little notebook. Burroughs also took up the study of ornithology at about this time. He had become fascinated with a copy of Audubon's Elephant Portfolio edition of *The Birds of America* in the library of the Military Academy. He bought binoculars. He invested sixty cents in an illustrated reference book for use in the field. He began recording his sightings of birds beside his notations on flowers. ". . . I am much interested in the birds," he wrote Benton, "at least of late I can think or talk of nothing else."

He devoured an essay by Wilson Flagg entitled "The Birds of Field and Forest" from an old (December 1858) edition of the *Atlantic Monthly*. After reading Flagg, he turned to Thoreau. Soon, he decided that he himself should try his hand at turning nature study into literature. He began writing a paper about the ornithological events of spring, tentatively calling it "The Return of the Birds." Here, in his first formal attempt at composing a nature essay, he married his growing knowledge of both flowers and birds. "The dandelion tells me when to look for the swallow," he wrote, "the dogtooth violet when to expect the wood-thrush, and when I have found the wake-robin in bloom I know the season is fairly inaugurated. With me this flower is associated, not merely with the awakening of Robin, for he has been awake some weeks, but with the universal awakening and rehabilitation of nature." [24]

Burroughs was "full of the birds," he would recall, when Emerson came to lecture at West Point in June of 1863 and Burroughs contrived to meet him. Benton, whom Burroughs had been unable to lure to Highland Falls with the promise of unmarried nymphs, was easily and quickly brought there with the promise of Emerson. The two young writers sought out their hero at his hotel, and spent an hour or more walking and talking with him. Burroughs, in the first flush of his infatuation with natural history and its literature, was full of questions about that other self-taught literary naturalist, Henry Thoreau. Thoreau, responded Emerson, was really more at home with animals than with people. He had, said Emerson, infinite patience with any beast and absolutely no patience to spare on any man. Emerson did the best he could not to dominate the conversation. He was plainly not interested in delivering a lecture to the two young fellows who tailed him as he carried his bag through the hotel lobby and did the paperwork of departure at the desk. He let them talk. He asked questions. He seemed eager to know their minds.

Eventually, after taking the measure of Burroughs and Benton, Emerson spoke more readily. Hearing that Burroughs was interested in natural history, he recommended a book by his cousin, the botanist G. B. Emerson, on the trees and shrubs of Massachusetts. After a question from Burroughs, he described David Wasson, a Unitarian minister and essayist of Concord with whom Burroughs had corresponded. Wasson, said Emerson, was "one of the best heads" among the Concord Transcendentalists, but "the most indiscreet—if medicine is prescribed for him, he will double or triple the dose." He went on to say that another worthy Concord citizen, Bronson Alcott, was eloquent with speech but not with pen. He instructed Burroughs and Benton never to miss a chance to hear Alcott talk, but explained that "something negative" happened to Alcott's inspiration whenever he tried to put pen to paper. "I get more pain than pleasure from his writings," Emerson said.

As Emerson spoke, he walked casually from the hotel to the boat landing, where his schedule called for him to catch the ferry across the river to the town of Garrison. Burroughs carried his bag for him—a shiny black oilcloth bag, he would remember. "We didn't cross the ferry with him," recalled Burroughs many years later. "I suppose our sixpences were pretty short. Standing at the very edge of the pier as the boat pulled away, we listened as Emerson continued to talk. When he could no longer make himself heard, he simply stared at us benignly with that angelic smile, and with his long arm waved us a sweeping farewell before turning toward the other shore." [25] His good-bye glance, Burroughs remembered, felt like a "benediction."

Burroughs and Benton told Elijah Allen the story of their encounter with Emerson when the three men camped in the Adirondacks during August. Allen reciprocated with tales of someone Burroughs and Benton found at least as interesting as they did Emerson: Walt Whitman. Allen had moved to Washington, D.C. several months before to open an army supply store. Whitman was another recent immigrant to the capital city, having moved there from Brooklyn in December of 1862 after going to Virginia to search out his brother George, who had been wounded at the battle of Fredericksburg. Whitman supported himself, Allen reported, with a job as a clerk at the Bureau of Indian Affairs, a branch of the Department of the Interior. Allen, who'd met Whitman at Pfaff's more than two years earlier, had struck up a close friendship with the poet in Washington. "Between Walt Whitman and me has passed the bond of beer, and we are friends," Allen had written Burroughs that spring. [26] "Walt strolled in today as he frequently does," Allen wrote in another note. "The whole front of our store is open and shaded with an awning, and is a cool pleasant place, coming in from the street. Sometimes when I am busy I'll see Walt's picturesque form in one of the many camp-chairs, a fan in his hand; and then, after while, he is gone. When I am not busy I sit down and talk with him." [27]

By the light of their campfire on the Boreas River, not far from Mount Marcy, Burroughs and Benton pumped Allen for information about the poet they both admired. The gray-bearded Whitman, Allen told them, was a man of about fifty years of age. (He was actually forty-four.) Allen explained that Whitman spent most of his free time either working on his cycle of war poems, *Drum Taps*, or doing volunteer work in the Army hospitals in and around Washington. Allen described the sight of Whitman, his arms full of bottled drinks and bags of fruit, walking briskly down the street on his way to do some good in the wards. Allen, who accompanied Whitman on a few hospital calls, was to write Burroughs movingly of how he'd watched Whitman's "large active sympathy reaching down to [a] homesick soul shivering within a shattered body, and lifting it into the light and warmth of love." [28] Whitman did not discriminate to whom he gave his care, said Allen. He tended to the Confederate wounded as quickly as he did the Union boys. He seemed to have no side to take. Whitman's only enemy, Allen told Burroughs, was the suffering.

In the midst of their talk of Whitman, Burroughs wondered aloud to Allen whether Washington was not a town he should try his fortunes in. He was increasingly unhappy with the remuneration associated with teaching school. Ursula seemed always to want more than he could afford to provide, and he was beginning to run into debt. "I refuse to scrimp on the needs of normal life," she wrote her sister. "I spend what I must spend in order to be respectable. John says I always spend more than is necessary, but that is not the case." [29] Thinking out loud beside the fire where six trout sizzled in the pan, Burroughs reasoned that he could not do any worse financially in Washington than he was doing in New York. It seemed that Allen, who did a brisk business selling field gear and cartridges to those members of the undersupplied Union army who had the price, was a success. Perhaps Burroughs could find relative affluence in Washington, too.

Allen tried to discourage him. Washington was a hard town, he counseled Burroughs. It was an overcrowded provincial city filled with former slaves, white refugees from the war-torn border states, and soldiers—many soldiers. The forests of downtown Washington were not made of trees, Allen told the budding naturalist, but rather of glistening bayonets. Allen made it plain that he felt he had "lucked" into a good business, and that many other civilians in the city were starving. Allen reminded Burroughs that he had not moved to the capital for pecuniary reasons in the first place. He had only gone there to be near his fiancee, Elizabeth Akers (the widow of the sculptor Paul Akers and a popular sentimental poet who published under the name "Florence Percy"). If it were not for Elizabeth, explained Allen, he would flee Washington immediately despite his flourishing trade at the army supply store of Allen, Clapp & Co. No matter how much money he made there, the town was still a "detestable place."

A detestable place, perhaps, but also to Burroughs's mind a likely escape hatch. And he was beginning to think he might be needing an escape.

4

WASHINGTON, WAR, &
WHITMAN

Where is the poet who strikes his roots down deep and draws up for us some
of the rude vigor and freshness of the earth itself? A poet in whom Nature
wells up full and lusty, overriding and keeping under all mere prettiness
and excrescence?

— Journal Entry, *August 7, 1865*

MAKING A SHORT VISIT to Washington, D.C., in March of 1912, the
seventy-five-year-old John Burroughs would write to a friend that
the place was full of nostalgia for him. This city, where he had spent
the decade of his life from 1863 to 1873, had changed dramatically.
No more was the town bordered by dense woodlands as it had been
when he'd first arrived there in '63. No longer were herds of cattle
(beef for the Army of the Potomac) chased down Pennsylvania
Avenue to pens beside the half-finished Washington Monument.
No longer was Walt Whitman on hand to amuse and delight and
challenge. It seemed the only remnant of the Washington he had
known so many years before was the dominating architecture of the
buildings of state: the White House, the Treasury Building where he
had been employed, and of course the Capitol itself. "The one thing
I see here as I go about that looks like an old friend, almost like the
face of a member of my own family, is the Dome of the Capitol," he
wrote. "It has figured in my dreams since I left Washington. Once I
dreamed of it as covered with farms and homes where some of my
people lived. How many times I have seen it rising over the hills as I
have tramped over the surrounding country, from all points of the
compass." [1]

In late September of 1863 Burroughs wrote Benton from Highland Falls that he was seriously considering joining the Union Army. He had proposed to the trustees of the school that they raise his wages, "and if they refuse to do it, I shall stop the school at once and shoulder a musket." [2] The idea of enlisting for battle was an extreme one, and short-lived on Burroughs's part. Yet the general unrest and unhappiness that triggered the notion was very real. He had found himself simply unable to maintain a household on the meager pay of the typical schoolmaster. He had gone deeply into debt. When the school trustees refused to increase his pay, Burroughs had no choice but to make a drastic move. By October Burroughs had quit his position at Highland Falls and was gone to Washington in search of a new beginning. Ursula stayed behind awaiting a call and some cash.

He began by sleeping on a cot at the back of Allen's store and taking whatever work was available. The first job he put his hand to that fall was with the Army Quartermaster's staff. The position involved the mass burial of black soldiers in graves segregated from those of their white comrades. With a bandana wrapped around his face, Burroughs joined twenty other workers in receiving wagons of days-old bodies from the front and bringing them to pastures just outside the city. These were privately owned fields that the federal government had requisitioned. Having set the carriages of the dead far enough away so as to avoid the stench, Burroughs and his co-workers would then dig huge mass graves. (Whenever possible—which was rarely—they used some of the precious supply of Union dynamite to blast out the enormous trenches.) Once the holes were dug, the carts would be drawn to them and the cadavers dumped in. Following this, Burroughs and the others poured white quicklime over the unknowing faces before covering them up with the Maryland earth. There were no formal religious rites. Occasionally one of the diggers would volunteer to read a prayer. There were many times when Burroughs would have to break away from the physical removal of the dead. While his fellow workers pushed the bodies from the carts into the holes, Burroughs would retreat to the nearby woods and vomit. When he returned to the city each evening, he was painfully aware of the "nearly dead" who were transported through town by the dozens on beds of straw in ambulance carts. Pained and emaciated faces, many yellowed with jaundice, huddled at the bottom of wagons and stared out between cracks in the siding of the hospital rigs.

Initially, Ursula was safely removed from such scenes. Back in New York with very little money, Burroughs's wife spent her time as economically as possible as the guest of relatives. "I do not enclose any money because I have none to enclose," John wrote Ursula. ". . . I have already borrowed some, and will have to borrow more, I suppose . . . Perhaps Amanda [her sister] can relieve you till I get replenished . . . After you are through visiting, you had better hire your board some place where you can get it for $2.50 or $3.00 per week, and as fast as I get any money I will send you some . . . Of our things at the Falls [Highland Falls] you had better sell all but a few . . . I think you could get money of your father to straiten [*sic*] our affairs there till I can earn some." He signed the letter "Your Good-for-Nothing John." [3]

In the same October letter he sent Ursula strangely mixed signals about the state of his desire to continue their marriage. He made the formula statements expected from any young husband embarked upon a long separation from a young wife: "I cry daily to the depths of my heart, but mean to harden myself and be a Stoic." At the same time, he told her "I am beginning to feel quite at home and can assure you appreciate my freedom. I am getting quite studious and think I shall do a big winter's work in the shape of study. Household cares and domestic duties, I think in time would about have spoiled me. There is nothing so deadening to intellectual pursuits." Elsewhere, to the wife that he had sent away to live off the charity of relatives until he could afford to send for her, he said: "You don't know how good it seems to eat a meal of victuals without having to cook it, or be disturbed by the remembrance of the after-clap of dish-washing; or to sit down by a fire you did not kindle, or are not obliged to replenish." [4] Ursula did not respond to his letters. There must have seemed little to say. How soon could she expect John to send money to pay their debts and her travelling expenses to Washington when the very idea of keeping house plainly repelled him? By mid-November, the burden of the burial detail having proved too much for him, Burroughs was out of work again. He had been paid thirty-eight dollars for twenty-three days worked. "I have lost my place and know not what I shall do next," he wrote Ursula. ". . . I hope you will see all my creditors there [in New York] and assure them that I will pay every farthing . . . If you have any money to spare, pay the small debts first . . . If I should get a place soon, I can send you some of the money I now have." [5]

He was still without employment a month later. Having been humbled by his inability to sustain himself in the new city, he seemed to gain a new respect for the stability of life he had enjoyed with Ursula. He also appeared to have made a decision that one's own home and hearth were well worth having, even if one did occasionally have to clean them. "I sleep on a little camp bedstead about two feet wide, and six and a half long, here in the store," he wrote Ursula. "Army blankets form the bed under me and the cover over me. Allen happened to have an old pillow his mother gave him and one case for it. On that rests my head. When the case is dirty, I turn it, and when both sides are soiled, I wash it here in the sink and dry it before the fire. I also wash my socks and handkerchiefs in the same way." At the end of the note he told her "I am not at peace, nor happy. I miss home and quietness, and a wife's love and influence." [6]

Day after day he knocked on the doors of various officeholders looking for appointment to any work in any department of the government. In Washington, if one did not work in one of the federal bureaus, then one was either a soldier, a menial laborer, or unemployed. Finally, on January 8, after many weeks of searching, he obtained a position as a clerk in the Department of Treasury under Hugh McCulloch. His salary was to be $1200 per year, a full third more than what he'd been making at Highland Falls. The job was acquired through the influence of Burroughs's congressman from his native Delaware County. In Burroughs's initial letter to Ursula after this success—written on his first day of work—he was again fluffed up and full of himself. "Write me how you are, and what you think of coming to Washington, in case I send for you. I shall be cruel and hard-hearted enough to exact some promises before you come." [7]

After having spent nearly three months fending off Burroughs's debtors and living on the charity of her family, Ursula seems not to have been in the mood to respond to a letter addressed in this tone. On January 20 a more contrite Burroughs wrote again. "I have been expecting every day to hear from you," he said. "Why do you not write and let me know how you are? . . . A man who has no female society here, of the right sort, is very apt to go to the devil pretty fast." [8] In another letter, the one that seems to have finally lured Ursula back to him, he conceded all that his wife had to put up with in the past. "I will not blame or recriminate," he said. "I know you have had a hard time of it with me . . . I see plainly what you have suffered . . . No friends, no society, no amusement . . . and, through so many past years, your sole companion a glum silent husband who talks little, and thinks less how he may seem to, or affect, others." [9]

In February of 1864, shortly after Burroughs's letter of contrition, the couple were reunited. Temporarily, pending payment of his backlog of debts, Burroughs moved his wife into a boarding-house that he himself described as dingy. "You must make up your mind that all boarding-houses are dirty," he wrote her by way of preparation, ". . . a light sweeping is all the house ever gets." But the tables were clean and the food adequate. Therefore Ursula was instructed not to have "too sharp eyes and peep around in holes and corners." [10] Their fellow boarders were mostly single men: either junior government employees or visiting lobbyists. The rooms were made up and the tables waited upon by black servants. During the workday week Ursula spent her hours alone with only the help for company. Then on Sunday, if the weather was inclement and her husband could not head for the woods, she would spend the day with him and whichever of his friends happened to stop by. This would more often than not be Walt Whitman.

BURROUGHS HAD BEEN INTRODUCED by Allen to Whitman almost immediately upon his arrival in Washington. The robust Whitman's face was shaggy with a frame of long beard and flowing hair. His grip was strong, his arms heavily muscled. The impression he gave, wrote Burroughs, was of an incredibly well-spoken lumberjack or ditch digger. He looked like a common farmer, but had "the manner and eloquence of genius and a look of infinite good nature." [11] Burroughs, in turn, cast an impression on Whitman that the writer described with a succinct, poetic image. "Burroughs's face," Whitman told Allen, "is like a field of wheat." One imagines the analogy Whitman was trying to draw: the naive twenty-six-year-old had a face full of wide-eyed, innocent expectation that was quick with a response to the slightest emotional breeze.

Although they had first met at Allen's store, it was not until they came upon each other on a lonely footpath under the trees by the Capitol one Sunday that they had a chance to talk. Whitman was journeying to an army hospital, his knapsack stuffed with snacks and gifts for the wounded men. Burroughs was birding. As quickly as Whitman issued the invitation for Burroughs to accompany him on his mission of mercy, that quickly was the invitation accepted by the young man whom Whitman immediately took to calling "Jack."

Most of Washington's army hospitals were buildings that had been hastily converted from other uses at the outbreak of the war. From 1863 through early 1865, Washington's hospitals held an average of 70,000 wounded—this in a city that had a normal residential population of just 60,000. Churches had been converted into wards. So had schools, taverns, the Georgetown prison, and the confiscated Alexandria mansion of General Lee. More casualties were housed in the Capitol Building and the patent office. Eventually, even the East Room of the White House was appointed to receive wounded. Many of the wounded were either illiterate or unable to write because of their injuries. Whitman was their constant volunteer secretary. He read aloud letters from home and helped the men write responses. Often he would quietly append his own notes to the letters that the patients dictated, explaining that he was a volunteer in the hospital and that he wished to doubly assure the family that their loved one was mending well. At Whitman's urging, Burroughs signed on for similar volunteer work.

Regular attendance at the hospitals was no light duty. Burroughs's experience with the gory burial detail served as good preparation for the hospital visits he shared with Whitman. As Whitman put it in a diary note, "As you pass by, you must be on your guard where you look." [12] The conditions were unsanitary, the wards overcrowded. Pallets of the wounded cluttered the corridors. One had to step over torsos in order to get anywhere. Amputations went on in the hallways. Boxes of bloody, amputated limbs were stacked beside corpses in the courtyards awaiting burial. As Stewart Brooks has pointed out in *Civil War Medicine*, amputation was to become the trademark of Civil War surgery. According to federal records, three out of four operations in army hospitals were amputations. The few surgeons operated on hideously tight schedules. Amputation was often the quickest possible treatment for a life-threatening wound. Many amputations were not at all necessary, just time-saving. Burroughs was regularly witness to the sight of this surgery during his rounds on the wards—yet it would be Whitman who would eloquently describe the terrible picture in *Specimen Days*: "What is removed drops horribly in a pail."

During these first months of acquaintanceship with Whitman, Burroughs's journal entries and letters to Benton reflected a devoted but unequal relationship between himself and the poet. Burroughs was cast as the earnest student thirsting for knowledge. Whitman fell all too easily into the role of guru. In December of 1863 Burroughs wrote Benton a letter that showed clearly the way the young man viewed the more mature Whitman. "I have been much with Walt. Have even slept with him," wrote Burroughs. "I love him very much. The more I see and talk with him, the greater he becomes to me. He is as vast as the earth, and as loving and noble. He is much handsomer than his picture represents him . . . I am convinced that Walt is as great as Emerson, though after a different type. Walt has all types of men in him, there is not one left out." [13] Awed in a way he would not be later in their friendship, the young Burroughs avidly embraced every view and notion expounded by Whitman. It seemed to the naive Burroughs that the poet could make no mistakes, could utter no thought that did not seem divinely inspired. "The more I see of Walt, the more I like him . . . He is by far the wisest man I have ever met. There is nothing more to be said after he gives his views," Burroughs reported confidently to Benton. "It is as if Nature herself had spoken. And so kind, sympathetic, charitable, humane, tolerant a man I did not suppose was possible. He loves everything and everybody. I saw a soldier the other day stop on the street and kiss him. He kisses me as if I were a girl." [14]

We know Walt Whitman was a homosexual. It is doubtful, however, that the relationship between Burroughs and Whitman was overtly sexual. Burroughs's effusions should not be taken out of context. The phrase "have even slept with him" meant in the common vernacular of the day to have shared a room—not a bed. Burroughs's mention of the fact that Whitman "kisses me as if I were a girl" should also be understood within the context of the mid-nineteenth century. Then as today in American society, most men did not make a habit of kissing other men. Men only kissed women. For one man to be kissed at all by any other man was to be kissed "as though one were a girl." And Whitman was famous for kissing everyone he called friend—male and female—in greeting and farewell.

Reading Burroughs's journal for the period, we do get a hint of sexual tension in the relationship with Whitman that the relatively innocent Burroughs himself appears not to have really understood. Burroughs sensed and recorded in his journal an undefined desire and fire in Whitman that made him uncomfortable and, in fact, plainly repelled him. "Notwithstanding the beauty and expressiveness of his eyes," reads one of Burroughs's journal entries, "I occasionally see something in them as he bends them upon me, that almost makes me draw back . . . [The look in his eyes is] dumb, yearning, relentless, immodest, inhuman." [15] If Whitman dropped hints, Burroughs probably either was cool to them or simply did not understand them. In either case, Whitman would have gotten less than an enthusiastic response.

Another fact that argues against sexual intimacy playing a role in their relationship is that Burroughs was not Whitman's type. There is no record of Whitman ever developing a romantic relationship within the circle of his literary and intellectual friends. The poet's lovers were invariably unlettered workingmen: firemen, soldiers, mechanics. Whitman's infatuation during the war years in Washington was with Peter Doyle, a paroled Confederate prisoner of war.

Nor was Whitman Burroughs's type. All the evidence suggests that Burroughs was not just heterosexual, but a voracious one at that. We already know that his amorous attentions with regard to one woman at least—Ursula—were extensive enough to make her complain that he only wanted her for her body. Through the Washington years and after, as Ursula continued to refuse him either partially or wholly, he sought outlets in casual relationships with a succession of anonymous women identified in his journal by initials only. Whitman, who was always constant to one man at a time and despised the notion of casual sex, penned several notes to Burroughs through the years chastising him for his unchaste behavior. "Your casual, selfish wantonness hurts 'Sulie [Ursula] more than she or anyone deserves to be hurt," wrote Whitman in one fatherly note. "The urges of your biology spark the one great and only flaw in your otherwise generous and noble character." [16]

The tie that bound Burroughs and Whitman was not sex. Rather it was their common devotion to literature and young Burroughs's need for a father figure and role model in letters. As is revealed in Burroughs's journals, Whitman seems to have helped the young writer focus and clarify his ambitions with regard to literature and nature. He told the young writer he believed that natural history prose, to be true to life, had to be inspired with a vision akin to poetry. There should be, said Whitman, an intuitive perception of truth; pure scientific observation was not enough. The most important discoveries in all the sciences seemed to Whitman to be born of what he called "a kind of winged, ecstatic reasoning, quite above and beyond the real facts," but based upon them all the same. [17] Thus it was that in natural history literature only the personal vision of the inspired artist could be counted upon to convey the essential reality of the natural world.

During every spare moment at his desk in the Treasury building, Burroughs practiced his craft as an artist committed to discerning and describing nature. He would "liberate the birds from the scientists," he wrote Benton. He would be an "Audubon of prose." Burroughs held fast to Whitman's dictum that it was impossible to adequately describe—or even grasp—the full power, beauty, and meaning of nature with the cold prose and calculated thinking of strict scientific summation. The eye of the painter, the ear of the poet—these things were necessary to understand truly what science might reveal. Although Eckermann could no doubt instruct Goethe in ornithology, could not Goethe instruct Eckermann in the meaning and mystery of the bird? With Whitman prodding him, Burroughs worked hard at developing a literature of nature that was in tune with the facts of natural history but also represented his own poetic vision of the life of the woodlands.

BY THE SPRING OF 1864, John and Ursula had moved out of the boardinghouse that Ursula despised and were keeping a rented home on Capitol Hill. Theirs was a little red-brick building that stood on ground now occupied by a section of the Old Senate Office Building. Burroughs had an acre of land, a plot of potatoes, many chickens, and a cow, Chloe, that he turned out to pasture on the common near the Capitol. Burroughs was to write to Benton back in New York that "My wife is quite well, and the cow also." [18] Whitman lived not far away in a tenement on M Street. Although Whitman made a fair salary as a government clerk—in excess of $1000 per year—he spent much of this on the fruit, candies, and gifts he distributed to soldiers in the hospitals. When he was done buying supplies for his "boys," Whitman was left with only enough money to rent a squalid room in a back-alley slum. Whitman's perennial shortage of cash was the chief reason why he was made a regular guest at John and Ursula's house for Sunday breakfast. Burroughs knew that without the invitation, Walt just might not eat.

Whitman's ritual tardiness on these occasions usually drove the punctual Ursula to distraction. "The coffee would boil, the griddle would smoke, and car after car would go jingling by, but no Walt," recalled Burroughs. "But at last a car would stop, and Walt would roll off it and saunter up to the door—so cheery, and so unaware of the annoyance he had caused." After breakfast, the friends would wander outside and have long discussions while sitting on "the cataract of marble steps" of the Capitol. [19] Although Ursula made no bones about the fact that she disliked Whitman's poetry, and that she did not care for poets and "scribblers" in general, she neverthe-less took a liking to Whitman as a person. Ursula made his shirts, darned his socks, and later, after paralysis disabled him, carried delicacies to his sickbed much in the same way that Whitman had carried them to the wounded in the hospitals. In fact, on Thanksgiving and other holidays, Whitman usually was able to cajole Ursula into baking cookies and pies for distribution in the wards.

Early in their stay at the house on Capitol Hill, Ursula and John had attic-room borders in William Douglas O'Connor and his wife Nellie. O'Connor was a poet turned short story writer, and one of Whitman's staunchest admirers. O'Connor and Whitman had met in Boston in 1860 where O'Connor, having just been dismissed from his editorial job at Philadelphia's *Saturday Evening Post*, was discussing plans for an antislavery novel with the then publisher of Whitman's *Leaves*, Thayer & Eldridge. Now in Washington, O'Connor was a clerk at the Federal Light House Board by day. By night and on Sundays he closed himself up in the dark attic and, stimulated by coffee and tobacco, wrote feverishly on a range of projects. Burroughs objected to what he called O'Connor's "sui-cidal" way of working at composition. When hoeing in his garden below, he would throw fresh plums up into O'Connor's open window "to remind the poor man that there was a good green world waiting outside for him." [20]

Ursula did not get along with Nellie O'Connor. While Ursula was somewhat provincial and plainly skeptical of nonconformists, Nellie in turn personified all things liberal and bohemian. Before her marriage to O'Connor in 1856, she had been active in the women's rights movement and had served on the staff of William Lloyd Garrison's abolitionist newspaper, the *Liberator*. Nellie was in the habit of throwing late-night parties with many of Washington's artists and writers in attendance. When she was out of the house, her husband would often sneak in girlfriends. Ursula seems to have minded this more than did Nellie, for Nellie was in love with Whitman and was constantly engaged in the frustrating business of trying to seduce him. Worst of all, as far as Ursula was concerned, Nellie never cleaned. Dust gathered on the stairs that led up to the O'Connor's attic room. Trash—consisting mostly of empty liquor bottles—accumulated. Ursula fumed, and then finally took it upon herself to clean the space unasked. Then she fumed again at the thought that she had become a maid for strangers. The O'Connors remained for only a few months. The strain on the household was just too great.

If living conditions inside the Burroughs home were less than ideal, so too were the conditions outside. Washington was an unsettled place during the Civil War. Confederate invasion was always an imminent threat. Refugee freemen blacks flocked to the town, where there were already too few jobs to go around. The limited sanitary systems of the city were fearfully inefficient and overburdened. Most streets were unpaved. Mud and dust were everywhere. There had been several major Federal building projects underway immediately before the war, including the half-completed Washington Monument and the new dome on the Capitol. The extensive construction had inhibited the putting down of sod over vast tracts of what is now the Ellipse and Mall. Major portions of this open space were being used for bivouacking soldiers and corralling Union beef. The few leaves of grass that grew in Washington seemed to come only from the brain of Whitman for transplantation into his book. Without lawns, the dry, sunbaked earth of the city was easily whisked up by the winds that came off the Potomac. Whitman would sometimes wear a bandana over his mouth as he walked from hospital to hospital. From Georgetown one day, Burroughs saw a whirlwind cloud of dust that actually blotted out his view of the Capitol dome for more than a minute.

At the same time that it was crowded with suffering and inconvenience, the town was also full of the sense of history being made. On a spring day in 1864, standing by Whitman's side at the corner of Newspaper Row, opposite Willard's Hotel, Burroughs watched Burnside's Army flow through the streets on its way to the Battle of the Wilderness. Forty thousand strong and including more than ten thousand black troops, the Army took over three hours to pass. That summer, Burroughs himself got a brief taste of soldiering when Confederates under the command of General Early threatened the capital. Rebel forces got as close as seven miles from the city limits. Burroughs was a member of a reserve unit comprised of volunteers from the Treasury Department. Twice a week, wearing blue army jackets and shouldering rifles, the clerks and accountants had been drilled. Now, with the Confederate Army close at hand, Burroughs and his coworkers took their guns and found their way to the front at Fort Stevens. "I lay most all Tuesday night in the rifle-pits with the veterans from the Fifth Corps . . . Many bullets came very close to me. How the soldiers did laugh to see me dodge!" [21] He spent only two nights at the front, and was relieved to return to the relative calm and safety of the city. He had not gotten off a single shot, although he told Whitman that he had "learned the song of those modern minstrels—the minnie bullets—by heart." [22]

Of course, the single dominating presence in Washington D.C. was Abraham Lincoln. Burroughs noted in his journals each time he observed Lincoln coming and going about town. When Burroughs went home to the Catskills, he would tell his admiring relatives of how regularly he found himself within sight of the president. Sitting by the fireside at the Roxbury farm, he explained to his delighted parents what had happened when he met Lincoln at a White House reception for Treasury employees. Burroughs passed by in line with hundreds of others who all waited anxiously to greet the president. "When my turn came I lingered a little, but was pulled along," he recalled. "I can feel yet the pull of his great hand as he drew me along past him to make room for those coming after." [23]

In the fall of 1864, Burroughs went home to Roxbury to vote for Lincoln in the national election. On the last leg of his trip, as he walked to Roxbury from the railway station at nearby Stamford, he was given a lift by a farmer. Talk turned to the war, and then to the president. The farmer's comments revealed him to be a Democrat, a Confederate sympathizer, and no friend of the Republican administration. Burroughs jumped out of the wagon and, according to his own account, swore loudly that he'd be damned if he would ride one foot further with a damned copperhead. The farmer tried to coax him back into the wagon but Burroughs, refusing to speak further, trudged angrily across the fields toward home.

Burroughs's extreme reaction to the farmer is as interesting as it is suspect, for the fact is that Burroughs's own beloved Whitman was something of a copperhead himself. Although devoted to Lincoln as an individual, Whitman was no abolitionist and had much sympathy with the Confederate cause. "My opinion is to stop the war now," Whitman argued in 1863. "In comparison with this slaughter," he told O'Connor, "I don't care for the niggers." In Whitman's estimation, slavery was less a sin than were the horrors he witnessed daily in the hospitals. Burroughs was to think back years later and fail to recall Whitman having one friend among the blacks of Washington. After watching the black regiments march in review with the rest of Burnside's Army, Whitman commented to Burroughs that, "It looked funny to see the president standing with his hat off to them just the same as the rest." Speaking to O'Connor one day, Whitman pointed to his head and said, "You know, those poor niggers just don't have much of anything up here." With the war moving to a close, Whitman saw the victorious North, with its four million new freeman, as being in the same bind as "the man who won the elephant in a raffle." [24]

Whitman's racism was one of the few of the poet's stances which Burroughs did not choose to blindly adopt as his own. With O'Connor, Burroughs viewed slavery as an abomination and the Civil War as nothing less than a holy crusade to end it. He likewise considered the black race to be fully equal to his own in both mental and physical endowment. In an essay of the late 1860s, "Winter Sunshine," Burroughs would particularly digress from his theme of Washington wildlife in winter to speak of the black men and women who he met so often in his walks about the capital. "I see myself in them," he wrote, "and what is more, I see that they see themselves in me, and that neither party has much to boast of." Burroughs pointed out that the black man "touches the Anglo-Saxon at more points than the latter is always willing to own." Burroughs went on to attack the stereotype of the lazy black, saying, "I know cases among our colored brethren, plenty of them, of conscientious and well-directed effort and industry in the worthiest of fields." In sum, wrote Burroughs, the black had in him "all the best rudiments of a citizen of the States." [25]

AFTER SPENDING A FEW WEEKS back home in the Catskills during the summer of 1865, Burroughs returned to Washington excited about having heard the singing of the hermit thrush during a hike on

Batavia Mountain. Speaking to Whitman about the bird, Burroughs explained his opinion that not even Audubon had gotten the description of the secluded thrush's flutelike, deliberate song quite right. Burroughs noted after their discussion that Whitman was "deeply interested in what I tell him of the hermit thrush, and he says he has largely used the information I have given him in one of his principal poems." [26] Whitman himself made notes: "Sings oftener after sundown . . . is very secluded . . . likes shaded dark places. His song is a hymn . . . never sings near farm houses—never in the settlement—is the bird of the solemn primal woods & of Nature pure & holy." [27]

At the time, Whitman was spending long hours trying to write an elegy for Abraham Lincoln, who had been assassinated in April. For months he had sought an image that would set just the right tone of dignified yet heartfelt grief. Now John Burroughs, Whitman's naturalist-in-residence, brought him the image on a plate. Within a week, Whitman used the mournful singing of the hermit thrush as the foundation for his classic memorial to Lincoln, "When Lilacs Last in the Dooryard Bloom'd," which was to be the principal piece in his collection of Civil War poems, *Drum Taps.*

> Solitary the thrush,
> The hermit withdrawn to himself, avoiding the settlements,
> Sings by himself a song.
>
> Song of the bleeding throat . . .

While Burroughs was visiting Roxbury, Whitman had suddenly found himself fired from his job at the Indian Bureau. The order to release Whitman had come down directly from Interior Department Secretary Harlan himself. Word had it that the action was caused by Harlan's discovery that a clerk on his staff was the author of an "obscene" book, *Leaves of Grass.* It was not long, however, before Whitman was reappointed to a new clerkship in the office of Attorney General James Speed. J. Hubley Ashton, then assistant attorney general, who was a Whitman admirer and a friend of O'Connor, arranged the new position. In the heat of the moment after Whitman's firing, O'Connor hurriedly wrote a stirring defense of Whitman as an artist. *The Good Gray Poet* was published in January 1866 as a pamphlet under the imprint of Bunce & Huntington, New York. Burroughs wrote Benton to persuade him to write a review of O'Connor's pamphlet for the *Radical*, which Benton subsequently did. At the same time, Burroughs was himself beginning to write a great deal on Whitman and his place in American letters. Slowly, methodically—and with much editorial input from Whitman himself—Burroughs began to assemble the chapters for his first book, *Notes on Walt Whitman as Poet and Person*.

In *Notes* (self-published during the spring of 1867), Burroughs suggested that *Leaves of Grass* could not be compared to any other contemporary poetry. The *Leaves* were absolutely new, both in the theory of art upon which the poems were founded and in the ends that the poet had in mind. That the literary establishment disliked Whitman was, wrote Burroughs, the best of signs. He warned against letting the literary standards of the nation be set by those far removed from the street, the tavern, the battlefield. "The question with me now is not what will conduce to the production of scholars," wrote Burroughs, ". . . for such obscure the true ends of literature as the priests pervert religion; but what comports with grand, primary bards upon whom a nation can build." [28]

While Burroughs believed Emerson had taken the highest step in morals and religion, he likewise believed that Whitman had taken it in art. Shying from didactic philosophy, the poetry of Whitman was not thought but rather an actual act, such as Creation. This transferred the work to a higher plane. The grand artist—Whitman—was not merely a knower and sayer, he was a doer. His art reflected his life personally and precisely. The universe he sang was uniquely his own. Whitman became in Burroughs's mind the ultimate model individual—the embodiment of the Emersonian ideal of the unapologetic, self-defined man. Burroughs wrote that Whitman was the poet of democracy not because he preached this as a doctrine, but because he predicated his poems on personal independence as a living, dominating fact.

In his later years, Burroughs was quite candid about the fact that substantial portions of *Notes on Walt Whitman as Poet and Person* were read and revised by Whitman himself. The poet reviewed sections as they were completed, discussed drafts with

Burroughs, and even wrote a section entitled "Standards of the Natural Universal." Whitman also supplied the book's title, several chapter titles, and wrote a large collection of "Supplementary Notes" that would be appended to the second edition in 1871. Burroughs saw nothing improper in this. He considered Whitman a great critic. He was in the habit of submitting all his manuscripts, even those on natural history, to Whitman for review. It would be Whitman who would title Burroughs's first nature book (*Wake-Robin*, 1871). Whitman, in turn, had a long history of ghosting his own reviews for *Leaves of Grass*, as well as numerous magazine and newspaper profiles of himself and his work. He had also put a final polish on O'Connor's *Good Gray Poet.*

Benton wrote a favorable review of *Notes on Walt Whitman as Poet and Person* for the *Radical* of November 1867. Thanking him for the review in a letter dated November 12, Burroughs informed Benton that the *Notes* were hardly selling at all: ". . . not fifty copies have yet been disposed of, which is proof, I think, that the book has something in it." [29] Soon Burroughs had all the remaining unsold copies of the print run stacked in piles in Ursula's otherwise tidy living room. Of course, the punctilious Ursula was not pleased. She chided Burroughs. Was this the literary life? First she had to put up with the mess of papers associated with his efforts at composition. Now she had to dust the bound books. Burroughs, undeterred, piled up four columns of the *Notes*, placed a board across them, and created a desk upon which to continue his writing.

Both O'Connor and Burroughs were actively promoting Whitman in every magazine they could get into. O'Connor not only used the essay form in advertising and defending Whitman and his work, but turned to fiction as well. *Putnam's Magazine* of January 1868 printed a short story by O'Connor entitled "The Carpenter." Whitman appeared in this strange, allegorical tale as the Christ—a miracle-working "gray redeemer" and "lover of soldiers" who healed the wounds of a war-ruined family and gave them a holy message: "Better than all is love. Love is better than all." Burroughs would reach a point where he was uncomfortable with the many comparisons with Christ that several of Whitman's admirers—especially O'Connor—applied to the poet. But he was not yet so reserved, and he wrote Benton to tell him that he thought O'Connor's story splendid.

The *Galaxy* of April 1868, carried Burroughs's most stirring defense of Whitman to date. In "Before Genius," Burroughs restated in brief most of his arguments from the *Notes*. He suggested that nature afforded the only adequate standard for a first-class modern artist. To elaborate was to no avail—but to hint, stimulate, and vitalize in and with nature was everything. "Nature is perpetual transition," he wrote. "Everything passes and presses on; there is no pause, no completion, and no exhaustive elaboration." To produce and multiply endlessly was the law of nature, without committing to any particular end or scheme. God did not pause to worry about how polished and presentable was the scattered pattern of a stand of woods. Something like this was in *Leaves of Grass*—"a hint, a word, a significant look, and the author goes on, follow who can." In this, *Leaves of Grass* moved beyond "the merely conventional and scholastic," in the same way that did the best works of Plato, Hegel, and Emerson. [30]

"Before Genius" had been written largely in response to recent articles in the *Atlantic Monthly* by the New England essayist, editor, and Unitarian minister Thomas Wentworth Higginson. Higginson had denigrated the work of Whitman while suggesting that cultural development hinged on strict appreciation of traditional forms. In Higginson's view, beauty and grace needed to be recognized as institutionalized requirements for all quality literature. Now, after Burroughs's indirect response in the *Galaxy* article, Higginson wrote to him and the two began a correspondence of friendly argument over Whitman and the value of his work. Burroughs had suggested that Whitman was exempt from traditional rules of style because of the raw, untamed nature of his subject matter and focus. Higginson wrote to say that he thought it a mistake to assume that there was any "incompatibility between native force and high polish." [31] In a second letter, Higginson was more direct in his assessment of Whitman. "His poems I read on their very first appearance, and with some disappointment; the attacks on them made me expect more from them than I got," he wrote. "This, you would say, was my fault; perhaps it was—at any rate, I like your loyalty to your friend. Afterwards I met the author, and was gratified to see his fine physique, that being rather a hobby of mine. In other ways he did not make so favorable an impression—seemed a little self-conscious and egotistical, I thought—though here, again, I may have done him an injustice. Several times I have gone back to him, trying to do him justice. Believing most heartily myself in whatever is broad, hearty, American; having found the roughest forest and border society palatable (to say nothing of the camp), I cannot quite understand why it is that he still seems to me crude, turgid and even morbid." [32]

Whitman was to be the only topic upon which Burroughs and Higginson could find grounds for disagreement. Higginson had been a financial backer of John Brown and was a commissioned Colonel in the U.S. Army during the Civil War. It was Higginson who raised the first all-black regiment to fight for the Union cause. Years later, Higginson would be responsible for introducing the world to the poetry of Emily Dickinson. For now, he wrote Burroughs that he was "happy to learn from one who appreciates Nature and Emerson and Aeschylus and Thoreau as you do . . . Your only two great Americans are Emerson and Whitman; mine are Emerson and Hawthorne: I am glad to have even fifty per cent agreement with one who writes so heartily." [33]

AT THE SAME TIME that he was eloquently defending Whitman in the press, Burroughs was working hard at fine-tuning his powers of nature observation. He studied carefully the works of Audubon, Eckermann, and Wilson; and he subscribed to all the Department of the Interior's publications on wildlife. Taking many hikes with Whitman and others in the forests that skirted Washington, he not only studied the birds through field glasses but also collected specimens. Burroughs often carried a cane gun with him on his walks. What birds he shot he then stuffed and mounted at a workbench in the basement of his home. He put together a glass case with fifty specimens for Ursula's front parlor, a case similar to that of native Catskill Mountain birds he had assembled for his mother. "As to shooting the birds," he wrote a correspondent in 1865, "I think a real lover of nature will indulge no sentimentalism on the subject. Shoot them, of course, and no toying about it." [34] On one particularly lovely Washington afternoon in the spring of 1868 he shot the last wild pigeon he would ever see. The species was to be extinct by the mid-1870s.

By the 1880s, Burroughs would develop a different attitude and a deeper sensibility with regard to taking specimens.

> I confess my excursions to the woods are often spoiled, or at least vitiated, by taking my gun and making it a specialty to obtain a bird. I am too much preoccupied and miss everything but the bird. I am not devout and receptive, but eager and inquisitive . . . [However, when I do not take my gun,] the kindly and hospitable influences of the air and earth come nearer to me; nothing escapes my eye, ear, or nose. A more intimate and harmonious relation is established between me and Nature. I do not outrage the woods; I do not hunt down a bird.

He would never fully give up the killing of animals. He would always take a specimen when he thought it necessary for study. And he would always be willing to kill any animal that he thought a pest, or that tasted good on the dinner table. Still, he did become more aware of the impact of modern man on wildlife, and he did eventually seek to minimize his own personal impact on the forest whenever possible.

Washington offered relatively mild winters compared to those Burroughs was accustomed to in the Catskills. Although the mercury occasionally sank to zero, the earth was never so frozen that at least some vegetation did not flourish. "I have found flowers here every month of the year; violets in December, a single houstonia in January." And so Burroughs could, without suffering too much cold, attend to his nature study year-round. On Sunday afternoons he would go beyond the boundary of the city, over Meridian Hill, and make the brief, ten-minute walk that would bring him to primitive woods. Washington, he wrote, "has not yet overflowed its limits like the great Northern commercial capitals, and Nature, wild and unkept, comes up to its very threshold, and even in many places crosses it." Sometimes he would go directly north of the Capitol Building for about three miles, past scattered Irish and black shanties, to come suddenly upon flocks of feeding snowlarks (regular visitors to the district in February and March). Then he'd wander farther, following the eastern branch of the Tiber, which was at that time lined with bushes and a rank growth of greenbrier, to a wilderness where sparrows, goldfinches, and golden-crowned kinglets nested. On other days, such as that of the second inauguration of Lincoln, Burroughs went the opposite direction and found, within two miles of the White House, "a simple woodsman chopping away as if no President was being inaugurated!" The benchmark of the history books for March 4, 1865, is the Lincoln inauguration. The benchmark for the same date in Burroughs's journal is something else again: "This day, for the first time, I heard the song of the Canada sparrow, a soft, sweet note, almost running into a warble." [35]

With Whitman, Burroughs was a regular visitor to the many public parks in Washington. The two also frequented the public gardens of the White House, where they could hear the veery thrush in the trees as well as the ruby-crowned kinglet. While great matters of state were debated and decided just a few yards away, Burroughs sat under a tree and relished the song of the kinglet: "the same liquid bubble and cadence which characterize the wren-songs generally, but much finer and more delicate than the song of any other variety known to me; beginning in a fine, round, needle-like note, and rising into a full, sustained warble." Similarly, Burroughs would often walk the grounds of the Capitol Building. Here, in the early spring, he would go to hear robins, catbirds, blackbirds, kingbirds, and wrens. And in February, on the grounds of the Smithsonian, he saw and heard the fox sparrow.

By far, Burroughs's favorite natural haunt in the area was Rock Creek. A large, rough, rapid stream, Rock Creek flows into the Potomac between Washington and Georgetown and has its source in the interior of Maryland. Its course, for five or six miles out of Washington, is marked by scenery similar to that of the East Branch of the Delaware. Burroughs wrote that Rock Creek "flows in a deep valley, which now and then becomes a wild gorge with overhanging rocks and high precipitous headlands, for the most part wooded; here reposing in long, dark reaches, there sweeping and hurrying around a sudden bend or over a rocky bed; receiving at short intervals small runs and spring rivulets, which open vistas and outlooks to the right and left, of the most charming description."

Though wild and rugged, the region was hardly unpopulated

during the warm weather months. It was a popular area to which young men of the city would repair to "bathe and prowl around, and indulge the semi-barbarous instincts that still lurk within them." When the Civil War was still on, these were usually Union soldiers on a day's leave or Confederates on furlough from prison camps. More often than not, Burroughs found "the pollution of their presence" a nuisance, these whiskey-filled roughnecks who shot guns "for pure hell and no other good reason" and spooked the very birds Burroughs was hoping to spot. [36]

Still, in spite of such distractions, Burroughs used Rock Creek as a place to shrug off everyday worries. With knapsack and notebook he descended to a free, untamed reality where wildflowers and birds were abundant. He came to know the Rock Creek area intimately and in all seasons. In each little valley or spring run he knew where to look for the first liverwort, lupine, mandrake, and bloodroot, as well as the hepatica, anemone, saxifrage, houstonia, and other signs of spring. Here he would come every first of May with the express purpose of hearing the wood thrush. Here he would come in December to discover the woods swarming with warblers, the birds exploring every branch and leaf, from the tallest tulip tree to the lowest spicebush, so urgent was their demand for food during their long winter journeys.

Burroughs attempted little or no composition in the field. Much of his writing was done either at home or at his mahogany desk that faced the iron wall of a vault in the Currency Bureau. Burroughs spent eight hours a day, five days a week at the Treasury, and was usually there a half-day on Saturday as well. Burroughs appears to have been highly efficient at accomplishing the expected amount of daily ledger work, and so had time within his office hours for composition. There at his desk he let his imagination run to the wide open fields and the wild woods of the countryside. Slowly, year after year, in odd spare moments at that accounting desk, he accumulated the skill in writing that gradually gained him ready acceptance for his outdoor sketches. Soon after the end of the Civil War these began to appear with some regularity in such publications as *Putnam's Magazine*, the *Galaxy*, the *Atlantic Monthly*, *Scribner's*, and *Appleton's*.

ENGLAND & EMERSON

No book can deeply please, or long last, that has not a good, lovable man
behind it. The final background of every book, or poem,
or essay, is the character of the author . . .

— *Journal Entry, February 11, 1871*

WHILE WE KNOW THAT Burroughs was experiencing exponential personal growth in the years during and immediately after the Civil War, we must also consider what life in Washington must have been like for Ursula. For that matter, what was her life with John Burroughs like in general? On many planes, John and Ursula's characters seem to have diverged. He had no aptitude for tidiness, nor any patience with the mundane, everyday practices that are necessary in every household to maintain order. Ursula, on the other hand, was a punctilious housekeeper. She was not happy unless her floor was spotless and her home completely free of dust. She spent all her days cleaning and complained that John did not spend his free time in the same way.

Another fundamental difference between the couple was the fact that John was gregarious to an extreme and Ursula not. Burroughs made it known to the many writers and artists who were his friends in Washington that they were always welcome to stop and visit, and that appointments were an unnecessary formality. Ursula, however, cherished her privacy. This is not to say that she was reclusive. She simply did not care to have stray members of Washington's bohemia tramping through her home at odd hours uninvited. John seems to have been unwilling to adjust his friend-filled, unkempt lifestyle to accommodate Ursula's needs. The resulting friction was never very far below the surface.

Ursula did not join him on his hikes to Rock Creek and other woodlands spots. This may have been her preference, but it is also clear that she was never invited to accompany her husband on these sojourns. In his journals he frequently spoke of the wild as not just an escape from the city itself, but also as a refuge from "domestic tyranny" and "henpecking." The woods, it seemed, were something to be experienced in the company of men alone. The fraternity of nature appreciation was to be exactly that: a fraternity. In the woods, men could forget about wiping their feet at the door. There were no rugs to beat, no crumbs that needed sweeping up. It was a place where boys could get away from their mothers and play without worrying about dirtying their hands or tearing their clothes. The journals are filled with such allusions. According to Burroughs's journals, Ursula often scolded him upon his return from a hike for having wasted time that could have been better employed around the house.

Another area of disagreement between husband and wife was his continued dedication to writing. Now that her husband had finally gotten what Ursula considered a "real" job, she wanted him to focus all his energy on doing well and advancing at the Treasury Department. Ursula remembered all too well the summer at Marlboro when they each had to pick strawberries at a local farm in order to buy bread for the table. So too did she remember the constant requests for loans that they had forwarded to both Burroughs's father and hers. To her mind, it was Burroughs's aspiration to be a writer that had been the root of these indignities. If she could only get him to set the "scribbling" aside forever, then she could be more confident about their future.

For his part, Burroughs seems to have gone through a subtle but definite shift in priorities following the episode of his financial collapse at Highland Falls. From that time on, he always put financial security ahead of literature. Only after his daily ledger work was done would he pull his manuscript book from the bottom drawer of his desk and continue work on the birding essays that might or might not sell. This focus on professional responsibilities allowed him to do well at the Treasury. Success on the job in turn enabled him to increase his income by steady advancement among the ranks of clerks. His annual salary was raised to $1400. And the magazines he was selling to with increasing frequency often paid up to $80 or $90 per essay. By late 1867 he had paid off all his old New York debts. With his financial horizon looking bright, Burroughs felt flush enough to buy land and contract for the building of a brick house on what was then the north edge of Washington. This building—dubbed by Whitman "The house that Jack built"—stood at number 1332 V Street. The site is occupied today by a school and a playground.

Ursula was quite pleased with her V Street house. After ten years of marriage, she and John finally owned the roof over their heads. The place consisted of a total of ten rooms, a large cellar, a coal- and woodshed, and several verandas. As usual, Ursula focused her energy on keeping the house impeccably clean. "Ursula does her own work," wrote Burroughs to Benton, "and even the cat wipes her feet on the mat before she ventures inside." [1] Being on the very edge of the city, he could turn his face north and be in the country or turn it south and be in the town. He had about a mile to walk to his office, although the streetcars that stopped within a block of his front door were also an option.

For Ursula, there was only one unhappy aspect to the new house. In order to make the payments on the place, they needed to take in tenants. This in itself might not have been so bad, but John insisted on leasing rooms to William and Nellie O'Connor. Why he rented to the O'Connors, whom he knew Ursula disliked intensely, one can only guess. On the O'Connors' side of the house there were soon dirty clothes strewn across the floor, empty beer bottles on the stairs, and late nights of drinking and loud talk with all the artist population of the city being made welcome.

One of the O'Connors' regular guests was Whitman. Another was Count Adam Gurowski. A former Harvard professor and reporter for Horace Greeley's *New York Tribune*, the socialist Gurowski had been expelled from Poland for having associated with revolutionaries and consorted in a plan to kidnap his cousin, the king. He had in turn been fired from his Harvard position for threatening the life of a dean with whom he'd had a disagreement regarding a lecture hall reservation. Gurowski was, according to O'Connor, "a maniac . . . a madman with lucid intervals," who was one day a genius of diplomacy and the next a raving lunatic with whom none could reason. [2] In 1862, Gurowski published a notorious book in which he suggested that practically everyone in wartime Washington, including Abraham Lincoln, was either a coward or a Confederate sympathizer. He had kind words for only three individuals: Grant, Secretary of War Stanton, and Whitman, who Gurowski wrote was "the incarnation of genuine American original genius . . . Walt alone in his heart and in his mind has a shrine for the nameless, for the heroic people." [3] Gurowski's book had prompted a libel action that cost him his job as a State Department translator. Downing whiskey after whiskey in the O'Connors' kitchen late at night, Gurowski would tell exotic tales of his sister-in-law who was a Bourbon princess, or of how he had lost his left eye in a duel. Lying in bed and trying to go to sleep, Ursula was able to hear the count's booming stories clearly through the wall as well as the raised voices of all the others as they debated and joked and drank. Were John beside her she might have turned over to ask him to go and quiet down the party, but he was usually next door himself.

One evening, Whitman chided Burroughs for leaving his wife alone in her "cold bed." Burroughs countered (so that no one else could hear) that his presence would add little warmth to the situation. Ursula, Burroughs told Whitman, brought "her own ice" to the bedroom. Not even a brass bed warmer could raise the temperature between the sheets where she lay "tense, nervous, unhappy, and too much concerned about sin." Whitman, for his part, refused to lay the blame upon Ursula. "You have not made her love you enough," he wrote shortly after in a jotted note to Burroughs. "You have not made her want to do for you, to bring you joy. It is you who are at fault." [4]

OSCAR HOUGHTON, OF THE Boston book-publishing firm Hurd & Houghton, had been aware of John Burroughs's nature essays for several years before he suggested that a few of them be drawn together to form a book. He'd always enjoyed the pieces when they appeared in the *Atlantic* and other popular magazines. When in the fall of 1870 he wrote Burroughs proposing the idea of a volume of essays and asking what Burroughs "might want" from the publication, the young author did not know how to answer. His previous book, *Notes on Walt Whitman as Poet and Person*, had been printed and bound at his own expense. He had no experience with publishing contracts. Burroughs took Houghton's proposal to Whitman, who in turn dictated terms that Burroughs jotted down and sent to the publisher for approval—one hundred dollars in advance, and a ten percent royalty on "cash received" for each copy sold.

The book was to be comprised by and large of papers previously published in magazines. Houghton supplied a list of his personal favorites. Burroughs spent several months pruning this list, adding a few stray essays that Houghton had not been aware of, and making final edits on all of them. As was his custom, he submitted the revised drafts of each essay to Whitman for his criticism and approval. Virtually all of Walt's suggestions were to be incorporated in the final revision. Published in the spring of 1871, *Wake-Robin* received immediate critical approval and general, though not dramatic, sales success. Reviewing *Wake-Robin* in the *Atlantic Monthly*, William Dean Howells said the book was one in which the "dusk and cool and quiet of the forest seem to wrap the reader . . . It is sort of a summer vacation to turn the pages . . . Perhaps it would be difficult not to be natural and simple in writing of such things as our author treats . . . but Mr. Burroughs adds a strain of genuine poetry which makes his papers unusually delightful, while he has more humor than generally falls to the ornithological tribe. His nerves have a poetic sensitiveness, his eye a poetical quickness." [5]

In these early essays, Burroughs was doing far more than simply listing his personal observations of nature. He was defining a form of creative prose that related the facts of nature accurately, yet infused them with touches of his own personal vision. Burroughs's instinct was purely literary; his ambition was art. Eight years after the appearance of *Wake-Robin*, he would address this point when commenting on comparisons of his writings to those of Thoreau and Gilbert White. "There is really little or no resemblance between us, " wrote Burroughs. "Thoreau's aim is mainly ethical, as much so as Emerson's is. The aim of White of Selbourne [*sic*] was mainly scientific. My own aim, so far as I have any, is entirely artistic. I care little for the merely scientific aspects of things, and nothing for the ethical. I will not preach one word. I will have a pure result, or nothing. I paint the bird, or the trout, or the scene, for its own sake." [6]

Burroughs did not just describe the trees, birds, mountains, and waterfalls. Beginning in *Wake-Robin* and carrying through in all his subsequent writings on nature themes, he endeavored to transport his readers to elemental nature through eloquent paragraphs that were truly art. His words were carefully contrived to stimulate a native imagination in the reader, leading him or her to discover the woodlands anew, with a freshly awakened eye and a keener sense of the oneness and fineness of the fabric that is the natural world. By the time of the publication of *Wake-Robin*, Burroughs's literary technique was carefully crafted to depict the immediate, total harmony between man and nature. Indeed, it was meant to paint a relationship closer than harmony: to reveal man as an element in nature, himself a miracle equivalent to the robin and the trout-filled headwater.

To achieve this, Burroughs embodied his observations of nature in narrative recollections of his own hikes and adventures in the wild. Many years later he would write, "If I name every bird I see in my walk . . . it is doubtful if my reader is interested. But if I relate the bird in some way to human life, to my own life—show what it is to me and what it is in the landscape and the season—then do I give my reader a live bird and not a labeled specimen." Although a creative writer in the way he presented the truths of nature, Burroughs made a point to never alter those truths for the sake of literary effect. "The literary naturalist does not take liberties with the facts," he wrote, "facts are the flora upon which he lives . . . To interpret nature is not to improve upon her . . . it is to have an emotional intercourse with her, and reproduce her tinged with the colors of the spirit." [7]

As an artist interpreting nature, Burroughs was never to become what he called "a strict man of science." He evolved not into a naturalist, *per se*, but into a new hybrid: a literary naturalist with a duty to record his own unique perceptions of the natural world. While remaining loyal to the truth of natural facts, he also remained true to his personal vision of these facts. In an essay of the 1880s, "Nature and the Poets," Burroughs explained his view of the relationship between nature and those literary artists who would try to depict her.

> The poet himself does not so much read in nature's book— though he does this, too—as write his own thoughts there . . . Of course, the poet uses the truths of nature also, and he establishes his right to them by bringing them home to us with a new and peculiar force. What science gives is melted in the fervent heat of the poet's passion, and comes back to us supplemented by his quality and genius. He gives more than he takes, always. [8]

In many ways, *Wake-Robin* was an intensely personal book for Burroughs. It was very much a chronicle of the last fifteen years of his life, during which he had matured from an unfinished youth into a refined and focused man who had grown through trial, hardship, and intense effort. In the essays "Birch Browsings" and "The Adirondacks," he recounted his camping adventures with Elijah Allen, Myron Benton and others in New York State during the early 1860s. In "Spring at the Capital" he spoke of the woodland rambles he'd shared with Whitman in Washington. Burroughs also made a point of including the very first nature essay he'd ever penned. In 1863, when he'd begun writing "The Return of the Birds," he'd been an impoverished and demoralized schoolmaster unsure of his prospects and unhappy in his marriage. He yearned to be a writer, but he knew that everything that had come from his pen had been "a fraud, a masquerade." [9] Now he had found his own genuine voice. The writing of "The Return of the Birds" had proved a critical event for Burroughs's development as a writer. He gave the piece a place of honor by positioning it as the opening chapter of *Wake-Robin*.

In the book's closing piece, "The Invitation," Burroughs proposed hiking and bird-watching as the ideal avocations—healthy, inexpensive, and endlessly intriguing. When one took to the woods, one returned with full vigor of body and full awakening of mind. Burroughs suggested that there was no saner way for the modern man to spend his free time than out amid wild nature. The forest provided the perfect escape from the cares of the town. The woods were a democratizing element—a world where money counted for little. All shared equally in the commonwealth of virgin forests, flowing waters, and blue skies. In days of increasing technology and bureaucratization, Burroughs invited his readers to the peace of the woods. There, he wrote, they might partake of a healing tonic unique to wild places away from cities, a tonic he believed vitally necessary for the health of the soul of man.

THE PROUD YOUNG AUTHOR made sure that several copies of *Wake-Robin* were among the things he packed when, in October of 1871, he and two other Treasury Department employees were dispatched on a two-month trip to England. Their mission was to convey fifteen million in new U.S. bonds and superintend destruction of the expiring notes. One copy of the book was earmarked for Emerson's long-time friend, Thomas Carlyle. Another he planned to give to one of the leading admirers of Whitman in England, William Michael Rossetti. Moncure Conway, an American admirer of Whitman then living in London, had promised to introduce Burroughs to both men. Conway was a Quaker minister, writer, and former abolitionist.

When Burroughs and Conway reached Carlyle's house in Cheyne Row, Carlyle was out for a walk. Carlyle's housekeeper invited the two Americans to wait. When Carlyle arrived, he was wearing a long gray coat and a slouch hat. Although an old man, his body was robust and his face quite tan beneath a mop of gray hair. Burroughs wrote that Carlyle seemed sobered by age. "His eyes were full of unshed tears, and whenever he lapsed into silence, there was a look of unutterable yearning in them." Carlyle rested his elbow on the table and leaned his head upon his hand as he listened to Burroughs's and Conway's conversation. He seemed, wrote Burroughs, like "a gentle affectionate grandfather, with his delicious Scotch brogue and rich melodious talk, overflowing with reminiscences of his earlier life, of Scott and Goethe and Edinburgh, and other men and places he had known. Learning that I was especially interested in the birds, he discoursed on the lark and nightingale and mavis." Carlyle told Conway and Burroughs an Arabian legend about Solomon's temple having been built amid the chirping of thirty thousand sparrows, then he expressed his own dislike for the common sparrow. Cocking his head on one side to imitate the "comical little wretch," he said it was so bold it would dispute passage up an alley with you. He laughed when Burroughs explained that the English sparrow had recently been introduced to America. "Introduced it, have you?" said Carlyle. "Well, you will rue the day ye did it!" Much as Burroughs did in his essays, Carlyle framed his remarks about the birds in episodes of his personal experience, and thus invested their songs "with the double charm of his description of his adventure." [10]

Carlyle and Burroughs discussed Whitman's recent pamphlet, the just-published prose work *Democratic Vistas*, in which the poet had quoted from Carlyle at length in arguing that American democracy in its present incarnation was a sham, a hypocrisy, a failure. During the Civil War, Whitman had unabashedly adopted the views of Carlyle, who had written that half a million Northerners and Southerners were losing their lives fighting "for the empty purpose" of emancipating "three million absurd blacks." Now, with the war finished, Whitman adopted another of Carlyle's social platforms.

It was the Scottish writer's diagnosis that democracy in England was suffering from a "foul elephantine leprosy" characterized by greed and industrialization. Whitman was quick to diagnose an American variant of the same disorder. "Never was there, perhaps, more hollowness of heart than at present, here in the United States," wrote Whitman. "Genuine belief seems to have left us. The underlying principles of the States are not honestly believ'd in." The spectacle, wrote Whitman, was "appalling." The great cities reeked with "respectable as much as non-respectable robbery and scoundrelism . . . The best class we show, is but a mob of fashionably dress'd speculators and vulgarians." Whitman said that no matter how great a success American democracy was in "materialistic development" and uplifting the masses "out of their sloughs," it was a complete failure in its social aspects "and in really grand religious, moral, literary, and esthetic results." The country grew larger and larger and richer and richer, but to no avail. "It is as if we were somehow being endow'd with a vast and more and more thoroughly-appointed body, and then left with little or no soul," wrote Whitman. [11]

Burroughs and Carlyle spoke about the subtle difference between Carlyle's view of the situation and Whitman's. Carlyle's view of democracy was virtually elegiac. His writings on the subject did not prescribe cures, but rather proposed prayers for the dead. As Burroughs pointed out to Carlyle, Whitman was far less pessimistic. Whitman believed that if handled correctly, the American and British "sickness" could prove to be nothing more than a transitional growing pain. For all its failures, modern democracy alone possessed the potential for true political freedom and "natural religion." Carlyle said he hoped Whitman was right, but that he'd wager Whitman was wrong. Before leaving, Burroughs gave Carlyle a copy of *Democratic Vistas* inscribed to him from Whitman with "true respects & love." He also gave Carlyle a copy of his own *Wake-Robin*.

Burroughs's next stop was the home of William Michael Rossetti, literary critic and brother to the poets Dante Gabriel and Christina Rossetti. William Michael had recently edited a special edition of Whitman's *Leaves of Grass* for British publication. Rossetti's edition was entitled *The Poems of Walt Whitman*. In it he deleted those poems that used the words "nipple," "venereal sore," "prostitute," and other phrases potentially upsetting to a genteel public. The book, Burroughs advised a correspondent at the time of publication, "looks first rate and, save for two or three very absurd and stultifying statements in the introductory essay, is all that we had expected." [12] Whitman had agreed to the editing process, without which Rossetti and his publisher would not have been allowed to print the book in Britain. Nevertheless, the poet soon complained that Rossetti's selection represented a "horrible dismemberment." In old age, Whitman would still be talking about the incident. "Rossetti said expurgate and I yielded," he told a friend. "Rossetti was honest, I was honest— we both made a mistake."

At dinner with Rossetti, Burroughs spoke about the British edition of the *Leaves* in glowing terms that, warned Burroughs, Rossetti must not expect to have echoed by Whitman himself.

Burroughs believed that Rossetti had done an admirable job in pruning the text of the book to get around British obscenity laws while at the same time keeping the essential inspiration of Whitman intact. Rossetti had refrained from using any poem that he could not print, unexpurgated, in its entirety as Whitman had written it. When a portion of a poem had proved offensive, he'd deleted the entire piece. A decade later, when a Boston publisher proposed printing a complete edition of the *Leaves* with offensive passages tidied up and certain key words replaced, Burroughs would not be nearly so receptive to the idea. At least Rossetti's approach had left *parts* of Whitman's work whole.

"I told Rossetti what you should also tell him," wrote Burroughs to Whitman in a highly unusual, scolding letter. "I let him know that he had done you an inestimable service by seeing your work through to press here in a fine edition that will certainly foster the growth of your reputation abroad. What matter that readers here do not get all of your poems right now in one complete collection such as that does not, even at this moment, exist in the States? Is it not better that they should get a few of your poems now and the rest later, rather than none at all, ever? Make no mistake about it: Rossetti is a friend, not an enemy. It would be prudent to treat him as such." [13]

Burroughs also wrote Whitman about his sight-seeing. "St. Paul's was too much for me and my brain actually reels . . ." he wrote. He said that he had never seen a building with "a living soul" before. "I saw for the first time what power and imagination could be put in form and design." The interior of the cathedral was grand, the enormous dome "other-worldly." The outside possessed "the beauty and grandeur of rocks and crags and ledges. It is nature and art fused into one." He spent as much time in the enormous crypt below the cathedral as he did the church itself. "Nelson's monument is the centerpiece, a grand black box of marble elevated above all others. The grave of [Christopher] Wren, the architect genius who created the church and dome above, is in an obscure corner and marked with a simple inlaid stone. There are a few other Wrens in the same corner. Poor Christopher, so eloquent above from this grave below." [14]

BURROUGHS HIKED EXTENSIVELY throughout the rural districts west of London. After just a few days of travel, he decided that he frankly loved the landscape, the people, and the pace of life in the British countryside. Burroughs found something eminently civilized in the ancient country seats of England. The rural districts of the United States seemed somehow unplanned and temporary—accidents of geography and history waiting for cities to spread and engulf them. But in Britain, the countryside gave one a sense of having been carefully planned. For generations, the character of whole districts had not markedly changed. Here, nature was completely domesticated, and reflected "the humanizing influences of so many generations."

As noted in Burroughs's memoir of his British journey, which was to be published in *Winter Sunshine* (1875), he admired particularly the enormous number of birds that populated the landscape.

> It was truly amazing. It seemed as if the feathered life of the whole continent must have been concentrated on this island. Indeed, I doubt if a sweeping together of all the birds of the United States into any two of the largest States, would people the earth and air more fully. There appeared to be a plover, a crow, a rook, a blackbird, and a sparrow, to every square foot of ground. They know the value of birds in Britain . . . How could an American see so much game and not wish to exterminate it entirely as he does at home?[15]

A general unwillingness to annihilate native wildlife was something Burroughs viewed as the critical sign of a major cultural difference between Britain and America. He came to believe that the differing sensibilities that led to the varying British and American approaches to nature appreciation and wildlife management were important. Not long after returning to Washington, Burroughs began work on "The Exhilarations of the Road," which ostensibly was an essay promoting the joys of hiking. In this and a later essay on the same subject ("Footpaths," in *Pepacton*, 1881), Burroughs used the simple art of walking as a metaphor by which to compare the youthful, loud, and unfinished culture of the United States with the more developed habits and manners of England.

In "The Exhilarations of the Road," Burroughs praised the British for having a land "threaded with paths which invite the walker, and which are scarcely less important than the highways." He bemoaned the lack of similar paths in the United States. Unlike their British cousins, Americans seemed in a great hurry to grasp any invention that would separate them from immediate contact with the natural world. Burroughs suggested that the American was incapable of amusement on a low key. The American demanded excitement, speed, and immediate gratification. "He has nothing to invest in a walk; it is too slow, too cheap." Americans craved the astonishing, the exciting, the far away, and did not know "the highways of the gods"—rural trails to natural cathedrals—when they saw them. This, said Burroughs, was "a sign of the decay of the faith and simplicity of man."

Burroughs speculated on what the cultivated habit of walking might do for the American national character. "I do not think I exaggerate the importance or the charms of pedestrianism," he wrote, "or our need as a people to cultivate the art." It would tend, argued Burroughs, to soften the national manners, to teach Americans the meaning of leisure, to reintroduce them to the charms of the open air, and, most importantly, to foster a bond between the race and the land. "Next to the laborer in the fields," wrote Burroughs, "the walker holds the closest relation to the soil; and he holds a closer and more vital relation to nature." Burroughs proposed walking as a cure for the brash brag and swagger of the stereotypical American. Perhaps the mortal pace of slow, two-legged locomotion would have a humbling effect. He wrote that the absence of footpaths such as those found in England was not so much the point as was "the decay of the simplicity of manners" that this lack implied.
16

Burroughs was not the first to endorse walking as a useful practice for an America in the midst of the birth pangs of the industrial revolution. The *Atlantic Monthly* of June 1862, published Thoreau's "On Walking," which had been put together from some of the late author's journal entries of the early 1850s. "How vain it is to sit down to write when you have not stood up to live!" wrote Thoreau. "Methinks that the moment my legs begin to move, my thoughts begin to flow." Burroughs's "Exhilarations of the Road" appeared in 1871. In this same period, Burroughs produced many magazine articles extolling the beauty of the Catskills. Soon, in some part because of these publications, tourists with backpacks began to migrate to Burroughs's home range. Through the mid-1870s, pilgrims were coming to the Hudson River and the Catskill Mountains in large numbers to view God's sublime handiwork for themselves. Local guides made good money conducting avid hikers to the Devil's Dance Chamber, the summit of Slide Mountain, and other choice Catskill sites.

By 1875 the *New York Times* would publish articles and editorials on the "walking mania" that was sweeping the eastern seaboard. For the first time, nature became something that the new middle class of the industrial state spoke of "getting back to." Throughout it all, Burroughs remained a proponent of walking as something therapeutic for both mind and body. But he was to go on record that no good could come out of the walking mania, *per se*. A fad instead of a natural, wholesome impulse, the walking craze was, so far as Burroughs was concerned, nothing more than "a prostitution of a noble pastime." [17] He would write to Benton to say that "only in our uncouth and unformed land of America could a simple walk be turned into a frantic cult. The fad of walking is no good precisely because it is a fad. These things by definition have no permanence whatsoever. The fad of hiking will fade away to be replaced by something less healthy next year—probably Bald Eagle plucking." [18]

WHEN BURROUGHS RETURNED HOME from England in December of 1872, he carried with him a sealskin jacket and a silk dress for Ursula, both of which he had bought in London. He'd purchased for himself a new suit of clothes, a winter overcoat, and an extra large leather trunk. Ursula's presents, he told her, were her rewards for being "a good girl" while he was away. The rewards were handed out despite the fact that in his absence Ursula's displeasure with the O'Connors had caused her to evict the couple. Burroughs seems not to have troubled himself too much over the O'Connor flap. There were more important matters to be concerned with. No sooner had he settled into his old routine when Ralph Waldo Emerson arrived in the Washington area. Emerson, wrote Burroughs to Benton, "unsettles me for a week, my planet showing great perturbation in its orbit whenever such a body comes in my neighborhood." [19]

Emerson lectured in nearby Baltimore. Burroughs went, bringing Whitman with him. Emerson did not remember having met Burroughs earlier at West Point, and Burroughs appears not to have bothered to remind him. Burroughs recorded in his journal that Emerson had visibly aged in the nearly ten years since their first meeting—his nose a bit more hooked, his hair thinner and grayer, his overall appearance more fragile. Yet his voice was still clear and resonant, "having the ring of purest metal." Whitman reintroduced Burroughs to Emerson. Burroughs wrote Benton that Emerson had received him "quite warmly, unusually so, Walt said." Emerson was familiar with Burroughs's name, and had read many of his pieces in the *Atlantic*. In fact, Emerson was versed enough in Burroughs's writings to put him "on trial" for a critical remark he had made in his essay "With the Birds" about a faulty observation reported by Thoreau. "I defended myself as well as I could," wrote Burroughs to Benton, "and explained how I had left it out of the book [*Wake-Robin*] because I had not been to the Maine woods, etc. He was good-natured about it. Said he had *Wake-Robin* on his table, and had looked into it with a good deal of interest. Thought the title a capital one—expected to see an older man in me, etc."

Burroughs was unimpressed by the lecture on "Sources of Inspiration" that ensued. When a little while later Emerson spoke once more, this time in Washington, Burroughs again went to hear him. The topic for the second lecture was "Homes and Hospitality"—another letdown. Each of the lectures sprang from old themes that Emerson had spoken upon at length more than twenty years before. "Viewed in the light of the wants or needs of the American people today," wrote Burroughs to Benton, "and of the great questions and issues about us, nothing can be more irrelevant or pitiful than these lectures he [Emerson] is now delivering." Burroughs believed that a degree of national innocence had been lost forever on the bloody battle fields at Antietem and Gettysburg. A radical transfiguration—"a giant, maturing step for the race"—had left America and Americans dramatically and permanently changed. Burroughs thought that Whitman's recent poetry in *Drum Taps* addressed head-on the harsh experience that had been the American decade just passed. But in Emerson's current work Burroughs detected no hint of the national watershed, the Civil War.

"What we need from our great father Emerson," he wrote Benton, "are words to heal us and help us deal with the pain of our maturing. As a nation we have left the joy of childhood to enter the uncertainty and pain of young manhood. We need our father's wisdom, comfort, and religion more than we have ever needed anything from him before. But wisdom and comfort and religion he does not give. He withholds his best from us when we require it the most." Coming from Burroughs, this in an interesting comment on the man he so often called his "spiritual" father. Burroughs had been left with deep feelings of abandonment and betrayal when his own father had withheld support for his continuing education and forced him out of the house to seek his bread. Burroughs probably did not realize the psychological linkage between the emotions he was feeling with regard to Emerson and those he had felt, years before, with regard to Chauncey.

Burroughs had another reason to be disenchanted with Emerson. While at first an outspoken admirer of Whitman's *Leaves*, Emerson had lately stood back as the book was attacked and banned. Privately, Emerson criticized Whitman's most recent additions to the book. His quarrel, however, did not center on issues of "decency," but rather concerned the actual workmanship and quality of the poetry itself. To Emerson, Whitman's later work appeared to be tossed off, the verse a bit too "free" and the content too widely scattered. Just a few weeks before Emerson's lecture at Baltimore, Whitman had received a note from a friend in Boston who'd had a chance meeting with Emerson on the street. When Whitman was mentioned, Emerson said, "Yes, Walt sends me all his books. But tell Walt I am not satisfied—not satisfied. I expect him to make the songs of the nation, but he seems to be contented to make the inventories." [20]

Burroughs wanted to discuss Emerson's opinion of the poet with him face to face. On the morning after the lecture on "Homes and Hospitality," as Emerson was about to depart Washington, Burroughs contrived to chance upon Emerson at Union Station. "I stood off at one side and saw him purchase his ticket," wrote Burroughs to Benton. "It was amusing to see what hard work he made of it, fussing and fumbling, at a loss to know what to do with his gloves, his umbrella, his parcels—very anxious and earnest, apparently charging himself: 'Now, Old Forgetfulness, don't leave your ticket or your money, or miss your train, as you have so often done before.'" Burroughs helped Emerson board the train and then sat down beside him.

> I drew him out on Walt and found out what was the matter. He thought Walt's friends ought to quarrel a little more with him, and insist on his being a little more tame and orderly—more mindful of the requirements of beauty, of art, of culture, etc.—all of which was very pitiful to me, and I wanted to tell him so. But the train started just then and I got off. However, I wrote him a letter telling what I thought, and sent him my book [*Notes on Walt Whitman as Poet and Person*]. I do not expect to hear from it, but I was determined to give him a shot.

For the moment at least, Burroughs was less than impressed with his one-time idol. He had traded one guru for another, Emerson for Whitman, and had not yet learned the true Emersonian lesson that it was folly to have any such thing at all.

ANOTHER YOUNG WRITER WHO made Washington his home in the late 1860s was Henry Adams. The grandson and great-grandson of presidents, the son of the ambassador to the court of St. James, Adams was thirty years old when he arrived in Washington in 1868 after having lived in England for several years. Burroughs and Adams seem not to have known each other, even though Adams, a freelance journalist, was a frequent visitor to the Treasury Department where he often called on Burroughs's boss, Secretary of the Treasury Hugh McCulloch. At this stage of his career, Adams had a particular interest in writing on monetary affairs. In articles for the *Edinburgh Review*, the *London Quarterly*, and the *North American Review*, Adams admiringly chronicled the deft financial maneuvering with which

McCulloch's department endeavored to remedy the economic disarray that had been left after the Civil War. A series of Adams's papers for the *Edinburgh Review* documented McCullough's attempts to bring the southern states, with their heavily damaged infrastructure and massive war debt, back into the economic framework of the Union without dragging the whole exchange system of the country down to depression and collapse.

Adams wrote that McCulloch "was no politician" and "had no party." He was a banker pure and simple, and an eminently capable financial tactician. After Lincoln's assassination, President Johnson kept McCulloch in place at the Treasury. In 1869, President Grant removed McCulloch and made a political appointment to fill his shoes. Adams called McCulloch's replacement, George S. Boutwell, "a somewhat lugubrious joke." He wrote that Boutwell "could be described only as the opposite of Mr. McCulloch," as someone who "meant inertia." Worse than that, Boutwell's political favors could easily be bought by special banking interests, and often were. Although Adams had himself supported Grant's candidacy, it did not take him long to sense that corruption was to be the order of the day under the new administration.

Someone else who sensed this fact was Burroughs's old friend Jay Gould. In the late 1860s, Gould was busy laying the foundation for what would eventually become one of the greatest personal fortunes in the land. In 1867 Gould had narrowly beaten a consortium of Boston investors headed by Henry Adams's brother, Charles Francis Adams, Jr., in a bid to control New York's Erie Railway. The battle was finally won by the highly public maneuvering of Gould and his partner Jim Fisk to deflate the value of Erie stock and then buy it in quantity, after which they easily seized control of the Erie board of directors. Gould experienced his next splash of publicity shortly after, when in 1869 he very nearly succeeded in using the Grant administration to help him corner the gold market. It was whispered that Gould had employed shady business practices. "It is said that I have bought government officials," Gould told one reporter. "If that were the case, then I would only say that I, like anyone else, can only buy what is for sale. In the unhappy event that government officials were open to bribery, then I would be well advised, though not pleased, to finance them before my competition did the same." [21]

In 1870 Henry and Charles Francis Adams collaborated on a book-length study of Gould and his financial empire. Charles Francis took on the history of the fight for the Erie Railroad. Henry, with his penchant for economic affairs, looked into the "Gold Corner." In *Chapters of Erie* the Adams brothers compared Gould to a wily, evil spider who routinely lured unsuspecting investors into multifaceted webs of finance and then feasted on their carcasses at will. When doing business, wrote Charles Francis, Gould would sink to any depth simply to achieve his ends. Gould, the Adams brothers concluded, was a monopolist and enemy of the common good. "It is scarcely necessary to say that he has not a conception of moral principle," wrote Henry.

After his vilification in *Chapters of Erie*, Gould became infamous. A mythology grew up around him: He was a man who fed on the betrayal of friends, fattened on the ruin of stockholders, and endeavored to lie and bribe his way to a position of power that raised him above the law. As Gould's biographer Maury Klein has pointed out, it is hard to exaggerate the degree of vituperation heaped on Gould in his own time. The financier Daniel Drew said Gould's touch was "death." James R. Keene, another Wall Street operator, denounced Gould as "the worst man on earth since the beginning of the Christian era. He is treacherous, false, cowardly and a despicable worm incapable of a generous nature." Joseph Pulitzer called him "one of the most sinister figures that have ever flitted bat-like across the vision of the American people." *The New York Times* would eventually editorialize that "the work of reform is but half done when the insidious poison of an influence like that of Jay Gould can be detected in politics, in finance, in society, and when people claiming to be respectable are not ashamed of being associated with such a man as he." [22]

Of course, Gould was no better and no worse than any other mogul of the Gilded Age. His larger-than-life reputation for evil was more folklore than fact. Gould was a shrewd businessperson. When he saw his competition make mistakes, he tried to profit from those mistakes. He was as heartless and conniving as any other successful entrepreneur before or after him. But, as Burroughs knew well, Gould was certainly not as malevolent as the press made him out to be. Burroughs wrote to his father of Jay Gould in November of 1871. "Jay has got himself a whole lot of enemies," he told Chauncey. "Everybody seems to think he is the worst kind of man since Judas. I tell them he ain't nearly so bad as is made out, but nobody listens." [23]

Despite his personal loyalty to Gould, Burroughs backed all the complaints Whitman put forth in *Democratic Vistas* about how American big business was corrupting the vision and promise of American democracy. "Our love of the heroic overrides our humanitarian feelings," Burroughs wrote, criticizing the cynical pragmatism that seemed to guide what masqueraded for American business ethics. "Our attraction for power blunts our sense of right. If a man steals a chicken we hold him in contempt, but if he steals a railroad we feel quite differently toward him. Anybody can rob a henroost, but it requires genius and capacity to steal a great corporate interest." [24]

6

RIVERBY

We talk of communing with Nature, but 'tis with ourselves we commune. Nature has nothing to say. It all comes from within. The air supports combustion, but 'tis the candle that burns, not the air. Nature furnishes the conditions—the solitude—and the soul furnishes the entertainment.

— ***Journal Entry**, November 27, 1877*

As the early 1870s progressed, Burroughs began to complain a great deal to Ursula about how he was having to do more than his share of the work at the Treasury Department. He was constantly filling in, taking on the tasks that Secretary Boutwell's political cronies, who occupied more and more of the desks adjacent to him, simply did not know how to do. Soon, he told her, he would have to make a change.

The change was made effective January 1, 1873. Burroughs had spent several months negotiating a new federal appointment as Special National Bank Examiner for districts along the Hudson River, several other sections of New York, and three counties of Virginia. It was a post he would hold for thirteen years. His first task was to be receiver for an insolvent bank in Middletown, New York.

He left Ursula behind. He had to see about purchasing a place for them to live in New York; and Ursula had to oversee their Washington home until it was rented or sold. It would be an entire year before she would be able to join him, although they would visit each other regularly. "I left Washington in great haste," wrote Burroughs to Whitman, who had not been in town when Burroughs departed, "and since I have been here have been in the midst of a very maelstrom of business, all new, all strange, and very mixed . . . I have really cut loose [from Washington], and do not expect to return except briefly. I can make more money here, be much freer, be nearer home [Roxbury], and have a new field of duties. My greatest loss will be in you, my dear Walt, but then I shall look forward to having you up here a good long time at a stretch, which will be better than the crumbs I used to get of you in Washington."[1]

With Ursula alone in Washington, Walt took on the task of keeping her company. Early in January 1873, Whitman made regular visits to the lonely Ursula, sometimes bringing her magazines with Burroughs's essays in them. (Missing her husband, she even deigned to read one, and wrote Burroughs with surprise: "It pleased me very much, some of it was real funny.") But after January 23, Whitman's visits stopped. The poet suffered a stroke resulting in a paralysis that left him bedridden for more than a month. On February 23, Ursula wrote John that she'd been to see Whitman, for whom she obviously had a genuine concern. "I called to see Walt yesterday and he is still confined to his room," she wrote Burroughs. "He says its not only been a stroke of the muscles but also of the brain, and will be a long time perhaps before he entirely recovers . . . I asked him if he did not think he had better come up here and stay with me, and I rather urged him to come for I felt sorry for him and told him I would do the best I could, but he said no and seemed to think he had better stay there."[2] She took the poet out for a carriage ride a few days later. "I expect Mrs. Burroughs here probably today with a carriage to take me out riding," Whitman wrote to his mother on February 26, "so you see I am beginning to sport around."[3] Burroughs was of course enthusiastic about Ursula's helping Walt. "I was glad to hear about Walt, and that you are so kind to him," he wrote her. In closing the letter, he added a catch-phrase she had heard many times before. "Love me, love Walt."[4]

Ursula had one other major charge in addition to watching out for Whitman: taking care of a twelve-inch brook trout that Burroughs kept in an aquarium in the study of his Washington house. He must have been nervous about how seriously Ursula would take this responsibility, for in letter after letter to her during this period we find the uncompromising reminder: "Feed my trout."

Burroughs spent much of his free time that spring prospecting for a piece of land. His long-term ambition was to put ledger books behind him forever and become a farmer and writer. His ideal was to be able to farm in season and then have every autumn and winter to work at his prose. "I come from a race of farmers," he wrote to a correspondent in Britain, "and have always had a hungering for the soil, and am now bound to take my fill of it and let the empty artificial world go its own way, which is not mine." [5] In working his own farm, he hoped to retreat not to a place but from a time—the industrial present. The things he would try to grow on his farm, he wrote Benton, would be the fruits of memory. His earnest desire was to reclaim and nurture the pastoral roots within himself by sowing them both in the land he cultivated and in the pages he wrote.

To this end, he looked extensively on Long Island and through-out the Hudson Valley for the right parcel of real estate. Finally, he settled on a nine-acre fruit farm on the west shore of the Hudson River at West Park, some ninety miles above Manhattan. The place was less than a day's ride from his family's home at Roxbury, yet close enough to the city so as not to be inconvenient. An additional favorable aspect was a large stone heap nearby, from which he planned to pull much of the material for the house he wanted to build. Besides that, the view from the property was truly sublime. The farm overlooked the broad sweep of the Hudson due north of Krum Elbow. Directly across the Hudson, at Hyde Park, the white facade of a robber baron's mansion loomed large. At the foot of Burroughs's sloping property, a gigantic icehouse owned by the Knickerbocker Ice Company sat on the riverside just beyond the edge of the last arable field. Out past the icehouse a regular traffic of steamboats, sloops, and barges paraded up and down the main thoroughfare of commerce for eastern New York.

In time, Burroughs would grow weary of the majestic scenery. He would write in the 1880s that a small river or stream flowing by one's door had many attractions over a large body of water like the Hudson. One could make a companion of a small stream; it could become something private and special. "You cannot have the same kind of attachment and sympathy with a great river," he wrote. "It does not flow through your affections like a lesser stream. The Hudson is a long arm of the sea, and it has something of the sea's austerity and grandeur. I think one might spend a lifetime upon its banks without feeling . . . at all intimate with it." [6] In the late 1890s, explaining why he'd built himself a cabin retreat in the hills above West Park, he would write that to a "countryman" like himself, not born to an extensive water view, such a thing became wearisome after a time. "He becomes surfeited with a beauty that is alien to him. He longs for something more homely, private, and secluded. Scenery may be too fine or too grand and imposing for one's daily and hourly view. It tires after a while. It demands a mood that comes to you only at intervals." Hence, Burroughs wrote, it was never wise to build your house on "the most ambitious spot of the landscape." [7] In the long run, he was sorry he'd done so himself. But location would only be one of the elements of his dream house that he would come to detest.

The deed for Burroughs's place was drawn up in mid-September of 1873. Shortly thereafter, work began on digging the basement of the house he had been sketching and refining in his notebook for months. Burroughs boarded in Middletown, but traveled to West Park regularly to superintend the building.

Whitman, who was now living with his brother George's family at their home in Camden, New Jersey, wrote Burroughs suggesting that he talk to George, a carpenter and civil engineer, about how to best go about putting the new house together. "There is his old Brooklyn partner," wrote Whitman, "who is also a natural builder and carpenter (practically and in effect) architect . . . My brother thinks (and I think so, too) that if you have not committed yourself, you could not do better than to get Smith to plan and supervise and practically work with you . . . an honest, conscientious, old-fashioned man, a man of family. . . youngish-middle-aged—you would like him—I do." [8] Burroughs did not look up Whitman's carpenter. Instead he used local contractors from Kingston and Poughkeepsie. He himself served as architect. After all his sketches, he made a scale pasteboard model of the Tudor-style house he wanted to build.

The house was planned and built without Ursula being consulted on any aspect. One imagines that Mrs. Burroughs might have liked to have had a word or two about the house that was to be her home for the remainder of her life. Judging from what finally got built, one also imagines the house may well have been improved by her suggestions. Instead of Ursula, it was Benton with whom Burroughs routinely discussed the project. Benton flooded Burroughs's mailbox with suggestions for the new dwelling. Benton's letters and postcards were full of advice in the form of both words and sketches that addressed every minute detail of functionality, convenience, and aesthetics.

Where Burroughs proposed quaint but impractical architectural details, Benton tried to restrain him, reminding him that the house should first be a useful and efficient tool for living and only secondly something beautiful. Burroughs suggested fancy leafing for the interior woodwork of black walnut. Benton reminded him that this would catch dust "fearfully," and that every speck would show up on the dark wood. "I imagine Mrs. Burroughs with a step-ladder, dusting them night and day," wrote Benton. Burroughs thanked Benton for his advice and then proceeded with the intricate black walnut finish as originally planned. Given Burroughs's constant protests over his wife's insistence on having a tidy household, one is almost tempted to wonder whether he purposely designed the dwelling in a way that would make housekeeping twice the chore it should have been.

It would take him only a few years to realize that in designing for beauty he should not have ignored the requirements of daily convenience. In later years he would look at the place and tell his son: "It's the most absurd house ever built." [9] The layout defied efficiency in all aspects of the life of the household: cleaning, heating, bathing. Dining room and kitchen were in the basement, with a door out the back of the place on the slanted hillside. Library, parlor, master bedroom, and bath were on the main floor, with a front door opening out to the elevated driveway before the house. Additional bedrooms were on the second floor. Narrow stairways connected the three levels. In the days of no running water, this was to mean hard housekeeping for the punctilious Mrs. Burroughs. Ursula was to find herself regularly dragging buckets of water up two flights of tight stairs from the basement to the high second-floor rooms in order to be able to clean them. Benton had strongly urged Burroughs to put a hand pump on the top floor of the house, but

Burroughs decided this was not necessary. The bath being on the main floor, with no water pump, posed an obvious problem. It would never be used. Instead, for the next twenty or more years, the Burroughs family would bathe in a portable copper tub that was hauled out onto the center of the kitchen floor every Sunday night and filled with water heated on the wood stove close by. Another ignored suggestion of Benton's was that Burroughs should include many large windows. As strange as it may seem, Burroughs installed hardly any windows at all. And those that were put in were small. "The place," he wrote a friend in the late 1870s, was "as dark as a basement on every floor. And I am to blame." [10] To top it all off, the heating was totally inefficient. The upstairs rooms were frigid in the winter. After the birth of their son, they would spend most winters boarding in Poughkeepsie rather than trying to endure the harsh season in the cold stone house at the farm.

What he lacked in practical design on the inside of the house he almost made up for in the aesthetic flair with which he contrived the outside. He was full of theories for assuring natural beauty in construction. In "Rooftree," an essay-length memoir of the building of his house, he argued that native stone should always constitute the main structure. "All things make friends with a stone house," he wrote, "the mosses and lichens, and vines and birds. It is kindred to the earth and the elements, and makes itself at home in any situation." He had precise notions on the subtle art of this kind of construction. The mortar between stones, he believed, should form a depression rather than a ridge. Then, when the rising or setting sun shown on it and brought out the shadows, it would appear dynamically "powerful and picturesque." He also insisted on unpainted wood for both the interior and exterior walls. "How the eye loves a genuine thing; how it delights in the nude beauty of the wood!" he wrote. "A painted surface is a blank, meaningless surface; but the texture and figure of the wood is full of expression."

It was, he maintained, imperative to build in harmony with the natural surroundings. "Disguise it as one will," he wrote, "the new house is more or less a wound upon nature, and time must elapse for the wound to heal. Then, unless one builds with modesty and simplicity, and with due regard for the fitness of things, his house will always be a wound, an object of offense upon the fair face of the landscape." He argued that the beauty to be strived for in exterior domestic architecture was the same negative beauty that characterized the best and most simple hangings, which were but backgrounds for great pictures. He pitied those, such as a few of his millionaire neighbors, who seemed to think a house should stand out and be more than the lives enacted in it. "Every man's house is in some sort an effigy of himself . . . ," he wrote. "When you seriously build a house, you make public proclamation of your taste and manners, or your want of these. If the domestic instinct is strong in you, and if you have humility and simplicity, they will show very plainly in your dwelling; if you have the opposite of these, false pride or a petty ambition, or coldness and exclusiveness, they will show also." [11]

The analogy is a tempting one. To what extent was Burroughs's house an image of himself? The exterior was designed to settle easily into the rural landscape and to convey modest, subtle refinement. Built into the side of the hill, the rock walls seemed a natural extension of the earth: wholesome, organic. Inside, however, the place was incapable of providing comfortable shelter for a family.

IN THE EARLY FALL Ursula came north for a brief inspection. She came in joyous expectation of seeing the site of the grand house that her husband had described so eloquently. He picked her up at the little West Park steamboat landing and brought her in a carriage to the new farm. In the gate and down the driveway they drove. "Here," Burroughs announced with satisfaction, pointing to a huge hole in the ground, "this is where our house is to be." Together they walked the perimeter of the rude stone foundation that walled the freshly dug cellar. She could not conceal her disappointment. "It seems so small!" she told him. In vain did he show her the plans and pace out the dimensions of each room—"So many feet this way and so many feet that, such a size to this room and such a size to that, but it was no use." She had not been close enough to the planning of the house; she could not conceive a grand reality rising out of the muddy ditch.

Ursula arrived to stay during the frigid January of 1874. She had overseen the sale of their Washington home and the shipment of their belongings. She traveled by train from Washington and disembarked at Poughkeepsie. John met her in a horse-drawn sleigh. The river was frozen. The horse pulled them swiftly across the ice, north to their farm just a few miles distant. When they came up across the snowy fields from the river and approached the nearly completed house, Ursula was genuinely surprised to find herself liking the look of the place. The snowbound house was fully enclosed. It looked complete, but the interior still had to be finished and several chimneys extended. Thus John and Ursula had to set up temporary lodgings in the dilapidated home that the previous owner had left: an old Dutch farmhouse with little windows set under the low roof. By this time, Burroughs had settled on a name for the farm: he called it "Riverby" (by-the-river, but pronounced *riverbee*). Ursula was not consulted on this either. Burroughs's letter to her concerning the name is phrased as an announcement rather than a proposal.

It was the height of the ice harvesting season on the river when Ursula arrived at Riverby. As their sleigh approached the farm, John and Ursula passed nearly a hundred men and perhaps twenty horses out on the river abreast of their farm. Daily, through the long winter, the couple could see from their house the dark figures of men and horses moving out on the ice: some of them marking lines in the ice for cutters to follow, others sawing, others corraling the huge floating blocks. The square rafts would be floated down an improvised canal to the icehouse. Workmen loaded the blocks onto the high elevators leading into the huge storage house. An unbroken procession of great crystal blocks slowly ascended. During the summer these blocks, each weighing between 250 and 300 pounds, would be placed in barges and brought to New York. Burroughs wrote of the ice as a typical farmer would, as though it were a crop. "In the stern winter nights," he wrote, "it is a pleasant thought that a harvest is growing down there on those desolate plains . . . [It] takes two or three weeks to grow . . . Men go out from time to time and examine it, as the farmer goes out and examines his grain or grass, to see when it will do to cut." [12]

Ursula was terribly alone that first winter. She knew no one in town; and her husband was usually away on bank examining trips most of the week. Shy and insecure, she did not make friends easily but nevertheless craved them. The best way to meet new people was to become a member of a church. But Burroughs refused to accompany her to services at the local Methodist meetinghouse, although he would drive her there. (Wanting no part of "the hocus-pocus," he tied up his buggy alongside those of the faithful, escorted his wife to the door of the chapel, and then took off for an hour's tramp through the winter woods, returning in time to drive Ursula back home.) She found herself having to explain the idiosyncratic behavior of her seemingly unsociable and irreligious husband. He embarrassed her, which made her even more shy and standoffish than usual. Eventually she would make friends, but the process was to be a slow one.

It did not help Ursula that John seemed always to be leaving. Burroughs would depart early every week in the fancier of the two Riverby carriages, sporting a smart black dress suit with a gold watch tucked into the vest pocket, a fine overcoat, and a satchel packed with ledger sheets. He looked every bit the part of the influential bank examiner, a duly authorized auditor for the federal government, as he went off to visit various institutions throughout the state. But he chafed in the suit, as he did in the job. Writing to Ursula during a week of prolonged court proceedings in Manhattan for the closing of an insolvent bank, he complained that he would "ten times rather be on the mountains with Eden and his hounds than here." Burroughs did not say he'd ten times rather be at home with her.

When he came home on Thursday or Friday, he was usually off again every day wearing rough corduroys and a wrinkled workman's jacket. Some apples were tucked into his pocket instead of a gold watch. And his destination was not the office of a bank, but rather the frigid quietude of the forest. When the milder weather came— their first spring at Riverby—the destination was more often his own orchard, where he had begun keeping bees.

Burroughs was industrious in getting his acres planted that spring. He had to be. The place was mortgaged. It needed to be made productive fast in order not to be merely an expensive luxury. A bank examiner could not afford a country estate. Besides, the faster the place showed a profit, the faster he would be able to realize his dream of abandoning ledgers and becoming a full-time writer and farmer. He had a great deal to learn about growing the farm's principal crops. His background was entirely in dairy farming. To master his new place, where there was not one cow, he turned to pamphlets from the Department of the Interior and books on practical farming by E. P. Roe, a Methodist minister who lived twenty miles to the south at Cornwall. Roe was also one of the best-selling popular novelists of the day. He lived at the former estate of Washington Irving's old friend, the New York editor Nathaniel Parker Willis, who had chronicled life on his acres overlooking the Hudson in the 1862 book, *Idlewild: The Making of a Home on the Banks of the Hudson*. Burroughs studied Roe's several books on horticulture carefully. His copies of Roe's books, which are still on the shelf of his study where he left them, are heavily annotated in pencil. He made notes up and down the side margins, adding to Roe's suggestions those he culled from the Department of the Interior's pamphlets.

He had a hired man now: Smith Caswell, a Roxbury neighbor who had married Burroughs's niece Emma Deyo. Smith and Emma moved into the old Dutch farmhouse after John and Ursula vacated it to take up residence in the stone house. It was Smith who saw to the day-to-day management of the farm while Burroughs was off "doing the banks," as he called it. At Riverby on the weekends, Burroughs carefully supervised and worked alongside Smith, who himself really only knew about dairying. The two pitched in together on every aspect of planning and tending the acres of strawberries, raspberries, apples, currants, and grapes. When Burroughs went away on banking business during the week, he left Smith with precise written instructions on exactly what needed to be accomplished. Burroughs was a fair but demanding boss. Smith was family, and Burroughs had a genuine affection for him as a friend. But he was also an employee whom Burroughs relied upon to produce. Burroughs had Smith cross off the tasks on the weekly laundry lists as he accomplished them, and write down the number of hours that each job had taken. From the written record that survives we can see that Smith was a trustworthy, hard worker. And Burroughs appreciated this. "Smith Caswell, my niece Emma's husband, is here with us now," Burroughs wrote Whitman. "He is my man Friday of the fields. A fine trustworthy fellow. A great help. Without Smith, all would be lost." [13]

Burroughs was active in the fields as well. "I have been all day digging a drainage ditch," he wrote Whitman in July. "The muscles throb with a healthy ache. I find the effort exhilarating. It is good to work up a sweat at least once every day and sustain it for at least an hour." [14] He wrote Benton of becoming better acquainted with the hoe than at any other time of his life. "The hoe feels as natural as a pen in my hand," he wrote. "It is a tool with which I write my wishes upon the land." [15] It was also a tool he hoped would prove more profitable than his pen, which was then yielding him only about a fifth of what he needed to live on. The wish he wrote on the land was that it should be bountiful and that it should free him from bank closings and restructurings. He wanted to be able to spend all of his todays nostalgically recreating a rural yesterday both on his farm and in his books. He wanted to be able to define himself solely via the creative processes through which he found his most vital link to the past: the processes of farming and writing.

THROUGH 1873 AND 1874, with a new fruit farm on his hands, a house to build, and duties as bank examiner taking much of his time, Burroughs did hardly any writing at all. When his next book, *Winter Sunshine*, was published in 1875, it contained only one essay written at Riverby. The bulk of the book consisted largely of papers composed during the Washington period, including those stemming from his British journey. The book was warmly greeted by the critical community. Writing in the *Nation*, no less a critic than Henry James said that *Winter Sunshine* was a "very charming little book . . . The minuteness of [Burroughs's] observation, the keenness of his perception, give him a real originality, and his sketches have a delightful oddity, vivacity, and freshness." An anonymous reviewer in the *Boston Gazette* commented that "Mr. Burroughs is one of the most delightful American essayists, and in the description of our out-door scenes, sports, and observations, we know of no one who excels him." Charles Dickens's old friend and publisher James T. Fields wrote Burroughs to thank him for sending out "a book like *Winter Sunshine* to charm and instruct the whole country." Burroughs's Irish friend Edward Dowden, a Whitman admirer who taught at Trinity College in Dublin, wrote to tell him that parts of the book were "like an immediate off-growth of nature, and as full of juice as a bonny-cheeked Newton pippin, or a red astrachan." [16]

Dowden had chosen his metaphors carefully. The one essay in *Winter Sunshine* that had been written at Riverby was "The Apple." The Hudson Valley is great apple country, and Riverby boasted a fine orchard of gillyflowers and spitzenbergs. Burroughs, an acquaintance would recall, was a great devotee of the apple. He was in the habit of comforting himself with an apple in the same way that others might smoke a pipe or cigar, or take a drink of liquor. There was invariably, in season, an apple or two in his pocket which, when bored, he would produce and eat. When on bank examining trips, he usually had several apples in his bag. He never used a knife. He preferred, he said, that his teeth have the first taste. After all, he said, the best flavor was immediately beneath the skin.

He loved orchards as much as he loved their fruit. In "The Apple" he wrote of how during his boyhood in the Catskills the apple tree had been a prized possession. He remembered how, when trees broke down or were split by storms, the neighbors would all turn out and work together to put the divided tree together again, fastened with iron bolts. In some of the oldest orchards one could still occasionally see a large dilapidated tree with the rusty iron bolt yet visible. Staring out the window at his own orchard, he wrote of his father's apple trees in the Catskills from which, in addition to apples, he had gathered a "crop of sweet and tender reminiscences dating from childhood and spanning the seasons from May to October." He had played among them as a child, mused among them as a youth, and walked among them as a thoughtful, sad-eyed man. His father had planted the trees, and he had pruned and grafted them, and worked among them until every separate tree had a peculiar character and meaning in his mind. Then there was the never-failing crop of birds—robins, goldfinches, kingbirds, orioles, starlings—all nestling and breeding in the branches of the apple tree. "Whether the pippin and sweetbrough bear or not, the 'punctual birds' can always be depended on," he wrote. "Indeed, there are few better places to study ornithology than in the orchard." Birds of the deeper forest also came to the orchard in their season. The cuckoo came searching for the tent caterpillar, the jay hunting frozen apples, the ruffed grouse seeking out buds, and the crow foraging for birds' eggs. [17] The orchard was a place, wrote Burroughs in a letter to Benton, where the great world of nature would invariably swing round to "the watcher who is willing to sit patient and wait it out." [18]

After composing "The Apple" in early 1875 he continued to find many essay topics in the domesticated nature close to home. In "The Pastoral Bees," he wrote of the hives he kept in the orchard. "My bees are working like beavers," he wrote Whitman during his first spring at Riverby, "and there is a stream of golden thighs passing into the hive all the time. I can do almost anything with them and they won't sting me. Yesterday I turned a hive up and pruned it, that is, cut out a lot of old dirty comb; the little fellows were badly frightened and came pouring out in great consternation, but did not offer to sting me. I am going to transfer a swarm in a day or two to a new style hive." [19] In his essay, he wrote that he always felt as though he were missing some good fortune if he was away from home when his bees swarmed. "What a delightful summer sound it is; how they come pouring out of the hive, twenty or thirty thousand bees each striving to get out first; it is as when the dam gives way and lets the waters loose, it is a flood of bees which breaks upward into the air and becomes a maze of whirling black lines to the eye and a soft chorus of myriad musical sounds to the ear." This way and that they would drift, first contracting and then expanding, "rising, sinking, growing thick about some branch or bush, then dispersing and massing at some other point, till finally they begin to alight in earnest, when in a few moments the whole swarm is collected upon the branch, forming a bunch perhaps as large as a two-gallon measure." Here they would hang from one to three hours, until a suitable tree in the woods was located by "scouts," or, until a suitable hive was offered by the smart farmer who would have honey for his table.

His parents had kept bees and he had learned the skill from them. Beekeeping, he said, was a "long and valued tradition" of all "wise and sane and good country-men."

> It was fabled that Homer was suckled by a priestess whose breasts distilled honey; and that once when Pindar lay asleep the bees dropped honey upon his lips. In the Old Testament the food of the promised Immanuel was to be butter and honey (there is much doubt about the butter in the original), that he might know good from evil; and Jonathan's eyes were enlightened by partaking of some wood or wild honey: "See, I pray you, how mine eyes have been enlightened, because I tasted a little of this honey." So far as this part of his diet was concerned, therefore, John the Baptist, during his sojourn in the wilderness, his divinity school-days in the mountains and plains of Judea, fared extremely well. [20]

"While I doubt very much that the taste of honey will, in these cynical times, turn one instantaneously into a poet or a prophet," Burroughs wrote in a paragraph of the original draft essay that did not make it to the printed page, "it can honestly be said that the succulent flavor of the sauce is enough to recommend it. No other benefit, mystical or otherwise, need be looked for." [21]

In "Strawberries," he again mingled his present day experience with cherished memories of youth. He wrote that when he was a boy and went forth with his hoe or with the cows during the strawberry season of early summer, he was sure to return at mealtime with a lining of strawberries in the top of his straw hat. "They were my daily food, and I could taste the liquid and gurgling notes of the bobolink in every spoonful of them; and at this day, to make a dinner or supper of a bowl of milk with bread and strawberries,— plenty of strawberries,—well, is as near to being a boy again as I ever expect to come." He went for the strawberries with the same voraciousness with which he went after the trout and the apple. Hiking through the woods for hours in quest of the wild strawberry, his appetite became "a kind of delicious thirst,—a gentle and subtle craving" for the past as well as for the berry. [22]

7

IMMERSION IN THE LOCAL

Without a center-board your sail-boat slides upon the water. It does not take deep hold of it. You cannot beat up to the wind. What is the center-board of a man's character—will, integrity, depth of purpose, or what?

— *Journal Entry, December, 1876*

IT WAS NO ACCIDENT of convenience that Burroughs found topics for literature right there on his acres at Riverby. As an artist interpreting nature, he had charged himself to become immersed in its local occurrences, investing his personality and love into the landscape of his own region as had Thoreau, and using his native terrain as a local lens through which to view things that were universal in scope. He would find big things in little. He would make the infinite leap from the eye of a sparrow.

In his 1877 book, *Birds and Poets*, Burroughs explained how he felt the "home instinct" affected his experience of nature for the better by making him a part of the landscape, one in tune and "in sympathy" with the mountains, fields, and streams in a way that no casual visitor could be.

> . . . when I go to the woods or fields, or ascend to the hilltop, I do not seem to be gazing upon beauty at all, but to be breathing it like the air . . . what I enjoy is commensurate with the earth and the sky itself. It clings to the rocks and trees; it is kindred to the roughness and savagery; it rises from every tangle and chasm; it perches on the dry oak

stubs with the hawks and buzzards . . . I am not a spectator of, but a participator in it. It is not an adornment; its root strikes to the center of the earth. [1]

It was, argued Burroughs, not just any random chasm or peak that could inspire such vision and emotion. The landscape for which one felt a "wholesome, home impulse" and in which one made an investment of years, sweat, and love—that was the only landscape one could find real joy in. "We have met before," he wrote in a journal entry addressed to the silent trees, gray rocks, and waterfalls of his home hills. "My spirit has worn you as a garment, and you are near to me." [2]

There was nothing provincial or limiting about Burroughs's regional bias. Burroughs was looking for the cosmic in the local. As he wrote in his journal:

The universe, eternity, the infinite are typified by the sphere. The earth is the symbol of the All, of the riddle of riddles. We speak of the ends of the earth, but the earth has no ends. On a sphere every point is a center, and every point is the highest point . . . There is no end to Space, and no beginning. This point where you stand, this chair, this tree, is the center of Space, it all balances from this point. Go to the farthest fixed star and made that distance but the unit, one in millions and sextillions of such distances, and you have only arrived at Here. Your own doorstep is just as near the limit, and no nearer. [3]

In the essay "A Sharp Lookout," Burroughs wrote that nature came home to one most when one was at home, that the stranger and traveler found her a stranger and a traveler also. St. Pierre had written that a sense of the power and mystery of nature would spring up as fully in one's heart after he had made the circuit of his own field as after returning from a voyage round the world. "This home feeling, this domestication of nature, is important to the observer," wrote Burroughs. ". . . the place to observe nature is where you are; the walk to take today is the walk you took yesterday. You will not find just the same things: both the observed and the observer have changed; the ship is on another tack in both cases." [4]

Modernity worked against the necessary bond between man and land. One of the chief things that Burroughs disliked about cities was that they were, by and large, filled with transients. The factories that rose with ever increasing frequency on the outskirts of New York, Pittsburgh, and other metropolises lured men from farms cradled in the rural countryside. These ugly, monotonous, urban landscapes did not inspire affection.

> There is nothing there to care for. So the unhappy man stays but a while and then moves on to another industrial place where there is nothing to love, another modern spot where people hate what substitutes for what might have been a real home, and where cynicism is the only thing that takes root. We know so little! Even the simple birds understand not to build their nests in a place that is unclean and unhealthy, where their nerves are rattled, where loud noises assault the ear and foul smells [assault] the nose. You would think the choice not a hard one. The choice is plainly between rural paradise or industrial hell. Why do we unconsciously shift one way and not another as a society? Perhaps there really is something like a stain of original sin upon us. Perhaps we really are banned from paradise. But does the fruit of the tree of knowledge have nothing but knowledge of factories and slums to give? Why not knowledge of the value of simple things, modest wants, agrarian independence, and the value of a kinship to place? [5]

The city was a machine filled with even more machines. "Slay the monster, cut open his stomach. There are but more monsters within," he wrote Benton. "We have mastered the art of making first-rate machines," he wrote Whitman, "but have, in the process, somehow lost the art of making first-rate men." [6] A visit to the 1876 Centennial Exhibition in Philadelphia did nothing to reassure him. The exhibition was a vast tribute to the era that Thomas Carlyle had called "the age of machinery in every inward and outward sense." Great halls of glass and iron, one of them said to be the largest in the world, housed the latest examples of modern invention as well as a dazzling array of futuristic prototypes of coming innovations. The exhibition took up 450 acres at Philadelphia's Fairmont Park, and was serviced by a new state-of-the-art railroad depot designed to handle two trains every minute. Between the day the fair was opened on May 10 and its closing six months later on November 10, eight million visitors—one out of every five Americans—were to wander the huge show and marvel at the fruits of American science and industry. The exhibition was the chief fascination of the country from its opening until late June, when the deaths of Custer and his men at the Little Big Horn claimed the national attention.

The heart of the exhibition was a linked pair of four-story-tall steam engines that supplied electrical current to some eight thousand presses, pumps, gins, and lathes in Machinery Hall. Burroughs was repelled by what he called the "Hellish cacophony" of pounding hammers, hissing steam, blowing whistles, and whirling turbines. "A bird had somehow gotten in," he wrote his brother Curtis. "It flew desperately across the high ceiling, above the tops of the screaming, frenzied, pulsing machines—desperate to get out, as was I. The poor cardinal, of course, made straight for a window and rammed head-on into the glass. I imagine he was singing through his whole ordeal, as they do in times of tension and fear, but I could not make him out through the racket of crazed inventions." [7]

In one corner of the hall, a small steam engine drove a dynamo invented by the Belgian, Zenobe Gramme, which in turn lit up a tiny arc in a glass globe. Another young inventor, Thomas Edison, was there not with the incandescent light he would one day perfect, but rather with his quadruplex telegraph system, the rights to which he had recently sold to Jay Gould. At the Massachusetts education exhibit there was a newly patented "speaking telephone" developed by a Boston University professor of speech, Alexander Graham Bell. President Grant was among those who used the device and then walked away astonished at having been able to hold a conversation with Don Pedro, Emperor of Brazil, who was sitting on the other side of the fairground.

"It is in these things of iron and steel," wrote William Dean Howells in his account of the show, "that the national genius most freely speaks." A German reporter wrote that in Machinery Hall "the diligence, energy and inventive gift of the North Americans celebrates its triumph over all that has ever been achieved by other nations in the invention and construction of machines." The British philosopher Herbert Spencer used the exhibition as an example when he optimistically suggested that the old military and feudal orders, founded upon theology, were inevitably bound to give way to a new industrial order inimical to militarism, founded upon the increased productivity made possible by the advance of modern science.

Amid the hosannas and hallelujahs to technology, however, a few voices were raised in protest and warning. Herman Melville's book-length poem *Clarel*, published that centennial year, cast science and technology as menaces to God, nature, and social order. "Always," wrote Melville, "machinery strikes strange dread into the human heart, as some living, panting Behemoth might." In his short story "The Bell Tower," Melville made a mechanical clock-figure strike its maker dead. "So the blind slave obeyed its blinder lord; but, in obedience, slew him. So the creator was killed by the creature." Among the clergy, the prominent New England minister George F. Wright asked in 1876 "whether in our religion there is moral power enough left to control and keep in harness the [technological] giant we have awakened." Henry Adams was equally disaffected. "Man has mounted science," he wrote, "and is now run away with. I firmly believe that before many centuries more, science will be the master of man. The engines he will have invented will be beyond his strength to control. Some day science may have the existence of mankind in its power, and the human race commit suicide by blowing up the world."

Ralph Waldo Emerson wavered on the subject of the machine. At first, he sensed the possible good of technology. He wrote that it could be used to help make land more fruitful and life more healthy and wholesome. In his later writings, however, he recognized that technology might easily foster materialism and dehumanization. "The machine unmans the user," he wrote. As he and the century grew older, Emerson came more and more to believe that industrialization debased humanity's vision and lowered its moral stature. Still, he did not condemn the results of industrial science outright. Instead, he asked for the development of the proper moral and spiritual leadership to govern technology and see that it was used wisely.

Burroughs found relief from the dark vision of Adams and Melville by working to build a life for himself based on the agrarian tradition he honored, and by making a point to regularly go to nature and find communion with her on her own terms. Writing of a camping trip that he made with Elijah Allen shortly before visiting the exhibition, Burroughs praised the rugged terrain around Peek-amoose Mountain, in the Catskills. The craggy face of the world in that wilderness was so rough that no railroad could intrude; no factory could impose. Nevertheless, while inhospitable to industry, the mountain, which was ladened with berry bushes and clear streams in which trout were plentiful, seemed a benevolent and welcoming host to all who approached in the right spirit. "It is our partial isolation from Nature that is dangerous," wrote Burroughs, "throw yourself unreservedly upon her and she rarely betrays you." [8]

BURROUGHS HAD BECOME A diligent, well-tutored field observer of nature. He was rigorous in collecting the facts he reported in his papers. Aaron Johns, a friend with whom he camped, hiked, and fished for trout on many occasions, wrote of Burroughs's intense habit of inquiry and study in the wild. Johns recalled that Burroughs "casually revealed, in tossed-off and relaxed comments, an almost encyclopedic knowledge of birds, flowers, trees, rocks." Burroughs was, wrote Johns, "surely the most serious, passionate, and genuinely intrigued of all amateur natural historians. When he came upon a flower he did not know, he pulled a sample and put it in his pocket, saying he would have to look it up when he got back home. When he heard a distant bird song he did not recognize, he jotted the song down in his notebook using a strange shorthand of high and low running lines and dots, then also recorded the altitude, the type of forest, and the season at which he'd heard the song that was now clearly a mystery he intended to solve." There was, Burroughs told Johns, always something new to learn in the woods. "The forest is full of questions," said Burroughs, "and finding the answers is half the fun." [9]

Burroughs did much birding during their week-long jaunt at Peekamoose Mountain, near the headwaters of Rondout Creek.

"The winter-wren, common all through the woods, peeped and scolded at us as we sat blowing near the summit," he wrote, "and the ovenbird, not quite sure as to what manner of creatures we were, hopped down a limb to within a few feet of us and had a good look, then darted off into the woods to tell the news." He also spotted the Canada warbler and the chestnut-sided warbler. "Up these mountain brooks, too, goes the belted kingfisher, swooping around through the woods when he spies the fisherman, then wheeling into the open space of the stream and literally making a 'blue streak' down under the branches." [10] He meticulously recorded the names of the birds he spotted in a little notebook, and made running comments beside some of the names. Next to the notation of "three yellow-backs" he commented that they had been spotted probing the flowers and buds with their beaks, "probably going for honey." [11]

Another who wrote his impressions of Burroughs afield was Edward Carpenter, a young Fellow of Trinity College, Cambridge, who came to America for the express purpose of meeting Whitman and several of the poet's key supporters in the summer of 1877. (Carpenter would later cause a scandal in his native England by living openly with a male lover.) Carpenter published an account of his visit to Burroughs at West Park in his memoir *My Days and Dreams.* He recalled "a long walk in the primitive woods back of his [Burroughs's] house, while he talked of Whitman and bird-lore." Carpenter's impression of Burroughs was that he had a "tough, reserved, farmer-like exterior, some old root out of the woods, one might say—obdurate to wind and weather . . ." but that he was also "a keen, quick observer, close to Nature and the human heart." In a letter to Whitman, Carpenter said that Burroughs seemed to him to be "a poet with field-glasses, a Thoreau but much more friendlier, who dresses the farmer, talks the scholar, and has studied well the book of nature." As Burroughs and Carpenter went up the road toward the woods, they passed "two or three locals—farmers—with each of whom JB stopped and gossiped in a relaxed manner. He appeared very much at home with them. He said he does not speak of literary things with his neighbors—that he doubts any of them know him as a writer of books, and that he prefers it that way."

Burroughs brought Carpenter to Black Creek, a wooded tributary of the Hudson that was fast becoming a favorite fishing and meditating spot for Burroughs. The stream originated in a pond about a hundred feet higher than the Hudson, and flowed roughly parallel to the river two miles inland, taking a northward course until it found an opening through the rocky hills. "Its career all the way from the lake is a series of alternating pools and cascades," wrote Burroughs. "Now a long, deep, level stretch, where the perch and the bass and the pickerel lurk, and where the willow-herb and the royal osmunda fern line the shores; then a sudden leap of eight, ten, or fifteen feet down rocks to another level stretch." [12] As Carpenter and Burroughs sat by one of the waterfalls, Burroughs "grabbed a butterfly but lightly, with thumb and forefinger, as it flitted by," wrote Carpenter to Whitman. "Then he held it out before me, named its species, explained how he'd derived this from its markings, and described with brief eloquence that was poetry the creature's cycle of birth, life, and death. As he let the little thing go with the breeze, he turned and said, in a conspiratorial whisper as though he did not want the butterfly to hear, 'They are beautiful, but they are really only food for blackbirds.'" [13]

As attentive as he was to the study of nature in the field, he was equally thorough in his library, where one wall was filled with books on natural history and another wall with books of poetry, essays, history, philosophy, and criticism. The wildflower he collected and put in his pocket while camping he later researched at home using a reference book. The birdsongs he annotated in his notebook he compared to descriptions by Audubon and Wilson, as he did birds that he sighted and did not at first recognize. He corresponded with other ornithologists and biologists, both amateur and professional. He was to have lifelong letter-writing associations with various bird-watchers, wildflower collectors, and other naturalists throughout the U.S. and Canada, many of whom he would never meet face to face.

WHEN VISITING PHILADELPHIA FOR the Centennial Exhibition, Burroughs stayed in the same rooming house as Anne Gilchrist. Gilchrist was an English woman in her forties who had fallen in love with Whitman through his poems, some of which inspired her to a "marvelously free, sensuous radiance exploding inside." She had recently migrated to America with her three children in order to be near the poet. Gilchrist had carried on an active, often passionate correspondence with Whitman for several years. Now, much to Whitman's chagrin, she had come to America in hopes of becoming his wife despite his warning her in a letter of his complete disinclination to "get hitched." She had been sure of her mission when, despite Walt's protests that she should not, she sailed for Philadelphia from Maidenhead on August 30, 1876. "I passionately believe there are years in store for us, years of tranquil, tender happiness," she had written him, "me making your outward life serene & sweet—you making my inward life so rich—me learning, growing, loving." Of course, when Gilchrist arrived in the United States she found that her poet of sensuality was not prepared to fulfill the most critical need of her love, although he did offer the love of friendship.

"Walt came over every evening from Camden and took supper with us," Burroughs wrote Ursula after his Philadelphia trip. When he returned to Philadelphia six months later, Gilchrist was no longer in a boardinghouse. She had established her own residence on the east end of the city, and there kept a spare bedroom for use by Whitman whenever he wanted it. Whitman was still making his home with the family of his brother George in Camden. "Returned yesterday from Philadelphia where I spent the night of the 15th with Walt at Mrs. Gilchrist's," he wrote in his journal for February 17, 1877. "After ten o'clock we went up to his room and sat and talked till near one o'clock. I wanted him to say how he liked my piece on him, but he did not say. We talked about it, what had best go in, and what were best left out, but he was provokingly silent about merits." [14]

The piece in question was Burroughs's essay "The Flight of the Eagle," which Burroughs had originally titled "The Disowned Poet." The essay was another marshaling of Burroughs's standard defense of Whitman as "the poet of the new, of freedom and sane sensuality." That Whitman reviewed and revised the essay dramatically before publication is evidenced by the copy of Burroughs's original manuscript in the Henry and Albert Berg Collection of the New York Public Library. The manuscript has been heavily overwritten with comments, corrections, and whole paragraphs in Whitman's hand. The emendations were made by Whitman some weeks after Burroughs's visit and then mailed to Burroughs at Riverby. Virtually all of Whitman's changes wound up finding their way into the final published piece. Thus Burroughs should not have been surprised when, after publication of the essay in *Birds and Poets*, the egocentric Whitman wrote to tell him: "I especially much like—and more like—the chapter about me." [15]

Birds and Poets, a book in which Burroughs comfortably mingled essays on natural history with those that were pure literary criticism, also included a detailed, critical essay on Emerson. This, the first piece Burroughs ever published on the great inspiration of his youth, was likewise the most unsympathetic essay he would ever compose about the Emersonian mystique and message. Burroughs at this time was still totally infatuated with Whitman, very much to the exclusion of all other influences. The fact that Emerson did not give more vocal support to Whitman still bothered Burroughs mightily. "I have felt pretty ugly towards Emerson," wrote Burroughs to Benton, "because he ignored Walt Whitman in his *Parnassus* [a poetry anthology Emerson had just finished editing]. I think Walt can afford to be overlooked, but I don't think Emerson can afford to overlook him." In a letter to Whitman after a camping and fishing trip on the Jacques Cartier River north of Quebec during the summer of 1877, Burroughs noted that he had paused in Concord on his way to Canada and had stood outside Emerson's house long enough to "admire the woodpile." He did not "bother," he wrote Whitman, to stop and pay a call. "I passed by Mr. Emerson's house and looked my defiance towards it," he wrote another correspondent. [16]

In "On Emerson" Burroughs suggested that as a phenomenon Emerson stopped somewhere short of greatness himself, while at the same time providing the spiritual release and impetus necessary to allow others—such as Whitman and Thoreau—to soar. From this statement, Burroughs proceeded to appraise Emerson not on the body of his own work, but purely on the basis of his views concerning Whitman. Burroughs trotted out his familiar barometer for gauging all intellectual wits and all individual philosophies: Those people who were keen enough to understand and delight in Whitman's greatness must have some merit. All who did not bow to the poet were suspect, and somehow lacking. Burroughs noted that much surprise was expressed in literary circles that Emerson did not follow up his first offhand endorsement of Walt Whitman with fuller and more deliberate approval. "But the wonder is that he should have been carried off his feet at all in the manner he was," wrote Burroughs, "and it must have been no ordinary breeze that did it . . . [Emerson's] power of statement is enormous; his scope of being is not enormous." Burroughs said the prayer Emerson had uttered many years before for a poet of the modern, one who could see in the present age the same carnival of noble notions and grotesque evils that had defined man through all times and cultures, was explicitly answered in Whitman. "But Emerson is baled by the cloud of materials, the din and dust of action, and the moving armies, in which the god comes enveloped."

He had decided Emerson was a bit too proper, too concerned with grace, elegance, art, to be able to fully relate to Whitman's poetry of "the street, the common man, the rough." A letter from Carpenter, who had proceeded to Concord after his stay at West Park, confirmed Burroughs's judgment. Carpenter wrote of having been invited to stay overnight with Emerson on the strength of a letter of introduction from Burroughs. "He was so good and gentle (by no means of the race of 'savage old men') that I could not feel angry with him," reported Carpenter. "He did not abuse Whitman, or rant against him in any way. He spoke of him more in sorrow than in anger. Said of course that he thought he had some merit at one time—there was a good deal of promise in his first edition— but he was a wayward, fanciful man. (It appears that Whitman took Emerson to see his Bohemian society in New York—and Emerson thought it very noisy and rowdy; and he couldn't understand his friendliness with firemen. In fact, Whitman baffled and puzzled him.)" [17] According to Carpenter, Emerson enjoyed a hearty laugh when Carpenter repeated a story Burroughs had told him: Burroughs had at first proposed *Nature and Genius* as the title for his new book, but changed it to *Birds and Poets* when Whitman criticized *Nature and Genius* as sounding "too Emersony altogether."

"I do not quite like the way you knights errant of Walt Whitman hound Emerson about that endorsement," wrote Benton to Burroughs. "He ought to have the rights of a man and perfect freedom in the Republic of Letters to say what he chooses on any subject, and let it drop when he chooses." [18] Burroughs heard similar murmurings from other quarters about his essay. "I have had no sign of what he [Emerson] or his friends think of it," he wrote Benton. "I met [Charles] Dudley Warner at Mr. [Richard Watson] Gilder's . . . he said much the same as you do." Higginson wrote Burroughs to mockingly "congratulate" him on having "so much confidence" as to be willing to "wrestle the grand old man, our father, down to the ground." Higginson added that he supposed Burroughs would sit on Emerson's back and hold him down in the dirt until Emerson said "'Uncle,' or, more appropriately, 'I love Walt, too.'" [19] James Russell Lowell wrote Burroughs that he thought the essay a bit "severe," and asked exactly what the credentials were that qualified "you, my so young Burroughs," to "suggest improvements for the mind that gave us 'Nature'." [20] Burroughs said in his defence that he hardly felt that he had really been criticizing Emerson at all, "but rather sounding him, and trying to determine exactly what he is. He is not a man to be criticized, but rather to be defined and appreciated." [21] He told Lowell he had nothing but respect for Emerson, who was the "sire" of whatever was good in the "small garden" of his intellectual curiosity. "He is the father of the writer that is me. He was the sower of the first seeds of my intellectual wits. Any criticism I ever offer will be tempered by the gentle love of a grateful son, with which it shall always be accompanied." [22]

8

FATHERHOOD

How true it is that every person has his or her permanent water-level, like a mountain lake. We can hold only just so much happiness . . . How much I love little Julian, and what a godsend he is to me, and yet is not my water-level permanently raised.

— ***Journal Entry, January 30, 1880***

WHEN STILL CONSIDERING THE purchase of the farm that was to become Riverby, Burroughs had written Ursula of a concern that was on both of their minds. "If we were not alone I should not hesitate about the . . . place," he wrote, "but the great bane of my life has been loneliness. We two are not enough in a house. I pine for a companion of my own sex; so, no doubt, do you. What shall we do? Can we make it up by dogs and cats, and a pig and a horse, a cow, hens, etc.?" [1] They had been married for thirteen years, and still the child that they wanted had not come. Writing to his Irish friend Edward Dowden, Burroughs congratulated him on the birth of a son and prayed "the fates" would "pass the favor round this way." [2] Of course, the strained nature of John and Ursula's sexual relationship was a likely contributing factor in their childlessness.

The problem was finally resolved on the early morning of April 15, 1878. Just before dawn, the forty-one-year-old Burroughs walked across a field to the north of his house carrying a bundle, a bundle that he handled gingerly, as though it were precious china that he dared not break. The contents of the rolled blanket moved slightly in his arms. A newborn baby boy blinked up and out at his father. The boy's mother, a young Irish maid at a nearby estate, had seen the baby only once and would not see him again. Within two days she would be on a clipper ship bound back to her homeland. This had been one of the things Ursula had insisted on in agreeing to accept John's child into the house as her own. Another had been that the boy should never be told that he had any mother other than Ursula. And another had been that there should be no more philandering by John. In the long run, only the first of Ursula's three demands would be met. [3]

A few weeks after the birth, Whitman came on a mission to see the new baby. He stayed a week at Riverby that June. During the visit, in thumbing through Burroughs's journal, the poet came across an entry that he found of special interest. "Saw three eagles today," Burroughs had written under the date January 29, 1878. "Two were sailing round and round, over the river, by the dock. They approached each other and appeared to clasp claws, then swung round and round several times, like school-girls a-hold of hands." [4] It was not long before Whitman turned the image of the tallon-clasped eagles into one of his *Leaves*. The brief poem, entitled "The Dalliance of the Eagles," was shot through with sexual energy building to a moment of climax. At the same time, it related a certain condition of casualness, if not anonymity, with the act of intercourse.

> Skirting the river road, (my forenoon walk, my rest,)
> Skyward in air a sudden muffled sound, the dalliance of the
>   eagles,
> The rushing amorous contact high in space together,
> The clinching interlocking claws, a living, fierce, gyrating wheel,
> Four beating wings, two beaks, a swirling mass tight grappling,
> In tumbling turning clustering loops, straight downward falling,
> Till o'er the river pois'd, the twain yet one, a moment's lull,
> A motionless still balance in the air, then parting, talons loosing,
> Upward again on slow-firm pinions slanting, their separate
>   diverse flight,
> She hers, he his, pursuing.

Whitman was to tell O'Connor that the poem was derived "in one part from Burroughs's journal, in another part from Burroughs."

Once the "rushing amorous contact" of the birds in the sky was culminated, they parted and each went on "their separate diverse flight"—"She hers, he his . . ." Burroughs and the woman who'd conceived his son had coupled briefly and then gone their separate ways. So too had Burroughs and several other maids of the neighborhood, not a few of whom had worked in the stone house at Riverby.

A relatively high turnover rate for maids was to become something of a tradition at Riverby through the 1880s and 1890s. Burroughs's usual explanation for the rapid change in staff was Ursula's habit of working household employees too hard. In fact, the trouble was more often that John developed—or at least tried to develop—a relationship with the maid that Ursula found intolerable. This is what Ursula's sister, Amanda North, wrote in a 1921 letter to Burroughs's authorized biographer, Clara Barrus. We have something by way of confirmation in a comment Whitman made in another letter to O'Connor. "John should show the same attention to 'Sula [Whitman's pet-name for Ursula] that he does to several other young—and not so young—ladies. Then they would get on better," wrote Whitman. "Knowing John, I would not make the futile suggestion that he dispose of the others. I would simply propose that he include Ursula on his dance-card." [5] The question, of course, is whether or not Ursula wanted to be included on the dance card. The indications are that she did not want to dance and that she did not want Burroughs to dance either, with anyone.

More than forty years later, at the close of Burroughs's life, the facts of Julian's birth were still to be a sore point with him. This was the one part of his story that Burroughs forbade Clara Barrus to include in her book. Thus we find the milestone event that was the arrival of a long-awaited son treated with just one terse sentence in Barrus's *The Life and Letters of John Burroughs*. "The year 1878 was comparatively uneventful," wrote Barrus, "with a few outstanding features, of which the birth of his son in April was the chief." [6] She gave no further details. Barrus was not prepared to state falsehoods, but at the same time she wanted to adhere to the dying Burroughs's injunction. [7]

The suppression of the story of Julian's birth went beyond skipping details in Barrus's biography. Either Burroughs or Barrus tore pages from Burroughs's journal for the months of March and April of 1878. In the correspondence of Burroughs and Myron Benton there is evidence of more tampering. Four letters, two from Burroughs and two from Benton, dated between March 29, 1878 and May 13, 1878, are missing from the file in the Berg Collection of the New York Public Library. The missing letters appear on the mastersheet of documents supplied by Barrus with the sale of the correspondence. According to a Berg Collection curator who investigated the matter, the four letters in question were not listed, however, on the catalog receipt of documents received by the Berg Collection from Barrus. Barrus hung on to them, and probably either destroyed them or gave them to Julian.

AFTER A SILENCE ON the part of Burroughs since May, Benton wrote in November of 1878 to warn him not to let fatherly duties keep him from old friends. He also wrote of how the advent of the child put the all-too-fast passage of time into perspective, and made more plain the way age colored one's view of the world with dimmer, grayer colors. "What a different world was that to our eyes in those first letters!" wrote Benton. "There was a freshness, a glory to everything that seems to have vanished." [8] Burroughs's reply is revealing, and reinforces our picture of the deep nostalgia that was a central element of his character. "Yes, it is a sad fact that life and the world lose their freshness and glory as we grow older," the new father wrote Benton. "The future becomes the past, and we turn more and more from what is, or is to be, to what has been . . . It is the pack at our back, the burden of memory, that grows more and more as the days pass."

He confided a similar emotion to his journal. "I look back at the work [my parents did]—the farm they improved and paid for, the family they reared, with unspeakable longing. How idle and trivial seem my own days!" [9] His natural sentiments were so turned around by his strange, backward-looking pessimism, that he went so far as to mourn that his new son had everything ahead of him, that he had only a future and no sublime, romantic past. "I look upon this baby of mine and think how late he has come into this world—how much he has missed; what a faded and delapidated [*sic*] inheritance he has come into possession of." [10]

In his journal Burroughs wrote that he cared little for the future, that time did not become "sacred" to him until he had lived it, until it had passed over him and taken a part of his soul away with it. "Here we stand on the marge of time," he wrote, "with all that growing past back of us, like a fair land idealized by distance into which we may not return."

His farm, as beautiful and productive as he eventually made it, would always be inadequate as compared to the farm he'd grown up on and made so perfect in memory. His books, for all their striving to invoke and reinvigorate the rural innocence of the past, he would come to view as nothing more than nostalgic, flawed, aide-mémoire for a nation of ever-expanding urban sprawl. And his family, Julian and Ursula, would always be a pale imitation for him of that other family of his childhood, the memory of which he would try to conjure up through ritual reenactments with Julian of the joys and sorrows he'd shared with his own parents. Beneath it all there would be a confused yet always constant love. But, increasingly, he loved things of the present most when they could be used as tools for resurrecting the past.

Both parents—the natural father and the adoptive mother—doted on their boy. "The youngster, by the way, is doing well," he wrote Benton in November of 1878. "His sense and his intelligence are very keen, and I think I see a future poet in him. He and I have great times already." [11] "Julian," wrote Burroughs to Whitman, "completely fills my heart." [12] The father took a serene delight in watching the transformation of the tiny baby into an inquisitive, babbling little boy. "He just now begins to use the word 'wish.' Among other things he says, 'I wish you get me seven league boots,'" wrote Burroughs to another friend. "His last [latest] want is that I should get him a little well, 'wiv' a bucket and rope, and a wheel to go round." As Burroughs sat in the library of the stone house and wrote essays, he could hear Julian "training through the house, running from the pantry and through the hall into the dining room, and back, for hours at a time. He toots long and loud and fills the low part of the house with the sound of his feet and his whistle."

In 1880, Burroughs would report to Benton that he and the

two-year-old Julian had "long walks and talks together. He knows the sparrow, the blue jay, and the robin. The crow he persists in calling a black robin . . . He said that one day a robin called him to come up in the clouds and sit down. He speaks of 'smooth' as an extraneous or independent something; of this or that he says, 'It has smoove on it'. . . . He asks ten thousand questions a day. He is a bright boy, and we love him more and more."

To the publisher James T. Fields he wrote that becoming a father was the best thing he had ever done for himself. "I love helping Julian find the secret doors of the world, and then watching his amazement as he opens them. It brings back the suggestion of youth and optimism to me. Fatherhood is a wonderful thing." [13] After an 1879 visit to Riverby, Whitman commented to Edward Carpenter in a letter that Julian was "plainly John Burroughs's first, best friend now—just as it should be. His love of the boy is like his love of the woods: effortless, natural, joyous. It is a wonderful thing to see."

Writing in his journal shortly after the death of his seventy-two-year-old mother five days before Christmas in 1880, Burroughs said that the two-year-old Julian was his "comfort" and his "life." The boy could not understand the death of his Grandma. "He insists with great emphasis, however, that Grandpa is not buried in the ground. 'Grandpa live,' he says, 'and coming to see Dudy this day.'" [14] The little boy played happily that Christmas. He did not know what day it was. He did not know to miss the Christmas tree that was not there and would never be there. He did not expect, and so did not miss, the presents that children in neighboring house-holds were delighting in. As Julian grew, his awareness of Christmas would increase. He would come to feel the lack of the tree, the gifts, the joy—and eventually even the religion.

"Poor Mother," Burroughs had written in his journal a few days before her death, "her mind is in fragments, like a shattered vase, she can fit only a few pieces together." The series of strokes that eventually killed her body first killed her mind. Burroughs was to comment to

Benton that it seemed "an ironic coincidence" that while his mother suffered "the loss of all her wit and reason," his "spiritual Father," Emerson, was experiencing a similar mental collapse. Thinking back on the twin destinies of the elderly Emerson and his own elderly Mother, Burroughs in old age would write his son: "I do not fear death, but I do fear the imbecility that too often comes before it." [15]

Burroughs first learned of Emerson's senility through second-hand accounts. Mrs. Gilchrist wrote Burroughs of an evening spent with Emerson and his wife in Concord during the fall of 1878. Burroughs wrote to Benton, reporting Gilchrist's impression of Emerson. "He is very serene and cheerful, remembers earlier things and events, but is fast losing his hold upon later. He saw Walt Whitman's photograph in her album, and on being told who it was asked her if he was one of her English friends." At one point during his dinner with Gilchrist, Emerson leaned across the table to inquire of his wife the name of his best friend. "Henry Thoreau," she answered. "Oh, yes, Henry Thoreau," he echoed happily. [16]

A year later Burroughs met Emerson at the seventieth birthday breakfast given by the *Atlantic Monthly* in Boston for Oliver Wendell Holmes. To Burroughs, it seemed that Emerson's mind was "like a splendid bridge with one span missing." The old man was "like a plucked eagle tarrying in the midst of lesser birds." John Greenleaf Whittier, the Quaker poet, stood next to Emerson, prompting his memory and supplying words that the once eloquent writer would have otherwise spent hours groping for. "When I was presented," recalled Burroughs, "Emerson said in a slow, questioning way, 'Burroughs—Burroughs?' 'Why, thee knows him,' said Whittier, jogging his memory with some further explanation."

In the autumn of 1881 the addled Emerson had something of a reconciliation with Whitman. The poet was entertained at the Emerson home during a trip to Concord. The occasion seems to have softened Whitman to Emerson, and in turn softened Burroughs. "I cannot tell you how sweet and good (and all as it should be) Emerson look'd and behaved," wrote Whitman to Burroughs from Concord. "He did not talk in the way of joining in any animated conversation, but pleasantly and hesitatingly, and sparsely—fully enough—to me it seemed just as it should be." [17] Later Whitman had more to say about his visit with Emerson. "I thought [Emerson] in his smiling and alert quietude and withdrawnness (he has a good color in his face and ate just as much dinner as anybody) more eloquent, grand, appropriate and impressive than ever, more indeed than could be described," wrote Whitman. "Isn't it comforting that I have had, in the sunset, as it were, so many significant, affectionate hours with him?" [18]

Emerson died on April 27, 1882. "Emerson died last night at 8:30 o'clock," wrote Burroughs in his journal. "At that hour I was sitting with Myron Benton in his house, talking of Emerson and his probable death. With Emerson dead, it seems folly to be alive. No man of just his type and quality has ever before appeared upon the earth." A few days later, on the 30th, Burroughs was still thinking about Emerson. "Today Emerson is to be buried, and I am restless and full of self-reproach because I did not go to Concord. I should have been there. Emerson was my spiritual father in the strictest sense. It seems as if I owe nearly all, or whatever I am, to him . . . I must devote the day to meditating on Emerson." [19] The result of his meditations was an appreciation that he published in the *Critic*. Before his death, wrote Burroughs, Emerson's mind had cracked the phial in which it was held and had begun to escape "like some rare essence that would no longer brook restraint."

BURROUGHS WROTE FOR THE love of it. But as time progressed he also wrote with an eye toward making the writing pay. Every two or three months, he used a page of his journal to sum up exactly what he had written recently and exactly what he had been paid for the writing. He told Benton that he needed to be "mercenary" about everything, even writing. "Not being as affluent as you, I must make the literature earn its own way. My many obligations insist on this—as does my wife." [20] In another letter to Benton he itemized his output for a given month, adding that "The *Atlantic* has two, the *Century* one, the *Critic* four. The rest I am still nursing . . . You see I do not let my strawberries rot on the vines as you do. I send them to market." [21]

When he determined to take his wife and four-year-old son to

England and Scotland during the spring and early summer of 1882, Burroughs jotted a note in his journal estimating how many essays he could likely mine from the trip, and what he would likely be paid for them. He sent a letter to his publisher saying that he thought he would get seven to ten good papers from the journey, and asking if there would be interest in a book. Houghton's answer was yes. He would be willing to pay a $700 advance for the book. Burroughs estimated he would get at least another $700 in serial fees from Richard Watson Gilder, editor of the *Century*. The trip would cost him about $300. As soon as the enterprise looked like it would more than pay for itself, he booked passage. He planned to leave Smith Caswell in charge of the farm. He arranged for a fellow examiner to handle any problems that came up with banks in his districts while he was away. With all these details tended to, John Burroughs took his family in tow and sailed from New York on May 5, embarking on a twelve-day voyage that ended in Glasgow, Scotland.

Shortly after his arrival in Scotland, John wrote his brother and fellow farmer Eden Burroughs a glowing description of the pastoral landscape that he found there. He had never seen such fine farmland. "The cattle are in the pastures up to their eyes, and are all fat enough for beef," he told Eden. "The oats and wheat are several inches high." In a little notebook kept during the trip he noted: "One of the first impressions is that the cattle and sheep have all got in the meadows, and one's impulse is to go and drive them out. Then look farther and see that there are no pastures as at home. It is all fresh and green and meadow-like." A similarly approving description went to Benton, to whom he contrasted the subdued, domesticated landscape of the Clyde with the countryside of the Hudson River Valley. "It looks as if it had all been passed through the mind and heart of man, and was still nature," he told Benton. "There is no hint of the savage and the sublime, as with us, but a human tenderness and beauty and repose, and pictorial effect impossible to describe." Much of the land was cultivated right down to the river bank. On every hillside was visible the result of many centuries of enlightened, dedicated husbandry.

At the same time, he told Benton that he noticed some "insults" to the rural British landscape that were unsettling.

There is a touch of industry on too many horizons. The foreground of the picture is pure, but the background has the stain of soot, the ring of metal. Look beyond the near, peaceful meadow to the distant river, and you find, amid the many farms, the inevitable single mill and all that goes with it: chimneys and the soot,—pipes running down and into the tide,—the pounding vibration and the harsh, rhythmic ring of automation,—the silence above and the stillness below the waters,—no fish, no birds, no toads, all who know better than man not to live by such a poisonous enterprise.

Thoreau's pristine Walden woods had been within a day's hike of the factories at Lowell. Burroughs's own rural home at Riverby was but fifteen minutes by boat from Poughkeepsie, where several factories lined the river shore. On his first trip to England, he had thought that the rural English landscape was far less corrupted by factories than its northeastern American counterpart. Now, in 1882, he saw more clearly that the British situation was virtually the same as the American one. The British, Burroughs wrote Benton, "seem no cleverer than we unclever Americans with regard to the negative potential for technology's impact on sceneries and souls." Though still beautiful in many vast expanses, the landscape of England was slowly turning, wrote Burroughs, from "a poem by Wordsworth to a painting by Turner. The place is rife with old beauty overshadowed by the dark evil of the modern." [22] Rural life in England was just as much threatened, if not more so, than rural life in the United States. An entire generation before Burroughs's visit, William Blake had written forlornly of England's "dark Satanic mills" with their fatal ability to transform the landscape, as well as the social order, for the worse.

Burroughs made a point in stopping at Carlyle's hometown of Ecclefechan, one hundred miles from Edinburgh. Writing from there to Whitman, he enclosed a daisy and a spray of speedwell gathered from Carlyle's as yet unmarked grave. Leaving Scotland, Burroughs and family then travelled to Wordsworth's Lake District, where Burroughs did a walking tour from Ambleside to Grasmere on a typically rainy British day. "As I scribble this beside the mossy stone wall," he wrote in his notebook, "the call of the cuckoo comes over Rydal Water—a blithe sound, hardly birdlike. Have just seen Wordsworth's house, and looked long at it, and at the grove of noble beeches in front of it, and at the mountains back of it, and thought of Emerson's visit here near fifty years ago." [23]

Burroughs also made a pilgrimage to Gilbert White's old haunts at Selborne and Wolmer Forest. The place, save for the inevitable mill on the horizon, had changed little since White's time. "Selborne is as provincial as my native Roxbury," he wrote Benton. The postman handed Burroughs his letters upon the street without asking his name. Burroughs was the only stranger in the place. At the hotel where he stopped, a copy of White's classic book on the natural history of the region could not be produced. Burroughs spent several hours searching for White's tomb amid the graves of the church where he had been parson. He finally found a plain slab with "G. W." inscribed on it. "There was no mark that indicated that the grave was more frequently visited than any other." [24]

Through most of these excursions into the country, Julian and Ursula remained behind in London. The three of them shared sightseeing in town. In a notebook entry for June 16, Burroughs recorded his son's reaction to St. Paul's Cathedral: "This is an awful high house, isn't it, Papa—three thousand acres high," said the boy in what Burroughs termed "a plaintive and mournful tone." [25] Julian enjoyed the London Zoo and insisted on being taken back there on three separate occasions. The boy was equally impressed with the Tower of London. To his brother Eden, Burroughs reported, "Julian keeps well and eats like a wolf." To Benton he wrote that "Mrs. B. has had some serious battles with the dirt of this country, but she keeps her courage up, and intends to fight it out on that line." Returning to Scotland at the end of July to board their boat home, he and Ursula made it their last business to hire a Scottish maid who they brought back with them to Riverby. The maid would not last long.

"It is good to be back," he wrote Benton from Riverby at the beginning of August. "I am now, after a run out home, regularly ensconced in my little hermitage, chewing the succulent cud of my English and Scotch memories. That green land with its sweetness and repose will long haunt my memory." [26] He methodically set to writing about, and paying for, his journey. He ground out a succession of papers that Richard Watson Gilder, editor of the *Century Magazine*, would buy immediately and publish sporadically: "Bird Songs, English and American" (*Century*, January 1883), "Nature in England" (*Century*, November 1883), "In Wordsworth's Country" (Century, January 1884), "A Hunt for the Nightingale"—reporting on his visit to Tennyson's hometown—(*Century*, March 1884), "British Fertility" (*Century*, May 1884), and "British Wildflowers" (*Century*, August 1884). All of these pieces would likewise find publication in the book of British sketches Burroughs had promised Houghton: *Fresh Fields*, to be published in 1884.

Burroughs spoke much of his recent experiences in England when he played host to Oscar Wilde at Riverby in August of 1882. Wilde had made a much-publicized lecture tour of the United States the previous year, and had returned to New York for the staging of his play *Vera, or The Nihilists*. Henry Abbey, the Kingston poet whom Wilde had paid a call on, brought Wilde down to Riverby for a visit. Ursula was much taken with Wilde, who told her she baked the best bread he had yet eaten in America. Julian, who was four years old at the time of Wilde's visit, would recall that Wilde helped him pick strawberries for lunch. Writing of the visit, Burroughs said his impression of Wilde was that he was "a splendid talker, and a handsome man, but a voluptuary." There was, wrote Burroughs, "something disagreeable" in the movement of Wilde's hips as he walked. [27] Wilde, for his part, wrote a friend that Burroughs was "far more charming than his rustic look would lead one to anticipate. He looks like the farmer that he is, but talks like the cultured man-of-letters that he also is. Very oxymoronic, but very gracious too. I did, however, want to take him out and buy him some clothes." [28]

Burroughs did not invite Wilde to go hiking, as was his habit with most guests. Perhaps he sensed that rough trails and steep hills were not the types of things that Wilde found entertaining. Instead, Burroughs and Wilde spent many hours sitting in rocking chairs in the summerhouse outside Burroughs's one-room bark-covered study, which he'd built the previous January overlooking the river. One topic of discussion was Walt Whitman, whom Wilde greatly admired. Wilde's mother had been among the first to promote Whitman's work abroad. Wilde himself had recently been to visit the old man in Camden, where he and Whitman toasted each other with elderberry wine and hot toddies. During the visit, Whitman had charged the young Englishman not to miss a chance to meet and speak with Burroughs. Wilde and Burroughs also spoke of Carlyle, whom both men had known, as well as their mutual friends Edward Carpenter and William Rossetti.

In addition to an appreciation of Whitman's poetry, Wilde and Burroughs shared a common dissatisfaction with the results of invention and technology. Wilde told Burroughs that he thought America to be the "noisiest" country that ever existed, with the increasingly industrial England running a close second. One was awoken in the morning not by the singing of the nightingale, but by a steam whistle. Burroughs noted in his journal that he and Wilde agreed that both England and America were failures in the manner in which they "applied science to living." [29] British cities, Wilde told Burroughs, were just as rank and unhealthy as American ones. Wilde added that unlike Liverpool and other "industrial pits" of the United Kingdom, New York at least had one truly great architectural marvel to boast of, one superb example of technology turned into use for good. That was the Brooklyn Bridge, which was just a few months away from completion after fourteen years of work. The bridge, Wilde told Burroughs, was "a poem of angularity." By designing for utility and strength, the architect Roebling had unwittingly ended up with "beauty of form." In a century, said Wilde, the bridge that was now so modern would be studied and hailed as a classic structure, an architectural treasure. While reserving judgment on the timelessness of the bridge's design, Burroughs agreed with Wilde's assessment that utility usually led to beauty. Wilde would remember Burroughs telling him that this was not just true of bridges. It was usually true of words as well. If one found something real that was worth saying, then the form would follow promptly. A genuine thought, said Burroughs, was almost always an easy one to express in an eloquent manner. [30]

Both Wilde and Burroughs were admirers of John Ruskin, who had long protested the indignities perpetrated on the English landscape by what Ruskin called "rank manifestations of the modern."

As early as 1866, Ruskin had written to mourn the demise of the British countryside. Ruskin commented particularly on a spot in the south of England, amid a region bordering the sources of the Wandle River and embracing the lower moors of Addington that Burroughs had visited and with which Wilde was familiar. "No cleaner or diverse waters ever sang . . . no pastures ever lightened in spring time with more passionate blooming," wrote Ruskin. The place had remained pristine for generations. But recently it suffered from "reckless, indolent, animal neglect" that had spoiled the waters and the woods. At the headwaters of the stream, by the town of Cashalton, "the human wretches of the place cast their street and house foulness . . . to diffuse what venom of it will float and melt, far away, in all places where God meant those waters to bring joy and health." [31]

Burroughs went into his study to find Ruskin's book, *The Crown of Wild Olive.* Then he read the passage aloud to Wilde, who sat rocking Julian on his knee. When Burroughs was done, Wilde commented that Ruskin was on the right track, but did not understand the whole of the "insidious" problem. The fact was, said Wilde, that it was impossible to get far enough away from the "damned machines." They would ferret one out no matter where one hid. Wilde waved his hand across the panorama of Burroughs's peaceful farm and the river below, and lamented that there was poison dripping somewhere right then that would one day flow to even that benign garden. [32]

9

A PLENTIFUL COUNTRY

*The story of Adam and Eve is a beautiful myth. There is an Adam and
Eve in Darwin's plan, too, but they were not set up in business on the
home-farm, their garden ready planted. They made their own garden, and
knew how they came by their acres . . . Grandfather Adam, who ate his
steak raw, and Great-Grandfather Adam, who had a tail, and lived in
trees, and had a coat of hair.*

— *Journal Entry, August 17, 1883*

THE AUTHORS' CLUB OF New York was being organized in the late
summer of 1882. Burroughs had initially indicated to Earl Clarence
Stedman, one of the chief advancers of the club, a willingness to be
among the charter members. Then, at a preliminary meeting, he
learned that Whitman would not be invited to join. As soon as he
heard this, Burroughs demanded his own name be removed from
the rolls. "In New York there is a society of authors of which I was a
member," he would tell an English visitor to Riverby, J. H. Johnston,
several years later. "Some two or three years ago they actually black-
balled Whitman . . . They would have done themselves infinite
honor had they elected him—I didn't propose him—but they showed
themselves contemptible little fools by refusing him." In 1886, after
visiting the club for one night with Gilder, Burroughs would remind
himself in his journal that this was the organization that had banned
Whitman. "Think what the hope of American letters is in the hands
of such men!" he commented to the privacy of his journal page.
"I sincerely pity them. They are mostly the mere mice of literature.
Such men as Gilder, Stedman, and DeKay recognize Whitman, but
probably the least one of the remainder believes himself a greater
man."

Burroughs vacationed with Whitman at Ocean Grove, New Jersey, in late September of 1883. They spent a week together by the sea, with Burroughs taking a few hours every morning to examine the books of a local bank. "Walt Whitman came yesterday and his presence and companionship act like a cordial upon me that nearly turns my head," wrote Burroughs in his journal for September 27. "The great bard on my right hand, and the sea upon my left—the thoughts of the one equally grand with the suggestions and elemental heave of the other." [1] Whitman seemed the equivalent of—or better yet, the human personification of—the ocean. "There is something grainy and saline in him," wrote Burroughs, "as in the voice of the sea. Sometimes his talk is choppy and confused, or elliptical and unfinished; again there comes a long splendid roll of thought that bathes one from head to foot, or swings you quite from your moorings." [2] The forty-six-year-old Burroughs would occasionally take off on long loops down the coast, or back inland, while the sixty-three-year-old Whitman moved slowly along the beach or sat in some nook sheltered from the wind and sun. When alone, Whitman spent most of his time scratching a new poem in his notebook, "With Husky-Haughty Lips, O Sea!"

In a letter written at Ocean Grove, Whitman described Burroughs going "up and down long stretches of this beach every day, his pants rolled up to below his knees, his right hand saluting to shade his eyes as he scans the scene up and down. He comes back to me, sits down, and talks for half an hour of the margin of shore where the tongue of the surf slips back and forth, opening his hand to show the life he's found an inch below the damp sand." Later Whitman noticed from a distance that down on the shore Burroughs made the acquaintance of "three very little girls with buckets." Burroughs spent nearly an hour crouched on the sand with them, using a bucket to dig a deeper and deeper hole from which he pulled "shells and strange creatures that he held out for the young ladies' astonished pursual [*sic*] and, providing, it seemed, a running narration through the whole exercise."

Whitman wrote that Burroughs was "looking like a man who is in the healthiest of middle-ages. His beard is half gray, his head half-bald, his body slim and muscled." Burroughs, wrote Whitman, "speaks much—speaks too much—about diet, a thing he is very careful of and has many theories upon. He is greatly concerned about my habits in this regard; I suffer his advice without argument, because I know it comes from love." [3] Burroughs was then a subscriber to the dietary theories of a widely published British physician, Sir William Thompson. "[Thompson] shows very convincingly that as our activities fail by the advance of age, we must cut down in our food," Burroughs wrote to Whitman shortly after the Ocean Grove vacation. "If not, the engine makes too much steam, things become clogged and congested, and the whole economy of the system is deranged. He says a little meat once a day is enough, and recommends the cereals and fruits. I think you make too much blood. The congested condition of your organs at times shows it. Then you looked to me too fat; and fat at your age clogs and hinders the circulation . . . In the best health we grow lean, Sir William says, like a man training for the ring." [4]

Burroughs was reading Darwin's *Origin of Species* during his stay at Ocean Grove. It was an appropriate place for him to read the book, since Darwin believed the ocean to be the cradle of life on earth. The poetry of Whitman, Burroughs reminded Benton in a letter from Ocean Grove, was rife with suggestions of "the grand drama of evolution." Whitman's masterpiece "Out of the Cradle Endlessly Rocking" had first been published in 1859, the same year as *Origin of Species*. The poem is packed with images of man emerging from oceans of both real and psychic depths. The child emerged after nine months' gestation in the ocean of the mother's body; the race emerged from the brackish depth of the primordial sea after the long gestation of eons. The process in each case, wrote Burroughs in a letter to Edward Dowden, was "at once a birth and a baptism. Birth, in the end, is the only real baptism. You yourself are your own priest." [5]

Reading Darwin's *The Descent of Man* that August, shortly before the jaunt to Ocean Grove, Burroughs had written that the book "convinces like Nature herself. I have no more doubt of its main conclusions than I have of my own existence." [6] Now, reading *Origin of Species* with Whitman at his side, he called it "a true wonderbook. Few pages in modern scientific literature [are] so noble as those last few pages of the book. Everything about Darwin indicates the master. In reading him you breathe the air of the largest and most serene mind." Darwin, wrote Burroughs, was "the first to open the door into Nature's secret senate chambers. His theory . . . is as ample as the earth, and as deep as time." Darwin's theory, Whitman told Burroughs matter-of-factly one night over dinner, was poetry "simple and straight—just like all the other great books of revelation." God had writ the verses in the truth of nature for Darwin, his instrument, to find and transcribe.

Burroughs was thinking and writing of little but Darwin when he returned to Riverby on October 1. "In the light of Darwin's theory, it is almost appalling to think of one's self, of what he represents, of what he has come through," he wrote in the journal. "It almost makes one afraid of one's self. Think of what there is inherent in his germ! Think of the beings that lived—the savage lower forms—that he might move here, a reasonable being! At what a cost he has been purchased! a million years of unreason for his moment of reason! a million years of gross selfishness, that he might have a benevolent throb!" He wrote that the "hyperbole" of the Church, which held that the salvation of modern man was "bought by the blood of Christ," was in the end at least an analogy for the truth. It seemed to him now that every child born was bought by the blood of countless ages of barbarism and countless lives of beings. "Out of an ocean of darkness and savagery is distilled this drop of human blood, with all its possibilities." [7]

In another journal note, Burroughs commented that Darwin's theory of the descent of man added immensely to the mystery of nature and to the glory of the human race. Suddenly, Darwin had presented man with the notion that greatness was not thrust upon him by divine whim, but was his own achievement. Darwin's theory tied man to the system of things, and made his appearance not arbitrary, or accidental, but a vital and inevitable result. No more did one have to live with the "mechanical, inartistic" view of creation that the Church proposed. If all the vast, complex forms of life were enfolded in the first germ—what would this say to man? Would it not mean that physical existence itself was literally the living body of God—a functioning organism of a vast, mysterious, all-embracing, and eternal power? "I believe this is the case," he wrote. "Here is my testament of faith." The religious vision he'd inherited from Emerson was now reconfirmed and brought into better focus by Darwin, who he called "another poet, another prophet." [8]

BURROUGHS TRAVELLED TO New York City on October 29, 1883, to attend a reception at the home of Richard Watson Gilder for the British poet and critic Matthew Arnold. Burroughs was primed not to like Arnold. He had a memory from nearly twenty years before in Washington at the time when Whitman was furloughed from the Indian Bureau for the publication of "obscene" poems in *Leaves of Grass*. After Whitman's firing, O'Connor had written to a host of leading writers of America and Europe, Arnold among them, to rally support for the poet. Arnold refused to protest the dismissal. In his response to O'Connor, he attacked the merits of Whitman's work. "As to the general question of Mr. Walt Whitman's poetical achievement," Arnold had written, "you will think that it savours of our decrepit old Europe when I add that while you think it his highest merit that he is so unlike anyone else, to me this seems to be his demerit; no one can afford in literature to trade merely on his own bottom and to take no account of what the other ages and nations have acquired." Arnold went on to add that not just Whitman, but all of America's intellect, must eventually come "in a considerable measure" into the European movement.

After that, Whitman detested Arnold. In commenting on Arnold's visit to America, Whitman had told a reporter that Arnold was bringing coals to Newcastle, for the country was already "rich, lousy, reeking with delicacy, refinement, elegance, prettiness, propriety, criticism, analysis: all of them things which threaten to overwhelm us." Arnold, Whitman wrote to Burroughs, was the spiritual leader of "the great army of critics, parlor apostles, worshippers of hangings, laces, and so forth and so forth—they never have anything properly at first hand." "Vellum?" said Whitman in refusing the fancy material for the binding of a new edition of *Leaves of Grass*, "pshaw! hangings, curtains, finger-bowls, chinaware, Matthew Arnold!"

Generally, of course, Burroughs was bound to detest anyone

who Whitman detested. Conveniently enough, Burroughs also had reasoned intellectual grounds for not caring for Arnold; he saw Arnold as an affront to his strong sense of American literary nationalism. Burroughs's devotion to the work of Whitman was in no small way related to the fact that he believed it necessary for American literary culture to develop as something separate from England's and the Continent's. He believed that the United States, with its dramatically different history and values, should make itself more than merely an intellectual colony of Europe. American democracy, Burroughs had written in *Notes on Walt Whitman as Poet and Person*, was something new on the landscape: something fundamentally different from any other experience of man. The dramatically new social and political phenomena ushered forth in the United States demanded a literature characterized by a dramatic iteration in form and scope. America's art, in order to be truly representative of the experience of the young, upstart country, must by necessity be as revolutionary in concept and execution as was the nation itself. A completely different rationale for literature, distinct from the European tradition, was in order.

"But what is that look I see, or think I see, at times, about his nose and upper lip?" Burroughs asked his journal after meeting Arnold. "Just a faint suspicion of scorn. I was looking for this in his face. It is not in his brow, it is here, if anywhere—the nose sniffs a bad smell . . . and there hovers about it a little contempt." Burroughs went on to comment that as Arnold talked to him, he threw his head back—"the reverse of Emerson's manner"—and looked out from under his eyelids, sighting Burroughs down "his big nose." This, wrote Burroughs, was "the critical attitude, not the sympathetic." [9]

Burroughs wrote Benton that Arnold was showing himself for the "great critic-pedagogue" he was in the lecture he had brought to the American circuit, a critique of Emerson. "He is asking for trouble in choosing to criticize an American subject on his American tour. I think it is a strategic error. I know that as an American I am not much of a mind to have Arnold come across the water to explain Emerson to me, any more than he would take kindly to one of us coming to England to finally clarify the motivations and meaning of Wordsworth." [10] Burroughs made a similar point in a postcard sent to Whitman. Was there not, Burroughs asked Whitman, behind

Arnold's choice of subject the inference that Americans were incapable of looking critically at their own literature? Was not the suggestion that Americans needed their English "parent" to come and point out what was good and what was bad? [11]

Burroughs heard Arnold talk at the Authors' Club in Manhattan on January 5, 1884. He shortly wrote no less than two essays on the subject of Arnold's speech. "Arnold's View of Emerson and Carlyle" and "Matthew Arnold's Criticism" would each be published in the *Atlantic Monthly* and then would appear again in his 1899 book of literary essays, *Indoor Studies.*

Arnold's view was that Emerson was not a great poet because his work had not the Miltonic requirements of simplicity, sensuousness, and passion. He was not even a great man of letters, said Arnold, because he had no instinct for style. Neither was Emerson a great philosopher, in Arnold's opinion, because he had no "constructive talent." He did not build a full system of philosophy.

It seemed to Burroughs that in criticizing Emerson, Arnold was criticizing a man of a fundamentally different order of mind than his own. Emerson, wrote Burroughs, was essentially religious and "filled with the sentiment of the infinite." Arnold, on the other hand, was purely a critical force—a "machine" of constantly balanced and heartless reason. All his sympathies were with the influences that made for scholarly correctness. Discipline, taste, and aesthetic perfection were primary with Arnold. Less important to him, wrote Burroughs, was the power and freedom of originality that was bound to characterize the best literary output of the United States. Burroughs suggested that though one could never doubt Arnold's ability to estimate a purely literary and artistic endeavor, it was by no means certain that he could fully appreciate or give justice to art which embodied character, patriotism, conscience, and religion.

Arnold, it seemed, was willing to sacrifice too much in the way of personal genuineness for adherence to form and tradition. "In the decay of the old faiths," wrote Burroughs, "and in the huge aggrandizement of physical science, the refuge and consolation of serious and truly religious minds is more and more in literature, and in the free escapes and outlooks which it supplies." The best modern poetry and prose admitted the reader to new and large fields of moral and intellectual conquest in a way "the antique authors" could not and did not aim to. "New wants, and therefore new standards, have arisen," wrote Burroughs. Purely literary writers, such as Shakespeare and Milton, "priceless as they are, are of less service to mankind in an age like ours, when religion is shunned by the religious soul." [12]

A TELEGRAM ARRIVED FOR Burroughs at Riverby late on the afternoon of January 8. His eighty-one-year-old father had suffered a stroke from which he was not expected to recover. The next afternoon, on his way back to Roxbury, he learned by telegram at the Kingston train station that his father was dead. He did not arrive at the home farm until after nightfall. He walked there from the Stamford train station "in the moonlight in a whirl of wind and snow." How lonely and bleak the old place looked in that winter landscape—"beleaguering Winter without, and Death within! Jane and Abigail were there with Hiram, and some of the neighbors." He did not go into the death chamber. Instead, he went to his own "sleepless" room— the room of his boyhood—while the wind buffeted the house. "How often in youth I had heard that roar, but with what different ears as I snuggled down in my bed while Mother tucked me in!"

Early in the morning he went down quietly, alone, to view the dead man. "The marble face of Death!," he wrote. "What unspeakable repose and silence there is in it!" The forty-six-year-old Burroughs looked down on the face of his dead father and took an inventory of their physical similarities. "I saw more clearly than ever before how much my own features are like his—the nose the same, only, in his case, cut away more at the nostrils. The forehead, too, precisely the same. Head nearly as large as mine." He commented that he had never before looked upon the sleeping face of his father in the morning without speaking his name, "and I could not refrain from speaking his name now, and speaking it again and again." [13]

Once more, as they had done with their mother, the brothers carried the body to the waiting sleigh. Once more the snowy winter landscape of the Catskills provided the backdrop for a day of mourning and burial. Once more he sat through a sermon he had no sympathy with, but that he imagined the corpse would have enjoyed. "[It was] a sermon as Father delighted in and would, no doubt, have preferred should be preached at his funeral." After the funeral service he wrote of his father, "Well, we shall meet again: our dust in the earth, and the forces that make up our spirits in the eternity of force. Shall we know each other then? Ah! shall we? As like knows like in nature. I dare not say farther than that." [14] The following spring, he would walk to the graveyard with his brother Curtis. "By Father's new-made grave I pause with such thoughts as few may know, and by Mother's and by the graves of all my dead," he wrote. "Curtis says to me, 'Here, I suppose, we will all lay one of these days.' 'Yes,' I reply, 'here is to be our last bed' . . . Whose place will be next to Father's, I mentally asked, and had my own thoughts." [15]

He had given his father a copy of his last published book, *Pepacton and Other Sketches*, and suggested that he read the first portion in a chapter entitled "Winter Pictures," which told the story of tracking a fox through the winter woods on Old Clump. He thought that his father, who normally only read religious tracts, would enjoy the piece since it spoke of experiences and landmarks that Chauncey would be able to relate to directly. On his last visit home before his father died, he asked whether or not the old man had read the essay. The answer was no, he hadn't gotten to it. So far as Burroughs knew, neither his father or his mother had ever looked into any one of his books that sat on the mantle above the fireplace at the old home. "Father knew me not," he wrote. "All my aspirations in life were a sealed book to him, as much as his peculiar religious experiences were to me." [16]

The death of his father triggered a round of introspection on the question of the radical difference between his religious needs and that of his parents. "I sit down to read [the Bible] as a book, a curious and instructive legend, and to suck the literary value out of it," he wrote, but "they sat down to read it as the autocratic word of God; to learn God's will toward them; and to feed their souls upon the spiritual riches it contains." Reading the Bible was a solemn exercise for his parents, but for John it was simply a search after truth and beauty. "There is perhaps more religion in the eye with which I read Nature, than there was in the eye with which they read it," he wrote, "and there was more religion in the eye with which they read the Bible than in mine." His father and mother no more doubted the literal truth of the Bible than they did the multiplication table. They saw no purpose in reasoning about it further. And this, thought Burroughs, had been their error. "When people began to reason about witches, belief in witchcraft ended," wrote Burroughs. "When you begin honestly to reason about the Bible, and to exclude all feeling, experience, sentiment, you cannot believe it other than a great primitive book." Burroughs believed that the Bible was the word of God only in the sense that all good and wise books and every wise word ever spoken by any man were the word of God. [17]

In a journal entry, he compared the idea of a personal God to the notion of Santa Claus.

> How much deeper and more painful a void would have been left in the minds of our fathers if they had suddenly made the discovery which their children have made, that their Santa Claus, the great Dispenser of the gift of life, was a delusion, a fiction, and that natural law brought all these things to pass! What a chill, what desolation, would have possessed their credulous souls . . . Fancy the state of orphanage which such a discovery would bring about in the hearts of our fathers! [18]

On another occasion he compared the idea of God to the sky. "What appears more real than the sky?" he asked his journal. "We think of it and speak of it, as if it were as positive and real a thing as the earth. It is blue, it is tender, it is overarching, it is clear. See how the color is laid on it at sunset. Yet what an illusion! There is no sky; it is only vacancy; it is only the absence of something." When one tried to grasp, or measure, or define God, one found that he was another sky—sheltering, overarching, but receding, vanishing before the closer search. God, he wrote, was the vast power or space in which worlds floated, but God himself was ungraspable, unattainable, "forever soaring beyond our ken." God, for Burroughs, was not a being, not an entity. Rather, God was that which lay behind all beings and all entities. [19]

In his 1900 book, *The Light of Day*, Burroughs would go on record with his vision of how man's sense of religion must shift with modern times, modern knowledge, and modern needs. In Central Asia, Burroughs explained to his reader, there was a famous rock called the Lamp Rock. Far up inside Lamp Rock was a cavern, at the heart of which a mysterious light shined by day. For generations, natives had venerated and worshiped this light, which was clearly a God of the highest order—so magnificently strong was the illumination that peeked out from the heart of the cavern's darkness. Then, finally, one brave soul found the courage to enter the cave and walk to its heart of light. Of course, it turned out that the mysterious glow came from a hole in the far end of the cavern. The God they all had prayed to for generations was nothing more than the simple light of day.

In Burroughs's *The Light of Day*, he argued that the traditional mythology of religious belief was just that, mythology. He admitted that the spiritual truths underlying tales of wonder and parables were themselves real and valid. They emanated from the depths of the human mind and had been created to meet certain fundamental psychological needs. While arguing against theology as such, he did not argue against the basic necessity for some religious aspect to life as a comforter and guide, and way of understanding the universe. Among the literary remains of his last few weeks of life we find this fragment:

> I have not tried, as the phrase is, to lead my readers from Nature up to Nature's God, because I cannot separate the one from the other. If your heart warms toward the visible creation, and toward your fellow men, you have the root of the matter in you. The power we call God does not sustain a mechanical or secondary relation to the universe, but is vital in it, or one with it. To give this power human lineaments and attributes, as our fathers did, only limits and belittles it. And to talk of leading from Nature up to Nature's God is to miss the God that throbs in every spear of grass and vibrates in the wing of every insect that hums. The Infinite is immanent in the universe.

JOHN BURROUGHS WAS ALWAYS a devotee of mountains. In a letter, he told his son he thought it no accident that mountains had always, through the history of man, held a special spiritual significance for whatever race or sect lived near them. The Arabs believed that mountains steadied the earth and held it together. For the Chinese, mountains were more often than not the abodes of divinities. The gods of Greece had lived on Mount Olympus. And in the Bible, mountains were repeatedly used as a symbol for what was great and holy. Jerusalem was spoken of as a holy mountain. It was on Mount Horeb that God appeared to Moses in the burning bush, and on Mount Sinai that He delivered to him the Law. [20]

Current visitors to the top of Slide Mountain, the highest peak in the Catskills, are greeted first by the sublime view and then by a plaque dedicated to the memory of John Burroughs who, as the sign says, was the first to introduce Slide Mountain to the world through his writings. It was not until age forty-seven that Burroughs, in July of 1884, first attempted the ascent of Slide. Through the past five decades he had fished every stream that it nourished, and had camped in the wilderness on all sides of it. Whenever he had caught a glimpse of its summit, he'd promised himself to set foot there before another season had passed. But the seasons came and went, and "my feet got no nimbler, and Slide Mountain no lower." Finally, he coaxed Myron Benton to join him on an expedition. After a full day of hiking, during which they approached Slide through the mountains on the east, Burroughs and Benton only managed to achieve the top of Slide's neighbor, Wittenberg Mountain. The view from Wittenberg, wrote Burroughs, was in many respects more striking than that from the higher Slide. Wittenberg perched one immediately above a broader and more distant sweep of country. Here, on the eastern brink of the southern Catskills, the earth fell away at one's feet and curved down through an immense stretch of forest until it joined what was then the plain of Shokan, and then swept away to the Hudson and beyond. Slide was some six or seven miles to the southwest of the spot where Burroughs and Benton paused for the night, but was only visible when Burroughs climbed a tree, saluted, and promised to call next time.

In June of the next year, Burroughs and Benton tried once

again to conquer Slide. This time they were reinforced by Burroughs's West Park neighbors, William H. Van Benschoten and his brother, Richard John Van Benschoten. Burroughs planned the hike with a line of red ink on a topographical map. He chose not to come at the mountain via the Big Indian Valley, from whence the climb is relatively easy. Instead, he informed Benton and the Van Benschotens, they would essay the highest peak in the Catskills from Woodland Valley—a steep and hazardous climb without a clearly blazed trail.[21]

With blankets strapped to their backs and a double ration of fruit and jerky in their pockets, the team set out from the foot of the mountain on a bright and warm June morning. The climb was steep and hard. The northern side of the mountain was thickly covered with moss and lichens, just "like the north side of a tree" wrote Burroughs. This made the rocks soft to the foot, and laid the scene for many slips and falls on the vertical slope. Everywhere stunted growths of yellow birch, mountain ash, spruce, and fir opposed their progress. "The ascent at such an angle with a roll of blankets on your back is not unlike climbing a tree," wrote Burroughs. "Every limb resists your progress and pushes you back." When they at last reached the summit, after seven hours of uphill climbing during which they had covered only about seven miles, they were exhausted.

At the top of the mountain they overtook Spring, which had been gone from the valley for over a month. On the summit the yellow birch was just beginning to hang out its catkins, and the claytonia was in full bloom. The leaf buds of the trees were about to burst, making a faint mist of green that, as the eye swept downward to the valley, gradually deepened until it became a dense, lush cloud of new green leaves. "At the foot of the mountain the claytonia, or northern green lily, and the low shad-bush were showing their berries, but long before the top was reached they were found in bloom," wrote Burroughs in his essay about the climb, "In the Heart of the Southern Catskills," which he published in the 1894 book *Riverby*. "I had never before stood amid blooming claytonias, a flower of April, and looked down upon a field that held ripening strawberries." Every thousand feet of elevation seemed to make about ten days' difference in the vegetation, so that the season was a month or more later on the top of the mountain than at its base.

They spent the night at the mountaintop, surrounded by the sublime view of Slide's sister mountains—Wittenberg to the east, Peekamoose with its sharp crest and Table Mountain to the south, Mount Graham and Double Top to the west, and Panther Mountain to the north. The party slept in a rickety bark hut placed at the summit many years before as a convenience to hikers. Burroughs and Benton gathered birch branches to plug up openings in the hut; the Van Benschotens gathered balsam boughs to make beds. They collected such meager firewood as they could without an axe: roots and stumps and branches of decayed spruce. Burroughs built a small fire in one corner of the shanty where a hole in the roof would allow the smoke out. Despite the fact that this was June, nightfall brought a sharp drop in the temperature. Benton found the fire inadequate. He spent most of the evening dancing around the mountaintop in a frantic attempt to keep warm.

The next morning, they descended in a snow flurry. The party cautiously made its way down along an ancient avalanche—the slide that had given the mountain its name. The perilously steep course dropped down from their feet straight as an arrow until it was lost in fog. "The rock was quite naked and slippery," wrote Burroughs, "and only on the margin of the slide were there any boulders to stay the foot, or bushy growths to stay the hand."

When Burroughs came to write of his excursion to Slide, he made special note of the pure streams that flowed down all sides of the mountain. "Civilization corrupts the streams as it corrupts the Indian," he wrote, perhaps recalling Ruskin's comments on the demise of pristine brooks in the British countryside. "Only in such remote woods can you now see a brook in all its original freshness and beauty. Only the sea and the forest brook are pure; all between is contaminated more or less by the work of man." In fact, much of the southern Catskills had long been contaminated by the work of man. Lumbering had gone on in the area since the Revolution. The Delaware River was large enough to accommodate the rafting of wood from Catskill lumber camps. Timber-cutting entrepreneurs could easily float valuable white pine from the Catskills all the way down to the lucrative markets of Trenton and Philadelphia. By the 1830s, tanners were stripping the bark from the hemlocks with a speed matched only by the cutters of the pines. When the superior pine became scarce enough, the tanners began to realize a double-profit from the hemlocks. After the bark was peeled, the hemlocks were rafted downriver to meet the growing demand for wood. At the same time, balsam firs were taken by the wagonload from Catskill mountainsides for use by landscape gardeners to ornament the grounds of Hudson Valley mansions.

By the mid-nineteenth century the depletion of the Catskills' reserves of pine and hemlock had begun to bring tanning and rafting to an end. The forests grew back, but with different trees than before. In the place of the early, virgin woodlands there now grew up a mixture of grasses, trees, and shrubs that all struggled against each other to build their place. In the end, it was the hardwoods—birch, ash, maple, and oak—that won the fight, forming dense stands of second-growth timber. These woods were in turn also harvested. Unlike the earlier trade in hemlock and pine, the Catskills' second generation timber industry did not rely on the rafting of goods to urban centers. Most hardwoods were milled right in the Catskills, where sawmills tooled to produce boards, planks, and joists were set up beside many a mountain stream.

One year after Burroughs climbed Slide in 1885, the same trek was made by the Honorable Townsend Cox, one of three newly appointed forest commissioners for the state of New York. Cox was accompanied by a large contingent of Democratic state officials (including John Burroughs's West Park neighbor, Judge Alton B. Parker, who would run against Theodore Roosevelt for the office of President of the United States in 1904). Cox was also accompanied by about a dozen newspaper reporters armed with notebooks and cameras. At the summit of the mountain, Cox took a little pad of paper from his pocket and began to read. He announced that from that day forward there was to be a new way of understanding and using the woodlands of the southern Catskills. Slide and the regions surrounding it had just been made part of a newly created State Forest Preserve. The state government would regulate all timber cutting in the future. The state-owned lands on Slide and in its vicinity, said Cox, were important to the people of the state because of the spring water originating on their slopes. On his way down the mountain, Cox stopped in the midst of a thick carpet of mosses and decaying vegetation. He picked up a piece of the forest floor, squeezed water from it, and explained how the spongy soil held rain water, purified it, and released it slowly to replenish rivers. This cleansing action of the forest was fundamental to the long-term water quality of Catskill creeks and streams, and in turn of the quality of the Delaware and Hudson rivers, by these tributaries fed.

Several weeks later, John Burroughs sent Cox an inscribed copy of his new book, *Signs and Seasons.* "For Townsend Cox," Burroughs wrote on the title page, "Who will help keep this a plentiful country,— Yours affectionately, John Burroughs." Below the inscription, Burroughs jotted a verse from the Old Testament:

> And I brought you into a plentiful country, to eat the fruit thereof and the goodness thereof; but when ye entered, ye defiled my land, and made mine heritage an abomintion.
> —*Jeremiah 1:6*

10

BARRENNESS

I do not write much, and probably shall write less in the future. My harvest is about gathered . . .

— *Burroughs to Benton, April 5, 1886*

BURROUGHS TOOK THE TRAIN south to Camden to visit Whitman in early March of 1887. The poet lived in a squalid little house that he'd bought, using his life's savings, in 1884. Burroughs found Whitman with a shawl pinned about him and a goat-skin across the back of his rocking chair. A chaos of letters, manuscripts, and books were at his feet. "Never saw such confusion and litter," wrote Burroughs in his journal, "bundles of letters, bundles of newspapers, cuttings, magazines, a cushion or two, footrests, books opened and turned down, dust, and above all the grand, serene face of the poet." Whitman told Burroughs he was doing no writing at all, and that "miscellaneous" was the word he would use to describe himself. Burroughs found the old man "alert and vivacious." They spoke of the health of the ailing O'Connor, of the approach of Burroughs's milestone fiftieth birthday in April, and of Swinburne, who both men agreed was a sort of "abnormal creature, full of wind and gas," with no lasting importance as a poet. "We have much talk, and it does me good to be with him again," wrote Burroughs in his journal. "He talks affectionately about Beecher just dead and says many things in his praise. We sit by the firelight till 9." [1]

In a round-robin letter to Burroughs and other friends, the semi-invalid Whitman had asked them to write to him as often as possible, for "Monotony is now the word of my life." [2] Burroughs was among a group that planned to help alleviate both the tedium and the financial crunch that their hero found himself the victim of. Since 1879 Whitman had given occasional lectures on the topic of the Lincoln assassination. The program included readings of the poems "When Lilacs Last in the Dooryard Bloom'd" and "Captain, My Captain!" And it included Whitman's personal reminiscences of wartime Washington and the immediate aftermath of the shooting. In April of 1887 Burroughs and a few other supporters arranged for the poet to deliver his talk once again. The place was the Madison Square Theater in New York; the date was April 14, the twenty-second anniversary of the Lincoln murder. The theater was half-empty, but among those who joined Burroughs to listen to Whitman's swan song were Mark Twain, Richard Watson Gilder, Lincoln's former secretary John Hay, General William T. Sherman, Andrew Carnegie, and the sculptor Augustus Saint-Gaudens. Burroughs shared a box at the performance with Charles Eliot Norton, the president of Harvard, and the poet James Russell Lowell. According to Burroughs's account of the evening, the performance garnered several hundred dollars for Whitman. During his brief visit to New York the poet lived in a regal style quite unlike what awaited him back at his tenement in Camden. Carnegie had arranged for him to stay at the Westminster Hotel in a suite of rooms once occupied by Charles Dickens.

By helping to organize the New York lecture, Burroughs once again demonstrated his steadfast loyalty to his old friend Whitman. However, his loyalty was now tinged with far more restraint than the younger, more ardent Burroughs had ever displayed. Though still a public defender of Whitman, he was beginning to distance himself from the dramatic rhetoric of the rest of the coterie that circled the aging bard.

Many of Whitman's small band of supporters had for years infused their admiration with semireligious overtones. The adulatory process had started in Burroughs's Washington attic, where O'Connor penned his story "The Carpenter" with its portrait of Whitman as a miracle-working Christ figure. Recently the Harvard-trained Unitarian minister William Sloane Kennedy had written that he felt Whitman the "equal, and in many respects the superior of the much misunderstood Jesus." [3] In a Christmas note to Whitman in 1890 Kennedy would go so far as to ask the poet, "Do you suppose in a thousand years from now people will be celebrating the birth of Walt Whitman as they are now the birth of Christ?" [4] Dr. Richard Maurice Bucke, physician and superintendent of the insane asylum at London, Ontario, who was to serve as Whitman's literary executor, said he experienced "a sort of spiritual intoxication" when in Whitman's presence, and that he believed Whitman to be endowed with "the highest moral nature."

In the self-absorption of an obscure old age, anxiously encouraging any move that might win the readership that had proved so elusive for so long, Whitman did little to gainsay such talk. In Burroughs's estimation, Bucke and the others lacked "balance and proportion" in their view of Whitman. Rhetoric implying dogma contradicted the very intent of *Leaves of Grass*. In *Literary Values* (1902), Burroughs would write: "Do the disciples of Whitman, who would make a cult of him, live in the spirit of the whole, as Whitman himself tried to live?—Whitman, who said that there may be any number of Supremes, and that the chief lesson to be learned under the master was how to destroy him?" [5] Where Whitman ranked was not as a prophet or a God, but as a very human poet.

Burroughs declined to attend when a seventieth birthday dinner, billed by Kennedy as the poet's "last supper," was held for Whitman at Camden in May of 1889. "I had not grown cold toward him," wrote Burroughs later, "but I saw less of him, and was not so active a disciple as I had been. I had absorptions of my own. Then the crowd that surrounded him was not altogether to my liking." [6] Burroughs made a habit of sending Walt fresh Riverby produce in season. One day in the autumn of 1888, when Whitman's secretary and nurse Horace Traubel walked into Whitman's bedroom with a basket of grapes just received from Riverby, Whitman exclaimed: "Agh! John Burroughs again! He still thinks of us here in our prison. John is good to us—good, good!" On the poet's birthday in 1891, Burroughs jotted him a postcard. "Walt," he wrote, "I keep your birthday pruning my vineyard and in reading an hour from your poems under my fig tree. Will let you eat your dinner in peace, as I shall want to do if I ever reach my seventy-second." [7]

A FEW MONTHS AFTER publishing another negative review of Whitman in the *Atlantic Monthly*, Higginson half-seriously sent a note to Riverby in which he inquired after Burroughs's health and expressed concern that Burroughs had not rushed into print with a response to Higginson's recent criticisms of "your dear Walt." [8] Higginson was correct in noting that Burroughs refrained from promoting or defending Whitman in the press through 1889 and 1890. The fact of the matter is that Burroughs was hardly doing any writing at all, about Whitman or about anything else. The book he published in June of 1889, *Indoor Studies*, was a collection of literary criticism written over the past twenty years. It featured no recent writings. The journal for 1890 records the composition of only two essays the entire year. One of them, "Country Notes," he called "of little worth—a mere potboiler." The other, a rambling philosophical reflection on "Faith and Credulity," he considered "rather feeble" and was surprised when a popular magazine, the *North American*, accepted it for publication. "I do no literary work," he wrote Benton, "though I have plenty of calls . . . The theological seems to be the last state of man—after that, barrenness." [9]

He had given up his bank examiner post in mid-1886. Now the farm, which had recently doubled in size when he went into debt to purchase an adjacent plot, took precedence over writing. "These lovely April days find me pawing the soil up here at a lively rate," he wrote to Hamilton Wright Mabie, editor of the *Christian Union*. "I am fairly besmirched with new earth from my head to my heels . . . You should see how fresh and tender the earth is here when we open it with our plow . . . You ask me for a piece. I will give it to you if possible. The feast of the soil will soon be over with me and then I will remember your request." [10] He wrote to Benton with a similar sentiment. "I find when I take hold of my farm myself, I can make it pay . . . and I see that in a couple of years I can be pretty sure of a good income from my fruit. Literature is quite neglected these days.

All requests for articles go quickly into the waste-basket. If my appetite for magazine-writing ever returns, then I may hang up my hoe for a season, but I propose to let my intellectual domain lie fallow for awhile." [11] In an apologetic, delinquent letter to another literary acquaintance Burroughs said, "I am a farmer these days and treat my correspondents shabbily, but my vineyard has no reason to complain." [12] In the message that Burroughs sent to be read at Whitman's seventieth birthday celebration in Camden he said that he was "sequestered . . . on the banks of the Hudson, delving in the soil and trying to give the roots of my life a fresh start."

Through the spring of 1888 Burroughs had invested heavily of himself and his equity to plant the Riverby acres. "I have been hard at work," the fifty-one year old Burroughs wrote Benton, "and have got my body so disciplined I can hoe potatoes all day without flinching. We put out an acre of early potatoes in April, and are now hoeing them. We have put out 2400 grape-vines, 2000 currant bushes, and 2000 hills of raspberries . . . I have not spent so happy an April for years . . . The hoe-handle is better for me now than the pen, and I mean to stick to it." [13] Two days later Burroughs sent Whitman the same message. "The world has not been so beautiful to me for a long time as this spring; probably because I have been at work like an honest man," he told the poet. "I had, in my years of loafing, forgotten how sweet toil was . . . I have taken to the hoe and crowbar . . . I write you amid the fragrance of clover and the hum of bees. The air is full these days of all sweet meadow and woodland smells. The earth seems good enough to eat." [14] Whitman commented on this letter to Horace Traubel, who was at that time in the habit of taking down in shorthand much of the daily conversation of the failing poet. "It is a June letter," said Whitman, "worthy of June, written in John's best out-of-doors mood. Why, it gets into your blood and makes you feel worthwhile. I sit here, helpless as I am, and breathe it in like fresh air . . . John has the real art—the art of succeeding by not trying to succeed; he is the farmer first—the man before he is the writer; that is the key of his success."

At the end of the 1888 planting season, Burroughs made an important strategic decision for the farm. In the future, he would plant only grapes. He had gotten a high market price for his potatoes in 1888, but had a poor yield owing to dry weather. "May get back the expense and a little more," he wrote in his journal with reference to the potatoes, "in which case the fun of the thing will not have cost me anything. All my hoeing, watering, killing of bugs, on Sundays and nights, will not cost me a cent." [15] He was confident that grapes— not wine grapes, but rather fancy table grapes such as his neighbors planted—would pay him better in the long run. "I shall plant largely Niagaras," he wrote a friend in September. "Van Benschoten's Niagaras have done so well, and yield so enormously, that I shall try more of them. He got 14 cents a pound. He must have cleared over $2000. I am more encouraged than ever. I see no reason why I cannot do as well and have an income by and by of $3000 from my fruit." [16] He also put in several rows of Concords and Delawares.

The journals for the next several years are full of references to his work in the fields. "Sitting in my vineyard, waiting for my part in putting up wire," he wrote in a notebook entry of early spring, 1890. "Zeke is at other end of row putting in staples. When he gets back here I rush in with nippers and tongs, cut the wire and stretch it, while Zeke drives home the staples." [17] In his first years at Riverby, Burroughs delegated much of the running of the farm. Now, although he still had hired help, he himself supervised and joined the help in accomplishing daily chores. "When there's a particularly hard job of work to be done on the farm, he does it himself," Whitman told Traubel. "He has hands there to help him, yet he chooses his own place, and that generally the most difficult one."

The introduction of full-scale grape growing to Riverby required detailed planning; the vineyard rows had to be laid out carefully so that the sloping hillside plot above the river could best meet the subtle needs of the easily damaged grape crop. Burroughs was up every morning at dawn, and at work at farm projects for a good twelve hours out of every day. There were vineyard rows to build, irrigation drains to install, a fruit house to construct, and many smaller projects to oversee. To maximize the return on his investment in land, he spent long hours removing rocks so as to make every last foot of every acre cultivable. "In a few days now we have made room for several more grape-vines by digging out the place-rock where it came to the surface," he wrote in his journal. "We broke the sleep of long ages of those rocks, sometimes with bars and wedges, some- times with dynamite." [18] At the end of these long days, after dinner, he would retire to his study on the brow of the hill, perhaps to read a little or perhaps to try to write a letter or two. He was usually asleep by nine o'clock and then up again at sunup.

Burroughs was eventually proved right in his assumption about the profitability of grapes. In early 1891 he noted that he was "Very busy with grapes till September 20. A fine season for shipping for the most part . . . Shipped 21 tons . . . Brought $2100. Shipped mostly to Boston. Am convinced that small baskets pay best." [19] His correspondence with Benton was now less an exchange between one writer and another than it was a comparison of notes between farmers. "The grape campaign was rather a trying one," he wrote Benton in 1891. "We had over twenty tons, and we bent all our energies to getting them off early. One day we shipped 4700 pounds and for ten days about one and 1½ tons a day . . . My grapes were fine, and were soon in demand in Boston, so that at the end of the season I have a very respectable bank balance . . . Some of my new grapes are disappointing, others are very promising. I think highly of the Winchell and shall plant it next year." [20] His income from the grapes increased dramatically in step with his expertise as a vineyard master and his sense of what strains would prove the most marketable. In January of 1893 Burroughs wrote Benton that his seventeen acres had brought in $4000 the previous season. His expenses were $1500. That left a good margin of profit, and then, as he told Benton, "we are free from it from October till April." [21]

JULIAN BURROUGHS WAS TEN years old in 1888 and had begun keeping a journal. The little diary, packed with brief anecdotes and pencil sketches, provides a splendid "boy's-eye view" of life at Riverby. "Tonight is my bath night. I hate it," Julian wrote. [22] The "bathroom" was up on the second floor of the stone house—a bare hall with a zinc tub. Hot water had to be heated on the kitchen stove and carried up two flights of stairs before being poured into the tub. On the numerous Saturday nights when the master of the house did not feel disposed to lug buckets of boiling water up the narrow stairs from the kitchen, a copper bathtub would be pulled out of the middle cellar, where it hung on a nail, and placed on the kitchen floor beside the stove. Then one at a time each member of the family would take their turn at getting clean. Almost as annoying as baths for Julian were boring grown-up conversations about topics only grown-ups could ever possibly be dull enough to find interesting. In November, Julian noted to his diary that "Everybody is talking about polyticks, it is a hard tug. Papa is demeratic this time."

The relationship that Burroughs had with his son Julian was intense and devoted. "I hate to see him go," wrote Burroughs of Julian after the boy departed with his mother for a visit to her family. "I shall be very lonely. He is all I have. He often tires me with his endless questions, but I find much companionship with him." [23] Burroughs taught the boy to play chess, and the two had spirited games every evening. "He pushes me pretty hard when we have a game," wrote Burroughs to Benton. "At checkers he easily beats me." After the games of chess or checkers the two read aloud to each other. First Burroughs read three pages, then Julian. "Reading *Tom Brown* with Julian these nights," he wrote in the journal for December 27, 1888, "and get very much excited over it myself." [24] They also read Stevenson's *Treasure Island* and Pyle's *Robin Hood.* After the reading of *Robin Hood* Burroughs crafted his son a real bow and arrow set with which to prowl the woods and imagine. The two attended West Point football games in the fall, skated on the frozen river in winter, boiled sap in the spring, and swam in the Hudson and Black Creek together in the summer. "Julian and I had a delicious time on the river bank under the trees" reads a representative August journal entry. [25]

In addition to a love of books and learning, Burroughs also was careful to impart to his son a love of hiking, fishing, and nature appreciation. The journal is full of entries that begin "Julian and I go to the woods." As soon as Julian was old enough, Burroughs took him along on camping and fishing trips into Woodland Valley (then called Snyder Hollow) in the southern Catskills. "We would roll two stones near each other," wrote Julian in 1915, "building our fire between them; then if a sheet of iron was to be had we put that over the fire, resting the edges on the stones, thus making a really good stove on which we fried our trout or bacon." Their bedrolls were two army blankets that Burroughs had bought in Washington during the war, and that now after many years of hard service were frayed and smoke-scented.

Many of the experiences that father and son shared wound up being recounted in Burroughs's essays. In 1891, Burroughs published a paper entitled "A Young Marsh Hawk" that told the story of Julian nursing back to health a sick baby hawk found near death in the woods. "Then began a lively campaign on the part of my little boy against all the vermin and small game in the neighborhood to keep the hawk supplied. He trapped and he hunted, he enlisted his mates in his service, he even robbed the cats to feed the hawk," wrote Burroughs. The premises were very soon cleared of mice, and the vicinity of chipmunks and squirrels. "Farther and farther [Julian] was compelled to hunt the surrounding farms and woods to keep up with the demands of the hawk. By the time the hawk was ready to fly he had consumed twenty-one chipmunks, fourteen red squirrels, sixteen mice, and twelve English sparrows." [26]

Burroughs sold "A Young Marsh Hawk" to the *Youth's Companion* for $80. When he mentioned this to Julian at the dinner table, the boy suggested that he should get some of the money from the essay in turn for his having done "all the work." Burroughs pointed to his son's plate. "You are eating your share of the profits right now," he said. [27]

A drawing in Julian's journal shows John Burroughs carving the Thanksgiving turkey with Ursula at the other end of the table and Julian in the middle. "We can have no conversation whatsoever," wrote Burroughs of Ursula in his own journal. "I sit meal after meal and hardly say a word, year in and year out." Stationed in the middle of the table between the two silent parents, Julian learned to be the spark of conversation and to do his best to kindle a familial mood. This, it seemed, he alone had the power to do. The one common bond of Ursula and John was their love for Julian.

"It is the oft-told story," Burroughs wrote in his journal. "A crude, undeveloped man marries a girl older and more experienced than himself. He develops, she simply hardens, and their interests diverge. In middle life they are far apart: she knows him not at all, does not share his real life, only his kitchen life. The things he lives for are nothing to her." He packed his journal with complaints and recriminations focused around what he perceived to be fundamental character flaws on the part of his wife. The objective observer who reads Burroughs's lengthy journal criticisms notices that the traits in his wife to which he objected were ones that many other people would call virtues. Burroughs complained about Ursula's "maniacal cleanliness." Her "ceaseless war upon dust and dirt" drove him to distraction. Another characteristic that he found annoying seems, reading between the lines, to have been Ursula's essential honesty. "She hates deception to the point of discarding all the disguises and half-tones of life," wrote Burroughs, "nothing but the bare, ugly prose left—no charm, no illusion, no romance." [28]

Others did not find Ursula so unpalatable. Whitman instructed his secretary Traubel never to write Burroughs without sending love to Ursula "for she, too, has been kind and noble to me and I want her to know that I think of her." Another friend of Burroughs who would think Ursula quite easy to get along with was Hamlin Garland, the writer of Western romance novels. Despite several years of acquaintance with Burroughs, and many meetings at literary functions, Garland had yet to lay eyes on the wife of the naturalist. In his diary, Garland recalled that Burroughs "seldom referred to her [Ursula] and, when he did, it was with a tone of veiled antagonism, as though his wishes and hers were habitually in opposition." Garland was expecting a witch, but instead found Mrs. Burroughs to be quite charming when he at last succeeded in urging Burroughs to bring her to a dinner at his house. "She made a pleasing guest," recalled Garland. [29]

Unable to focus kindly on each other, John and Ursula instead focused on Julian. In late December of 1888 there was a special program at the West Park school to mark the beginning of Christmas vacation. The children were each to read their own original compositions. John and Ursula both showed up to hear Julian read his piece: "Papa's Dogs." Burroughs came home with the firm belief that his boy was "decidedly the best of all of them." In his journal he wrote, "I am glad to see [Julian's] mind take this turn. He does not look far off for a theme, like the other boys, but writes about something near at hand that he actually knows about. His essay was in my own vein and vastly more promising than anything I ever did at that age. It was a real piece of writing about my dogs.

How curious it was to me to see him stand up there and read an original essay." [30]

The bond between father and son was subject to stress at least once a year. Burroughs was not content to simply ignore Christmas. He had, instead, to chide both Ursula and Julian for wanting to be given "some trash" every 25th of December. Year after year Julian would be confronted with his schoolmates' questions after the holiday recess. What had he gotten for Christmas? The answer was always "not a thing." [31] Christmas, Burroughs told his son, was "a fraud based on a folk-tale" and a time when people extended a little more effort than usual in "pretending" to be Christians. He scoffed at the tale of the Nativity, saying that talking donkeys were not a miracle. The world was full of jackasses blessed with the gift of speech. When the boy asked about the magical, bearded friend of children called Santa Claus, Burroughs threatened to wait up for the "intruder" on Christmas Eve and teach him the definition of the word "trespassing." When the boy broke down in tears, his father smilingly consoled him with the words, "Now, don't you worry about Christmas. Just leave Christmas alone and then it can't do you any damage." [32]

At the start of 1889, after another miserable Christmas with John Burroughs, Ursula and Julian went to a boardinghouse in Poughkeepsie to escape the isolated inconvenience and dull severity of Riverby in winter. Burroughs had planned to stay on at Riverby and work in his study, but heavy snow drove him to town as well. Occasionally he would take a horse-drawn sleigh up to the farm to collect his mail and perhaps do some work in the study. On other days he walked about Poughkeepsie with Julian. Work had recently been finished on a new cantilevered railroad bridge over the Hudson. Julian and John would often cross the tracks that approached the huge structure on their walks. "Papa thinks of going over," wrote Julian. A few days after this remark, the boy recorded the fact that he and his father had climbed a ladder to the top of the high stonework on the Poughkeepsie side—"Papa helps me." This seems to have been a dry run: Julian did not object to the height so long as Burroughs held him close. The following Saturday, after dinner, Burroughs and son set out to cross the bridge. They did not say a word to Ursula about the planned adventure.

Julian wrote that "I am doubtful and don't know what to say, but I go." They took the ferry to the west side of the river, walked past the railroad station at Highland, and up a "very steep patch all ice" to the start of the bridge. A thin ladder went up to the tracks on the bridge. Although the boy did not know the exact height, the fact is that the Poughkeepsie railroad bridge, which still stands, towers 212 feet above water level. The hike across that Burroughs embarked upon with his ten-year-old son in the dead of winter was a very dangerous, foolhardy adventure. "We walked and walked," recorded Julian.

> Papa throwed great snowballs, when they hit the water they made a great noice, and threw a little snowball at the old ferry, it hit right near a man and he looked up at us. Papa acted silly, he run danced jumped and capered about right out on the ties, he sung and hooted and acted like mad . . . It went all right until we got to this [the Poughkeespie] side thair the plank walk ended and Papa had to carry me I was very frightened and clung to Papa with all my might, the ties wer evry which way and Papa had to jump, one place there was know ties and a man had to carry me over.

Ursula was livid when she heard of the dangerous episode. Burroughs moved into Julian's room at the boardinghouse, and shortly after, on March 5, made a trip to New York for a few days. "Papa went to New York this morning. I have my room all to myself and I am a little lonesome," wrote the boy.

In New York, Burroughs visited Richard Watson Gilder and accompanied him to a dinner at the Fellowcraft Club. It was at this dinner that Burroughs first met Theodore Roosevelt. The two men shared a table with Elizabeth Custer, widow of George Armstrong Custer. A dedicated amateur naturalist, Roosevelt excitedly told Burroughs of how he had come upon his books while in England, and how *Birds and Poets* and *Locusts and Wild Honey* had made him homesick due to their being so "thoroughly American."

The thirty-year-old Roosevelt was already an author himself, having written a naval history of the war of 1812 and several other works. The grandson of one of New York City's first millionaires, Roosevelt was then serving as a federal Civil Service Commissioner.

Roosevelt was a friend of Jacob A. Riis, who the following year would publish *How the Other Half Lives*, a photo essay on tenement life. Roosevelt was also an associate of John Jay Chapman, the reformer and essayist who lived not far from Burroughs at Rhinebeck on the Hudson. Chapman, who had married into the wealthy Chanler family of Rhinebeck, was the author of an enthusiastic biography of the abolitionist William Lloyd Garrison as well as *Practical Agitation*, a spirited guide to organizing and propagandizing. Chapman had opened a clubhouse for young people in the notorious Hell's Kitchen section of New York. Roosevelt and Riis both made a habit of stopping off at the club to visit with the boys. Roosevelt told Burroughs that he often recommended the naturalist's books to the youths he met at Chapman's storefront, as he felt that Burroughs's works emphasized "all that was good and important in life." Burroughs was skeptical. He wondered out loud to Roosevelt what slum youths, trapped in the city, would find useful in the homey woodlore of *Signs and Seasons* and other such books. In his notebook during the train trip home, Burroughs wrote, "How different is the life of Julian—in the country with fresh air, good books, and parents with a measure of leisure—from that of the boys that Chapman and Roosevelt want so much to help." [33]

When Burroughs had left Poughkeepsie for New York in the wake of the railroad bridge escapade, he and Ursula were not on speaking terms. With his business in New York completed, Burroughs returned not to Poughkeepsie, but to Riverby. Burroughs lived in his little bark study for more than a week, cooking in the fireplace and sleeping on the floor. It was not worth the bother to open and heat the stone house just for himself. One afternoon as he glanced out his study window, Burroughs was shocked to see his little boy, nearly frozen, hiking up the trail from the river.

As he would on more than one occasion, Julian had taken it upon himself to play peacemaker between his feuding parents. The ten-year-old had walked all the way across the ice and up the river from Poughkeepsie to West Park on his own. The distance was more than seven miles. The temperature was in the teens. "I get up home and find Papa in the study," he chronicled. With Julian there, Burroughs opened the stone house and started a fire in the Franklin stove. "I am very cold at bed time," wrote Julian, "I leave on my undershirt and put on Papa's socks and I got warm by the oven and then went up to bed. I slep with Papa and we had a sopestone [bedwarmer]." Burroughs recorded the more important aspect of the visit in his journal. "Julian came up last night and makes my heart glad for a few hours," he wrote. "In the evening we discuss our family difficulties. He stoutly takes the side of his mama, and with tears in his eyes lectures me on my duty to her. He cannot see the merits of my side of the case at all. He takes entirely her view; it is the irony of fate. We return to Poughkeepsie together." [34]

BURROUGHS'S BROTHER HIRAM HAD become a problem. After their father's death in January of 1884, the simple, reticent man had remained at the old home in Roxbury alone. He did not care to leave but could not afford to stay. There was a mortgage on the place. Bills were due and Hiram had no money. Burroughs lent him $1100. Then in 1887 he signed a second mortgage and advanced Hiram more money that totalled nearly $3000. Now, in the late autumn of 1889, Hiram was not able to make his payments to either Burroughs or the bank. Burroughs himself was overextended, having borrowed heavily to increase his Riverby acreage. There was nothing further he could do to help his brother. He was forced to call in his note and put Hiram out of business. "Went to Roxbury last Monday to look into Hiram's matters," he noted in a journal entry of early November, 1889. "Spent two days in the village; very wretched; did not go up to the old place—too painful . . . Hiram's outlook very bleak. He must give up the old place. I shall probably lose heavily by him . . . I wanted to see him keep the Old Home, but clearly he is not competent to manage the farm." [35] Burroughs wrote Hiram explaining things, and naming a date in early December when they were to meet at the office of a Roxbury attorney to draw papers giving title to the farm over to Burroughs.

When the day arrived, Hiram did not appear at the lawyer's office. Feeling saddened and betrayed, the younger brother hiked from town across the hills to the farmstead, expecting to find Hiram there. The place was vacant. Hiram had gone away to avoid him. Burroughs lay down to sleep in his old bedroom, but could not. His

John Burroughs at age 20 during an 1857 visit to Chicago. He would cut off the long bohemian locks at Ursula's insistence on his return to New York.

View of the Burroughs homestead, October 25, 1895. John Burroughs's boyhood bedroom is in the front corner of the second floor, the window open. In the foreground are John Burroughs, his brother Curtis, and Curtis's son, another John Burroughs.

Chauncey Burroughs, John Burroughs's father, photographed in 1879.

Amy Kelly Burroughs, John Burroughs's mother, photographed in 1880 shortly before her death at age 72.

Ursula North, the future Mrs. John Burroughs, photographed in 1857 at age 21.

John Burrroughs, schoolmaster, photographed at age 25 in 1862, the year he met Myron Benton.

Walt Whitman photographed in 1884.

Julian Burroughs, age 7, and his dog in the doorway of the house at Riverby, 1885.

Members of the Harriman Expedition to Alaska at Dutch Harbor, 1899. John Burroughs is at center. Edward H. Harriman is at far right.

John Burroughs and John Muir standing on the Muir Glacier during the Harriman Expedition.

John Burroughs and a young friend looking down at Slabsides from Julian's Rock in June of 1900.

John Burroughs and President Theodore Roosevelt by the fire in Yellowstone Park, 1903.

John Burroughs photographed in front of his study at Riverby with Julian and Julian's family, in the summer of 1908. Granddaughter Elizabeth, age 5, sits on the lap of Julian's wife Emily. Ursula, age 3, sits on her grandfather's lap. A grandson, John Burroughs II, would be born a year later. Photo courtesy: The Bettmann Archive.

The Muir/Burroughs party descending the Bright Angel trail into the Grand Canyon in 1909. John Muir is at top, Burroughs third in line, and Clara Barrus between them wearing white.

A group of Vassar students visiting with Burroughs at Slabsides.

John Burroughs and Henry Ford in Detroit in June of 1913.

John and Ursula Burroughs at Woodchuck Lodge during the summer of 1915. He is 78, she 79.

Above: John Burroughs and Clara Barrus on the porch of the Nest at Riverby, May 26, 1917. Burroughs's wife had died two months earlier.

Left: One of the busts made by the sculptor Cartaino Sciarro Pietro during a 1915 visit to Woodchuck Lodge.

The Ford camping party at Horseshoe Run, near Leadmine, West Virginia, on August 10, 1918. From left to right: John Burroughs, Henry Ford, Edsel Ford, Harvey Firestone, and Thomas Edison. The man at far right is unidentified.

Above: John Burroughs and Hamlin Garland on the steps of Woodchuck Lodge, summer 1920.

Left: John Burroughs and his grandson, John Burroughs II, photographed in May of 1919 when Burroughs was 82 and his grandson 10.

John Burroughs at his desk at Slabsides on November 7, 1920, less than five months before his death.

mind turned, with a curious mixture of sympathy and rage, on his fugitive brother. It was likely that Hiram had absconded to Eden's farm, so Burroughs walked there—another four miles—the following morning. "As I reach the house I see Hiram through the window. I felt ashamed and humiliated for him," wrote Burroughs in his journal. "I go in and greet them all, barely speaking to Hiram. He looks confused and guilty. I quickly open on him and tell him the sheriff is in possession, and that he is to be sold out . . . I try to show him how utterly hopeless it is for him to go on with the farm without ruining me." The next day, Burroughs and Hiram hiked together through wind and snow toward Roxbury. "As we toil up the mountain, I note how troubled and careworn he looks. He stoops as if bearing a great burden . . . I know how he is weighed down, but nothing can be done. He has lost the battle; the old farm and home he cannot keep. I am powerless to help him more. The roof over my own head is threatened." Approaching the lawyer's office, Hiram walked behind his brother "as if I were leading him with a rope—leading him to the slaughter. I could fly to get away from this painful business." Before the day was done, Hiram signed papers deeding the farm and all his personal property over to Burroughs. "Then we go to the Old Home. I sleep near him in the old chamber, or try to sleep, as he does; but neither of us sleep much." [36]

Burroughs spent four days at the home farm with his brother, during which time he rented the place to a young farmer of the neighborhood. Then Burroughs returned home to Riverby and Hiram went to live with Eden. In time, the new tenant would fail in Hiram's wake, and Burroughs would turn to another brother to pick up the mantle of maintaining the family homestead. "I am going to put my brother [Curtis] on the old farm," Burroughs wrote Benton in October of 1891. "He has a family of three boys and two girls, and so is strong-handed enough to put the work through, and as they all seem really in earnest, I am going to give them a chance." [37] John Burroughs's long financial struggle to keep the home farm in the hands of his family had more than two decades more to run.

11

WHITMAN LAND

Never a morning does Julian start off for school but I long to go with him, to be his mate and equal; to share his enthusiasms, his anticipations, his games, his fun. Oh! to see life through his eyes again! How young the world is to him, how untried, how enticing!

— *Journal Entry, October 13, 1895*

WHEN YOU DRIVE THROUGH West Park today, the New York State historical marker that greets you at the junction of Route 9W and John Burroughs Drive tells you he lived at West Park from 1873 onwards, and then points you away from Riverby, to the woods two miles inland where one will find the rustic cabin called "Slabsides" that Burroughs built in 1895. The little cabin resides in a bog that in Burroughs's time was a celery swamp. The bog sits at the center of a bird sanctuary that is owned by the John Burroughs Association, an organization founded after Burroughs's death in 1921 and endowed by several of his wealthy friends including Henry Ford, Helen Gould Shepard, Harvey Firestone, Thomas Edison, and Edith Carow Roosevelt (the widow of Theodore Roosevelt). Go to Slabsides today and look in the windows; you will see the furnishings and books just as John Burroughs left them seventy years ago. A fedora hangs from a peg in the wall. A Vassar pennant is tacked up beside it. There is a rickety table piled with books, pads, and pencils. And there are two rocking chairs that, in fair weather, Burroughs used to haul out onto the porch. The pennant was a gift to Burroughs from one of the hundreds of Vassar college students who came to visit him from nearby Poughkeepsie during the twenty-five years he used

Slabsides as a second home. Many of these "Vassar girls" were in training to become teachers; most were enthusiasts for the fashionable turn-of-the-century hobby of bird-watching.

Burroughs would meet the parties of young ladies at the West Park train station and then lead them on a steep hike of a mile and a half through the woods to the cabin. After showing them his shack—for it is little more than that—he would lead them on a trail through the hemlock woods that he had come to call "Whitman Land." It was in these woods that he'd walked with Walt during the poet's frequent visits to West Park in the late 1870s. A regular stop on Burroughs's tour was the cascading rush of Black Creek, where Whitman had paused to take out his pad and pencil and jot down the note that became "An Ulster County Waterfall" in *Specimen Days*. Black Creek was, wrote Whitman, "a stream of hurrying amber" running through a "primitive" forest that was "druidical, solitary, and savage . . . shade overhead, thick underfoot with leaves—a just palpable wild and delicate aroma." Enveloping the restful scene, Whitman had written, was "the monotone and liquid gurgle from the hoarse, impetuous, copious fall—the greenish-tawny, darkly transparent waters plunging with velocity down the rocks."

Walking through the same woods of which Whitman had written, Burroughs spoke to his guests as much about Whitman as he did about birds and wildflowers. He also spoke to them of conservation, discussed the New York State Audubon Society of which he had recently been appointed the first vice president, and decried the practices of poachers who raided nests for eggs in order to service the private, glass-encased collections of those "desicated mortals" called "closet naturalists." He said he hoped his guests would not turn into closet naturalists—that they would learn to seek out nature on its own terms, alive in field and wood, and not "stuffed and mounted in the bowels of some dark museum." [1] As the students sat on the rocks outside Slabsides and ate their picnic lunches, Burroughs would stand on the steps of the cabin, a worn copy of *Leaves of Grass* in his hands, and recite "Out of the Cradle Endlessly Rocking." Then he would speak of the fragile green earth, and the Darwinian childhood through which it had been the cradle for the race.

Whitman had died in 1892, the same year as Jay Gould. From the date of the poet's death through to the end of the decade the memory of the life and work of Whitman dominated the thoughts of his friend and apostle John Burroughs. After Whitman's death, the poet seemed suddenly to be the only subject that Burroughs could muster enough enthusiasm to write about. In 1894 he had produced *Riverby*, the first volume of his nature essays to be published in seven years and a book that included no piece of writing less than three years old. After so long a hiatus, Burroughs's readers were chagrined to read in the preface to the new book that this would probably be Burroughs's last collection of out-of-door papers. To his journal he confided, "For a quarter of a century I have been writing these [nature] books—living them first, and then writing them out. What serene joy I have had in gathering this honey! And now I begin to feel that it is about over with me. My interest, my curiosity, are getting blunted." [2] For the prior two years he had been writing almost exclusively on the subject of Whitman, and he would continue to do so until, after four drafts, he would fitfully and with many doubts as to its value send to press his book, *Whitman, A Study*, in 1896.

AFTER TWO YEARS OF immersion in farm work, hardly touching pen to paper, Burroughs felt his muse (what he defined as "a strange combination of desire, skill, and inspiration") slowly rise once again. [3] The essays began to come to him after the harvest of 1891. Farm management still preoccupied him, but he was able to produce a few pieces for the *Youth's Companion*, *McClure's*, the *Independent*, and other publications.

The joyous tone of his woodland essays gave no hint that Burroughs himself was in a state of depression, and was undergoing what later generations would call a mid-life crisis. In the journals for this year he referred to himself again and again as an orphan. His mind dwelled upon his losses and failures, and his increasing age (he was fifty-four). He spoke of looking back over every book he had written and finding each of them wanting in some major way. He expressed similar dissatisfaction with his married life. On a particularly bad day, the most useful thing to do seemed to be to choose a gravesite. In a note dated November 6, he spoke of pausing in the local West Park cemetery where many of his acquaintances were buried. "I linger about the graves," he wrote, "[and consider] whether or not I want to be buried here. The old Baptist burying-ground at Home is offensive to me. Had rather be buried beside my dogs; or else in one of the old fields at home." [4]

In contrast to Burroughs's humble plans, Whitman had built for himself a grand tomb in Harleigh Cemetery, Camden. A fund had been raised by Burroughs and others to to help the destitute poet "maintain a comfortable home." Upon receipt of the cash, Whitman took the terms of the gift to mean "eternal home." Instead of using the money to pay off the mortgage on the tenement he'd purchased a few years before, the poet began construction on an exorbitantly expensive mausoleum at Camden's Harleigh Cemetery. He did this much to the chagrin of Burroughs and other contributors who had donated dollars in the belief that without such funds the poet would have to default on his mortgage loan and be put out on the street.

Burroughs had been to visit Whitman the previous Christmas, by which time the poet had obviously begun to fail. "Walt on the bed with eyes closed," he wrote in his journal for Christmas Eve, "but he knows me and speaks my name as of old, and kisses me. He asks me to sit beside him awhile. I do so, holding his hand. He coughs feebly . . . asks about my family and sends his best love to Wife and Julian. Gives me two copies of his complete poems just out. He tells me where to find them. After a while I go out for fear of fatiguing him. He says, 'It is all right, John,' evidently referring to his approaching end." [5]

As Whitman neared his end, Burroughs meditated on death and its meaning. In tandem with this, he made note of the passing of a Roman Catholic cardinal whose obituary he read in the newspaper. Burroughs's journal records the newspaper report that the cardinal spent his last conscious hours imploring God to have mercy upon him. "He was firmly possessed with the Christian idea that he was about to go from a place where God was not, to a place where God is and abides," wrote Burroughs. "And that there was great danger that his God would be displeased with him, and would punish him. How curious, how curious! Poor Man! Why could he not have died in peace?" [6]

Whitman died in relative peace on March 25. Burroughs went immediately to Camden. "Look upon Walt's face long and long," he wrote. "Cannot be satisfied—it is not Walt—a beautiful, serene old man, but not Walt. After awhile I have to accept it as him—his 'excrementitious body,' as he called it." [7] Burroughs, Thomas Eakins, Moncure Conway, Robert Ingersoll, and Julian Hawthorne were among the honorary pallbearers who saw Whitman to his last resting place at Harleigh Cemetery. With characteristic lack of reserve, William Sloane Kennedy said after the event that he felt as if he had just been in attendance at "the entombment of Christ." [8] Grief-stricken, even Burroughs would briefly give in and proclaim to the privacy of his journal that "W. W. is the Christ of the modern world—he alone redeems it, justifies it; shows it divine; floods and saturates it with human-divine love." [9]

In the Berg Collection at the New York Public Library there is an unsigned, undated manuscript that is evidently the draft of a speech Burroughs intended to give at a gathering of Whitman's friends a short time after the death. Did this meeting of the apostles ever take place? We do not know. But in the draft speech Burroughs urges his listeners to think of themselves as "the elect, the blessed few" who were lucky enough to know and understand Whitman and his work during the master's own time on earth. It was not given to the masses to see Whitman; this felicity was denied them. The "great army of the Philistines" knew him not at all. "Do we not pity them?" asked Burroughs. "What a privation it is." [10] Elsewhere, in a journal note for April 15, Burroughs recorded that he was "fairly well these days but sad, sad. Walt constantly in mind. I think I see more plainly how Jesus came to be deified—his followers loved him; love transforms everything. I must still continue my writing about him." [11]

When Burroughs returned to Riverby after the funeral, he immediately began his spring planting. Again he bit into the great apple of the earth with his plow and found it sweet and appetizing, yet the new furrow was more eloquent and pathetic to him than ever before. "The world is so sweet, so benignant these days," he wrote, "yet my thoughts are away in that Camden cemetery where the great one lies." [12] On April 6, he addressed Whitman directly in his journal: "Again, dear Master . . . the swelling buds and the sprouting grass; again the robin racket in the twilight; again the long-drawn tr-r-r-r-r-r-r-r of the toad in the gloaming; again the tender ditty of the sparrow; again the waterfowl streaming northward; again the 'fields all busy with labor'—but thou, thou in thy tomb!" [13]

Following the death of the poet, whenever Burroughs touched pen to paper at the end of his day of work in the fields he wrote of nothing but Whitman. He was embarked on what he described to one correspondent as a "flood" of writing on Whitman. Even though it was planting season, Burroughs was to publish four articles about Whitman in the first month after the poet's death. "Walt Whitman, Poet of Democracy" appeared in the *Christian Union* for April 2, "Walt Whitman" appeared in the *Critic* of April 2, "Walt Whitman After Death" was published in the *Critic* on April 9, and "The Poet of Democracy" appeared in the May issue of the *North American Review*. Between 1892 and the end of 1896 Burroughs would publish no fewer than eighteen major essays on the poet, as well as the book *Whitman: A Study*.

A month after the funeral, Burroughs played host to Whitman's friend and literary executor, Dr. Richard Maurice Bucke. "Dr. Bucke came this morning," wrote Burroughs in the journal for May 1. "I did not use to like Dr. B., but since the death of W. my heart has softened towards him, and I begin to feel a strong attachment." Bucke was the most charismatic of all Whitman's devotees, and the one with the greatest religious fervor. As a young man he had been a railroad hand, a wagon-train driver, and a miner in the Utah and Nevada territories. One night at Riverby the Doctor regaled the fourteen-year-old Julian with the story of how he had helped stand off a Shoshone war party for half a day on the banks of the Humboldt River. Bucke then took off his prosthetic shoes and showed the astonished boy where one foot was missing and the toes of another gone, amputated after he had nearly died of exposure and starvation during an attempt to cross the Sierra Nevada in winter.

Bucke had first discovered *Leaves of Grass* in 1868, when he was thirty. In 1872, after an evening spent reading Whitman, Wordsworth, Shelley, Keats and Browning, he experienced what he described as an unforgettable moment of "illumination," "exultation," "Brahmic splendor," and "immense joyousness." He felt as though he were at the center of a "flame-colored cloud," and he "knew," with a certainty he had brought to no other knowledge before, that "the foundation principle of the world is what we call love, and that the happiness of everyone is in the long run absolutely certain." [14] From that day forward, Bucke dedicated much of his time to the study of what he called "spiritual evolution." He published a book on the subject in 1879, entitled *Man's Moral Nature*, and also authored a biography of Whitman in 1883.

With his infirmities, Bucke was incapable of walking the rocky trail beside Black Creek; thus Burroughs had to forego showing him the spot of which Whitman had written in *Specimen Days*. Instead, they sat under the shade of a pine tree by Black Creek Pond, a far more accessible section of the stream, and talked for several hours. "[Bucke's] idea now is that there is such a thing as Cosmic Consciousness," wrote Burroughs to Myron Benton, "that it is a new sense of power developing in the race; and that Walt had it in a preeminent degree—Paul had it, Buddha, and Mahomet. I fear he will ride the idea too hard." [15] Bucke was to publish his theory in the 1901 book *Cosmic Consciousness*. A few years later, William James would quote at length from Bucke's book in his *Varieties of Religious Experience*.

In discussing Whitman's "cosmic consciousness," Bucke elevated the poet to the status of prophet. According to Bucke, Whitman had experienced one supreme moment of illumination—as powerful and instantaneous as the conversion of St. Paul—and then had begun to write the *Leaves*. Bucke believed that like other prophets, Whitman had been an instrument of his message, a voice set upon earth to articulate the inspiration of divine love. Burroughs was to maintain a polite public silence on Bucke's ideas. In 1901, when writing a note to another physician, his confidante Clara Barrus, who was then working at the asylum for the insane at Middletown, New York, Burroughs would comment that he had always suspected that lunacy was contagious. "A friend of mine, Dr. R. M. Bucke, who has charge of the asylum at London, Canada, has caught a little of it, I think." [16]

Another topic that Burroughs and Bucke discussed during the doctor's visit to Riverby was Higginson, who had taken the occasion of Whitman's death to publish an editorial in the *New York Evening Post* suggesting that the dead man had led a less than "wholesome" life. Burroughs was fast to fire back in a paper published on April 9. "I have known Whitman for thirty years," he wrote, "and a cleaner, saner, more wholesome man in word and deed, I have never known. If my life depended upon it, I could not convict him of one unclean word, or one immoral act." Of course, the unspoken part of Burroughs's argument is that he and Higginson had fundamentally different views on what constituted "unclean" and "immoral." Part of Higginson's attack had suggested that Whitman's late ill-health was the result of the poet being in the last stages of syphilis. To this Burroughs also responded, but guardedly. "That Whitman's life was entirely blameless in this respect [sexual irregularities] I am not prepared to say, because I do not know," said Burroughs. "I think it highly probable that it was not, but that his partial paralysis was in any way traceable to any such cause, I am very sure is not the case." [17]

JOHN BURROUGHS AND SEVENTEEN-YEAR-OLD Julian spent most of the spring and summer of 1895 engaged in backbreaking labor. Two miles inland from Riverby, in a desolate bug-ridden hollow surrounded by second-growth maples, they blasted rocks to drain a lonely swamp of several acres. Then they dug out stumps of dead trees to clear the rich black soil that Burroughs had decided would be ideal for the cultivation of celery. "The vineyards at Riverby were then all in bearing," wrote Julian many years later. "They were well managed by our man 'Hud.' Father therefore had lost some of his early interest in the grapes. Here in the woods he found a new land to conquer, new problems to solve, new conditions, a new industry." Slowly through the summer, the land yielded to the labor of father and son and became a level floor of deep, black, muck soil. "All day in the swamp . . ." Burroughs wrote in the journal for May 1. "Break through the rocky barrier today and let the water out. I lay a long time on the rocks." [18] A few weeks later he wrote a friend, "I am again deep in my beloved muck-swamp, but the thing fights back with poisoned sumac." [19] He wound up doing much of the work with blisters and sores on his hands and arms from the sumac, but soon he had nearly 30,000 celery plants in cultivation.

Several years later, when Benton asked why he had decided to build himself a second home at a swamp that lay not three miles away from Riverby, Burroughs answered candidly that it was to free himself from "domestic tyranny." [20] He wanted a place to which to retreat on the numerous days when he began to find Ursula's company tiresome. To people other than Benton, Burroughs submitted a range of reasons for the construction of the cabin. Some were told that he'd built the place to get closer to wild nature; others were told he'd built it as a sanctuary in which to write; and still others were given to understand that it was a retreat from "the extensive water view" offered by Riverby, of which he had begun to grow weary. To Julian he explained the cabin as a potential home for the itinerant and bankrupt Hiram. But the fact was that he built the place in order to be able to get away from his wife.

Burroughs began building the cabin in late November. He positioned the structure on a gray stone ridge that formed an island at the edge of the swamp. After he and a carpenter set up the frame of the house, Burroughs laid the stone chimney with the help of a mason. "Still warm, 60 degrees in the coolest spot," he wrote in his journal for December 20. "I sweat at my work. How I enjoy it! Chimney nearly to the roof. Will [McLain] and I are pushing it up, happy all day long." An expert in the delicate and subtle art of chimney building, Burroughs was always to be justly proud of the hearth at Slabsides, which offered an excellent draft. "Before I built the [chimney] for my cabin," he wrote his friend, the photographer Clifton Johnson, "I went around hunting for old chimneys, and I'd poke my head into the fireplaces and look up them. I think I discovered the secret of a good draft. It is to have the throat of the chimney long and narrow and the flue above very big . . . I couldn't ask for one that would draw better [than the chimney at Slabsides.]" [21] The cabin was close enough to completion by Christmas that he was able to use it to entertain some friends from Poughkeepsie, among them Congressman Ed Platt. As usual, Julian and Ursula were left to see to their own Yuletide. Two days after Christmas, he wrote to Hamlin Garland to tell him, "The chimney is finished and we are putting on the slabs." [22] The weather remained very mild through January, and Burroughs went to the cabin every day with a hired man, Andrew Vanderwater (Van), to do the finish work on the interior.

Yellow birch poles from the surrounding woods made the frames of the porch. There was a roomy veranda with a rustic railing of cedar posts, a sloping roof, and a wide door with a latchstring. In the first years of the cabin, the cedar rafters had all the shaggy bark still on them, but these were soon stripped by wood borers which left in their wake a delicate tracery on the smooth wood. Burroughs covered the seams of the plain boards of the interior with split-birch saplings. He constructed much of the trim and furniture himself from what wood he found near at hand in Whitman Land. A yellow birch partition separated the living room and bedroom on the main floor. Stairs led to the loft, which held a guest bedroom and attic with extra cots. The bedsteads were made of native birch. The legs of the tables and windowseat were crafted from sumac limbs; they all had a spiral twist from the imprint of the climbing bittersweet. Several of the walls had built-in bookshelves. Burroughs's desk, a plain board supported by tripods of sumac, was quickly stacked with books and papers. In the far corner was the kitchen with its dish cupboard and basin, and the gasoline stove that he used only occasionally. He preferred to do his cooking over the open hearth fire.

"HAVE YOU READ *Wealth Against Commonwealth?*" Burroughs asked Benton in a letter during the summer of 1896. "If not, get the book. It is a great book of the kind. It makes me so mad that I can't read it long at a time. It tells how the people are robbed by the trusts and combines. Get it. Price $1.00." [23] A former editor of the *Chicago Tribune*, Henry Demarest Lloyd, had written an article in 1881 entitled "The Story of a Great Monopoly." The piece was a detailed exposé of the operating standards and procedures of the Standard Oil Company. It portrayed Standard Oil and other trusts as the enemies of honest competition and, therefore, the public good. The article had been rejected by the *North American Review* on the grounds that it was probably libelous. William Dean Howells, who was about to resign his editorship of the *Atlantic* and felt he had nothing to lose, purchased the piece for the March 1881 issue. When it appeared, the article struck a chord in the public mind. The March *Atlantic* went through seven printings as its publisher scrambled to meet the demand for extra copies. Soon the article was reprinted in England and circulated in Australia. The piece supplied the germ of what became Lloyd's book *Wealth Against Commonwealth*, which was published in 1894.

The book seems to have briefly radicalized Burroughs. Immediately after reading it, Burroughs sent a series of letters to the editor Richard Watson Gilder, urging him to make his magazine, the *Century*, into a forum for attacking "the greed of monopolies" and the "insolence and tyranny of railroads" [24] Gilder did not take up the cause. He wrote back to say that the *Century* emphasized literature that was meant to entertain, not disturb. "That is why we end up taking so many of your pleasant papers," wrote Gilder to Burroughs. "They do not offend. They do not condemn. They do not leave one discontented. They breed joy in the world as it is."

Although he would shortly lose his unquestioning commitment to Lloyd's ideas, Burroughs was for the moment dedicated to the reform movement. Burroughs's reading of Lloyd's book colored his view on topics that had long concerned him. After reading *Wealth Against Commonwealth*, he penned a short essay in which he, in a critical defense of Whitman, pointed out that the unhappy social facts of the day were more than just economic and political truths, but were also poetic truths as well. The paper was entitled "The Poet and the Modern," and was published in the *Atlantic Monthly* of October 1896. In it Burroughs explained why he believed that only a poet with the originality and force of Whitman could create poetic literature equal to and reflective of contemporary America.

> A sordid motive like money-getting does not awaken poetic enthusiasm. A manufacturing town is ugly. The roundhouse or machine-shop of a railroad is not a place where one would care to linger . . . What shall we say then? The modern age in its material and industrial aspects is unpoetic, or anti-poetic, and it is so because there is less free play of man in it, of human qualities and emotions, than in the world of the past . . . The movements of our population,

the setting up of new states, the tides in politics, the fall of political leaders, strikes and lockouts, etc., all these are themes as fruitful in poetic motifs as the wars and social upheavals of the past . . . The great social cankers and ulcers of our day, the greed of capital, the grip of the millionaire, the fury of faction, the vulgarity of wealth, the hollowness of society, the heroism of labor, etc., all afford artistic motifs to the man who is capable of seizing them and using them. He will need a powerful human equipment; no dainty, fine-drawn, attenuated poetling will do here. [25]

The "body-killing and soul-blighting occupations" peculiar to industrial civilizations were not in themselves suggestive of "poetic thoughts," wrote Burroughs; but if Dante had made poetry out of hell, could not a writer copious and powerful enough make poetry out of the vast and varied elements of industrial civilization?

"The Poet and the Modern" was to form part of what Burroughs eventually published as *Whitman, A Study* in 1896. In this book, Burroughs argued that if one came to Whitman with a purely critical frame of mind, a frame of mind begotten by books and not by life, and approached Whitman as "a professor and a judge," then both critic and subject were sure to suffer. When reading *Leaves of Grass*, one did not encounter highly stylized writing "got up for the occasion." Instead, one encountered a real man as he lived and breathed, and as he walked the streets—"a figure divested of artificial and conventional vestments." If one dipped into the *Leaves* looking for a poet instead of a man, one was bound to be repelled. "The poetry is there, of course," wrote Burroughs, "but it must be come at by a kind of indirection" that called for the sacrifice of one's "critical pride and equipment." Critics wishing to understand him had to divest themselves of their traditional theories and canons.

Burroughs noted that the problem many formal critics had in accepting Whitman was that their sense of poetry as craft—as something wrought—was stronger than the sense of a need for life and reality in art. These cold purveyors of literary theory valued "the shadow more than the reality." Burroughs noted that while many outside the literary establishment could easily accept Whitman as a major force, third- and fourth-rate critics and poets routinely rejected him. So, said Burroughs, did "gentlemen" and "ladies." So did all figures at peace with the established art, commerce, and religion. Burroughs proposed that while the "apostles of the gospel of the cultured, the choice, the refined" played a necessary part in civilization, this did not mean that other points of view were necessarily "ungood." *Leaves of Grass* did not recommend revolution, or mob violence, or any form of criminality. It merely recommended "largeness, health, robustness, charity, love, contentment, faith . . . and freedom for every slave on the face of the earth." In this it was the most wholesome book ever written.

Burroughs went on to explain that Whitman had not been opposed to culture and refinement as such, so long as these were not achieved at the expense of "native human traits." He had not disliked gentlemen, but had preferred common people and was "probably most content in their society." Whitman glorified Lincoln, "but it was not for his gentlemanly qualities." The Lincoln that Whitman honored was the human being beneath the expensively tailored suit. Had he not, in poem after poem, praised the common soldiers with the same verve as he had their commander-in-chief?

In *Whitman, A Study*, Burroughs credited the poet with political beliefs that did not fit with the facts of the poet's repeatedly stated opinions. With the influence of Lloyd's book still fresh upon him, Burroughs forced Whitman into a mold of political radicalism. Burroughs suggested that Whitman would have endorsed any political platform that was based on a respect for "the virtue and intelligence of the common man." He also said that Whitman believed "the soul object of any worthwhile government should be the preservation of liberty." At the same time, Burroughs added, Whitman condemned "the exploiting of the many for the benefit of the few" and that he was "enraged by the arrogance of wealth." [26] In fact, Whitman had disparaged virtually all liberal causes of his day—including abolition, unionism, and universal suffrage. While he wrote poetry of personal liberation, he had supported the public status quo.

"I will not gloss over the appalling dangers of universal suffrage in the United States," Whitman had written in *Democratic Vistas*, his manifesto of 1871. "In fact, it is to admit and face these dangers that I am writing." In the same book he had railed against the rise of "infidelism." Whitman quoted from Carlyle's "Shooting Niagara," where the author said that extending the vote to the English working class, as mandated by Disraeli's Reform Bill, would signal the death-knell of Britain in that it assured the rise of "blockheadism, gullibility" and "bribeability" in public office. Suffrage, wrote Carlyle, would allow for mob rule through the ballot box. By allowing for a one-man, one-vote system (the same system that Americans had affirmed after the Civil War with the Fourteenth and Fifteenth Amendments to the Constitution), England seemed to Carlyle to be launching herself over Niagara Falls in a barrel, to certain doom. In *Democratic Vistas*, Whitman warmly endorsed Carlyle's sentiments. The poet wholeheartedly urged the strict restriction of the vote in the United States. ("I had no idea he was so conservative," William Douglas O'Connor had written to Burroughs after reading Whit-man's book.[27])

After four years of steady effort, Burroughs knew, even as *Whitman, A Study* rolled off the press, that he had been less than candid in his portrayal of the poet. As always when writing of Whitman, he had endeavored to put his friend's best face forward. He was honest with himself about this. "I shall never be able to tell how much I am warped or biased in Whitman's favor, so that I am barred from taking an independent view of him," he wrote in his journal. "I would give anything to be sure that I see him as he is; to be his judge, and not his attorney. I early fell into the way of de-fending him, and it may be, *may be*, that I can take only an *ex parte* view of him. The moment I begin writing about him I become his advocate. My mind slides into the old rut at once. I must think further about this."[28]

Of course, Burroughs *was* Whitman's attorney and not his judge. (Burroughs was disturbed when William Sloane Kennedy wrote to congratulate him on the book, which Kennedy described as "a fine piece of proselytizing literature."[29]) Being the work of a loyal friend writing about a much loved associate, it was unavoidable that the book should end up being a defense and not a true critique. Still, it is immensely valuable as an intimate memoir of the poet by one who knew him well, a detailed account of Burroughs's own personal view of the *Leaves* and their importance, and a testament of personal devotion and friendship. Also, of course, it was one of the few accounts of Whitman by Burroughs that did not get revised and corrected by Whitman himself. In the end, it was, like of all of Burroughs's writings on Whitman, a study in hero-worship. Vachel

Lindsay would write that "John Burroughs's Whitman is a bigger man than Whitman himself."

Burroughs was getting from two to five cents a word for his magazine publications in the early 1890s, and only a few hundred dollars guarantee on each book published by Houghton. In the winter of 1892–93, he came upon another way, in addition to writing, to milk dollars from his intellectual wits. Mark Twain and other popular authors were making good money on the lecture circuit. Now Burroughs became an occasional lecturer and after-dinner speaker for hire.

His first engagement was in late February 1893, at the Authors' Club in New York—the Club he was still refusing to join because of its mistreatment of Whitman. "Spoke for the first time and did fairly well," he confided to his journal. "Papers say my speech and J. Jefferson's [the actor] were the speeches of the evening. With practice I think I could beat any of them." [30] Ursula did not object too strongly to this new diversion of her husband's, as his speaking fees were substantial for the day—usually around $150. On March 24 he made a speech at a dinner to honor the humorist Thomas Bailey Aldrich at a private men's club in Manhattan. "Did not do so well as at the Authors' Club dinner," he recorded in his journal. "[I] ate too much, and drank too much champagne." [31]

Burroughs continued to be a speaker for hire through 1896 and early 1897. He soon came to hate the lecture circuit, but wanted the cash it generated. He needed to pay tuition for Julian, who enrolled at Harvard beginning in the fall of 1897. (Burroughs had made up his mind to support his son in education for as far as the boy wanted to go. "You won't have the rug yanked from under you, like I did," he wrote Julian.) And then personal appearances seemed to help the sale of his books. At least that was what Oscar Houghton kept telling him. For these reasons he forced himself each winter through rounds of speech-making that he clearly did not enjoy.

On an evening that must have been typical for the reticent, high-strung Burroughs, he uncomfortably addressed a hall of listeners in Doylestown, Pennsylvania, in 1896. "Do not speak easily and smoothly," he commented in his journal. ". . . the audience not very sympathetic . . . Room too close. My undershirt is wet with perspiration when I have finished." He saw people asleep in his audience. "Was more nervous than ever before, and felt yesterday like canceling all my engagements. I am no doubt shortening my life by this foolish lecturing business." [32] A few days later he spoke to yet another anonymous Pennsylvania crowd. "Not in good form," he reported. "Can't see the faces of the people, nor see my notes—footlights glaring in my face. Once the audience tittered—in derision, I think. I can't recall at what, probably at my awkwardness and failure to see my notes." [33]

Moving from hotel room to hotel room through the winter months, he yearned for the peace and solitude of Riverby and Slabsides, for casual overalls instead of the fancy white collar and tie demanded by the circuit, and for the company of anyone other than the strangers who always seemed to want more from him than he was prepared to give. "I seem like a man who in some unguarded moment has been caught by the skirts in some piece of machinery which is slowly but surely drawing him in," he wrote a friend regarding his lecturing, "maybe to his destruction, certainly to the destruction of his peace of mind." [34] There were occasional good evenings when his speech came off without a hitch and when he chanced to meet someone who impressed or pleased him. Burroughs had just such an evening when he spoke for the Phi Beta Kappa Society at Yale in early 1896. The talk—which on this one rare occasion was on a topic he enjoyed, Whitman—went well. At a reception after the lecture he was introduced to Helen Keller. "A visible soul," he wrote of Keller in his journal. "[I] am strangely affected by her; can hardly keep from tears. She repeats my poem, 'Waiting.' Says she believes it all. So happy, almost ecstatic, all soul and feeling. Quite handsome, except her eyes." [35]

Burroughs's agent for his lecture tours was Major James B. Pond, who owned and operated the Boston Lyceum Bureau. Founded in 1868 by James Redpath, the Bureau had at various times included among its clients Wendell Phillips, Charles Sumner, Henry Ward Beecher, Mark Twain, and Thomas Wentworth Higginson. In return for a ten percent commission on Burroughs's lecture fees, Pond advertised Burroughs's availability, made bookings, arranged his itinerary, and collected the money from the individual local promoters. To his speakers, Pond offered an assurance of good money with a minimum of effort. To the local lyceum groups, he offered a complete, balanced selection of programs that he could customize to meet prescribed tastes and budgets.

Thirty years before, Bronson Alcott had used his lyceum lectures to promote education reform; Emerson, to espouse his philosophy of moral sentiment; and Frederick Douglass, to advance abolition and black suffrage. During the Gilded Age, the intellectual tenor of the lecture circuit changed in concert with the sympathies and interests of the era. The lecture-going public demanded talks that ratified and promoted the money-getting motto by which they lived. They wanted to be told that wealth, and the quest for wealth, were noble things. One still occasionally found Henry Demarest Lloyd on a lyceum stage giving voice to his notions of labor and capital. And British imports such as Wilde and Arnold could generate crowds for an hour or two of literary discussion. But the most popular lyceum draws were the Rev. Lyman Abbott speaking on "The Ministry of Wealth" and Thomas Wentworth Higginson discoursing on "The Natural Aristocracy of the Dollar." Abbott used his lyceum speech to propose that no means of acquiring wealth could be termed "wrong," since the rich could only have achieved their good fortune by the will of God. Higginson, in turn, painted the country's economic landscape as a battlefield where those who were naturally superior in intellect would always rise to power, there to serve the good of all.

When Burroughs first approached Pond with the idea of scheduling some lectures, he did so with three proposed programs. One talk was to have been on "Walking," another on "Walt Whitman: Neglected Master," and a third on "The Religious Sentiment of the Woods." Pond refused these ideas, and instead insisted that Burroughs discuss "The Biologic Origin of the Ruling Class." This Burroughs seems to have been willing enough to do, for despite his attraction to the ideas of Lloyd he had an equal if not greater affinity for the fundamental notions of social Darwinism. He did not view the line of demarcation between worker and master in racial terms. Instead, he believed that every ethnic group produced its share of "leaders and followers, lions and sheep." As a part of his speech, he quoted a few lines from Lloyd's *Wealth Against Commonwealth* and then said that it was incumbent upon the biological supermen to see to the well-being of their lesser fellows and to "conquer the temptation to avarice as totally as they conquer all other things of this world." These natural masters-of-men should mold themselves into benevolent fathers-of-men with their children's best interest always at heart.

Burroughs usually opened his remarks with the observation that, as was necessarily the case with all sacred things, no part of nature was unwholesome or impure. As Marcus Aurelius had said, "Nothing is evil which is according to nature." Yet, continued Burroughs, there were aspects of nature that, though unsavory, were "unmistakably useful and positive forces" toward the good of the whole. The most important of these, Burroughs proposed to his audiences, was the biological law that declared the supremacy of the strong over the weak, the fit over the less fit. This Darwinian fact, he said, was one that gave pause when applied to human history and to the relations among human beings. "Nevertheless," he told his listeners, "we would be denying the reality of science did we not use the enlightened lens that Darwin supplies through which to view the drama of human politics and business." Burroughs made the case that under the law of variation some individuals had a fuller endowment of vital energy and intelligence than others. Under a severe strain and trial, the favored ones would always endure and succeed while others failed and perished. Not every acorn became a tree. Burroughs told his audiences that the beneficence of nature was manifest in every form of power—be it business power, military power, or intellectual power. Success in business, in the professions, on the farm, and in manufacturing inevitably came to those who deserved it, said Burroughs. Amid the natural competition that went on in every town and city, success of one man over another was not usually the result of violence or wrong. "Men of high purpose and noble character tend to succeed in business and professional life," Burroughs told his audiences. "The millionaires add to the positive health and well-being of all." [36]

Burroughs sugarcoated the message, but his was in fact the same cynical interpretation espoused by other social Darwinists, including Herbert Spencer. The British social philosopher suggested that the cutthroat competition of laissez-faire capitalism be viewed as a device serving to eliminate those of weak mind and body. Spencer had proposed that the best source of progress was the initiative provided by the threat of failure and poverty. Progress could only occur if the fittest were allowed to fight their way to dominant positions in the economy. The unfit would have to suffer the consequences brought on by their inefficiency. Legislation designed to protect the little man, said Spencer in an essay, was legislation meant to preserve dead wood. Any law that protected the weak against the strong would encourage mediocrity and the eventual downfall of the country.

Social Darwinism appealed to Burroughs's love of logic. Yet the gross injustices that it was often used to justify seemed to him "worse than unsavory." The injustices—child labor, strike breaking, company towns, trust scandals—were a fatal flaw in Burroughs's neat plan for a dreamworld run by good-hearted, paternalistic natural masters. Occasionally, when the real-world implications of social Darwinism became too much for Burroughs to deal with, he wavered in his allegiance to the ideology. Two days after delivering "The Biologic Origin of the Ruling Class" in Bethesda, Burroughs wrote Richard Watson Gilder to chide him for his ongoing refusal to use the *Century* as a podium to attack the business trusts and monopolies. "I am glad to hear what the wealth of New York is doing and proposing to do for the poor there," he wrote Gilder, "if only the wealth of N.Y. and of other places would not make them poor in the first place! . . . The wealth, the learning, the conservative of a country are nearly always on the side of the oppressor." [37] Three days later he was on the road again, touting the "inherent positive force of the wealth created by the natural elite" in a speech delivered at Albany. [38]

THE MEASURE OF LEGAL PROTECTION that Burroughs was not willing to extend to the working class he was nevertheless willing to extend to birds. John Burroughs accepted appointment as the first vice president of the New York State Audubon Society in 1897. "I know your Society will frown upon the milliner's use of bird skins," he wrote to a founder of the organization in accepting the honorary position. "I hope it will also discourage the senseless collecting of eggs and nests which so many young people take up as a mere fad, and which results in the destruction of so many of our rarer birds."

One animal that was particularly victimized at the turn of the century was the bald eagle. At Slabsides, Burroughs would occasionally be visited by an eagle that would perch on a dead pine tree at the top of the nearby summit that Burroughs had named "Julian's Rock." "Sometimes, as I look out of my window in the morning, I see the eagle upon his perch, preening his plumage, or waiting for the rising sun to gild the mountain-tops," wrote Burroughs in "Wildlife About My Cabin" (in *Far and Near*):

> When the smoke begins to rise from my chimney, or he sees me going to the spring for water, he concludes it is time for him to be off. But he need not fear the crack of a rifle here; nothing more deadly than field-glasses shall be pointed at him while I am about . . . I once heard a collector get up in a scientific body and tell how many eggs of the bald eagle he had clutched that season, how many from this nest, how many from that, and how one of the eagles had deported itself after had had killed its mate. I felt ashamed for him. He had only proved himself a superior human weasel. The man with the rifle and the man with the collector's craze are fast reducing the number of eagles in the country. Twenty years ago I used to see a dozen or more along the river in the spring when the ice was breaking up, where I now see only one or two, or none at all. In the present case, what would it profit me could I find and plunder my eagle's nest, or strip his skin from his dead carcass? Should I know him better? I do not want to know him that way. I want rather to feel the inspiration of his presence and noble bearing. I want my interest and sympathy to go with him in his continental voyaging up and down, and in his long, elevated flights to and from his eyrie upon the remote, solitary cliffs. He draws great lines across the sky; he sees the forests like a carpet beneath him, he sees the hills and valleys as folds and wrinkles in a many-colored tapestry; he sees the river as a silver belt connecting remote horizons. We climb mountain-peaks to get a glimpse of the spectacle that is hourly spread out beneath him. Dignity, elevation, repose, are his. I would have my

thoughts take as wide a sweep. I would be as far removed from the petty cares and turmoils of this noisy and blustering world. [39]

Burroughs had no argument with serious students who occasionally took specimens from the woods for scrutiny. He had done enough of that himself in the past, and would again in the future whenever he thought his need to be genuine. It was the professional collector who looted the groves and orchards to service the collections of the closet naturalists whom he thought truly villainous.

> Robbing nests and killing birds becomes a business with him. He goes about it systematically, and becomes an expert in circumventing and slaying our songsters. Every town of any considerable size is infested with one or more of these bird highwaymen, and every nest in the country round about that the wretches can lay hands on is harried. A large business has grown up under the influence of this collecting craze. One dealer in eggs has those of over five hundred species. He says that his business in 1883 was twice that of 1882, in 1884 it was twice that of 1883, and so on. Collectors vie with each other in the extent and variety of their cabinets.

Burroughs reminded his readers that his own essays had always emphasized the study of wildlife as it thrived in its own habitat. Burroughs urged people to leave wild nature in the woods where it belonged, and not to try to drop her into vials of formaldehyde and drag her back to some dark room in the city for scrutiny. He wrote that the closet naturalist was probably "the most wearisome and profitless creature in existence." With his piles of skins, his cases of eggs, his "laborious feather-splitting," and his outlandish nomenclature, he was not only the enemy of the birds, "but the enemy of all those who would know them rightly." Burroughs had more sympathy with the birds than with the poachers. If one had to be shot, let it be the latter. "The professional nest-robber and skin-collector should be put down," wrote Burroughs, "either by legislation or with dogs and shotguns." [40]

THE HARRIMAN
EXPEDITION

*I suppose that one reason why, during my Alaskan trip, there was all the time
an undercurrent of protest and dissatisfaction, is the fact that I have passed
from the positive to the negative side of life, when we begin to take in sail;
when we want less and not more; when the hunger for new scenes and new
worlds to conquer is diminishing . . .*

— Journal Entry, January 30, 1900

IN THE LATE 1890s, as Burroughs's books began to reach a wider
audience, people began to drop in on him. One visitor who arrived
at Slabsides without an appointment was young Lyman Ward. His
experience of Burroughs on this occasion was typical of most who
took it upon themselves to intrude on the writer's space without
invitation. Ward, like others, was greeted with a degree of warmth
and cordiality that did not belie Burroughs's general dissatisfaction
with his growing lack of privacy.

Ward was living at West Point, some thirty miles to the south
of West Park. After having read some of Burroughs's books, he
decided to pay a call on the naturalist. Ward took his bicycle and
boarded a northbound train. He was at West Park within an hour.
He went to Riverby first, and was told by a workman he might find
Mr. Burroughs in the study. The door was ajar, but the master was
not at his desk. It was then suggested that Ward try Slabsides.
Armed with directions supplied by another workman, Ward pedaled
the winding uphill road and eventually came upon the rough house
in the woods. Here again, he found Burroughs absent. "I was
obliged to give up my quest as it was nearly nightfall," wrote Ward,

"and sought out the little railway station to take the first train to West Point."

But he was in luck. Ward had hardly seated himself in the waiting room when he saw through the window a solitary figure in the open pasture beside the station, and knew at once that it was John Burroughs. "I rushed across the railway track and clamored over the stone fence and was soon shaking hands with the man I had been looking for all afternoon," wrote Ward. Burroughs was clad in stout corduroy trousers, with rough brogan shoes. He had come to the depot to meet his wife, who was coming up from New York. "We had an hour or longer perhaps for a visit," recounted Ward. Burroughs spoke like "the average New York rustic" and "seemed more like a farmer than a writer of books." He was much interested in Ward's bicycle, and said he would buy one himself if he lived in level country. "But," he said, "I could not make my trips through the woods and over the mountains with a bicycle." Ward mentioned that he was very much interested in first and rare editions of Emerson, Whitman, and other writers of Burroughs's acquaintance. Burroughs responded, very bluntly, that he was not. The cheaper the book, the better he liked it. Indeed, he said, he owned no first editions of his own books. The two talked on and on. In the midst of it, Ursula came and went away with some friends to Riverby. Burroughs stayed with Ward until the southbound train whistle was heard, and then disappeared into the falling darkness as he took the path toward Slabsides. [1]

As a young reporter for *Success Magazine*, a not-yet-famous Theodore Dreiser turned up at the Slabsides doorstep on a June afternoon in 1898. Like Lyman Ward, the cyclist from the year before, Dreiser found the master of the house not at home. Dreiser did not have an appointment. There was, however, evidence of life in the unlocked cabin. Dirty dishes were on the homemade table; hot coals glowed red in the fireplace. So Dreiser sat down in one of the chairs on the porch to wait. In due course, Burroughs came strolling out of the woods with his sleeves rolled up, wearing a straw hat.

Once again, Burroughs was good-natured about the intrusion. He allowed Dreiser to interrogate him on his ideas about success, and suggested that he thought success to be something best got at through the following of one's own personal tastes and pleasures. "If

I ran after birds only to write about them," said Burroughs to Dreiser, "I should never have written anything that anyone else would care to read. I must write from sympathy and love—that is, from enjoyment, or not at all." While they were talking, Burroughs kindled a fire and prepared supper for his sudden guest. Then, as it began to turn dark, he lit a lantern and accompanied Dreiser down the long hillside path to "put him right," as he said, on the road to the railway station. Once Dreiser was safely on the main road, he stood for a few minutes and watched as Burroughs retraced his steps up the steep path, lantern in hand, the little light bobbing up and down and finally disappearing. [2]

One of the first invited guests at Slabsides was John Muir in July of 1896. Burroughs had been casually acquainted with Muir ever since meeting him at the home of the *Century Magazine* editor Richard Watson Gilder in the mid-1880s. Now, in 1896, hearing that Muir was spending a few weeks in the northeast, Burroughs invited him to spend a day and a night at West Park. Muir rode the train up the Hudson from Manhattan and disembarked at Hyde Park. Burroughs and Julian rowed across the river to fetch him. While Julian rowed back to Riverby, Burroughs told Muir that they would be going to Slabsides to sleep. Julian recalled that Muir responded, "Oh, anywhere there in the woods will do; I'm at home anywhere out-of-doors." Muir indicated the shadowed woodlands in a general way with a wave of his hand.

Years later, in his unfinished autobiography, Julian would comment on Muir, who impressed him greatly. "Only among hoboes and the truly great do we ever see such mental poise, such complete triumph over things material," he wrote. Julian's father also spoke at length on Muir in his journal. "I met him at Hyde Park. A very interesting man, a little prolix at times," wrote Burroughs. "You must not be in a hurry, or have any pressing duty, when you start his stream of talk and adventure. Ask him to tell you his famous dog story [*Strickeen*] . . . and you get the whole theory of glaciation thrown in. He is a poet and almost a Seer. Something ancient and far-away in the look of his eyes. He could not sit down in a corner of the landscape, as Thoreau did; he must have a continent for his playground." [3] The two men stayed up late speaking mostly of Emerson, who had been the hero of both of their youths and whom

Muir had coaxed into visiting Yosemite in 1872. On the next morning, Burroughs took Muir on a hike through Whitman Land that included a stop at Black Creek falls.

Lenora Sill Ashton, who with her sister and parents lived across the river in Hyde Park, was another visitor to Slabsides. Writing in the April 1921 issue of *Audubon Magazine*, she recalled the days so many years before when Burroughs had befriended her and her family. Lenora and her sister were avid bird-watchers. Occasionally Burroughs would row himself across the river to visit with them and compare field notes. "John Burroughs was interested to hear the tales we young people had to tell him," she wrote. "The days of those visits of John Burroughs to our house were Red Letter ones, but the trips we made to see him at Slabsides held wonder hours for us."

On the day of the girls' first visit to the cabin, Burroughs met them at the little West Park dock and then escorted them on the hike up to the cabin. After they walked up the steps, Burroughs paused, holding the latchstring in his hand. Below the latchstring, acting as a doorknob, the girls saw a curiously gnarled piece of the root of a tree. "That," he said, "is a queer piece of root that I found when we were digging up stumps for the celery garden. When the girls from Vassar come I tell them it is the Japanese emblem for Slabsides." Burroughs then pointed to some holes in the slabs surrounding the door. "There is where some woodpeckers have been tapping on my house," he said. "They think they have discovered a new kind of tree where a giant woodpecker has come to live."

He invited the girls to join him in an ascent to Julian's Rock, from which four states could be seen. On the way up, he pointed to tracks in the forest mud, explained their origin, and imagined what woodland adventure or tragedy might have been the result of the woodchuck's tracks coming so close behind those of the rabbit. Occasionally he stopped dead in his tracks, his hand held up to signal silence for those behind him, and listened to the distant singing of birds. Then he would utter one word—such as "whip-poorwill" or "robin" or "blue jay"—and proceed up the trail.[4]

One of the many photographers who visited Slabsides was Herbert Angell, a young man who came to the cabin to make photographs for the magazine *Country Life in America*. In the 1960s Angell wrote a memoir of his experience. Angell wrote that being "a callow youth" at the time, he was at first "overawed" by the presence of the famous Burroughs. This wore off quickly, however, after a few minutes in the company of the personable, unpretentious author. Burroughs met Angell at the West Park railway station and insisted on helping carry his heavy photographic outfit up the steep road for the mile and a half walk to Slabsides. This was in the day of large cameras and glass plates; neither man's load was light.

Angell was about twenty years of age and his host sixty-two. "But so far as hill-climbing ability was concerned I had no advantage, for John Burroughs trudged along, seemingly without effort, entertaining me with talk of how he had come to select the site for his cottage retreat." Angell and Burroughs spent most of the day making photographs in and around Slabsides, by Julian's Rock, and at Black Creek. They took a break at one point and Burroughs prepared lunch for the young photographer. Later, as the sun slowly disappeared behind the hemlocks, he escorted Angell back down to the rail station. Once again, Burroughs insisted on lugging a tripod and a heavy box of photographic plates.

BURROUGHS'S NEXT MEETING WITH John Muir was to be when they both took part in the Harriman Expedition to Alaska, in 1899. Railway magnate E. H. Harriman—a business adversary of Jay Gould's son and heir George Gould—had been instructed by his doctors to abstain from work for a period of several months. Harriman chose to use the free time to underwrite and take part in a comprehensive exploration of the Alaskan territory for the purposes of cartography as well as the chronicling of the wildlife, flora, fauna, and other natural resources of the region, and the habits and culture of the native inhabitants. The expedition would make maps for the United States Geological Survey, collect natural history artifacts and anthropological relics for the American Museum of Natural History, and produce a documentary book on the Alaska wilderness to be published by Doubleday, Page & Co.

To this purpose, Harriman assembled an impressive array of over forty scientists, scholars, artists, and writers to accompany him on an extended trip through the territory. Burroughs was made the official historian of the expedition. Muir was along as the authority on glaciers and mountain geology. Among the others in attendance were George Bird Grinnell (an expert on Indians and Indian culture), Louis Agassiz (the Harvard biologist), R. Swain Gifford (the landscape painter), and the explorer Frederick Dellenbaugh. The party also included Harriman's wife and children. Young Averall Harriman was to become a special friend of Burroughs during the trip; seventy years later the former governor and ambassador would still recall kayaking lessons he received from Burroughs in a harbor of Puget Sound. [5]

A private train of what Burroughs called "palace cars" pulled out of Grand Central Station on May 23, 1899, carrying most of the expedition staff. Two and a half hours after the departure of the northbound train, Burroughs looked forlornly out the window, across the Hudson to West Park, where his wife stood in the summer house frantically waving her apron in farewell. He would be gone until August. "Have I made a mistake in joining this crowd for so long a trip?" he asked his journal. "Can I see nature under such conditions?" As the official historian, Burroughs was charged to make a daily record of what was seen and experienced through the course of the expedition, and then to write a formal account for publication.

Each man had a semiprivate stateroom and bath. The train carried one butler for every two expedition members. The depression of a button beside Burroughs's berth would summon a manservant at any hour of the day or night. "The furtive fellow sneaks in at odd moments and upsets my balance," Burroughs wrote to Julian. "I blink and my clothes are laid out for dinner. There is something mystical about these silent retainers: elfish. They are here, yet not here: an invisible hand making all fall into place. I am not used to being so comfortable, but might very well get used to it! I suppose I should not be concerned that the help are dressed better than I am." [6] Three meals per day—"more like banquets than meals," Louis Agassiz would remember—were served in the spacious dining car. After dinner the men would sit with cigars and brandy, two things Burroughs did not have a taste for, and discuss the upcoming adventure as they watched the continent roll by. "Mr. Burroughs and I would usually excuse ourselves from this part of the daily round," recalled Agassiz, "and go find a room without smoke in which to talk of birds." [7]

They were in Seattle a week after the departure from New York. On May 31, they boarded the steamer that Harriman had chartered for the voyage north, the *George W. Elder*. Here the Californians in the party, including John Muir, joined with those from the eastern seaboard. The steamer was a large iron ship specially fitted for the expedition. Her coal bunkers were full, and she was provisioned for a cruise of two months. There were plenty of willing hunting parties among the expedition staff who expected to be able to supply the boat with venison and bear meat once they reached Alaska. Still, Harriman took the precaution of bringing along eleven fat steers, a flock of sheep, several dozen chickens and turkeys, a cow for milk, and a span of horses. The horses were to be used to transport the hunters and their traps inland and then again to pack out the game. "The hold of our ship looked like a farmer's barnyard," wrote Burroughs. "We heard the mellow low of the red steer even in the wilds of [the] Bering Sea." (The horses were to prove useless in the subarctic snows of Alaska. Harriman would wind up trading them at Kodiak for two skins of the rare and coveted black fox.) Harriman also brought along one steam and two naphtha launches, several folding canvas canoes, and many guns.

The forty members of the group, combined with the officers and crew of the ship, made for 126 bodies in all. Burroughs's roommate for most of the train trip had been Professor B. E. Fernow of Cornell, a forester "and a good fellow." Now, on the *Elder*, Burroughs had his own luxurious stateroom on the upper deck. John Muir was in the cabin next door. Writing to a friend from British Vancouver, Burroughs said he thought he was the most untraveled man in the group. "Many of them," he wrote, "know all this Alaskan and Western world as well as I know Julian's Rock." Half joking, he complained that it was a "fearfully and wonderfully learned" crowd. The botanists and zoologists spoke Latin most of the time, while the geologists had a jargon all their own. "I keep mum lest I show my ignorance. Oh, these specialists, who cannot see the flower for its petals and stamens, or the mountain for its stratification!" [8]

Every night during the voyage, the expedition staff would gather to amuse each other with stories, songs, or lectures. One evening the captain of the *Elder* sent up a stoker and a deckhand to entertain. One of them sang a song; the other gave a lively dance on a hatch cover brought in for the purpose. Not to be outdone by anyone from the forecastle, members of the scientific staff volunteered to perform. "John Muir did a neat double-shuffle," the biologist Frederick Coville would remember, "immediately followed by Mr. Burroughs, who, to the astonishment of everybody, stepped forward to the hatch-cover and gave an admirable clog dance, evidently a hang-over from boyhood days." On other evenings, members of the scientific staff gave formal lectures: the oceanographer Ritter spoke about the shore forms of sea life, the climatologist Brewer discussed the weather and ocean currents of the Alaska coast, and Charles Keeler did an hour on the coloration of local birds. Expedition photographers processed their film in a darkroom specially installed on the ship, and showed slides every evening of the day's events: Mr. Harriman bagging a Kodiak Bear, or the young Fred Dellenbaugh carrying the weary, sixty-two-year-old Burroughs on his back across a rushing, knee-deep creek of chill arctic waters. As is evidenced by his clog dance and a lecture he gave on the wildflowers of the Alaska coast, Burroughs did his best to be sociable. He tried to be a regular part of the evening entertainments. But there were nights when he wished he were home. "The company is a fine one but I do not mix easily with a lot of men," he wrote to a young friend. "Women like me better than men do, and understand me better. Men are worldly and seldom dreamers, as I am. I like Gifford, the artist, and two or three others, best; we affiliate; we love things."[9]

It was a white man's mission, this trip of Harriman and his crew: a trip to document the natural history of a conquered land and to collect the totem poles, burial garments, and other artifacts of a decimated ancient culture. During the first week of June they visited Metlakahtla, the Indian mission settlement on Annette Island. Here, wrote Burroughs, they found "one of the best object lessons to be found on the coast, showing what can be done with the Alaska Indians." One hundred frame houses surrounded a large, imposing wooden church, a schoolhouse, a town hall, and a vast canning plant where seven or eight hundred Tlinkit Indians, formerly fishermen and hunters, worked. The Indians, said Burroughs, had been brought "from a low state of savagery to a really fair state of industrial civilization" by William Duncan, a Scottish missionary who had founded the town twelve years before. Burroughs visited the paternalistic Duncan at his house where the preacher explained how he supervised the business enterprise of the canning plant, served as mediator in all local disputes, and was leading the program to make sure the natives abandoned their native tongue—which Burroughs called "a vague, guttural, featureless sort of language." Fred Dellenbaugh, who accompanied Burroughs on the call to Duncan, argued with Duncan that the tribal language should be preserved, at least until some linguist was able to document its vocabulary and syntax. "Document it quickly then," retorted Duncan, "for it has never brought them anything but barbarity and Godlessness and I would have it die right here and now."

Duncan had the tribal leaders bring Grinnel, Dellenbaugh, Harriman, and Burroughs to what the disapproving Dellenbaugh called "a barren, wasted place" a kilometer or more away from the very last of the houses. Here lay the remains of the Indians' last traditional village: the place where they'd been camped when Duncan found them. Forgotten, unrepaired totems leaned this way and that in silhouette against the afternoon sky. The doors of abandoned ceremonial huts flapped in the wind, revealing intricately sewn blankets and garments stacked haphazardly inside. Beautifully carved wooden canoes lay piled one upon the other, protruding from under a mound of snow. "They had left their culture to rot in that spot of woods," Dellenbaugh remembered. "They had dumped it all right there where Duncan told them to leave it—the heritage of a thousand years."

Harriman bought most of the totems, blankets, clothing, and huts from Duncan for a few hundred dollars. The Indians helped to knock down the huts and carry the totems that were then packed away securely in the hull of the *Elder*. Burroughs wrote condescendingly in his journal of the "childish" enthusiasm with which the smiling Indians went about the task. Commenting on the character of the natives, he noted that they compared "favorably" with the "more quarrelsome" plains Indians, who "did not know how to adapt." The Alaskan Indian, wrote Burroughs, "takes more kindly to our ways and customs and to our various manual industries." Something Burroughs failed to notice, or at least to mention, was that the Alaskan Indian had also taken to the white man's taste for liquor. The Tlinkit men poured out of the canning plant at the end of the day, their cash pay in hand, and walked directly to the row of taverns that lay across the muddy street. Reverend Duncan had brought more than just Christianity and modern commerce to Metlakahtla.

Below Haenke Island, north of the Russell Fjord, the expedition came upon an encampment of Tlinkit Indians who still lived in the way handed down to them by their fathers. This tribe lived in tents and bark huts. They hunted the hair seal amid the drifting icebergs cast off by the Turner and Hubbard glaciers. This was their summer camp. They were laying in a supply of skins and oil against their winter needs. The beach by their huts was redolent with seal oil. The dead carcasses of the seals lay in rows upon the pebbles in front of the huts. The woman and girls skinned the seals, cutting out the blubber and drying it in pots over smouldering fires. "The Indian women frowned upon our photographers, and were very averse to having the cameras pointed at them," wrote Burroughs. "It took a good deal of watching and waiting and maneuvering to get a good shot. The artists, with their brushes and canvases, were regarded with less suspicion." Dellenbaugh commented to Burroughs that he doubted Duncan's Indians back at Metlakahtla, laboring all day indoors at the canning plant as they did, had as healthy an existence as did the Tlinkits out here who had kept to the old tribal ways.

It is a telling fact that in Burroughs's journal, as well as his final published account, he seems to have been far more interested in the landscape of Alaska than in the native peoples who populated it. In his memoir of the journey entitled "In Green Alaska," the Alaskan Indians received about four pages of discussion out of more than one hundred total pages of text. The native residents of the territory were far less important to him than the glaciers, mountains, and other magnificent displays of nature.

Perhaps the one element of scenery that struck him the most was the Muir Glacier. He was to call it the most outstanding spectacle to be found anywhere upon the continent. It was, he would write, "savagely majestic" with its crumbling wall of ice two hundred and fifty feet high stretching across the full mouth of the inlet, the foot of the wall choked with ancient icebergs. Burroughs was also much taken with the glaciers of the Gustavus Peninsula, which is now a part of the Glacier Bay National Park. Today the place is very much as Burroughs and his companions found it: the perfect spot at which to witness what Burroughs called the "terrible labor throes" of the glaciers as huge sections of ice "calve" off them into the sea. The Harriman Expedition scientists came to the conclusion that this was a relatively recent deposit of glaciers, not much more than a century old. The botanists found a first generation growth of trees, none of them over forty years old. Far up the mountainside at a height of about 2000 feet they came to the limit of the younger growth and struck a well-defined line of much older trees. This seemed to suggest that within the previous hundred years an ice sheet 2000 or more feet thick, and older and larger than the Muir Glacier, had swept down the valley and destroyed the forests.

"We saw world-shaping forces at work; we scrambled over plains they [the glaciers] had built but yesterday," he wrote. "We saw them transport enormous rocks, and tons on tons of soil and debris from the distant mountains; we saw the remains of extensive forests they had engulfed probably within the century, and were now uncovering again; we saw their turbid rushing streams loaded with newly ground rocks and soil-making material; we saw the beginnings of vegetation in the tracks of the retreating glaciers." Daily they witnessed the formation of the low mounds, ridges, and bowl-shaped depressions that would come in time to form the diverse landscape of the new-made land—all the while with the muffled thunder of the falling bergs in their ears. "Here, with this violence, is how God builds his world," Burroughs told his journal.[10]

High, huge rocks—granite-ribbed and snow-crowned—towered high above the *Elder* on both sides of the Gustavus Peninsula inlet. One day at the peninsula Burroughs took off on his own and climbed to the shoulder of a huge granite ridge on the west, against which the glacier pressed and over which it broke. Huge masses of ice had recently toppled over, and a great piece of rock hung on the very edge. Windrows of soil and gravel and boulders were clinging to the margin of the ice. All was poised on the brink of dramatic shift. But as Burroughs watched, not a pebble fell. "All was silence and inertia," he wrote. "And I could look down between the glacier and the polished mountain side; they were not in contact; the hand of the sculptor was raised as it were, but he did not strike while I was around; in front of me upon the glacier for many miles was a perfect wilderness of crevasses, the ice was ridged and contorted like an angry sea, but not a sound, not a movement anywhere."

The expedition ended when the *Elder* dropped anchor at Safety Cove in Puget Sound on July 28. Burroughs was back home on August 9. "I found . . . that the bottom had not dropped out of things during my absence," he wrote Muir in early September. "Indeed, I am beginning to suspect that the sun would rise and set just the same, and grapes would continue to ripen, if I were to vanish for good and all." [11] Julian had been there to help oversee the farm. Burroughs wrote Benton that he felt "delightfully dispensable."

Burroughs dedicated most of the autumn of 1899 to the writing of the account of the expedition that he had promised Harriman. "I am over here at Slabsides," he wrote in November to Julian, who had returned to Harvard. "I keep pretty well and am working on my Alaska trip—have written about 10,000 words. The *Century* paid me $75 for two poems [two of three poems written during the Alaska trip]—three times as much as Milton got for *Paradise Lost*. The third poem I shall weave into the prose sketch. The *N. Y. World* sent a man up to see me a couple of weeks ago to get me to write 6 or 7 hundreds words for their Sunday Edition. They wanted me to write on the Thanksgiving Turkey! Offered me $50—they wanted it in two days. Of course, I could not do it off hand in that way. So I fished out of my drawer an old MS of about 1000 words that I had rejected and sent that. They used it and paid me $30. It was in the *Sunday World* of November 19." [12]

He was spending much time at Slabsides, though not sleeping there regularly. The cabin had become a retreat for writing. "I have just come over to Slabsides, have built a big fire, and am writing you in front of the leaping flame," he wrote in December to Clara Reed, a Vassar student who had been to visit him with her classmates the previous September.

You have never seen my open fire. It is a spirited affair, and puts a new face on things in a twinkling. Then, you know, I cut my own wood, and so have relations with it from the stump. I built the chimney also, and that improves the draught. I bake my potatoes in the ashes, and broil my chops over the coals, and that makes us still better acquainted. An open wood fire ventilates the mind as well as the room. All my blue devils go up the chimney with the smoke . . . One wants about the same virtues in an open fire that he does in his friend—warmth, glow, music, but not too much pyrotechnic. I dislike the butternut people who, under the heat of conversation, snap and bang all the time . . . But how I am running on about this fire! [13]

When Julian returned from Harvard to spend Christmas with his parents, Burroughs was still at work on his chronicle of the Alaskan trip. The father interrupted his work on New Year's Eve, the last day before the cusp of the new century, to tromp through the woods above Black Creek with Julian. That evening, as the two sat warming their feet by the fire in the study at Riverby, Burroughs made a fitting note in his journal with which to begin a new era. "To be remembered in art or literature, or in almost anything else, you must do something unique, and that no one else could do," he wrote as Julian stoked the hemlock coals of the fire. "The secret of your power lies in the breadth of your relation to mankind and to common nature; in the richness and fullness of your human endowment. But immortality is the result of something above and beyond all this; something which is your own, and must suffuse and color and shape all the rest. The universal and the special, the general and the particular, must be blended and harmonized." [14]

13

ENTER
CLARA BARRUS

*You see what my peculiarity, maybe weakness, is—I idealize everything. The
thought of a thing after it is past is more to me than the thing itself.*

— *Burroughs to Clara Barrus,*
June 12, 1902

BURROUGHS WAS BUSILY AT WORK on his 1902 book, *Literary Values,*
when, in September of 1901, he made the acquaintance of Clara
Barrus, a physician associated with the state psychiatric hospital at
Middletown, New York. She was thirty-three years of age and unmarried. She was also slim, short, brunette, and extremely bright.

The two had exchanged several letters through the summer.
Their correspondence had begun in May with a sugarcoated fan
letter from Barrus. "I never before yielded to an impulse to write to
an author, but tonight it seems less like an intrusion—more like a
paltry payment on a long-standing debt. Will you take it as such?"
she wrote. "When the dandelions laugh at you in the grass, and the
meadowlarks call, and the orioles sing, 'Will you, will you really,
truly,' remember that one of your grateful readers is, through these
messengers, thanking you better than she can herself?" [1] Luckily for
Barrus, Burroughs was in the habit of answering all his mail, and he
promptly responded to her note. "Full of self-criticism and self-
dissatisfaction as I am, letters like yours of the 12th always make me
a little more tolerant of myself," he wrote in what was something of
a standard, though certainly sincere, letter sent to all anonymous

admirers, "I thank you for your kind sympathetic words . . . The genuine responses that come to an author from his unknown readers, judging from my own experience, are always very welcome. It is no intrusion but rather an inspiration." [2]

He probably did not expect to hear from her again, but he did. Several notes traveled back and forth: more praise from Barrus, more modest thank-yous from Burroughs. Finally there came to Barrus just what she was fishing for: an invitation to visit Burroughs at his cabin.

On an appointed September morning, Barrus arrived in West Park by train. Burroughs was there waiting for her, anticipating what he thought would be just another day at Slabsides shared with a devoted reader of the type he often tried to make himself available to. As usual, there was no mention of going to Riverby. As soon as he had checked to make sure that the young lady was well shod for the steep walk over the mountain to the cabin, they began the hike. He walked briskly with an agility that belied his years. On the way up the mountain, he pointed out the section of the woods that he had named "mount Hymettus" in his essay "An Idyll of the Honey-Bee." When Barrus asked if there were still bee trees there, he confirmed that there were but then dashed her hopes when he did not propose an excursion to collect some of the sweet nectar. Instead he wearily commented, "Yes, wild honey is delectable—I pursued that subject till I sucked it dry."

At Slabsides, the two spoke of the usual subjects: Whitman, birds, Emerson. When they eventually got round to talking about Barrus's work with psychiatric patients, the otherwise gentle Burroughs surprised Barrus by angrily declaring that President McKinley's assassin should be hung, whether insane or not. Burroughs further puzzled Barrus when he asked whether she did not think it a wasteful expenditure to try and salvage such "human derelicts" as were found in most asylum halls. Burroughs boiled a chicken. After they were done eating he escorted her down the mountain to catch the train back to Middletown. He promised that he would see her again soon.

At the time Barrus met him, Burroughs was sixty-four and in robust health. His frame was strong, his carriage erect. "His large,

superbly formed head, when uncovered, was his distinguishing fea-
ture," wrote Barrus admiringly. He had a full head of white hair
which he wore a trifle long and that curled softly at the neck.
Sideburns wound into the solid white mustache and the ample,
wavy beard. His deep-set, blue-gray eyes, with flecks of brown in the
iris, Barrus described as "young eyes, eyes that seemed to bear on as
they looked." His skin, she wrote, was "fair pink, healthy, and fine-
grained." In fact, she said, his "whole physiology showed fineness of
texture and organization." Years later, she would write of how she
had been taken by the sight of his sturdy back and shoulders, his
broad chest, his well-knit wrists, and the hands that were "brown,
firm, well-shaped, and unpliable, showing long familiarity with
manual work in the open." Barrus found him infinitely intriguing
and attractive, as he did her. [3]

Just a few days after Barrus's first visit to him, he wrote to her,
addressing her as "Little Sister" and signing himself "With much
love." By December, after several trips by Barrus to Slabsides, the
relationship had ripened into an affair. He spent much time with
her in Middletown, and sent roses when he could not manage a visit.
"How nicely you have feathered your nest, and what a charming
nest!" he wrote her after one excursion. "Mine seems cold and barren beside it." He went on to say that he was becoming conscious of
a great loss in not having known her years before. "All the beautiful
springs and summers that are past and you not a part of them for
me." [4] His message was painfully clear. The house with separate
bedrooms that he shared with Ursula was cold and, quite literally,
barren. The nest with one bed that he shared with young Barrus in
Middletown was splendidly feathered, comfortable, joyous, free.
The previous years of his life were somehow less to him because he'd
spent them with someone other than Barrus. "If I could always be
surrounded by the gentleness and consideration you could give me,"
he wrote her, "how different my life would be." [5]

As interested as Barrus was in Burroughs as a man, she seems to
have been equally interested in positioning herself as his literary col-
laborator. Just a few months after the beginning of their relationship, Barrus volunteered to proofread the galleys for a poetry anthology he had just finished editing on commission for McLure Phillips
& Co., titled *Songs of Nature*. Burroughs detested proofreading and

copy editing. He was delighted when Barrus volunteered to take a stab at the project. He wound up being so pleased with Barrus's work that he announced a decision to send her all his proofs in the future.

Shortly thereafter he forwarded to Barrus the complete collection of his journals through the 1880s, notebooks he had nursed and cherished for years. "No one else is interested in them," he wrote Barrus in the note that accompanied the soiled, rumpled notebooks.

> I would like you to have them all when I am gone. I am truly surprised at your interest in them, but I know you would not make believe . . . [I do not] expect you to read them all—only here and there, where you get some real glimpse of me. I looked into some of them last night. They seem too sad. I seem to have put all my sunshine into the books and all my gloom into the diaries. Remember they were written for my eye alone—a sort of cemetery where I could turn and mourn over my vanished days, and vanished thoughts. [6]

In January he was again at Middletown. Barrus was reading proofs for *Literary Values,* and Burroughs was putting the finishing touches on another piece of commission work, a brief biography of Audubon for the Beacon Biography Series. Although Burroughs was an admirer of Audubon, the biography project was somewhat uninspired and definitely a "work for hire." He had accepted Beacon's proposal for pecuniary reasons, and he mechanically churned out an acceptable (though hardly noteworthy) short narrative rehashing the substance of Audubon's journals as edited and published by the artist's daughter, Maria Audubon. Barrus helped greatly with the Audubon project. As a journal note of January 13 indicates, she was becoming indispensable in more ways than one, even though she had only known Burroughs for five months. "Work on *Literary Values* and the Audubon book. Feel unusually well," he wrote during a stay in Middletown. "Dr. Barrus, at the Hospital, more than kind—helps me with much proof; type-writes the *Audubon.* A very keen, appreciative mind, of more ready service to me than any woman I ever met. Would like to write my life. I should like her to do it, if it is ever done—have named her my literary executor—the most companionable woman I have yet met in this world—reads and delights in the same books I do—a sort of feminine counterpart of myself." [7]

Burroughs viewed Barrus as the antithesis of Ursula. She was, in Burroughs's parlance, "Whitmanesque." She was a "new woman" who had the capacity to be his true emotional and intellectual equal. She was somewhat like Ursula in that she was jealous and possessive. However, unlike Ursula, Barrus was to be not merely possessive of Burroughs the man but also of his fame. The renown that Ursula disparaged and thought unimportant, Barrus in turn thought more important than anything else about him. Already, five months into their relationship, she had made sure she was designated both his literary executor and his authorized biographer. Already, on Burroughs's regular trips to Middletown, he routinely carried valises packed with invaluable letters, manuscripts, and memoranda from his days with Whitman in Washington, and from other important periods of his life. These Barrus would keep to herself until long after Burroughs's death. Even Julian Burroughs, in putting together a short memoir of his father in 1922, would not have access to the papers.

On February 15, 1902, Burroughs sailed with Julian for a few weeks on the island of Jamaica—a trip paid for by the Hearst organization in return for an article about the island. He left Barrus in charge of seeing the Audubon book through press. It would be the only book he would ever dedicate to anyone, and he would cryptically dedicate it to Barrus, as "C. B." A short while later, when writing out a copy of his poem "Waiting" for Barrus, he added a verse that he told her was to be hers alone, and that he did not include in subsequent reprints of the poem.

> The law of love binds every heart,
> And knits it to its utmost kin;
> Our lives cannot flow long apart
> From souls our secret souls would win.

In *Literary Values* BURROUGHS picked up the threads of thought from many of his magazine articles since the completion of the

Whitman book in 1896. One of his finest moments as a writer on literature, *Literary Values* focused on contemporary trends in criticism, and on the issue of genuineness in both criticism and art. William Dean Howells had recently published *Criticism and Fiction*, in which he said that the critic's job was merely to "classify and analyze the fruits of the human mind as a naturalist classifies the objects of his study, rather than to praise or to blame them." Criticism, according to Howells, should limit itself to description and interpretation, and not endeavor to estimate the relative or absolute quality of a work of art. In Howells's view, the critic had no more business to condemn an unappealing poem, novel, or essay than did the botanist to trample a plant because he did not find it pretty.

Tackling this question in an essay titled "Criticism and the Man," Burroughs acknowledged that to classify and analyze the fruit of the human mind was certainly one function of criticism, but only one. Art had a direct relation to life. The critic, therefore, was honor bound to consider how true and how important these relations were in a given work. The critic was examining a human product, not a natural phenomenon, and should feel free to accept or reject after comparing, weighing, and appraising. Burroughs called false Howells's analogy between literary criticism and the pursuit of natural science. All products of nature had an inherent, self-defining perfection. There could be no judgment as to the fineness of one bird over another, no "best" chosen from among wildflowers. But all things of the hand of man—be they literature, architecture, theories of science, or modes of religious thought—could and should be appraised on their merits and demerits, and graded against the best that had yet been thought and done in the world.

From this definition of the role of the critic, Burroughs went on to make a case for critical literature that was itself art. The best criticism, wrote Burroughs, was that which was infused with the heartfelt emotion and concern of the critic himself. Burroughs sought criticism that rose organically from the author's passions, affections, and biases, criticism that was much more than just a dry scholarly summing up. He craved the full mind of the critic. The most interesting and meaningful considerations went beyond mere intellect and portrayed something of the living, breathing man behind the point-of-view. "In many of the authors of whom Sainte-Beuve writes I have no interest, but I am always interested in Sainte-Beuve's view of them," wrote Burroughs. "Criticism that warms and interests is perpetual creation, as Sainte-Beuve suggested. It is a constant combination of the subject with the thought of the critic. When Mr. [Henry] James writes upon Sainte-Beuve we are under his spell; it is Mr. James that absorbs and delights us now. We get the truth about his subject, of course, but it is always in combination with the truth about Mr. James."

Saying that it is not truth alone that makes literature, but truth plus a man, Burroughs suggested that while one might not care for Carlyle's literary judgments, one was still affected by his quality of mind and flashes of insight as well as his "burden" of conscience, power of portraiture, and "heroic moral fiber." Likewise, if readers were to estimate Ruskin by the soundness of his judgments alone, they should miss the important part of him that, as well as being a critic of art, was also a prophet of a way of life.

Clearly, what attracted Burroughs to the likes of Carlyle, Ruskin, Emerson, and Thoreau was the deeply personal way in which they looked at all topics falling under their scrutiny. In "Style and the Man" Burroughs stated his preference plainly, and at the same time enunciated the standard to which he made his own nature writing and criticism adhere. "All pure literature is the revelation of a man," he wrote. "In a work of true literary art the subject matter has been so interpenetrated and vitalized by the spirit or personality of the writer, he has become so thoroughly identified with it, that the two are inseparable."

As a corollary to this line of thinking, it was obvious that true, total communication from author to reader demanded an unstudied style that was itself a purely natural extension of the author's intellect. Throughout the papers "Style and the Man" and "Literary Values" Burroughs made no bones about his displeasure with "wordsmiths." He was unimpressed by writers who showed off with an endless vocabulary and intricate verbal somersaults. In Burroughs's estimation, well-honed literary craftsmanship was not something to be prized in and of itself. Rather, Burroughs valued the sincere over the skilled craftsman. He praised the man who picked up his pen solely for the sake of communicating a point-of-view uniquely struck from the roots of his own feelings, knowledge, and meditation. The best and only worthwhile style flowed from honesty; and it offered something rarer and finer than mere studied eloquence.

"Indeed," wrote Burroughs, "perfect workmanship is one thing; style, as the great writers have it, is quite another. It [good style] may, and often does, go with faulty workmanship." The memoirs of Ulysses S. Grant were a case in point. By simply telling his story in unassuming, conversational prose, the unliterary Grant achieved something wonderfully rich in his first and last attempt at authoring. Burroughs railed against the writer who appeared to wield his language "as an instrument or a tool, something exterior to himself." He did not want to be conscious of a writer's vocabulary in such a way as one got a sense that words were "the garments and not the tissue of his thought."

It is not surprising that the specter of Whitman loomed large through the various essays in *Literary Values*. The poet's ghost was especially present when Burroughs lighted on the topic "Recent Phases of Literary Criticism." In this essay, Burroughs continued the strain of thought which had begun with his earlier reflections on the poetry of Whitman, the economics of Henry Demarest Lloyd, and America's emerging industrial state. Burroughs picked up the flag of those who said that criticism was divided into two schools: the aristocratic and the democratic. The aristocrat cared little for reality in poems or stories. Surface beauty was paramount. The democrat, on the other hand, demanded reality. Even in its most brutish forms, the actual physical world held the only actual beauty there could ever be. "So far as good taste means 'good form,' and so far as good form is established by social and conventional usages of the fashionable world, the poet of democracy has little to do with it," wrote Burroughs in *Literary Values*.

In a related paper, "Democracy and Literature," Burroughs argued with opinions Sir Edmund Gosse expressed in his *Questions at Issue* (1893). Despite the fact that Gosse had earlier gone on record as being an admirer of Whitman, in his 1893 book he wrote that "democracy in literature" represented nothing better than an incursion of the loud, the vulgar, and the cheap and meretricious. "The aristocratic tradition," wrote Gosse, "is still paramount in all art. Kings, princesses, and the symbols of chivalry are as essential to poetry, as we now conceive it, as roses, stars, or nightingales." Sir Edmund said that nothing but a great poverty would be left once this romantic tradition was done away with. In response, Burroughs wryly pointed out a few of the things that could be counted upon to endure after aristocratic cliché had vanished. "We shall certainly have left what we had before these types and symbols came into vogue," wrote Burroughs, these being nature, life, man, and God.

NEARLY THIRTY YEARS BEFORE, Burroughs had spent long, happy days digging out stone for the house he was building at Riverby. Now, in the spring of 1902, he occupied himself even more joyously in a similar pursuit. Accepting Burroughs's invitation to return to the farm and manage it, Julian was building his own home on the brink of the hill overlooking the vineyard, several hundred yards to the north of his mother and father's place. The wedding of Julian Burroughs and Emily Mackay, a young lady whom he had met in Cambridge, was to be on September 25.

By the end of March, the cellar was completely dug, and the masons were due to start laying foundation walls. Very pleased at the prospect of having his son decide to stay by him and make a life at Riverby, Burroughs made a momentous decision. "I have made up my mind to give Julian a deed on my Riverby property, and have done with it," wrote Burroughs to Barrus. "I shall have Slabsides left, and all my books . . . and I need no more." [8] Burroughs also retained title to the stone house and the study at Riverby, but signed over all the remaining acreage to his son as a wedding present.

Julian accepted the gift with no small amount of trepidation. He had many other intriguing options. A local Boston paper had offered him a position as a sports writer and photographer. Several of his Harvard professors had urged him to become an architectural apprentice, believing he had more than enough talent to pursue a career in that field. His classmate Raymond T. Bond was heading for New York City, where he meant to make a name for himself in book publishing. He urged Julian to follow. They could share rooms to save money and work together to found their fortunes in the book business. All of these interesting possibilities were more than counterbalanced by the unspoken but nevertheless obvious opinion of his parents that their lives would be the less if he did not return to them.

Like his father, Julian was reticent and easily swayed by pressure, especially when the pressure was applied by the two single most important figures he had known. Now he was stuck. He really couldn't do anything but come back to Riverby. He knew that he was still the one vital link between his parents. He knew that without his presence Riverby would be unlivable for either of them. There were to be many times in the coming decades when he would deeply regret what he came to see as his surrender in returning to Riverby after Harvard. There would be many days when he would speculate on other paths he might have taken.

Julian designed the new house himself. In doing so, he used the uncomfortable, inconvenient, and inefficient home his father built thirty years before as a reverse model. The stone house had been set into a hillside with many flights of stairs, numerous halls, and few windows. It was damp in summer, cold in winter. Julian had not forgotten that as a boy, when studying in his room in the stone house during winter, he had routinely worn a hat, coat, and gloves to keep himself warm. Now, as Julian drew the plans for his new home, he made sure to design something more livable. He created a house that sat well above the ground, and got plenty of sun and air from large, strategically placed windows. He did not build with stone, but with a wood frame covered by butternut, oak, and chestnut slabs. He covered the gable ends with hemlock shingles that would age to a rich red russett.

Julian's father threw himself wholeheartedly into the construction. ". . . have walked eight or nine miles today, looking up lumber for Julian's house, part of the way through woods and across swamps (I have just been drying my feet by the open fire)," he wrote Barrus on March 31. He dedicated his sixty-fifth birthday to manual labor on the project. "I spent the day with Ed, my nephew, digging out stone for Julian's house," he wrote Barrus. "I have enjoyed it much. I am always happy in spring digging out rocks and stones to build something with." [9]

The joy Burroughs took in the raising of Julian's new walls was tempered by tragedy. On May 7, Hiram showed up at Riverby. He was plainly not well, but had not been to see a doctor. Burroughs took him to one at nearby Rondout. A cancerous condition in the bowels, complicated by a hernia, was diagnosed. Hiram passed a bad night on the 8th; ". . . he thought he was going to die, as did I," Burroughs wrote. "He has lost his grip on life. I fear to have him leave me." [10] Within weeks Hiram died at the house of their brother Eden. "He had been around on Sunday as usual, and at nine had taken his lamp and gone to bed," wrote Burroughs, "and there his journey in the world had ended. He had said to Eden during the day that he should never take care of any more bees, and had told Bruce to take good care of his tools. He seemed to feel that his end was near." [11]

Hiram was buried at Hobart in the Catskills on the thirteenth. The next day, John and Eden returned to the grave.

> After breakfast Eden and I went down to the grave. The coverlid of the turf was already pulled over dear Hiram. We stood long by his grave. A finer locality for a village cemetery I never saw. A large, gentle, gravelly knoll, with the clear brook sweeping around its base on the one side, beyond which is a beautiful rolling landscape with its green hills, its grazing herds, its dark patches of pine woods, and then the encircling mountains, still brown and leafless. I almost envy Hiram his last resting place. [12]

Hiram, who was Julian's favorite uncle, was missed that September at Julian's wedding. The wedding took place at Keene Heights, now called St. Hubert's, in the Adirondacks. "Emily's grandfather (eighty tomorrow) officiating—pretty affecting sight," wrote Burroughs in his journal. "With what long sad thoughts I witnessed it all! Age and youth, face to face, under such significant conditions— the evening greeting and encouraging the morning, the fall congratulating the spring. My father and mother were married over seventy-five years ago; I was married over forty-five years ago; and now Julian and Emily begin the same journey together." [13] After a brief honeymoon, the couple arrived at Riverby on September 30 to begin housekeeping. "Julian and Emily unpacking and gleeing over their china, cut glass, silver, checks, etc.," Burroughs wrote. "Happy couple! When I was married our presents did not amount to one toothpick." [14]

Reflections on the ebb and flow of life, and the ongoing chain of human lives and losses, were compounded by the death of Myron Benton on November 25. The loss of Benton was a profound one. "He was one of the few farmers of real culture—a man of fine literary tastes, but a born countryman and lover of the soil," wrote Burroughs in his journal on the evening of Benton's death. "Tall, quiet, canny, lingering over the flavor of things, dwelling upon the quaint, the beautiful, the picturesque, fervently attached to his old home, always adding something to its beauty . . . gentle, genial, mellow, unobtrusive; his own native, meandering Webatuck in human form." [15] Burroughs told Julian that after Whitman's death, the other deaths he had most felt the full force of were those of Benton, Emerson, his father and mother, and Hiram. "All deaths of friends and kin weigh on one, but those deaths were the hardest. Those deaths left the biggest voids for me."

Burroughs brought Barrus with him to Benton's funeral at Troutbeck on November 27. She had never met Benton. He introduced her to Myron's brother Charles as his "literary assistant." Charles Benton, who like Myron and their cousin Joel Benton was a writer, would remember that Barrus made a poor first impression. He did not like the way she behaved when viewing the corpse, which lay in a coffin in the middle of the living room at Troutbeck. "She stared at Myron in his casket with a fervent curiosity that was repulsive: as though he were some sort of objet d'art of which she had heard tell for decades and for which she had waited on a line for hours in the rain to get a glimpse of. She seemed a little too pleased to be a part of the occasion." There was, wrote Benton in a letter to Richard Watson Gilder, an element of "hunger" about Barrus. She had, he wrote, an insatiable desire for any ghost, manuscript, letter, or corpse that lingered from the personal history of John Burroughs. She did not give the impression of having an identity, personality, or past of her own, so intent was she on absorbing and controlling those of Burroughs. She announced to Charles at some point during the day that she had been named by Burroughs as his authorized biographer, "and on that authority began to 'grill' me," complained Benton to Gilder.

"The dirt was not fully in Myron's grave but she was asking me, in the coach going back to the house, about the letters—all of John's letters to Myron—and what our plans were for them," recalled Benton. Somewhat irritably, Benton told Barrus the the letters would be John's now, of course, to do with as he pleased. "Then she started to mention the Thoreau letter, but John cut her off and turned the conversation back to the topic of his friend and my brother, who we had just seen buried." [16] Once they'd returned to Troutbeck from the gravesite, Barrus urged a hike to Mulberry Rock, which she was anxious to see. The excursion did not come off. "I will bring you back there on another, happier day," Burroughs wrote her somewhat apologetically a week later, "and show you the spot where Myron and I spent the day we met. I do want to share everything about and of myself with you, you know." [17]

14

THE NATURE FAKERS
& ROOSEVELT

To treat your facts with imagination is one thing, to imagine your facts is quite another.

—*Journal Entry, October 24, 1907*

IN MID-MARCH OF 1903, Burroughs received a handsomely engraved invitation to a dinner Andrew Carnegie was giving at his Manhattan home to honor Sidney Lee, the British Shakespearean scholar. Carnegie had little idea who Lee was, but the men whom he paid to advise him on such matters assured him that many of the best writers in the country could be coaxed to a table if they knew it was being assembled to honor Lee. Carnegie liked to associate with writers. He fancied the idea of being the benefactor of a literary salon that would have his Fifth Avenue home as its hub. Through dinners such as the one for Lee, Carnegie used his wealth to draw around him those authors he most admired.

According to his journals, part of the reason why Burroughs made a point of trying to be on hand for this and other of Carnegie's parties was that he remembered how kind Carnegie had been to Whitman during the last years of the poet's life. (Carnegie had not given charity outright to the destitute Whitman, but he had made a point of buying conspicuous quantities of the final edition of *Leaves of Grass*, and of making sure the poet's last public readings were all "sold out" even though they might have been ill-attended.) One also senses, however, that Burroughs was a regular participant in Carnegie's entertainments simply because he liked to associate with men of wealth and power. This had been Burroughs's chief fascination with E. H. Harriman. Now another ruler of the world beckoned and Burroughs ran to the call.

Some other writers who were occasionally invited to Carnegie's feasts objected to the idea of literary artists serving as instruments for the personal amusement of a millionaire. Hamlin Garland was particularly disgruntled by the fact that "money could command genius and genius would obey." Garland posed a question in his diary that went to the heart of the issue: By what authority besides that of the dollar did the iron merchant Carnegie bring these men of arts and letters to his palace? At the March party for Sydney Lee—where Gilder, William Dean Howells, and other literary luminaries were present—Garland whispered to Burroughs his candid belief that the unliterary Carnegie without all his millions "would not interest any of us."

Burroughs's journal note on the event records only "a fine evening at Andrew Carnegie's—Mrs. Carnegie very charming." Garland used his diary to note the evening's ostentatious program with dismay: The guests were led by a group of Scotch pipers into the dining room. Carnegie himself served as toastmaster. His introductions, which he read from little cards handed to him one at a time by a butler, had obviously been prepared for him. Garland wrote that Carnegie was plainly in "a false position . . . it was clearly evident that he would have been helpless without the actual text of his commendation."

The responses by Carnegie's guests were, according to Garland, "able and tactful." Indeed, this was just the kind of literary commerce Garland would have reveled in had it not been for a persistent sense of his host's helplessness. As each man rose to speak for the entertainment of all, but most especially the entertainment of Carnegie, Garland realized his own remarks would be the fee he had to pay to partake of the feast. Carnegie was to provide the place and the bread; his guests were to supply the entertainment. At another Carnegie dinner a few months later, Garland refused to speak. Later in the evening Garland told Burroughs, "I shall accept no more of these invitations." To this Burroughs replied, "You may not have another." And indeed, Garland did not. Burroughs, on the other hand, would be asked to return again and again and would always cheerfully pay for his supper with a generous portion of after-dinner remarks. [1]

NEARLY TWENTY-FIVE YEARS before, Burroughs had published the essay "Nature and the Poets" in the *Scribner's Monthly* of December 1879. In that essay he'd criticized a number of the country's leading poets for inaccurately depicting nature in their verse. A few weeks after publication of the essay, he was chagrined to find himself sitting at the same table as several of the writers he had commented on in his paper. The occasion was Oliver Wendell Holmes's birthday breakfast in Boston: the same gathering at which he saw and spoke to Emerson for the last time. His "victims" as he'd called them in a letter to Whitman, among whom was John Greenleaf Whittier, were all gracious to the somewhat embarrassed Burroughs. At the Sydney Lee party, Burroughs suffered a similar embarrassment. He was tense and uncomfortable the moment he discovered the name of the young man with the expectant, somehow sad face who stood shaking his hand. It was someone he hadn't expected to bump into here: the naturalist and writer Ernest Thompson Seton. Another victim, and, as luck would have it, another gracious one.

Burroughs had issued a stinging criticism of Seton in an essay published by the *Atlantic Monthly* just a few weeks earlier. The complaint that Burroughs had lodged against Seton was that he often misrepresented the facts of nature for the sake of literary affect. In the course of the evening at Carnegie's, Seton never mentioned Burroughs's attack on him in the *Atlantic* essay entitled "Real and Sham Natural History." Instead he spoke of his own admiration for Burroughs's books, how he had grown up with them, and how Burroughs had helped shape his ambition to become a naturalist and a writer. In the end, Seton wound up greatly impressing the older writer with his grace and wit. "He behaved finely and asked to sit next to me at dinner," wrote Burroughs to his son. "He quite won my heart." [2]

Seton's *Wild Animals I Have Known* was populated by a host of beasts who routinely accomplished fantastic feats of wit. A cunning fox deliberately lured the hounds at his heels to a trestle where he "knew" they would meet and be killed by a passing train. "The presumption," wrote Burroughs in his *Atlantic Monthly* essay, "is that the fox had a watch and a time-table about his person." In a more melodramatic tale, a mother fox went to a farmhouse at night to rescue her youngster who had been captured by the evil human inhabitants of the farm. Unable to free him from his chains, she gave her child poison by which to deliver himself from the hand of man through suicide. "Suicide?" wrote Burroughs to Garland. "Do foxes really think to imagine the idea of suicide when they have not first grasped the concept of life as separate from death? Suicide? Why, first they've got to figure out that they are alive." [3]

> Mr. Seton says in capital letters that his stories are true, and it is this emphatic assertion that makes the judicious grieve. True as romance, true in their artistic effects, true in the power to entertain the young reader, they certainly are; but true as natural history they certainly are not. Are we to believe that Mr. Seton, in his few years of roaming the West, has penetrated farther into the secrets of animal life than all the observers who have gone before him? There are no stories of animal intelligence and cunning on record, that I am aware of, that match his. Gilbert White, Charles St. John, Waterton, Wallace, Darwin, Jefferies, and others in England,—all expert students and observers; Bates in South America, Audubon roaming the whole country, Thoreau in New England, John Muir in the mountains of California and in the wilds of Alaska have nothing to report that comes within gunshot of what appear to be Mr. Seton's daily experiences. Such dogs, wolves, foxes, rabbits, mustangs, crows, as he has known, it is safe to say, no other person in the world has ever known.

After publication of Burroughs's "Real and Sham" paper, President Theodore Roosevelt wrote to Seton to urge him to stick to genuine, observed animal behavior and to clearly document any and all statements he made in the future with relation to wildlife. "Burroughs and the people at large don't know how many facts you have back of your stories," wrote Roosevelt to Seton. "You must publish your facts." [4] At the same time Roosevelt also sent a letter to Burroughs. "I was delighted with your *Atlantic Monthly* article," wrote Roosevelt. He went on to say that he had "long wished that something of the kind should be written. The fashion of the books you are criticizing was of course set in Kipling's jungle stories, but equally of course the latter are frankly fairy tales, and so they can do only good . . . But when the people like those you criticize solemnly assert that they are relating exact facts they do positive harm." [5]

Seton took Roosevelt's advice to heart. He discontinued his light, quasi-factual animal story books. Instead he focused on comprehensive scientific works, and began to produce such classics as *Life Histories of Northern Animals* and *Lives of Game Animals*. Shortly after their meeting at the Carnegie dinner, when Burroughs visited Seton at his New York apartment, he was intrigued and gratified to find the bookshelves packed with an extensive collection of sketches, measurements, and records stained with the mud and blood of the field. In a letter to Garland, Burroughs eventually granted that young Seton was indeed, despite his "unfortunate lapse" in *Wild Animals I Have Known*, a serious and dedicated field naturalist. After Burroughs's death, Seton's *Lives of Game Animals* would become one of the first books to receive the John Burroughs Medal for excellence in nature writing.

Another target of Burroughs's "Real and Sham" article was Reverend William J. Long. Long was a graduate of Harvard (1892) and Andover Theological Seminary. He also held M.A. and Ph.D. degrees in Divinity from Heidelberg University, and had studied at the Universities of Paris and Rome. In 1903, when Burroughs first raised his name in "Real and Sham Natural History," Long was pastor of the First Congregational Church in Stamford, Connecticut, and the author of three popular children's books: *Ways of the Wood Folk*, *Fowls of the Air*, and *School of the Woods*. According to Long's introductions to his nature books, he was an intimate student of the outdoors, having gained his experience of birds and mammals through more than twenty years of roughing it in the great northern forests. He had, he said, followed the animals in all seasons of the year, sometimes alone, and at other times in the company of trappers and Indians. The knowledge of trappers, he assured his readers, "is fatal in its accuracy." He had more than once gone "fifty miles off course" to interview them.

In his *School of the Woods*, Long stated that after "many years of watching animals in their native haunts," he was unalterably convinced that instinct did not play an important role in animal development. Knowledge, wrote Long, was based purely upon training at the hands of parents. Burroughs was aghast at the statement. Animal instinct was real, obvious, and well-documented as a natural phenomenon. That it ruled the woods was a scientific fact. In his "Real and Sham" paper, Burroughs told the story of a woman who came to him not long after reading one of Long's books, saying she'd overheard a robin "teaching" its young to sing. But, countered Burroughs, among robins the young do not sing until the second year, and then only the males. "If they are taught," he asked, "why don't the females sing? Is the singing school only for boys?"

In a magazine article, Long allowed how he'd had a peep into the kingfisher's "kindergarten." He saw the old birds go fishing downstream and return with small minnows which they placed in a shallow pool near the main stream. They then brought their young to the spot and demonstrated the art of diving for shiners.

> If [Long] had said that he saw the parent birds fishing with hook and line, or dragging a net of their own knitting, his statement would have been just as credible. Why should anyone palm off such stuff on an unsuspecting public as veritable natural history? When a man, writing or speaking of his own experience, says without qualification that he has seen a thing, we are expected to take him at his word.

Long responded to the charges in Burroughs's "Real and Sham" paper with an article published in the May 1903 edition of the *North American Review*. The thrust of his defense was that animal behavior was so diverse that no man could justifiably condemn any observations made by another as false. By way of illustration, Long described his recent experience with two Baltimore orioles. The birds exhibited behavior so incredible that Long said he'd dared not print it until he had verified it with "secondary observation." According to Long, the birds were constructing a nest in a buttonwood tree and encountered difficulties, not being able to find branches sufficiently stiff and straight to support the nest. Undismayed, they flew to the ground where they found three sticks of a size, and at once tied them together in a perfect triangle. The skill they demonstrated in doing this was remarkable, for, "at each angle they fastened one end of a cord and carried the other end over making it fast to the middle of the opposite side. Then they gathered up the loops and fastened them by the middle all together, to a stout bit of marline." Their staging now completed, they flew with it into the buttonwood tree and suspended it about two feet below a stout limb, the marline being "tied once around the limb, and, to make it perfectly safe, the end being brought down and fastened to the supporting cord with a reversed double hitch, the kind that a man uses in cinching a saddle. Moreover the birds tied a single knot at the extreme end lest the marline should ravel in the wind."

In September of 1903, Long published another fantastic wildlife story in *Outlook*. In "Animal Surgery" he suggested that animals practiced "a rude kind of medicine and surgery upon themselves." To support his statement, he then went on to describe the behavior of a woodcock that, he claimed, had a broken leg and "deliberately put it into a clay cast to hold the broken bones in place until they should knit together." [6] This time Burroughs was by no means the only naturalist to come down on Long. William Morton Wheeler, Harvard's eminent entomologist, attacked Long in the February 26, 1904, issue of *Science*. "Mr. Long virtually claims that a woodcock not only has an understanding of the theory of casts as adapted to fractured limbs but is able to apply this knowledge in practice," wrote Wheeler. "The bird is represented as knowing the qualities of clay and mud, their lack of cohesion unless mixed with fibrous substances, their tendency to harden on exposure to air, and to disintegrate in water . . . But the mental horizon of Mr. Long's woodcock is not bounded by the qualities of mud. He is familiar with the theories of bone formation and regeneration—in a word, with osteogenesis, which by the way, is never clearly grasped by some of our university juniors." Frank M. Chapman, Director of the American Museum of Natural History, wrote a letter to *Science* in which he said that Long had placed on record "more remarkable statements regarding the behavior of birds and mammals of New England than can be found in all the authoritative literature pertaining to the animals of this region." [7]

Theodore Roosevelt wrote to Burroughs about "Animal Surgery," saying that he had "never read such nonsense" in his life. [8] At first, Roosevelt maintained a public silence on the debate over what came to be called "nature faking." He wrote private letters counseling Seton and encouraging Burroughs, but he made no public statements concerning the issue. This changed in the spring of 1907, when he made comments that were published in the June issue of *Everybody's Magazine*. "You will be pleased to know," wrote Roosevelt to Burroughs shortly before the magazine appeared, "that I finally proved unable to contain myself, and gave an interview or statement, to a very good fellow, in which I sailed into Long and Jack London and one or two others of the more preposterous writers of 'unnatural' history . . . I know that as President I ought not to do this; but I was having an awful time toward the end of the session and I felt I simply had to permit myself some diversion."

Reading Roosevelt's letter, Burroughs was surprised to see Jack London's name brought up. Burroughs had not mentioned London in his "Real and Sham" paper. The author of many famous wolf and dog stories of the Alaska wilderness, London had always made a point of labeling as novels such works as *The Call of the Wild* and *White Fang*. Since London said outright that his were works of fiction, and not scientific reportage, he and Burroughs had no argument. The two men had never met, but they'd exchanged some correspondence and were on good terms. They shared several common acquaintances, among them Upton Sinclair and Richard Harding Davis. Burroughs did not at this point know the thrust or context of Roosevelt's statements with regard to London, as the June 1907 issue of *Everybody's Magazine* containing the article had not yet been published. Nevertheless, Burroughs sent a preemptive note to London warning him of the Roosevelt remarks and apologizing in advance for any discomfort they might cause.

As Roosevelt was well aware, Jack London was not only one of the most popular writers of his day, but also a Socialist. Roosevelt had long disliked London's politics. Now he decided he disliked the writer's natural history almost as much. Roosevelt had recently read Jack London's *White Fang* (1906), a sequel to *The Call of the Wild* (1903). While *The Call of the Wild* showed a domesticated dog slowly returning to a state of complete, untamed nature, *White Fang* reversed the transformation and followed a wild wolf through the process of becoming a tamed servant of man.

Roosevelt charged that a wolf-dog and bulldog in *White Fang* "fought in an impossible fashion" during one of the central scenes of the book. "I can't believe that Mr. London knows much about the wolves, and I am certain he knows nothing about their fighting, or as a realist he would not tell this tale," said Roosevelt. He also argued over the likelihood of another part of the story, where he believed a lynx weighing about twenty pounds killed a much larger wolf-dog. Roosevelt complained that in "the real world" the fight would have definitely gone the other way. Roosevelt should have read the novel more carefully. London had the wolf-dog kill the lynx, not the other way around.

From a public relations point of view, the president's "diversion" was an expensive one for him with regard to Jack London. The novelist got the better end of the publicity stick when he published a reasoned, respectful, but to-the-point reply in *Colliers*. "President Roosevelt does not think a bull-dog can lick a wolf-dog," wrote London. "I think a bull-dog can lick a wolf-dog. And there we are. Difference of opinion may make, and does make, horse-racing. I can understand that difference of opinion can make dog-fighting. But what gets me is how difference of opinion regarding the relative merits of a bull-dog and a wolf-dog makes me a nature-faker and President Roosevelt a vindicated and triumphant scientist." [9]

Reverend Long did not fare as well as London, although he too responded to the attack made on him by Roosevelt in the *Everybody's* article. Roosevelt had gone after Long with an especially big stick, saying that it was a "genuine crime" that Long's books, aimed as they were at children, gave such a false impression of the ways of wildlife. There was no more reason, said Roosevelt, "why the children of the country should be taught a false natural history than why they should be taught a false physical geography."

It was not a common occurrence for a private citizen to be singled out for attack by the president of the United States. Following Roosevelt's interview in *Everybody's Magazine*, Long was stunned to find his parsonage besieged by reporters. In short order, Long replied to Roosevelt with an "open letter" that accused him of taking advantage of his high office in a debate that did not involve politics. There were only two noticeable things about the president's interview, wrote Long, "its bad taste and its cowardice." In a second open letter, Long shrewdly used material from Roosevelt's own books, *Hunting Trips of a Ranchman* and *The Wilderness Hunter*, to attack the president. He characterized Roosevelt as "a man who takes delight in whooping through the woods killing everything in sight . . . He doesn't know what a square deal means, either for wild animals or men." Furthermore, he said he thought it ridiculous for Roosevelt to assume the guise of naturalist when he was in fact nothing but a hunter. "Who is he to write, 'I don't believe for a minute that some of these nature writers know the heart of a wild thing'?" asked Long. "As to that I find after carefully reading two of his big books that every time Mr. Roosevelt gets near the heart of a wild thing he invariably puts a bullet though it. From his own records I have reckoned a full thousand hearts which he has thus known intimately. In one chapter alone I find that he violently gained knowledge of eleven noble elk hearts in a few days." [10]

Long had some success in painting Roosevelt as a murderer of wildlife. The facts were certainly on the minister's side when he shifted the argument away from the accuracy of his nature observations and onto the buckshot-heavy woodland habits of the president. As was usually the case, however, Roosevelt was to fire the last round. The final chapter in the nature faker controversy was written shortly after, in the September 1907 issue of *Everybody's*, where Roosevelt had arranged that a symposium be published entitled "Real Naturalists on Nature Faking." The symposium gathered together many of the most eminent field naturalists in America, all who denounced Long's natural history as being nothing more than trite fiction. William T. Hornaday, Director of the New York Zoological Park (now the Bronx Zoo), led off the symposium with a skeptical critique of Long and his writings that was to set the general tone of all the subsequent papers. "Whenever Mr. Long enters the woods," wrote Hornaday, "the most marvelous things begin to happen. There is a four-footed wonder-worker behind every bush and a miracle every hour. Only the Omnipotent eye could see all the things that Mr. Long claims to have seen." J. A. Allen, Curator of Mammalogy and Ornithology at the American Museum of Natural History, criticized Long for his statements that "real" naturalists who attacked him were just jealous because his books were forcing theirs out of the market. C. Hart Merriam, Chief of the United States Biological Survey, suggested that Long was possessed of a "Creative Memory." Merriam wrote that a nature writer "blessed with the Creative Memory does not have to go about wasting valuable time waiting and watching for animals to appear and do something." The final paper in the Symposium, entitled "Nature Fakers," was authored by Roosevelt himself. "We abhor deliberate or reckless untruth in this story of natural history as much as in any other," he wrote, "and therefore we feel that a grave wrong is committed by all who, holding a position that entitles them to respect, yet condone and encourage untruth." [11] In the end Long was to fade, and to publish very little in the future.

After the strange intellectual exercise of the nature faker debate was over and done with, Jack London sent a brief note to Upton Sinclair in which he described the entire controversy as having been worthless. "The whole argument was without any point at all," wrote London to Sinclair. "Only rich hobbyists like Roosevelt and his aristocratic band of happy hunters could bother to spend so much time and energy debunking what was already fourth rate literature to begin with. Men beg for bread in the streets—and Roosevelt and Burroughs confine their muckraking to the defense of accuracy in nature writing!" Sinclair jotted, "He's right, you know!" in the margin of London's letter and forwarded it to John Burroughs. Burroughs tucked the letter into his copy of London's *The Call of the Wild*, but before he did so he answered Sinclair's comment with one of his own: "Yes, I know." [12]

THE WILDLIFE OF THE American West had been hideously abused during the previous fifty years. In 1846, John James Audubon had visited the Yellowstone region and the Badlands, where he was the first to identify the Badlands variety of bighorn sheep. "No one," wrote Audubon, "who has not seen the Mauvaises Terres, or Badlands, can form any idea of these resorts of the Rocky Mountain Rams, or the difficulty in approaching these animals." However difficult it was to approach them, it was not difficult enough. The tasty bighorns were to be extinct by 1908. The antelope were not much better off. Only by the grace of emergency federal protection in 1910 would the species avoid extinction. In the winter of 1906 the very last band of the once plentiful Arizona (or "Merriam's") elk met its end in the Chirichuas Mountains. The last great buffalo slaughter had taken place in 1882, the year of Emerson's death, in North Dakota. When the young Theodore Roosevelt arrived to begin ranching in the Badlands two years later, he rode his horse through the decaying carcasses of thousands of buffalo from the 1882 killing.

Amid all this carnage there had been, during the same decades, at least a few positive steps toward conservation and sound wildlife management. When he succeeded to the presidency on the death of William McKinley in 1901, Theodore Roosevelt became heir to a program of forest reclamation and preservation that McKinley in turn had inherited from previous presidents. The federal government had established a Bureau of Forestry in 1891, a full decade before the Roosevelt presidency. The first national park had been designated in 1864 at Yosemite Valley. A war-weary Abraham Lincoln signed the bill. Lincoln's personal secretary John Hay, who had lobbied his boss in favor of the establishment of the park, wrote to his friend Henry Adams that the giant mariposas would, like the blacks, be "henceforth and forever free." In less than ten years, the federal park program had become a "system" with the establishment of Yellowstone in 1872. Twenty-eight years later, in 1900, McKinley saw to the funding of Mount Rainier and Crater Lake parks.

Under Gifford Pinchot, Roosevelt's appointee to head the Bureau of Forestry, the Forest Service fostered a utilitarian approach to the management of watersheds. Pinchot defined conservation as the sound and careful economic exploitation of resources. Despite the outrage of John Muir and others, Pinchot encouraged the flooding of Yosemite's Hetch Hetchy Valley as a reservoir for San Francisco. Pinchot was also the first to sanction limited lumbering on federal lands. Other of Roosevelt and Pinchot's actions were better received by conservationists. One of Roosevelt's first acts as president was to launch a system of federal wildlife refuges modeled along the lines of those that had been pioneered by the Audubon Society. "I need hardly to say how heartily I sympathize with the purposes of the Audubon Society," he had written in a letter to Frank Chapman in 1900. "I would like to see all harmless wild things . . . protected in every way." [13]

Roosevelt the hunter put a great weight on the word "harmless." In company with many other naturalists and conservationists who wanted to be seen as preserving wildlife while still being able to hunt, Roosevelt branded certain breeds of predatory animals as outlaws and rogues that must be annihilated for the good of other beasts. Wolves and coyotes fell into this class of wildlife, as did cougars, other wild cats, and bear. John Burroughs was perfectly at ease with the logic of predator control, and saw nothing wrong with the killing of what Roosevelt termed "criminal vermin." Burroughs shared in the common belief that all creatures who were not benign and picturesque needed the bullets and buckshot of man to keep them from overpowering and destroying more docile species.

In early 1903, when Roosevelt asked if he might have Burroughs's permission to dedicate his new book, *Outdoor Pastimes of an American Hunter*, to him, Burroughs replied without hesitation that this would please him greatly. "I know it will be a solid contribution to natural history," he wrote the president, "as well as to the literature of big-game hunting—all your hunting books are that." [14] In his memoir *Camping and Tramping with President Roosevelt* (1907), Burroughs would say that he had never been disturbed by the president's hunting trips. "It is to such men as he that the big game legitimately belongs," wrote Burroughs, "men who regard it from the point of view of the naturalist as well as from that of the sportsman, who are interested in its preservation." [15] In a letter to his son, Burroughs revealed the essence of his point of view on the subject, which represented the ultimate in natural pragmatism.

"Nature does not care whether the hunter slay the beast or the beast the hunter," he wrote. "She will make good compost of them both, and her ends are prospered whichever succeeds." [16] Ultimately, he thought, the debate over to hunt or not to hunt did not matter.

In the late 1880s Roosevelt had helped found the Boone and Crockett Club with George Bird Grinnel, the editor of *Forest and Stream.* The club included among its members Senator Henry Cabot Lodge, Elihu Root, Generals William Tecumseh Sherman and Philip Sheridan, and Francis Parkman. The Boone and Crockett Club was part a private men's association, part an ad-hoc organizer of rich men's hunting expeditions on the range, and part conservation lobbying machine. The club never failed to bring its not insignificant influence to bear in support of legislation to protect range animals from commercial exploitation, as when it helped push through the Park Protection Act of 1894. As John Muir was quick to note, however, the political agenda of the Boone and Crockett Club was actually a subtle deceit. The club sought to guard buffalo and other wild herds of the western plains from professional hunters only so as to leave something for amateurs such as themselves to shoot. While the club lobbied intensely to limit or eliminate the opportunities for commercial hunters and trappers to work federally owned lands, it in turn also lobbied to allow virtually unlimited sport hunting in the same wilderness. Muir had no patience with this "sham" preservation: ". . . the pleasure of killing is in danger of being lost from there being little or nothing left to kill," he wrote.

Burroughs was in no position to criticize the president as Muir had, even if he was of a mind to, which he wasn't. In his journals and his letters to Barrus, we sense a hero-worship at work in the Burroughs-Roosevelt relationship that is reminiscent of that in the early relationship between Burroughs and Whitman. He had always defined himself largely by the company he'd kept. This was most certainly the case during the Washington period when the young, idealistic Burroughs found Whitman's genteel poverty appealing, his obscurity noble. By the turn of the century Burroughs's value system had changed. He still saw his own personal worth reflected in whom he called his friend. But those he sought now were not struggling, condemned poets, but rather men of undisputed wealth, power, and fame. He could never quite believe his luck in having made it to the pinnacle of social status with moguls and statesmen. In his journals and letters he regularly expressed private astonishment that he should be traveling in such circles as those of E. H. Harriman, Andrew Carnegie, and Theodore Roosevelt. To the new friends who added so much to Burroughs's sense of self-worth, he could refuse nothing and forgive everything. He frankly idolized them all. And he would frequently demonstrate his willingness to inconvenience himself in order to share their company and goodwill, as when he agreed to travel with Harriman to Alaska and with Roosevelt on a grueling camping expedition through Yellowstone Park in April of 1903.

Roosevelt had written Major John Pitcher, superintendent of Yellowstone Park, several months previously proposing a presidential trip in the spring. The note included a query about the practice of killing mountain lions within park boundaries, as Roosevelt was interested in bagging a few of the "rogues." The newspapers soon got wind of Roosevelt's plan to hunt in Yellowstone. The *New York World* editorialized that, "Folks on the inside here say Mr. Roosevelt does not care shucks about the park. What he wants to see is game and lots of it." The *New York Times* commented that "The image of the President of the United States thundering through a wilderness preserve with shotgun in hand is not one that we would care to contemplate." Realizing he'd made a serious blunder by proposing to hunt at Yellowstone, Roosevelt made two fast moves to remedy the situation. First, he put out a press release denying any plans to hunt during his two-week visit to the park. Second, he invited John Burroughs to be his companion on the trip. Roosevelt wrote his eldest son that by having the gentle, nature-loving Burroughs with him, he (Roosevelt) would be like "the town's prize burglar attended by the Methodist parson." In his letter of invitation to the sixty-six-year-old Burroughs, Roosevelt assured him he would endure "neither fatigue nor hardship" during the excursion, and would have "all the comforts attendant to traveling with the presidential entourage." [17] What he did not mention was that the presidential entourage planned to have a fairly rough time of it, and that fatigue and hardship were relative notions.

Just a few days after the Carnegie dinner for Sydney Lee, Burroughs spent the evening of March 31 as Roosevelt's guest at the White House. "I reached here at 6 ½ tonight," he wrote to his son on White House stationery, "was very cordially received by the President and dined with him at 7½ and am now at 10 in my big room ready for bed. I found your letter and others here. We start in the morning." [18] The next day, the presidential party began its journey west in a private train that took them on a roundabout whistle-stop tour ending at Yellowstone. Burroughs traveled with the president in the chief executive's private railroad car. A decoy engine traveled a mile ahead lest there be explosives wired to the track by anarchists or socialists or nature fakers. On the second day of the journey, Roosevelt's secretary let slip that one of the reasons Burroughs was along was to dispel the notion that this journey was just another presidential hunting jaunt. Burroughs was not at all bothered by the idea that he was present merely as a foil against bad publicity. "The yellow journals so exaggerate his [Roosevelt's] hunting trips, and make so much capital out of them, that the president is greatly annoyed," wrote Burroughs to Barrus. "But I have disarmed the yellow journals, so you see I have been of some use already." [19] He cast himself in the role of servant, and was completely satisfied to play it, at least for the moment.

As Burroughs was soon to learn, a conspicuous amount of socializing was required of anyone who would travel with the president. At each major town, there was a reception committee to be greeted, then a parade, then a speech by Roosevelt, and then often a formal luncheon or dinner. Roosevelt gave from eight to ten speeches every day of the trip, sometimes for only a few minutes from the rear platform of his private car, sometimes for an hour or more in some large hall.

At a lonesome point in the heart of the Dakota Badlands, Roosevelt ordered the train stopped so that he might enjoy a meal of smoked venison with the foreman of his old ranch from the 1880s and another cowboy friend from the same period. Both were simple, unlettered cowmen. Both made their lives on the desolate plains. Neither man was, as Burroughs put it, "at all eloquent." They were in their fifties. They wore suits that had obviously been bought for the occasion, and appeared to be uncomfortable wearing them. "The men, I thought, seemed a little embarrassed by his [Roosevelt's] open-handed cordiality and good-fellowship," wrote Burroughs. "He himself evidently wanted to forget the present, and to live only in the memory of those wonderful ranch days." After the cowboys departed, Burroughs commented to Roosevelt that few men in his station would bother to renew such friendships. "Then I pity them," Roosevelt replied. [20]

In procession at the University of Chicago, several professors pulled Burroughs aside and said his visit was an honor for the school. At Madison, Wisconsin, Burroughs found Governor La Follette pumping his hand and saying that meeting Burroughs was one of the great experiences of his life—"that he read me when young, and that he loved me, and he told me so a second time with visible emotion." In St. Paul, amid the crowd cheering for Roosevelt, Bur-roughs spied a group of girls who carried a big banner with the inscription: "John Burroughs Society." The girls pushed their way through the crowd and handed him a bouquet. Always, there were the few faces in the president's audiences that were there more for Burroughs than they were for Roosevelt. "In his presence my light is invisible to the crowd," wrote Burroughs, "but when I am separated from him it shines to a few—usually women who smile and bow and wave to me." [21] At Fargo, North Dakota, some women recognized him and called his name. He commented to his journal that they were "probably teachers." To Julian, Burroughs wrote, "So you see your Dad is honored in strange lands—more than he is at home."

Many teachers brought their classes out to see Burroughs and Roosevelt. The time of the passing of the presidential train had been publicized both in the cities and in the hinterland. At one point, as the train rolled through a vast and lonely prairie after a city stop that had exhausted the president, Roosevelt spied a little brown schoolhouse in the distance. The schoolteacher and her brood were standing outside, waving to the train. "We were at luncheon, but the president caught a glimpse ahead through the window, and quickly took in the situation," wrote Burroughs. "With napkin in hand, he rushed out on the platform and waved to them. 'Those children,' he said, as he came back, 'wanted to see the president of the United

States, and I could not disappoint them. They may never have another chance. What a deep impression such things make when we are young!' " [22]

At Yellowstone, Roosevelt and Burroughs spent two weeks exploring the wild landscape. Near Fort Yellowstone, at Mammoth Hot Springs, the party got their first taste of the characteristic scenery of the park: huge, boiling springs with columns of vapor ascending to the heavens. Their odor, Burroughs said, suggested "the traditional infernal regions." The springs stood high on an enormous mound above the village on the side of the mountain. Terraced and scalloped and fluted, they suggested some vitreous formation, "or rare carving of enormous, many-colored precious stones." To Burroughs it all looked "quite unearthly."

Still farther up the mountain, Burroughs and Roosevelt came upon the Stygian Caves. These little pockets in the rocks ("well holes in the ground at your feet") were filled with carbon dioxide. Roosevelt sunk a lit torch into one, and it was extinguished as quickly as if it had been dropped into water. "Each cave or niche is a death valley on a small scale," wrote Burroughs.

A mile beyond the Stygian Caves, the party arrived at a large, steaming pond of an acre or more in size. A pair of mallard ducks were swimming about in one end of it, the cool end. "When we approached, they swam slowly over into the warmer water," Burroughs recalled. "As they progressed the water got hotter and hotter, and the ducks' discomfort was evident. Presently they stopped, and turned towards us, half appealing, as I thought. They could go no further; would we please come no nearer?" [23]

Roosevelt had assured the finicky Burroughs that he would experience no discomfort or inconvenience during the trip. Nevertheless, the nervous, self-conscious Burroughs found himself being called upon to ride on a horse for the first time in many years, and to go skiing for the first and last time of his life. Wherever possible, Burroughs was driven in a buggy or pulled in a sleigh through the early spring snowdrifts, for he was not an adept horseman and did not care to ride a mount if it were not absolutely necessary. Unfortunately, there was one picturesque gorge of the park where neither buggy nor sleigh could pass, and where it was absolutely necessary for Burroughs to ride on his own. He put off the excursion for three days. While Roosevelt and the others went on ahead, Burroughs claimed a stomachache and stayed behind in a warm room at Fort Yellowstone.

But then he had to follow. "Except for an hour's riding the day before . . . I had not been on a horse's back for nearly fifty years," he wrote, "and I had not spent as much as a day in the saddle during my youth. That first sense of a live, spirited, powerful animal beneath you, at whose mercy you are,—you, a pedestrian all your days,—with gullies and rocks and logs to cross, and deep chasms opening close beside you, is not a little disturbing." Horse and rider cautiously made their way along the narrow path on the side of the steep gorge, with the foaming torrent of the Yellowstone rushing along at its foot. Upon finally reaching the bottom of the gorge, Burroughs unhappily found himself having to ford the rough and rocky Yellowstone River atop a nervous and quarrelsome mount. Burroughs was annoyed at his inconvenience, but also relieved when he at last reached the small cluster of tents that formed the president's camp.

Camp was broken every day, and the party moved on ten or fifteen miles farther along the course of the Yellowstone. Burroughs usually took up the rear of the procession. Roosevelt was always running at the lead. "I hurried along as fast as I could, which was not fast; the way was rough,—logs, rocks, spring runs, and a tenderfoot rider," Burroughs recalled. Now and then Roosevelt would look back, see the slow progress Burroughs was making, and beckon impatiently. "Once or twice I lost sight of him . . ." wrote Burroughs. "The altitude was great, and the horse was laboring like a steam engine on an upgrade. Still I urged him on." Once camp was reached, Roosevelt would often be in the mood for more riding and exploring. Burroughs routinely begged off and stayed behind. He was content to lounge with off-duty Secret Service agents, or fish for the large cut-throat trout that made its home in the Yellowstone.

In the park's geyser region, at an altitude of about 8000 feet, all of the party—even Roosevelt—resorted to riding in big sleighs through the heavy banks of spring snow. Each sleigh was drawn by four horses and carried up to five men with gear. The snow was about four feet deep except near the geyser formations themselves where the subterranean warmth kept the ground bare. Roads had been broken through the snow, and the snow packed down for good sleighing by advance teams from Fort Yellowstone. Roosevelt and Burroughs shared a sleigh. The president insisted on riding in his preferred seat beside the driver. Burroughs rode in the back. Whenever the sleigh would strike a bare patch of ground and begin to drag heavily, Roosevelt would bound out nimbly and take to his heels, running beside the sleigh in order to lighten the load. For the sake of appearances, Burroughs would reluctantly follow suit, grumbling to himself all the while. "Walking at that altitude is no fun . . ." he would write. And running was even less fun.

He was in a foul mood by the time they arrived at the geysers; he was in just the right frame of mind to hate whatever natural spectacle had made him suffer the discomfort of running beside the sled for as much as twenty minutes at a time. "As one nears the geyser region," wrote Burroughs, "he gets the impression from the columns of steam going up here and there in the distance—now from behind a piece of woods, now from out a hidden valley—that he is approaching a manufacturing center, or a railroad terminus." Once he got close to them, he found the geysers as aesthetically pleasing as a manufacturing center. He went on record as thinking them at best boring, at worst downright ugly. "Steam and hot water are steam and hot water the world over, and the exhibition of them here did not differ, except in volume, from what one sees by his own fireside."

He was put off balance by boiling lakes and steaming rivers. They seemed like a hellish corruption and mistake of nature. Burroughs caught trout one afternoon on the edge of one of the steaming pools in the Madison River. The water seemed "blood warm." He guessed the trout found better feeding here than in the chillier sections of the river. They were certainly plentiful enough. "On the table they did not compare with our Eastern brook trout," he wrote. Home was looking better and better every day.

The last sojourn of the party was up to the Grand Canyon. When they reached the Canyon Hotel, the snow was very deep and had become so soft that the only way they could reach the overlook was on skis. The president had used skis before, but Burroughs had not. He quickly came to grief. "The snow gave way beneath me," wrote Burroughs, "and I was soon in an awkward predicament. The more I struggled, the lower my head and shoulders went, till only my heels, strapped to those long timbers, protruded above the snow. To reverse my position was impossible till some one came and reached me the end of a pole, and pulled me upright." The canyon itself was nearly free from snow. Burroughs called it "a grand spectacle, by far the grandest to be seen in the Park." Across the head of Yellowstone Falls there was a natural bridge of snow and ice, on which coyotes passed. Roosevelt jokingly wondered out loud whether Reverend Long had not seen the coyotes build the bridge.

After Yellowstone, Roosevelt proceeded on to Yosemite where he planned to spend several days with John Muir. Burroughs, having had quite enough of trail life, broke away from the presidential party in order to visit with some friends in Washington State, Montana, and Idaho, and to speak at a few schools that had requested a visit from him. "The schools here have shown me much attention," he wrote Roosevelt from Spokane on May 5. "My books are much better known and appreciated than I had expected . . . Squads of school boys, too, come to see me and bring copies of my books for me to write in, and I talk to them about you, and I am sure to tell them that you do not smoke or use tobacco in any form . . . I do not conceal from myself the fact that so much of the attention I receive comes from my having been so recently with you and your companions in the Yellowstone Park." In Montana, Burroughs attended a council of chiefs at one of the Indian agencies. Addressing the beaten, demoralized, and cynical warriors who now lived their lives out at squalid reservations, Burroughs condescendingly spoke of having been with the "Great Chief" in Yellowstone Park. He praised Roosevelt as a friend of the land under whose stewardship the great herds were returning to the plains. When he told them of the three thousand elk he had seen one day in the park, they grunted loudly, "whether with satisfaction or incredulity, I could not tell."

After sharing the intimacy (and inconvenience) of trail life with the domineering Roosevelt, Burroughs's awe of the president seems to have succumbed to a moderating impulse. He still thought highly of Roosevelt, but would no longer willingly be a subservient partner in their friendship. In February of 1906 Roosevelt's young niece, Corinne, attended a White House luncheon where she was seated next to Burroughs. The president, according to Corinne, turned to Burroughs and said, "John, this morning I heard a chippy sparrow and he sang, 'twee, twee', right in my ear." Burroughs shook his head. "Mr. President," he said, "you must be mistaken. It was not a chippy sparrow if it sang, 'twee, twee.' The note of the chippy sparrow is 'twee, twee, twee.'" From that moment, recalled Corinne, the president of the United States and the naturalist ignored all others at the table and launched into an argument, loud and protracted, as to whether the chipping sparrow's song consisted of two notes or three. After lunch, Burroughs joined the Theodore Roosevelts senior and junior for a seven-mile hike during which they visited Burroughs's old haunts along Rock Creek. Once again, Burroughs found Roosevelt's frantic speed to be too much for his taste. "We saw no birds," he wrote exasperatedly to Julian, "they could not keep up with us. I haven't walked at such a pace in years." [24]

In May of 1908, Burroughs and Roosevelt went birding at Pine Knot, Virginia. They named over seventy-five species of birds, "he [Roosevelt] knowing all of them but two and I knowing all but two." It had not been Burroughs who had kept score so precisely, but Roosevelt. Burroughs told Julian he was growing tired of how the president insisted upon turning literally everything—whether it be spotting birds, hiking, or quoting poetry —into a competition.

THE GRANDFATHER

Joy in the universe, and keen curiosity about it all—that has been my religion. As I grow old, my joy and my interest increase. Less and less does the world of men interest me, more and more do my thoughts turn to things universal and everlasting.

— *Journal Entry, February 18, 1910*

BURROUGHS HAD NOT EXPECTED to launch a four-year controversy with his "Real and Sham" paper in 1903. He had meant the article to be just that, an article, and not the manifesto for a movement. Once he saw what he'd started, however, he happily wrote highly priced essays to service the demand for his comments concerning the ongoing argument. Burroughs found editors standing in line to bid for new essays related to the controversy. He could count on getting upwards of three hundred dollars apiece for such papers as "The Wit of a Duck," "Animal Communication," "What Do Animals Know?," "Do Animals Think and Reflect?," and "The Literary Treatment of Nature," many of which he would collect in his 1905 book, *Ways of Nature.*

In "The Literary Treatment of Nature," Burroughs listed the contemporary nature writers who impressed him. Seton had not yet made his list of favorites. Burroughs was especially taken with the work of Bradford Torrey, Dallas Lore Sharp, and Rowland Evans Robinson. All three of these men mimicked Burroughs's style of "ramble" essays and focused largely, like Burroughs, on wildlife as found in local, domesticated settings such as city parks and pastoral farm neighborhoods. In his classic study of natural history literature *Back to Nature*, Peter Schmidt has included Burroughs, Torrey, and Sharp in a literary movement that endeavored to combine the virtues of country life with the advantages of city culture. Schmidt correctly suggests that the "Arcadian myth" of "middle-class intellectuals" such as Burroughs and company was concerned less with rejecting urban society than with a move to join the urban state with the joys and satisfactions of country life.

Bradford Torrey's articles and books—most notably *The Foot-Path Way* (1902)—recounted his adventures as a bird-watcher in and around the city of Boston. Torrey never took his readers more than ten miles from downtown. Dallas Lore Sharp found commercial success with books that told of his amateur wildlife studies near his Massachusetts farm. In Sharp's first book, *A Watcher in the Woods* (1903), he told of counting thirty-six species of birds nested within a quarter mile of his house. This was the same density and variety, he argued, that one could find in most areas of remote wilderness. Thus, a harmonious coexistence between urban man and wild nature was most certainly possible. And thus, by implication, was the segregation of pristine wilderness from timbering and other forms of development unnecessary, just as Roosevelt's man Pinchot was always arguing. Rowland Evans Robinson's *In New England Fields and Woods* (1896) addressed the joys of hiking and wildlife appreciation, but not the critical issue of vanishing wilderness.

It is interesting to note the writers on nature and conservation who did not make Burroughs's list of favorites. One of these was John Charles Van Dyke, whose books *Nature for Its Own Sake* and *The Desert* were published in 1898 and 1901 respectively. Van Dyke was less interested in picturesque animal lore than he was in making an argument for dramatically expanding the practice of preserving pristine wilderness. Another writer on nature themes who Burroughs ignored was Winthrop Packard. At the time that Burroughs wrote "The Literary Treatment of Nature," Packard's essays were already appearing regularly in the *Century*, and he would publish several books (including *Wild Pastures*, *Wildwood Ways*, and *Wood Wanderings*) between 1908 and 1910. Burroughs was never to take public notice of the young writer who protested the way the "trolley tripper" was invading the quiet pond in the wild wood to build his bungalow on its shore, sink his tin cans in its waters, and scare the bullfrogs with his phonograph. It was all well and good to write essays sending people to the open woods in the way that Burroughs did, but how could one make sure those people behaved themselves once they got there? Packard argued for laws "to protect nature from the so-called nature lovers."

Unlike John Burroughs, Van Dyke and Packard had—along with John Muir—been greatly influenced by George Perkins Marsh. President Lincoln read Marsh's 1864 work *Man and Nature* shortly before he signed the legislation that created Yosemite National Park. In what is generally regarded as the seminal work in American conservation literature, Marsh analyzed the decline of ancient Mediterranean and Near Eastern civilizations in terms of watershed abuse, and warned against a similar mistake in America. Marsh demonstrated the way in which man had become a major technological force with a frightening new ability to change the environment drastically and permanently. His message was plain: In the face of expanding industry and population, wilderness had to be recognized as something of inherent value, the preservation of which was essential for the common good. Citing Marsh's articulation of such an important notion, Lewis Mumford, in *The Brown Decades*, identified the 1864 publication of *Man and Nature* as the fountainhead event of the American conservation movement. So far as we can tell, Burroughs never read the book or noticed the fountainhead.

Burroughs's vision was far less radical than that of Marsh and his intellectual heirs. Burroughs dreamed of taming the wild landscape of America in a sane and careful manner, largely to the exclusion of cities. His ideal wish was for the rural districts and regional, agricultural economies to ripen to splendid maturity through generations of careful nurturing. He wanted less a country that was wilderness than he did a country that was a garden. Muir, Packard, and Van Dyke recognized Burroughs's romantic vision for what it was, a lost possibility from an age before the dominance of machine industry. Muir and others of his school believed a firm line had to be drawn to protect the lands of the West against exploitation by timber, oil, and coal interests. They were the first environmental activists. And Burroughs was not one of their number.

🍃

EARLY ON THE MORNING of July 10, 1903, John and Julian Burroughs got into the best of the several wagons at Riverby, which Julian had painstakingly cleaned the night before, and rode down to the little West Park landing on the Hudson River. There were a few curious people gathered at the spot. All of them were local workingmen well known to both father and son. All were dressed in their Sunday best even though today was not Sunday. Burroughs expected some company here at the normally lonely dock, but had hoped the crowd would not be too large. "This won't be bad," he whispered to Julian. "I was afraid the whole town would be here!" After about half an hour of waiting, during which Burroughs joked and gossiped with his neighbors, a large white ship emerged out of the mist of the river to the south. A few of the workingmen applauded at the sight of the yacht, which flew the ensign of the president of the United States. [1]

After the ship was at anchor, President Roosevelt appeared on deck in a white linen suit and straw hat. He waved to Burroughs and called out, "How are you, Oom John?" ("oom" is Dutch for "uncle.") Then Roosevelt and his wife Edith got into a little speed launch that took them to the pier. The tide was low, and the president's launch wound up floating far below the dock. Roosevelt climbed up the side of the pier holding onto a half-rotten mooring line for leverage. Then he and Julian Burroughs reached down together to help Mrs. Roosevelt up out of the boat. Roosevelt gave Burroughs a hug. He patted the naturalist's trim stomach, and allowed how he hoped "Oom John" was "eating regular." This was probably an allusion to Burroughs's many complaints during their Yellowstone trip as to the lax, random schedule of meals. After this small talk, Roosevelt noticed the men who stood a few feet away in silent awe. Without hesitation, he walked over to them and shook hands. Burroughs introduced Roosevelt to the group which included one Charlie Burger, a veteran of the Civil War. "You were in the big war," said Roosevelt to Burger. "I was in the little [Spanish-American] war."

The president and Mrs. Roosevelt were scheduled to have lunch at Slabsides. Upon being informed that the cabin was two uphill miles from the spot where they stood, Roosevelt announced that the wagon Burroughs had brought would not be necessary. They would all hike to the cabin. The small party—which consisted of Burroughs, the president and his wife, Julian, and a few of the president's aides—stopped at the railway station where Burroughs wired the local congressman, Edmund Platt of Poughkeepsie, and asked him to join them at the cabin. While Burroughs sent his telegram, Roosevelt passed the time of day with the astonished station agent. Then the party headed up the rough trail to the cabin.

Several years later, when the Whitman biographer Bliss Perry made the same climb with Burroughs, the subject of the Roosevelt hike came up. "Halfway up the hill 'Uncle John' paused to ask me solicitously: 'Are you sure this hill isn't too steep for you?'" Perry recalled. Perry was forty-five, and had retained what he called "a boyish pride" in his physical stamina. Burroughs was in his seventies. Perry had been "holding back" for fear of tiring his host. He replied to Burroughs's query, perhaps a little dryly, that he thought he could make it. "You should have seen Theodore climb this hill!" exclaimed Burroughs. "He clenched his fists and gritted his teeth and came up like a race-horse!" "I thought you said Mrs. Roosevelt was with you," Perry remarked. A puzzled look came over Burroughs's face. "She was," he said, "and there was something queer about it. She didn't seem to make the slightest effort, and yet she got to the top just as soon as he did!" [2]

At the cabin, Burroughs went with a pail to fetch water from the spring for the parched first couple. Then he sat with the Roosevelts in the cool breeze on the porch and spoke of Reverend Long. Burroughs brought out a magazine illustration from Long's article where he'd described the orioles' string-hung nest. Roosevelt joked about the drawing of the nest. "Long might just as well say Jenny Wren built herself a log cabin with a bark roof—a miniature Slabsides—as to claim that an oriole did that." Roosevelt told Burroughs of a recent conversation he'd had with Lyman Abbott, editor of the *Christian Union*, which was the magazine where many of Long's articles appeared. Abbott had told Roosevelt that Burroughs possessed not enough imagination, and Long too much. "I told Abbott that Long had no imagination in the true sense at all,—that exaggeration and falsifying were not imagination, but yellow journalism," said Roosevelt.

Julian was dispatched around town with a message for the

neighbors. Anyone who wished to meet the president should go down to the dock at 2:00 P.M. Burroughs would be happy to introduce them. The word having been spread, Julian appeared at Slabsides holding a cherry pie that Ursula had sent up. Burroughs cooked and served lunch. Mrs. Roosevelt helped to rinse the Slabsides-grown celery. Burroughs broiled two chickens in the fireplace and baked potatoes in the coals. Congressman Platt arrived in time to share the feast. After lunch, Ursula showed up in her phaeton carriage driven by the hired man from Riverby, Hudson [Hud] Covert. In due course, she and Mrs. Roosevelt got into the wagon for the short ride to Riverby. This time Julian took the reins. Hud joined Burroughs, Roosevelt, and Platt for the hike back to the farm. At Riverby, Ursula served homemade ice cream. Here the party was joined by Julian's wife, Emily, who was pregnant with the couple's first child. Roosevelt was taken with Julian's newly built home. He praised it as being "original and American" in contrast with the enormous mock Roman villa that the Vanderbilt family maintained directly across the river.

"Then we walked down to the dock where quite a crowd had collected," Burroughs recalled in his journal. "I introduced every man, woman, and child to him . . . and at 2:10 they were off. He waved to us from the deck . . . I am quite a lion here now, and people are driving in to congratulate me." [3]

THE PUBLICITY OF THE nature-faker controversy combined with that of the Yellowstone trip to make John Burroughs's a household name. He was now a figure of notoriety beyond the quarters of his quiet following of serious readers. While Burroughs had previously been a respected author with a definite, wide, and established readership, he now became a persona. People began to know him who did not first know his books. Houghton Mifflin saw steadily increasing sales of the Burroughs backlist in the years immediately following the turn of the century. He even had an official fan club, several members of which he'd seen waving a banner at the Roosevelt rally in St. Paul. Sponsored by Houghton Mifflin, the John Burroughs

Society was promoted in grammar and high schools where Burroughs's books were used. It was a unique marketing tool. Part natural history society and part book club, the society offered members discounts on Burroughs books ordered directly from Houghton Mifflin. It also sent them newsletters salted with "special messages" from Burroughs as well as nature quizzes and contests tied directly to a thorough knowledge of his writings.

Intent on keeping their star nature writer in the public eye, Houghton Mifflin dispatched photographers to Riverby and Slabsides to capture the sight of Burroughs in his native haunts. Burroughs seems to have enjoyed the attention, at least most of the time. Like the mature Whitman, the mature Burroughs was always willing to pose. Eventually he would even entertain motion picture crews and lead them into the heart of Whitman Land. And he would let the Victor Company record him reading from his poems. "I went Thursday morning and bawled my 'Waiting' and 'The Return' into the end of a horn," he wrote a friend. "I am sure the record will not sound like me, except the slight hesitations here and there. I was nervous, and in no condition for such a thing." Listening to the record today, the reader one hears is obviously uncomfortable. His voice tenses and cracks again and again; the cadence of the recitation is not natural. He sent a friend a copy of the Victor record catalog, in which artists were listed alphabetically. "Burroughs, John" was followed by "Caruso, Enrico." Burroughs scrawled a note on the page. "Poor Caruso!," he wrote. "All that practicing just to end up in such bad company!" Burroughs occasionally acknowledged and condemned the ham in himself. He was to confide to Barrus that he admired his fellow author William Dean Howells, because "he doesn't have any of my vulgar craving for adulation."

In October, 1904, his first nature book in eight years was published. *Far and Near* presented in its entirety his chronicle of the Harriman Expedition, which he titled "In Green Alaska." It also served up a rich helping of natural history essays composed since the publication of *Riverby* (1896). These included "Wildlife About My Cabin" and "Babes in the Woods." (The latter piece recounted his adventures hiking in the area of Black Creek with a young weekend guest at Slabsides, Theodore Roosevelt, Jr., who was referenced simply as "a boy named Ted.") The majority of these essays were a return to Burroughs's old, beloved style of nature writing, packed with personal experiences in field and wood and full of vibrant first hand description. "In my preface to *Riverby* I told my readers that that was probably my last out-door book," wrote Burroughs in his Introduction to *Far and Near*. "But my life has gone on, my love of nature has continued, my habit of observation has been kept up, and the combined result is another collection of papers dealing with the old, inexhaustible open-air themes." [4] Of course, the open-air themes were also what sold best. Houghton Mifflin encouraged Burroughs to pursue these industriously, although they would loyally publish whatever he produced.

The Houghton Mifflin publicity department was charged with making sure Burroughs was in all the right literary clubs and at all the right literary functions. November 1905 found him one of nine people sitting around a table for a dinner to found the American Academy of Arts and Letters. Beside him, making jokes about the birds he expected at any moment to see fly out of Burroughs's beard, sat Mark Twain. In December of the same year, Burroughs attended the seventieth birthday dinner for Twain held at Delmonico's. Burroughs was one of more than forty guests including Willa Cather, Richard Watson Gilder, Andrew Carnegie, and Emily Post. After a cocktail reception, they all filed into Delmonico's red room to the music of a forty-piece orchestra borrowed for the evening from the Metropolitan Opera. Amid potted palms and huge gilt mirrors, the party dined on fillet of kingfish, saddle of lamb, Baltimore terrapin, quail, and redhead duck washed down with sauterne, champagne, and brandy. After the feast, they sipped claret and embarked upon five hours of toasts, poems, and speeches. [5] Burroughs recorded in his journal that Twain "was of course amusing, but most of what he said, spoken by anyone else, would have sounded flat and absurd." Burroughs and the other guests each had their pictures taken "in the strange new Holland light that kills all the pinks and reds, and makes you look like an old Pompeian bronze. Our lips were black, and our faces showed us all with Addison's disease . . . We were all presented with a small plaster cast of Mark Twain—not very good." [6]

❦

ON A SUNNY DAY in October of 1904, residents of rural Huntington, Long Island, noticed two strangers poking around the old abandoned Whitman homestead. It had taken several hours of investigating before the two men, John Burroughs and Bliss Perry, were able to find the building that was Whitman's birthplace. Perry, then at work on his monumental biography of the poet, had intrigued Burroughs several months before with the prospect of ferreting out the lost farm of Whitman's boyhood. Now, after talking to a few older residents of the village who still remembered the Whitmans of over eighty years before, they had found the spot—"a lonely farmhouse fast going to ruin . . . The old kitchen with its oaken beams was full of rubbish." Burroughs and Perry sat on the crumbling front steps, the colorful leaves of autumn blowing up against their feet, and ate the box lunches they'd brought along with them. Burroughs told Perry what he could remember of Walt's tales of a boyhood spent among these North Shore hills.

Burroughs allowed Perry access to all of his correspondence with Walt. He entertained Perry at Slabsides and took him on a hike to see the falls at Black Creek that had so impressed Whitman. And he wrote Perry nearly twenty letters packed with personal recollections of the poet. Published in 1906, the Perry biography was the book that began to turn the tide of critical opinion in Whitman's favor. After the book's publication, Burroughs wrote to Barrus that although the biography left much to be said, it yet came "nearest to being an adequate account and estimate of Whitman of any life of him that has appeared." [7]

At the dawn of Whitman's rehabilitation, Burroughs found many people coming to him for reminiscences of the man behind the *Leaves*. He tried his best to be candid and forthright with all inquirers. To one correspondent, Burroughs admitted that Whitman had not been entirely above reproach in the way he'd conducted his personal life.

> Christ-like, Walt seemed to prefer the company of publicans and sinners to that of the "best society" of his time. He doubtless found more reality there. Whitman identifies

himself with sinners in his poems in a way that to me does not suggest the "semi-hobo," but suggests the god. I love to dwell upon his divine commonness . . . I have occasion to be astonished more and more frequently at the way his soul is marching on. I meet people wherever I go, especially among women, who are coming under his spell. One thing I plume myself upon in this world, and that is that I saw the greatness of the poet from the first—that no disguise of the common, the near, the rough, the "tramp," could conceal from me the divinity that was back of it all, and challenged me to the contest. Familiar intercourse with him did not blur this impression. That head, that presence, those words of love and of wisdom convinced like Nature herself. I pitied those who saw him, and yet saw him not. [8]

Elsewhere Burroughs confessed that Whitman, through most of his career, had been lacking in something that society much prized and could not get along well without—taste or, as Burroughs described it, "a delicate appreciation of the finer relations of men in the social organism." But, continued Burroughs, if Whitman had had "taste," then he could not have written *Leaves of Grass*. "He was a barbarian, entirely of the open air as opposed to parlors and libraries," wrote Burroughs. "[Whitman] ignored, or was insensible of, the conventional proprieties and reticencies and modesties, that make social life possible. This is the price he paid for the elemental power and quality of his work that makes it so much in the spirit of creation itself." [9]

While helping Perry with his Whitman book, Burroughs was also preparing to publish his first and only book of poetry. In 1862, after reading the poem "Waiting," Myron Benton had told Burroughs not to seek a future in poetry. Whitman, too, had gently tried to push Burroughs away from poetry in favor of "the prose that you make so much your own." [10] Burroughs himself, in a candid moment, once said "I often think of myself as a flying-fish, compared to a bird, when I try to write poetry—the creature is so mechanical; it spins along, but there is no flight—no soaring." The editors at Houghton Mifflin did not share his reservations about his poems. They asked him to collect into one volume some thirty nature poems he'd composed at odd moments through recent years. He wrote Julian that he doubted the literary merit of most of the pieces, but that nevertheless Houghton Mifflin had encouraged him that a book of them would find its place in the market. *Bird and Bough* was published in March of 1906.

With regard to *Bird and Bough*, even the hero-worshiping Barrus, who was ready to adore everything and anything that flowed from the pen of Burroughs, admitted that Burroughs's "qualities as a poet were revealed in his poetic interpretations of Nature [as manifested in his prose writings], rather than in his verse." The reviewer in the *North American* would say of *Bird and Bough* that Burroughs's readers loved him so much they could forgive him anything—except his poetry. To his credit, Burroughs wrote candidly of the deficiencies of his poems in a paragraph originally intended to be part of the preface to *Bird and Bough*, but removed by the editors at Houghton Mifflin before publication. "I have a fairly well-founded conviction that my verses contain more truth than poetry," wrote Burroughs. "But if one cannot attain to poetry, truth is not to be despised. There is a good deal of sound natural history tucked away in these lines."

The poems were simply not very good. "The Bobolink" is representative of the pieces in *Bird and Bough*.

> Daisies, clover, buttercup,
> Red-top, trefoil, meadow sweet,
> Ecstatic wing, soaring up,
> Then gliding down to grassy seat.
>
> Sunshine, laughter, mad desires,
> May day, June day, lucid skies,
> All reckless things that love inspires,
> The gladdest bird that sings and flies.
>
> Meadows, orchards, bending sprays,
> Rushes, lilies, billowy wheat,
> Song and frolic fill his days,
> A feathered rondeau all complete.

Pink bloom, gold bloom, fleabane white,
 Dew drop, rain drop, cooling shade,
Bubbling throat and hovering flight,
 And jubilant heart as e'er was made.

He wrote a friend soon after publication of the book that the poems of *Bird and Bough* were "all art, all form, untouched by any depth of vision into the spiritual resonance of Nature." [12] Where Whitman had defied form, Burroughs clung to it. Tight little quatrains danced uniformly up and down the pages. Burroughs the poet described a simplified, picture-book vision of the wild. The nature of *Bird and Bough* did not build up and lay low, did not spring from dark depths, and gave no hint of the grand struggle of evolution or the constant, roundabout dance of life and death that circled to create the universe. Burroughs seemed somehow incapable of communicating in verse the realistic image of the woodlands he achieved in his prose writings. One reads *Bird and Bough* and wishes Whitman had still been available to read and revise, or better yet to simply veto publication and be done with it.

JOHN AND URSULA BECAME grandparents in the autumn of 1903 with the birth of Emily and Julian's daughter Elizabeth. In 1905 there was another granddaughter, Ursula. And in July of 1909 a grandson and namesake, John Burroughs II, was born. Burroughs went by Julian's place every day to visit the grandchildren, as did Ursula. Just as Julian had once been the one common passion that bound the couple, the grandchildren now became the one thing they shared and enjoyed together. The delighted grandfather filled his journals with tales of Julian's children, just as his journals thirty years before had been filled with tales of Julian. "Elizabeth has got so she giggles out-loud at my antics and grimaces," he wrote in one characteristic entry a few months after the birth of the first grandchild. When Julian's Cambridge friend, the violinist Edith Trowbridge, came to visit, Burroughs was highly amused by baby Elizabeth's negative reaction to the beautiful music with which Edith entertained the family every night of her stay. "Her violin alarmed Elizabeth greatly," wrote Burroughs to Barrus. "They are going to try it on her again today. I doubt if animals, or man at the animal stage, have any appreciation of harmonious sounds, or of perfumes." [13]

He had plenty of leisure in which to amuse himself with Julian's family. The vineyards belonged to Julian now. Burroughs took no part of the profits for himself, and in turn did not concern himself with the management of the grape business. He would help his son at harvest time by stepping in to oversee a few of the more than thirty temporary workers employed every autumn to bring in the grapes, but beyond that he had no involvement at all. The days, by and large, were devoted to reading, writing, and contemplation. He roamed the woods a great deal, walking several miles every day that was clement in either winter or summer. He entertained reporters and students at Slabsides, often showing up at the cabin some minutes after the scheduled guests had arrived and not occasionally heading away through the woods while his company were still finishing their lunch on the Slabsides steps. The cabin was no longer a place where he spent a great deal of time. Through countless magazine articles and news photographs, Slabsides had become famous. It was the place where strangers dropped in on him. He did not go there when he did not want to be disturbed; and with each passing day he wanted less and less to be disturbed.

He was in his late-sixties. At Riverby, he and Ursula occupied separate bedrooms just as they had for more than fifteen years. In fair weather, he sometimes slept in his room at the stone house. On other nights, depending on his mood (or perhaps Ursula's), he made a bed for himself on a cot in the study. During the winters, Ursula continued her habit of thirty years and boarded in Poughkeepsie. The stone house was usually shut down for the season. Burroughs would make camp by the fireplace of the study, preferring that to "supping with traveling salesmen in Poughkeepsie." Here he had his comfortable cot, plenty of wood for the fire, and most importantly his desk and books. He did his cooking in a little kettle on the hearth, or else took supper with Julian and Emily. When the snows came and made the passage of carriages down the steep Riverby driveway almost impossible, Burroughs would enjoy "a sweet, splendid isolation." He was content, the grandfather, to wait out spring here with his grandchildren nearby and his journal pages empty, receptive, waiting to be filled.

> Is there another so-called literary man who spends his time as I do, in the solitude of the country, amid the common people? Here I sit, night after night, year after year, alone in my little study perched upon a broad slope of the Hudson, my light visible from afar, reading an hour or two each evening, and then to bed at nine. No callers, no society . . . every day in winter the same. What long, long thoughts I have! What constant retrospection; what longings for the old days and people! The world goes by me afar off. I hear its roar and hubbub, but care little to mingle in it. It is mostly vanity and vexation of spirit. [14]

He used his journal to chronicle his daily round: Up in the morning before daylight to lend a hand getting breakfast, then fifteen minutes' walk to the post office and back. Then building a fire in the study; a little reading, and, at nine, to work with his pen until noon. Then dinner, and a few chores, followed by the sawing and splitting of wood for the next day. Then a walk to Slabsides, or elsewhere. Then a little reading and dozing in his study, which was followed by "supper and darkness again." On his morning walks to the post office he carried a large berry basket filled with outgoing letters. He would use the same basket to bring home the incoming mail, which was usually plentiful. He spent several hours a day on his correspondence. He answered every letter he received.

He made trips to visit Barrus in Middletown every week or so, often staying two or three days at her little apartment near the hospital. In the summers, the two usually spent a week or two together at Byrdcliffe, the artist colony at Woodstock, New York. "There are some artists here whom I knew in N.Y.," he wrote to Julian. "The fine library here is the chief attraction . . . Tell your Ma I will write her . . . Kiss the children for me." [15] With Julian, he seems to have been matter of fact about his relationship with Barrus: discrete but at the same time candid and unapologetic. Julian, for his part, was shrewd enough to realize that any sign of resentment would only strengthen Barrus's position with Burroughs by making him feel ostracized from his family. The son was unhappy with the relationship, but went along. When, in the fall of 1906, Julian proposed a trip to East Hampton from West Park in his motor launch, Burroughs brought Barrus instead of Ursula on the voyage with Julian's family and Emily's sister Laura.

Burroughs was now giving all his writing to Barrus for review, criticism, and what he called "grammar inspection." He religiously adopted the suggestions for changes she wrote in her tight, neat script down the side margins of his manuscript. At the same time, he filled whole tablets with reminiscences and passed these on to her for eventual use as part of the biography he had authorized her to do "one day when I am cold." [16] Barrus was nothing, Burroughs's granddaughter Elizabeth would recall, if not "ambitious." [17] Barrus soon gave up her medical practice in order to devote herself to the full-time cataloging of Burroughs's past. She began to create elaborate files on Burroughs cross-referenced by topic and year. When Burroughs visited her apartment, he would lounge on a couch beside the bulging drawers within which resided all the scraps, remnants, and voluminous records of his life. Here Barrus assembled not only Burroughs's own reminiscences, journals, and manuscripts, but also those of people who had known him. She wrote old acquaintances for recollections. She collected worn copies of magazines in which had appeared the ancient, naive writings of the young Burroughs. She once even wrote Julian to ask for his boyhood diaries, "which are most appropriately a part of my collection for the light they would shed on your father." She was angry when Julian answered that he would keep the diaries, along with several hundred pages of childhood recollections that his father had penned and given to Julian as a gift.

Burroughs's ongoing affair with Barrus made Ursula bitter and resentful. He, in turn, was annoyed and impatient with her resentment. He paid her back with pettiness. On their fiftieth anniversary in 1907, he went off hiking in the Catskills without even leaving her a note saying where he was. After five decades, the sad cycle of their relationship was as inevitable as it was routine. He felt she did not respect him enough. He repeatedly compared the high regard that association with the rich and famous brought him in distant places to the low regard in which he believed he was held in his own home. "Think of me," he wrote Barrus, "the Henpecked, riding down

Pennsylvania Avenue in a carriage beside the President of the U.S., and treated by him as a friend and equal." [18] "How strange and absurd it all seems to me," he wrote to Julian, "no honor at home, and overwhelmed with it abroad." Ursula let him know she was highly amused when he was invited to receive an honorary LL.D. from John Muir's old school, the University of Wisconsin. "Mrs. Burroughs half-jocosely said, 'They might as well confer the degree on an old cat,'" recorded Burroughs in his journal. Then he asked a question of the unanswering page: "How shall a man be a hero in his own family?" [19]

IN FEBRUARY 1909 BURROUGHS and Barrus left Ursula behind and journeyed west on a trip that was to last until May. Their first stops were the Petrified Forests of Arizona and the Grand Canyon. They visited both places in the company of John Muir.

At the Grand Canyon, Muir led the two easterners to the rim and waved his hand as if to unveil a great sculpture, saying "There! Empty your heads of all vanity, and look!" Muir took the Burroughs party down the perilous Bright Angel trail by muleback. They descended 4000 feet using a four-foot-wide path that zig-zagged into the abyss. "There were places where if the mule had stumbled, or made a miss-step, both mule and rider might have gone down 2000 feet," wrote Burroughs to Ursula; ". . . the awful gulfs that constantly opened up below us fairly made our hearts stop." [20] Muir's long monologue on the geology of the canyon sparked Burroughs's imagination. He filled his journal with discussions of the poetry that lay in the slow action of rock and water.

> How geologic time looks out from the ledges and walls of gray rocks unmindful of us human ephemera that pass! It has seen the mountains decay and the hills grow old. The huge drift boulders rest on the margin of meadows and fields, or stand sentry to the woods, and though races and kingdoms pass, scarcely the change of a wrinkle disturbs their calm stone faces. Yet time gets the better of them also. The frowning ledge melts as inevitably as a snowbank.

Following the encounter with Muir, Burroughs kept house in Pasadena with Barrus for a month during which he penned the first draft of "The Divine Abyss," an essay on the Grand Canyon. Then the couple traveled to Yosemite to meet up once again with Muir and take part in a Sierra Club outing. During this trip Muir took Burroughs to view Yosemite Falls, El Capitan, the redwoods, and other popular sites of the park. Burroughs and Barrus were on a tight schedule, however, and did not have time to view the giant sequoias, nor to climb to Glacier Point. Muir would write later to chastise them for this. "I puttered around here for ten years," wrote Muir to Burroughs, "but you expect to see everything in four days! You come in here, then excuse yourselves to God, who has kept these glories waiting for you, by saying 'I've got to get back to Slabsides,' or 'We want to go to Honolulu.'" Muir had also wanted to show them Merced Canyon and Hetch Hetchy. But Barrus wanted to get to Hawaii.

The trip to the islands was free. It had been paid for by the Hawaiian Promotion Company, a public relations firm whose business it was to publicize the island paradise's potential as a vacation spot. All that was asked of Burroughs was that, upon his return to the mainland, he write one magazine article touting the spectacle of Hawaii's natural wonders. The promotion company's guides made sure that Burroughs missed no experience. He rode a surf canoe and partook in native feasts. He sent Ursula an article clipped from a Honolulu paper with the headline "Burroughs Eats Two-Finger Poi." And he went on a ten-mile hike in the tropical woods with the governor of the islands.

Burroughs had not expected to enjoy it here, but he wrote Julian of the delight he was taking in the "blue and purple sea." He was also pleased with a trip to the top of the volcano Haleakala. As Burroughs looked down into the extinct crater of the volcano, it suggested "a burnt out Purgatory." He described as "wild and unfamiliar and elemental" the colors of brick red and dull plum, and the soot and black lava flows that defined the pit. Burroughs and his party stood at the edge of the crater till the light was gone and the stars came out, and the Southern Cross hung low in the sky. They also visited the active volcano Kilauea, on the island of Hawaii. Burroughs wrote to his brother Curtis that the sight of seething lava he'd been treated to from the top of that crater realized in full the hell of which their forefathers had been so afraid.

When they returned to California, Barrus and Burroughs spent one more day with Muir at the latter's home in the Alhambra Valley. It was on this day that Muir showed Burroughs what were literally barrels of notes from his early wandering years, including his Sierra studies and drawings. Burroughs urged Muir to shape this raw material into books. Back at Riverby that summer, Burroughs would write Muir to emphasize this point. "Are you making headway with your writing?" Burroughs asked. "The world wants all that harvest of yours thrashed out and made into crisp, sweet loaves, such as you know how to make." [21]

That fall, Burroughs wrote an essay on Yosemite, a paper that included views divergent with Muir's on the role of glaciation in the formation of the region. (Muir believed glaciation to be the prime shaper of these mountains, while Burroughs adopted a view expressed by other geologists that erosion actually played a much larger part in the process.) Burroughs sent the manuscript to Muir for criticism. Muir's response did not hold anything back. "I have read your Yosemite Ms. and can make nothing of it. You saw so little of the Valley, I think you had better say little or nothing of its origin. Leave it all out is my advice. It can do no good to yourself or others to try to tell what you have had no chance to know." Muir asked Burroughs to compare "this haphazard brazen ignorance with the careful, loving, life-long bird studies that have made you famous . . . Your impression of the Valley as scenery everybody will enjoy reading, without any blurring origin stuff." [22]

Writing of the argumentative, challenging Thoreau, Emerson had described his friend in terms that Burroughs thought could also describe Muir. "If I knew only Thoreau, I should think cooperation of good men impossible. Must we always talk for victory, and never once for truth, for comfort, for joy?" asked Emerson. Thoreau always had "some weary captious paradox to fight you with" and with which to waste one's "time and temper." Although Burroughs genuinely liked him, he knew that the Muir was at heart another Thoreau. "Muir was not too complacent and deferential," wrote Burroughs. "He belonged to the sayers of No. Contradiction was the breath of his nostrils." Now, with Muir's judgment of "haphaz-ard brazen ignorance" lying on his desk, Burroughs lost his temper.

> You did sit down on my Yosemite paper with a vengeance. Such wholesale condemnation is apt to defeat itself . . . Did you ever agree with any man upon any subject whatever? I really think, dear Muir, that your Scotch pig-headedness stands as much in your way in the pursuit of truth, as my "brazen ignorance" stands in my way . . . I considered carefully all you had written on Yosemite before finishing my paper, but your main conclusion was so at variance with the opinions of other geologists, and with common sense, that I could not accept it. [23]

Muir responded immediately with a note that was conciliatory, but at the same time not a retreat. "Now, dear Burroughs, don't waste your good nature. I only did as you requested with the Yosem-ite geology, but you give me no thanks—only the other stuff . . ." wrote Muir. "If instead of stubbornly sailing to Hawaiian moweries and volcanoes you had allowed me to take you to the head fountains of the Merced and Tuolumne on the High Sierra, you would have got lessons in ice action and water action, and on the relationship of the great Valley to existing and ancient glaciers, at its head and on either side of it." Muir went on to say that there was little to be gained from the studies of the region that had as yet appeared in books, and still less in squabbling controversy. "Only long plodding observation in the field yields anything worthwhile, at least to poor dreamy wanderers as dull as I. Earth sculpture, and the life and beauty that go with it, is a noble study, and now that you have got Yosemite on the brain, why not come back again? I'd be delighted to have you in spite of your rank Scotch stubbornness, and you might perhaps learn to endure or ignore my glacial behavior and airs. Anyhow, I am with all good wishes . . . faithfully your friend." [24]

Burroughs ended up editing from his Yosemite paper much of what had displeased Muir. "The Divine Abyss," his essay on the Grand Canyon, underwent similar cuts when it appeared in the July 1909 issue of the *Century*. Burroughs wrote Muir that the editors of the magazine "could not stand all that geology, so I cut much of it out." In another letter to Muir, Burroughs mentioned that he was to have a paper in the May *Atlantic* entitled "Through the Eyes of the Geologists." He did not send this article to Muir for pre-publication review. Instead he told Muir that he should read the piece when it appeared in the magazine and "unhesitatingly" forward any criticism. "I will not squeal, sit down upon me ever so hard." [25]

Muir took him up on the invitation. After the publication of "Through the Eyes of the Geologists," Muir wrote Burroughs that he had no doubt the piece would be "enjoyed by a wide circle of readers who are compelled to take their geology at second or third hand." Elsewhere in the letter, Muir added that "I have been hidden down here in Los Angeles more than a month, and with the aid of a good stenographer and typewriter have completed another book— *My First Summer in the Sierra* . . . The original notes were written forty-one years ago, when I did not know much about the geology of the Sierra, or about glaciers. Therefore I suppose you will like it better on account of its glacial poverty." [26]

16

THE WIDOWER

I often wish I had never seen a Ford car or any other. All such things create wants which we never knew before. Life is simpler and more satisfying without them.

— *Journal Entry, September 18, 1916*

WHEN HENRY FORD GAVE John Burroughs a Model T in January of 1913, it was Julian, not John, who took lessons in its operation from the Ford mechanic who delivered the present. Julian, in turn, instructed his father on how to run the car.

It took John some months to become a true master of the machine. He suffered several mishaps in the process. In April he ran the car into a locust tree just within the Riverby gates after returning from a quick trip to nearby Port Ewen. The forward spring was bent in the crash, preventing the engine from being cranked. Ford sent a mechanic to tend to the problem. Burroughs wrote in his journal how the "blind, desperate" automobile scared him. "How ready it is to take to the ditch, or a tree, or a fence! I fear I have not the mechanical type of mind ever to feel at my ease with it, or to feel perfect master of it." [1]

Soon there was another mishap. With Julian at the wheel, he'd driven with Emily and the grandchildren to Woodchuck Lodge, the little house on the corner of the home farm where he'd spent a part of the previous two summers. Julian's family was to stay with Burroughs for several weeks, but Julian had to get back to West

Park. Burroughs drove Julian to the railway station, and then came back to the homestead farm with his two granddaughters. "Return in good shape with the girls;" he recorded, "but, in driving the car in the old barn, get rattled and let it run wild; it bursts through the side of the barn like an explosion." There was a great splintering and rattling of boards and timbers. The car stopped with its forward axle hanging over a drop of fifteen feet at the rear of the elevated building. As the front wheels dropped, the car fell on its fly wheel. That alone kept it from going all the way through the wall and crashing on the sharply graded hill below. Luckily, he had let the two little girls out of the car before entering the barn. "I am terribly humiliated," he wrote that night, and "scared at my narrow escape." [2]

Despite the accidents and his initial nervousness, he soon felt confident enough to run the car all over Ulster County. "Mrs. B. and I had a beautiful run to Clintondale," he wrote in an April journal entry. "No more perfect day ever came down out of heaven." [3] A few days later he wrote, "Drive the car out beyond Pleasant Valley alone. Get stuck. Think car broken in turning around. Send for help. Car all right." On May 3, he recorded "A run to Highland through the fresh, fragrant May air." As his confidence in driving the car grew, so did the speed at which he drove it. His granddaughters still recall many nerve-rattling drives with their grandfather who came eventually to take a great joy in high acceleration.

In June 1913 Burroughs visited Ford in Detroit to thank him for the car that had nearly killed him. Ford paid for the trip. Burroughs wrote Barrus on June 5 that Mr. Ford was "pleased with me and I with him. His interest in birds is keen, and his knowledge considerable. A lovable man." Without consulting Burroughs, Ford had arranged a hectic round of public events for the naturalist during his visit to Detroit. "Yesterday morning I was coaxed down to the central high school, 'just to show myself to the young people—not to speak a word,'—the old story," he wrote Barrus. ". . . I was led like a lamb to the slaughter. The room was packed with 2600 pupils, all excited and expectant. Such a clapping as there was when they saw me! [I was led up to a] wide platform, but Mr. Ford . . . refused to follow, and left me to my fate." [4]

One afternoon, while they ate lunch at Ford's private bungalow in the woods near his home, Ford mentioned to Burroughs his plan to make a trip that autumn to Concord, Massachusetts, to visit the haunts of Emerson and Thoreau. Since it had been through Burroughs's books that Ford had been introduced to the work of the Transcendentalists, would Burroughs care to join him on the pilgrimage? Ford would be making the trip by car, of course, and would be happy to stop and pick Burroughs up at his home. Burroughs readily agreed to the proposal. And so it was that during the first week of September Ford and a fleet of cars arrived to set up camp in the orchard by Woodchuck Lodge. After spending several days at the lodge, during which Ford's mobile camera crew shot films of Ford and Burroughs hiking the hills of the old home, the two men departed for Concord. Burroughs recruited Emerson's and Thoreau's old friend, the educator Franklin Sanborn, to show Ford around Emerson's house, Walden Pond, and Sleepy Hollow Cemetery. As a young man infatuated with Whitman and annoyed with Emerson, when Burroughs had the opportunity to call at Emerson's house and find the man himself at home, he'd instead contented himself with just looking at the woodpile. Now that Emerson was long gone, Burroughs walked with Henry Ford through the musty, unoccupied rooms.

A fleet of Ford cars and trucks complete with chauffeurs and attendants accompanied the two men on the trip. One truck was a traveling field kitchen. Another carried seven tents for Ford, Burroughs, and Ford's staff. Other vehicles carried Mr. Ford's wardrobe, newsreel cameras of the Ford publicity department, a portable refrigerator, a dining tent with an upright table that seated twenty, and gasoline-powered electricity generators. Burroughs and Ford each had a private ten-by-ten tent complete with portable floor, electric light, folding cot, mattress, blankets, sheets, and pillows. When Burroughs woke in the morning, his freshly pressed three-piece suit was waiting for him. A clean, starched collar lay on the shelf beside his portable washstand. "The tent has more comforts than does Slabsides," he wrote Julian.

This was the first of many camping excursions that Burroughs was to make with Ford. The following February he would find himself at a luxurious campsite on the outskirts of the Everglades, near Fort Meyers, Florida, with both Henry Ford and Thomas Edison. Later years would see him on camping trips with Ford,

Edison, and Harvey Firestone in the Smoky Mountains (1917), the
Adirondacks (1918), and the Green and White Mountains (1919).
As was the case with every other move the carmaker made, the
camping adventures of Ford and friends (who called themselves
"The Vagabonds") were captured by the newsreel cameras of Ford's
publicity department and packaged for showing in movie theaters
throughout the country. MILLIONS OF DOLLARS WORTH
OF BRAINS OFF ON A VACATION read the heading of one
newsreel story, with the subtitle GENIUS TO SLEEP UNDER
THE STARS. The pictures cranked out by the hand-held movie
cameras are still here for us to see: choppy black and white images of
overdressed, seemingly nervous, and painfully self-aware men wandering through the woods in suits and ties, trying desperately to look
as if they are having fun despite the presence of the cameras. Here
they are posing stiffly on an unmoving old waterwheel. They smile
and nod to the camera. Edison swats a fly. A shot from a later
expedition shows them rolling up their trousers and wading into the
waters of a Catskill trout stream. In a clip that did not make it to
movie theaters, we see Ford take three steps, fall on his rear, then
turn to the camera and angrily motion for it to be turned off. In
another clip Ford and Burroughs have a contest to see who can split
logs the faster. Ford wins.

While Ford's cameras saw to the film documentation of the
journeys, Burroughs kept his own chronicles of the adventures. "I
am writing this on my knee beside the camp-fire at 7:30, while
breakfast is being got ready," he wrote one morning during the
Smoky Mountain trip. "Mr. Ford is standing with his back to the
fire on the other side, talking with a caller. Mr. Firestone is warming
his hands over the coals. Edison is not up yet—yes, he is just out,
holding his hand in front of his face in mock repentance for being
up so late. He is a great character, and we are all devoted to him.
Whenever the cars stop he gets out, collects a handful of flowers and
brings them to me—half a dozen times each day—and I name them
for him." Ford was the most energetic of the campers. "When we
have settled on a camping site," wrote Burroughs in 1918, "Mr.
Edison settles down in his car and reads or meditates; Mr. Ford
seizes an axe and swings it vigorously till there is enough wood for
the campfire."

As had been the case on his excursions with Harriman and Roosevelt, the finicky Burroughs insisted on his comforts. "It is the old story—dinner at 8 or 9 P.M." he wrote angrily in his journal of the 1919 trip through the Green and White Mountains. "I have just told Mr. Ford I must have a warm dinner in the middle of the day or I quit. Edison is dictator. He shuns all the good state roads and hunts up rough, hilly dirt roads . . . Mr. Ford says I shall have the warm dinner . . . I will not live on cold snacks." His excursions with the Vagabonds were often followed by notes of apology from Burroughs for complaints and demands made along the way. "I am aware that I whimpered and grumbled a great deal on the trip," wrote Burroughs to Edison after the 1919 expedition, "but you must charge that to my age. I really had a wonderful time and got a large slice of our geography very vividly impressed upon my memory, to say nothing of the impression made upon some of my posterior muscles." To Firestone he wrote after the same trip, "I did not quite cease grumbling and groaning till I got home. Well, you see allowances must be made for [an old man]; he is an old baby, and is entitled to a little indulgence on that score. No doubt I made myself disagreeable at times." [5]

Burroughs's diary notes of the Concord trip, his very first auto voyage with Ford, are full of adoring portraits of the carmaker with whom, like Roosevelt and Harriman before him, Burroughs was plainly infatuated. Burroughs wrote of Ford's response when encountering a poor family that had just been burnt out of their home. "The old man and his wife sit there under the trees looking pretty forlorn," wrote Burroughs. "Mr. Ford gave them a hundred dollar bill, which brought tears to their eyes and halting words of thanks to their lips. Then when he heard of the girl [their granddaughter] who had got ready to attend high school this week, but whose clothes were now all burned up, he gave them another hundred, which did, indeed, astonish them, and made their tears flow afresh." Burroughs frankly idolized Ford. "Notwithstanding his practical turn of mind," wrote Burroughs of Ford, "and his mastery of the mechanic arts . . . he is through and through an idealist. This combination of power and qualities makes him a very interesting and, I may say, loveable personality."

There was one aspect of Ford's personality, however, which the adoring Burroughs plainly, and without apology or acquiescing silence, did not adore. Ford was a rabid anti-Semite. Burroughs refused to go along. Just as he had vocally disagreed with Whitman's dislike of blacks, so now did he use every opportunity to quarrel with Ford's bigotry against the Jews. The topic made for lively conversation at many a campsite, as Edison was also an entrenched Jew hater. In his logs of the camping trips with Ford, Edison, and Firestone, Burroughs unhappily chronicled the round of Jew-baiting that took up more and more of the after-dinner conversation. "Mr. Ford," wrote Burroughs in his diary of the 1919 trip through Vermont and New Hampshire, "attributes all evil to the Jews or the Jewish capitalists—the Jews caused the war, the Jews caused the outbreak of thieving and robbery all over the country, the Jews caused the inefficiency of the navy of which Edison talked last night." At one point in the conversation, when explaining how the Jews controlled Wall Street, Ford used as an example Jay Gould— the bearded manipulator of stocks and bonds who many, including Ford, assumed must have been a Jew or, as Ford put it, "a Shylock." Burroughs gleefully recorded in his journal that he "took a distinct pleasure in informing Mr. Ford that all Jay's people were Presbyterians."

When Burroughs visited Washington D.C. in January of 1913 with Ernest Thompson Seton to lobby in support of the Weakes-McLean bird protection bill, Ford saw to it that a car and chauffeur were at Burroughs's disposal. Likewise, when Mr. and Mrs. Burroughs went to Georgia a year later to spend much of February there, Ford again provided an automobile. In certain moods, he loved hot-rodding over the hills in his Model T. In other moods, he despised the machine.

> Yesterday we sent the car back to town . . . and I took a five-mile walk . . . I saw what a fraud the car is—how much it had cheated me out of. "Afoot and lighthearted," you are right down amid things . . . How familiar and congenial the ground, the trees, the weeds, the road, and the cattle look! The car puts me in false relation to all these things. I am puffed up. I am a traveler. I am in sympathy with nothing about me. [6]

WHILE URSULA AND JOHN were being chauffeured about the south, Clara Barrus's first book, *Our Friend John Burroughs*, was published by Houghton Mifflin. The adoring chapters in the book discussed Burroughs's work hardly at all, and instead focused on building up a cult of personality about the man himself. Barrus wrote that she would feel guilty and selfish to experience the inspiring presence of John Burroughs at close hand unless she should "try to share it, in a measure, with less fortunate friends of Our Friend." The book was full of intimate, adoring portraits of Burroughs as an eminently modest yet great man, a lover of humble pursuits and pleasures who was at home in the company of presidents and moguls. "Is there another literary man anywhere," asked Barrus, "now that Tolstoy has gone, who is so absolutely simple and unostentatious in tastes and practice as John Burroughs?" [7]

Burroughs, who in the tradition of Whitman had read and revised all of Barrus's pieces, insisted that Houghton Mifflin bring the book to press. The ever-loyal firm acquiesced to this demand by one of its best-selling authors, but they were nervous about the project from the first. In fact, the editors did not like the book at all. They did not think that Barrus's overblown, artificial portraits of Burroughs would sell. To safeguard their investment, they insisted that the volume also include childhood reminiscences penned by Burroughs. All of the advertising for the volume emphasized that though authored by Barrus, the book included extensive autobiographical sketches by Burroughs. In fact, Burroughs's sketches took up a full 146 of the book's 279 pages.

The occasion of publication was followed by a revealing letter from Burroughs to Barrus. "Mrs. B read your book . . ." he wrote. "She said it made her nervous, you praise me so much, make such an ado over me . . . It irritates her to hear me praised or made much of. She said last night: 'Do you think you deserve all that praise? If people only knew you as well as I do.' She is the one that deserves the praise. She really thinks she has made me." [8]

In writing *Our Friend John Burroughs*, Barrus made what would prove to be a serious mistake, one that not even Burroughs anticipated when reading and approving her manuscript. Throughout her extensive portraits of Burroughs at his various homes, Barrus emphasized what a democrat he was, how open he was to guests, and how anxious he was to have personal contact with his readers. Had not Barrus's fan letter to her favorite author resulted in the very closest of personal friendships? She let the readers of *Our Friend* know in no uncertain terms that it had. And Barrus emphasized that although Burroughs was a man of the woodlands, he was by no means a hermit. "I question whether there is any other modern writer so approachable," she wrote. [9] The pages of *Our Friend* are full of stories about uninvited strangers receiving a hospitable greeting from the benevolent Burroughs. In point of fact, as Burroughs increased in age he was very quick to grow weary of company that was not of his own choosing. But this truth was not in the book. What was in the book, though Barrus probably didn't realize it at the time, was an invitation to all who ever wanted to see and shake hands with a famous man, to all who could claim to be a fan of Burroughs and his books. Of course, *Our Friend* mentioned the villages in which one could find Riverby, Slabsides, and Woodchuck Lodge. Barrus also included details from which it was easy to deduce at what times of the year the naturalist could be found at either West Park or Roxbury.

When Burroughs returned to New York that spring, he felt that his privacy was being more regularly invaded than before. At Woodchuck Lodge that summer he wrote in his journal that he was beginning to feel uncomfortable whenever he heard an automobile on the road out front of the house. "So many of them stop here," he commented. [10] In the autumn he would write from Riverby to a friend, complaining that strangers were dropping in on him in "masses" and "through the mails make many demands upon me." In his journal he noted wearily, "Surely the public is wearing a path to my door. More and more people come to see me. Probably no other American writer was ever so run after. It is a doubtful compliment." [11] To his son he wrote that he felt like "an unfenced common—people run over me and through me." He also complained to Hamlin Garland. "What shall I do," he asked in a letter to Garland, "to check this unwanted flood of company?" Though there is nothing to show that he realized it, the truth is that Burroughs had Barrus's book, a veritable blueprint for invasion, to thank for the nuisance.

Nonetheless, Burroughs was gracious to all callers. The guests he seems to have most genuinely enjoyed were young people: both schoolchildren and college students. "A young man from Portland, Oregon, took part of my day yesterday," he wrote Barrus in a letter. "A bird enthusiast with a pile of photographs to show me, very interesting, but I hated to have the thread of my thought snapped. Still I feel that I ought not to deny myself to such young fellows—often my own intellectual children." [12] The man in question was William L. Finley, destined to become a noted nature photographer.

Another college-aged visitor, Harriet Geithmann, arrived two years after publication of *Our Friend John Burroughs*. On a late October day Miss Geithmann and three other Columbia University students came up to West Park by train, without an invitation, in hopes of meeting the naturalist. When they disembarked at West Park, the stationmaster told them how to get to Burroughs's farm. Arriving at Riverby, they were greeted by a hired hand who directed them to the study. There they found Burroughs sitting by the hearth. He seemed unsurprised when he looked up from his work and saw the faces of three strangers. There was a hint of whimsical, happy resignation in his manner. He had been writing some letters, but set these aside and invited the students in. Burroughs fielded questions about Whitman and bird lore for about an hour, and then announced that he had an errand to run. Noticing that the girls had a basket lunch with them, he said "You girls can either eat your lunch here in the study or out-of-doors and I'll be back at two." He gave them some apples from the orchard and some grapes. When he returned, he suggested that the girls come with him to Slabsides, "his other study in the hills." As Miss Geithmann wrote, "That was our goal and to have the Master with us was in the nature of a miracle. He got out his Ford and we all piled in." By the time the day ended, Burroughs had invited the girls to have an overnight campout at Slabsides the following spring.

As he grew older, he began more often than not to take the car up to Slabsides. When Ruth Drake, a young woman admirer with whom he had corresponded since she was a little girl, came for a visit on a clear spring day in 1915, the seventy-eight-year-old Burroughs apologized for taking her to Slabsides in his auto. He said he hadn't slept very well the night before and didn't feel quite up to a hike that day. The road up the mountain was unpaved, and in places quite steep and winding. "I trembled every inch of the way for he went so fast and the curves were so treacherous," recalled Drake. "I think he was chuckling inside all the way for I guess he saw I wasn't as composed as I might be."

When they got to Slabsides, both the inside and the outside of the cabin was strewn with rubbish. Burroughs explained that on the previous day "gangs of schoolchildren and adults from New Paltz Normal and Kingston High School" had been to visit the cabin. He had walked over in the morning to open the cabin and visit with them briefly. Then he had gone back to Riverby to do some writing, leaving them to their lunches and their hikes. Late in the day he'd driven the car back to the cabin to lock up. That was when he saw the trash, but it had been too late to do anything about it. "One would think that people allowed such privileges would have better sense than to leave the amount of rubbish around that they did," wrote Drake. "Boxes, banana peels and so forth were scattered about the outside as well as in." Miss Drake helped Burroughs clean up, tossing the trash into the fireplace. Burroughs went about the task stoically, without complaint. Looking through his journal notes for the day, we find no mention of the garbage left by the thoughtless guests.

JULIAN HAD BUILT HIS father a fine oak writing table for the long summers at Woodchuck Lodge. Burroughs put the table in the sunny parlor that he originally planned to use as his study. But then the tourists starting knocking on the door, the grandchildren arrived to spend weeks running through the downstairs rooms, and Burroughs lost interest in his unquiet study. His only alternative was the old barn where he had stared with terror into the darkness of the hayloft when a boy. Now every morning of summer, after breakfast, he put his manuscript in a picnic basket along with a book or two and some fruit, and walked the two hundred yards up the quiet country road to the dilapidated barn. For his first two summers at the lodge, an old dry-goods box, which previously had been used as a hencoop, served as his writing table. At the start of the third summer, he made himself a rude table of cast-off boards that would remain his hay-barn desk for nearly ten years. At the opposite end of the barn he hung a hammock. The building was still in use for nonliterary occupations. As the season progressed, the piles of hay in the mows built up around the man who labored every morning with pen and paper, creating many of the essays that would go to make up *The Summit of the Years* (1913), *The Breath of Life* (1915), *Under the Apple Trees* (1916), and *Field and Study* (1919).

The writing he engaged in during the long summer hiatuses at Woodchuck Lodge ranged from the sublime to the feeble, from the inspired to the purely commercial. In such essays as "The Noon of Science" and "The Phantoms Behind Us" he took up the crisis of faith confronting modern man in the wake of the great scientific revelations of the late nineteenth century. Then there were essays that Barrus arranged for him to do on assignment for large sums. These were usually on light topics that did not genuinely interest him, such as an essay on "How I Can Do More Work at Seventy-Seven Than at Forty-Seven" for the *Ladies Home Journal*.

As usual he drew his best inspiration from what he found immediately around him. In "A Hay-Barn Idyll," which was published in the 1913 collection *The Summit of the Years*, he recounted his observations of a junco that had built its nest in a loft of the barn. In "The Circuit of the Summer Hills," also published in *The Summit of the Years*, he spoke of the scenic landscape of the home farm, with all its youthful associations.

> The peace of the hills is about me and upon me; the leisure of the summer clouds, whose shadows I see slowly drifting across the face of the landscape, is mine. The dissonance and the turbulence and the stench of cities—how far off they seem! The noise and dust, and the acrimony of politics—how completely the hum of the honey-bee, and the twitter of the swallows blot them out! In the circuit of the hills the days take form and character . . . The deep, cradle-like val-

leys, and the long flowing mountain-lines, make a fit re-
ceptacle for the day's beauty . . . The valleys are vast blue
urns that hold a generous portion of lucid hours. [13]

Breaking the idyllic tranquility of the place was the fairly regular blast of the master's rifle. He carried his gun with him around the
property and made it a habit to shoot every woodchuck he saw. "I
am writing this in my orchard-camp under the apple trees, with my
rifle standing at my elbow," he said in a letter to a friend. "The
woodchucks are doing their best to make the place justify its name. I
kill about three a day. If we could only eat them as they eat our
garden-truck, we would not need to call at the butcher's, or visit our
neighbor's hen-roosts." [14] He collected the pelts of the 'chucks he
killed, and eventually made them into a heavy winter coat. The
sculptor Cartaino Sciarro Pietro, who visited the lodge to do a statue
of Burroughs, had to put up with Burroughs regularly jumping up
from the spot where he posed in the meadow to seize his rifle and
shoot at 'chucks.

Pietro positioned Burroughs lounging on a big rock in the old
pasture upon which he had played when young—he called it his
"Boyhood Rock." Burroughs sat cross-legged on the rock, leaning
back on his right hand, shading his eyes with his left hand as he
looked across the valley. The pose went well with the title Pietro had
in mind for the work: "The Seer." But it was a hard position for
Burroughs to sustain for long hours while the fastidious Pietro
slowly crafted the clay model from which he would fashion the
larger statue in his Manhattan studio. Burroughs found the posing
uncomfortable and what was worse, boring. Barrus would come up
from the lodge to sit beside the Rock and read aloud to him from
Twain's *Joan of Arc* in order to make the time go faster. Every day,
at a different and completely unpredictable hour of his choosing,
Burroughs would suddenly climb off the rock and announce that he
was done. It made no difference at what point Pietro was in his
project, or whether or not he had reached a logical place for a break.
"He's the one who is getting paid for this, not me," Burroughs told
Barrus. "Let him work it out." (Pietro was on a commission from
Henry Ford.)

One early morning, before Burroughs went up to Boyhood Rock to begin his posing, he and Barrus were surprised to hear loud yelling from the pasture. Looking up to the field, they saw the sculptor and his assistant rushing wildly about, throwing sticks and stones at the astonished cows. When Burroughs got up to the spot, he discovered that the browsing cattle had eaten off the carefully modeled feet of the clay man. Pietro was in tears. Several days of work had been ruined. Burroughs showed no sign of caring about the sculptor's problem. His first instinct was to glance anxiously about the field to the lumbering cows and inquire, "Do you suppose they ate enough clay to poison them?"

A few days later, Burroughs announced to Pietro that he was going to Onteora Park with Hamlin Garland and other friends for the weekend. Further work on the statue would just have to wait. Pietro did not appreciate the delay. He revenged himself over Sunday by creating a small statuette of Burroughs on the veranda of the lodge which, while the clay was still soft, he put into a series of absurd poses. Pietro corrected the posture of the figurine before the clay hardened. The statuette was sold to Helen Gould Shepard, the eldest daughter of Jay Gould, for $5000. Pietro's wasted Sunday proved profitable after all.

"Pietro left Thursday," wrote Burroughs to Julian in late August. "He took away three J. B.'s in plaster." Other visitors came and went. The artist Walter Otto Beck painted him on the veranda of the lodge. Ida Tarbell, journalist and biographer of Lincoln, came to sit on the porch and listen to his reminiscences of Lincoln and the city of Washington during the Civil War. Helen Gould Shepard was a regular guest. Mrs. Shepard had purchased the old Gould farmhouse and donated it to the town of Roxbury as a library. She had also financed the building of a large Episcopal church in town that she dedicated to the memory of her father. And she established her own summer home nearby. Occasionally she would come with her car and take Burroughs for drives. They went over to the graveyard where many markers bore the names of either "Gould" or "Burroughs" and where Jay Gould had erected a granite obelisk over the graves of his parents and grandparents. Helen also brought Burroughs to visit Furlow Lodge, the princely log palace that her older brother, George

Gould, had built on the shores of Furlow Lake, where Burroughs and Jay Gould had trouted in their youth. [15]

Ursula Burroughs spent only a few weeks at Woodchuck Lodge every summer. "She does not like woodchucks nor Woodchuck Lodge as I do, nor a lodge in the wilderness, like Slabsides," he wrote a friend. "She is an impeccable housekeeper, and my likes and ways about a house are a sore trial to her." [16] Likewise Julian spent little time there, as he had responsibilities with the grapes at Riverby. Barrus was often with Burroughs at the lodge, and Emily and the grandchildren made extended visits. His grandson, John Burroughs II, camped in the orchard. Burroughs cooked on an open fire with the boy, and showed him how to skin woodchucks. After the 'chucks were skinned, Burroughs and the boy buried their carcasses in the garden. Then Burroughs showed John how to tan the pelts. He regularly took all three grandchildren—Elizabeth, Ursula, and John—swimming at nearby Stratton Falls. And he took them round the neighborhood of Roxbury and Hobart in the car to visit their many cousins.

FROM MID-1914 ON, the single dominating fact on the horizon for John Burroughs, as for so many other Americans, was the war in Europe. That summer, he often asked Barrus to put "La Marseillaise" on the Victrola. One night when someone started playing a record of "Die Wacht am Rhein," Burroughs instantly called out, "Don't play that—I never want to hear that again!" He despised the German war machine. "If I could forge my pen into a sword and run it through that world-scoundrel, the German Kaiser, a few times, I think my liver would turn over and wake up," he wrote to a friend. "I cherish one hope, that the War will put an end to militarism, and that every crowned head on the continent will fall. I can see no other good likely to come out of it." In his journal he expanded on this: "Write a little, but not with much zest. The terrible war oppresses me. That war-drunk Kaiser my special detestation. He will ring ruin upon his country, and great injury to the whole world. But if the militarism of which he is the embodiment is crushed and cast out by the war, there will be a great gain." From the quiet solitude of

Woodchuck Lodge, unable to get the carnage in Europe out of his mind, he took to writing letters about it to the *Times* and other New York papers. While America was still officially neutral, Burroughs made it plain in public places that he was not neutral. In letter after letter he itemized the crimes of Germany. He thought and wrote about little else than the war through 1914 and 1915.

In the fall of 1915, when Henry Ford was planning his famous, ill-fated "Peace Ship" voyage to bring a halt to the belligerencies in Europe, Burroughs told the automaker candidly that they had a disagreement.

> I have such affection for you and admiration for your life and work that I hesitate to speak any discouraging word about any worthy scheme you may undertake. God knows we all want peace—a real enduring peace and not a mere truce. I would give all of my little pile to bring about such an end, but the day has not yet arrived when peace can be had. To stop the war now would be like stopping a surgical operation before it is finished. The malignant tumor of German militarism must be cut out and destroyed before the world can have a permanent peace. The Allies will cut it out, give them another year.

That December, when the Peace Ship was at dock in New York preparing to go to sea, Burroughs went aboard and spoke with Ford. "He might as well try to hasten spring as to hasten peace now," wrote Burroughs. "I told him as much."

He was fascinated and appalled by the military machinery that made this war so much more gruesome and horrific than those before it. Submarines stalked and sank civilian cruise ships. First-generation war planes dropped crude bombs with fatal inaccuracy—aiming at troops or command posts but hitting cathedrals and schools instead. Mustard gas destroyed the lungs of soldiers in its windward path; then the killing wind kept moving on to where civilians huddled for shelter behind the lines of combat. Innocent noncombatants were routinely involved in the fray by the power of technology. Burroughs was depressed by the spectacle.

He turned to Emerson for solace and sanity. In a paper of the period, "Emerson and His Journals," Burroughs recommended the

Transcendentalist as a "hopeful and courageous force" that could be of value to young people in those troubled days. Emerson, wrote Burroughs, offered an antidote to "the pessimism and materialism which existing times tend to offer." Emerson had been an unconquerable optimist. "He saw clearly how good comes out of evil and is in the end always triumphant. Were he living in our day," wrote Burroughs, "he would doubtless find something helpful and encouraging to say about the terrific outburst of scientific barbarism in Europe." [17]

The progress of the war was the most important thing on his mind. Whether at Riverby or Woodchuck Lodge, he waited impatiently each morning for the newspaper. He was intolerant of any interruption that would keep him from reading it. As the war grew in its impact on Europe, so too did it grow in its impact on his nerves. He was suddenly truculent, curt, and easily exasperated by irrelevant conversation. He could put up with no argument that endorsed Germany's cause. When in discussions of whether or not the United States should enter the war, he was intemperately fierce and vindictive. On one afternoon at Woodchuck Lodge, when Barrus unwittingly introduced Burroughs to a friend who was a pacifist, there was a predictable result. As was usual these days, Burroughs brought up the subject of the war. In turn the philosophy of Barrus's friend was explained. Burroughs stood up, said, "You are a very foolish and naive young lady," and abruptly left the veranda. In a few minutes Barrus and her guest heard the sound of the elderly Burroughs ringing blows with his axe on the woodpile.

He saw the war as a great tragedy, and the German Kaiser as its sole founder. Sharing the popular naivete of the day, he sincerely believed President Wilson's admonishment after the entry of American forces that this would be the war to end all wars.

> If the Allies are victorious—and they must be—it will be the death of militarism, and all armaments will dwindle instead of increase as they have in the past forty years, and thus an enormous burden be taken from the people. Half the money spent for armaments every year among Christian nations would greatly ameliorate the condition of all classes of people, and banish many of the most cruel diseases from the world.

The war, he told Julian, had to have the highest of goals: the defeat of militarism as a concept. Without this, it would be nothing more than a grotesque burlesque of mechanized death and "unholy fire." Just as the abolition of slavery had given the carnage of the Civil War meaning, so now must a higher purpose make noble the Allied dead. Without this, all who suffered would be doing so in vain.

Burroughs became deeply depressed by the news of the thousands of Americans killed—among them several young men whom he knew and held in high esteem. Theodore Roosevelt's son Quentin, with whom Burroughs had hiked and fished, was to die in France in 1918. So too would Joyce Kilmer, the author of the poem "Trees," who had come to Woodchuck Lodge to meet Burroughs not long before going overseas. Elbert Hubbard, who had been to visit at Slabsides in the 1890s, died in the sinking of the *Lusitania.*

BARBARISM CAME IN MANY forms, scientific and otherwise. In many ways the natural ebb and flow of life was more barbaric than anything man could devise. In the fall of 1916, the seventy-nine-year-old Burroughs learned that Ursula, who had been his wife for over fifty-nine years, was soon to die. "We took my wife away to the [Battle Creek] Sanitarium at Middletown on Saturday, and I am to go over in a day or two and see how she is getting on," he wrote a friend in early November. "She is very feeble and the diagnosis [prognosis] is almost hopeless—a cancerous condition of the bowels is feared . . . I must stick by her in these hours of feebleness and pain."

He journeyed to Middletown on the 9th and found his wife very tired and discontented. X-rays had confirmed the doctor's suspicions. "I had long ago made up my mind that she could not get well, but when they told me what they saw, and that she could probably not live more than a month or six weeks, it came like a fresh blow. It cut me through and through. I return on 4:20 train." He went back to her on the twelfth. "I fear she grows weaker," he reported to his journal. "I sit by her and do all I can for her. Oh! how emaciated she is! Wants to talk with the doctors about her case. I tell her a part of what they say—that it is serious, and the chances are against her; but I tell her to will to get well. She says she will do all she can." [18]

With Ursula in the hospital, John was almost completely alone at Riverby except for Hudson Covert and Covert's family. Burroughs slept and cooked in the study for several weeks. "I am fearfully forlorn here now," Burroughs wrote Barrus after his wife entered the hospital, "both houses dead." Julian and his family no longer lived at the farm. Though Julian still managed the vineyard, he had moved north one mile to a residence on the estate of the Standard Oil tycoon Oliver Hazard Payne, where he had accepted the position of superintendent. He'd had a hard time in recent years making Riverby pay enough to support his family in the face of competition from California growers who could plant and harvest year-round and deliver grapes at much lower costs than most eastern growers. With a salary plus house and board at the Payne estate, Julian could rent out his home at Riverby and count whatever money he made from the grape crop as pure profit. Barrus had leased Julian's house, which she dubbed "the Nest." But that fall she was delivering a course of lectures on psychiatry in New York and would not return to Riverby until December.

From the Sanitarium in Middletown Ursula went to Vassar Brothers Hospital, in Poughkeepsie, for several weeks. Then, when the doctors there could do no more for her, she was brought home in mid-December. Ursula wanted to go back into her own home, but it was decided that it would be too hard to care for her there in that house of so many stairs. The other home at Riverby, the one that Julian had built and that Barrus was now renting, would be more comfortable both for the dying woman and for those who had to nurse her. Ursula was installed in a front bedroom.

Returned from her lecture stint in Manhattan, Barrus administered painkillers as necessary and otherwise saw to Ursula's comfort. Naturally, there had always been great tension between the two women. They had never spent much time in each other's presence. Now, for all practical purposes, this trend continued. The painkillers left Ursula unconscious for twenty hours out of every day. The two women—doctor and patient, mistress and wife—barely spoke.

"My poor wife does not mend," Burroughs wrote in a letter to Theodore Roosevelt shortly before Christmas.

We brought her here from the hospital over two weeks ago, as the doctors there said they could do nothing for her. She suffers a great deal and is a great care. I have no plans for the winter but to stay here and do all I can for her. I do some writing, some reading, some wood splitting, some walking, and a good deal of musing before my open fire . . . I feed the birds in front of my window, and play Santa Claus to a chipmunk nearby who is evidently short of winter stores.

Initially, Burroughs moved into the house with Barrus, Ursula, and a nurse. But then he moved out again, retiring once more to his cot in the study. He wanted to be able to put some distance between himself and his wife's suffering. Both Julian and Barrus were concerned for Burroughs, who was being worn out by the deathwatch and who was obviously entering into a state of depression. Early in December, when the American Institute of Arts and Letters awarded him a gold medal for excellence in belles-lettres, the event did nothing at all to brighten his spirits. "A great surprise, but, near eighty, it means little to me," he told his journal. [19] On the evening of the award ceremony he stayed away, preferring to spend the time with Ursula. "How can I go there for that medal—such a mockery—with poor 'Sulie lying there slowly dying?" he asked in a diary note. During Christmas week he wrote an article on "The High Cost of Dying" for the *New York Tribune.* In January, his friend the editor Hamilton Wright Mabie died. Burroughs wrote at length in his journal of "the bleak eternal darkness and stillness" that he assumed must now envelope the man.

January 3 was Ursula's birthday, her eighty-first. Burroughs sat by her side on the bed and heard her whisper that she hoped she would live as long as he did, and he as long as she, but neither of them any longer than that. Early the following morning he awoke to the distinct possibility that her wish might be coming true. He came in from the study before dawn, pale and frightened, and knocked on the door of Barrus's bedroom. He had spent two hours trying in vain to replace a hernia that had previously always yielded easily to his manipulations. It took Barrus another painful fifteen minutes to do the job. Burroughs told her later that he thought ominously of his wife's remark of the day before. His brother Hiram had died from the complications of a hernia.

As Ursula's illness dragged on, Julian and Barrus decided that something must be done to remove Burroughs from the prolonged tension of the deathwatch. Likely at the instigation of Julian, Ford invited Burroughs to join him on a short cruise through southern waters in mid-February. Ford had a voyage planned from South Carolina to Cuba and back. At the urging of everyone around him, Burroughs accepted. He claimed that he had never been the same man physically or emotionally after witnessing his mother's death, and he sincerely believed that at nearly eighty he could not endure another such ordeal. "She barely realizes that I am off," he wrote of the heavily sedated Ursula, "yet she asked me how long I would be gone." He stood by her bedside, gazing on her emaciated face that was yellow with jaundice. "I rested my face on hers a moment and said good bye." He could no longer feel the acute sense of loss and mourning that he had known two months before, immediately after the devastating news of the doctors' diagnosis. Though Ursula lingered, he made a conscious decision to move on. "She is almost the same as dead to me now," he wrote on February 18, the day of his departure for Charleston, where the Ford yacht *Sialia* was moored. "I would weep if I could. How pitiful it all is! Oh, if she could only be spared the suffering—if she could only go to sleep and not wake up!" [20]

The end came for Ursula two weeks later. Sitting in a white suit and straw hat on the upper deck of Ford's yacht, moored in the middle of Havana Harbor, Burroughs was handed a telegram. "In the afternoon, at three, as I sit alone on the upper deck reading an editorial in the *N.Y. Evening Post* on Mr. Howells's eightieth birthday, a telegram comes from C. B. saying my wife died peacefully yesterday—a blow I have been daily looking for, and which I thought I was prepared for," he wrote in his journal for March 7. "Here in this peaceful harbor, on this calm summer day, with the big ships coming and going about me, came this sad news. A long chapter in my life, nearly sixty years, ended." [21] Several days later he wrote to Barrus "I rejoice that I was not there; and that you and Julian did not want me; and that she did not miss me." [22]

He sought the consolation of nature. "The Ford party all off fifty miles into the country to visit the Rosario plantation," he wrote. "I have no heart to go with them, but crave a little solitude on the nearby hills. The launch puts me ashore on the N.E. side, and I walk up on the ridge overlooking the sea. Even Nature in her harsher aspects in the tropics soothes and heals. I stand and loiter long on the breezy ridge and look North upon the great blue crescent of the sea. I have but one thought and am glad to be alone with it on the hills." [23] Two days later, as the yacht pulled out of Havana, he looked off yearningly toward the green and brown countryside where he had walked with his sorrow. "I left something of myself on those hills," he wrote. "I lived in that solitude one hour of intensified life. No other point in the horizon so attracts me now. Thoughts of my poor lost one consecrate those hills. Oh, if she could only know how my heart went out to her that day!" [24]

He was home at the beginning of April, just in time to turn eighty quietly at Riverby among his family. He sat for a long time in the upstairs room of Julian's house where he had parted from his wife for the last time. He grilled Julian and Barrus for every detail of his wife's last hours, just as he had once interrogated his brothers and sisters for all their impressions of his father's death struggle. He felt a terrible sense of guilt over not being with Ursula at the time of her death, just as he had felt guilty about not being with his father. It was as if he could assuage this guilt by forcing himself to listen to the grim details of the final hours of she who died while he was safely away, out of sight and sound of her agony. It was an act of penance for him to hear the terrible story told. He tortured himself further by filling his journal with vivid, secondhand descriptions.

In the succeeding weeks, Burroughs and Barrus went through the hundreds of letters and telegrams of sympathy, and Burroughs answered every one. "I have come back into this shadow," he wrote in one note, "but I know that Death was a blessed release to her, and that thought helps to salve my wounds. We had lived together nearly sixty years, and, notwithstanding the disharmonies, her death leaves a great void in my life." [25]

He would live without her for four years, and would never quite get used to her being gone. At the same time, he plainly relished the absence of that part of her that he'd found annoying—the part of her that knew him better and longer than any other person, the part that was unawed by his fame, remembered his failures, and knew his fallibilities. His longing for the dead Ursula was laced with a nostalgia

292 / JOHN BURROUGHS

that quickly succumbed to the reality of his true emotions that had been so petty with regard to her for so long. "The house is like a tomb," he wrote in his journal the following autumn. "Felt her loss afresh when I went over to the kitchen door and found the leaves clustered there as if waiting for something. They were waiting for her broom. For over forty years it had not failed them, and now they lay there, dulled and discouraged." In the same entry he said that he never could have believed that he would miss Ursula so much. "Yet I do not want her back—but if I could only know she were well and happy somewhere in the land of the living." [26] He wanted her alive and happy; he wanted her safely away from care and suffering; he wanted her out of the cold, black hole of death; but he did not want her within sight of his eyes or within sound of his ears.

On a sunny morning in mid-May, more than two months after her death, Burroughs set out on his final errand for Ursula. Julian, Barrus, and Burroughs met the undertaker at the gate of the cemetery in Kingston where Ursula's body had been stored in a rented crypt. Four grave diggers loaded the casket into a hearse and the party drove to Tongore. In his journal, he described his wife's last resting place in detached, matter-of-fact detail. "Five feet deep into an old glacier hill," he wrote. "The bottom into two feet of sand, the upper part gravel and drift. It is a grim joke to say I never looked into a healthier grave—the drainage perfect. In the rear of her father and mother, instead of beside them, as I had expected." Over his father's objections, Julian insisted that a minister be present and that prayers be said. When the services were done, Burroughs walked away to the sound of dirt falling upon the coffin. "A beautiful spot, a beautiful view," he wrote. "I could see the schoolhouse where I began my career sixty-three years ago, and many farmhouses of those whose children came to school to me."

After the service, Burroughs had Julian drive him the short way to the school where his professional career had begun. "The little school ma'am was very gracious," wrote Burroughs. "She knew of me, but did not know that I had preceded her in that school by more than sixty years. No legend of me in the place, it seems. I told the staring children that I had been a teacher there sixty-three years ago, but that I did not see a face there I had seen then. They looked very solemn at my attempted joke." [27]

THE LAST HARVEST

This I know too: that the grave is not dark or cold to the dead, but only to the living. The light of the eye, the warmth of the body, still exist undiminished in the universe, but in other relations, under other forms. Shall the flower complain because it fades and falls? It has to fall before the fruit can appear. But what is the fruit of the flower of human life? Surely not the grave, as the loose thinking of some seem to imply. The only fruit I can see is in fairer flowers, or a higher type of mind and life that follows in this world, and to which our lives may contribute.

*— From "**Facing the Mystery**," written two*
months before his death

AMID THE PILE OF CONDOLENCE letters was a piece of mail that had evidently been posted before the death of Mrs. Burroughs, or in ignorance of it. It was a happy note from Miss Geithmann, who with her friends had dropped in to see him the previous fall, and to whom Burroughs had extended an invitation to sleep over at Slabsides come spring. Now she was proposing to take him up on his offer. It must have been a relief to him to be able to write a letter about something other than loss and grief. "If the weather keeps mild," he wrote to the girl, "the arbutus will be in bloom from about April 18 to May 1. I expect now to be here during that time and shall be glad to show you the sweet secret of the woods and put you all up at Slabsides."

At age eighty, Burroughs had sharply curtailed the amount of time he was willing to spend with visitors. Although he still did his best to accommodate his public, his best now involved considerably less personal involvement. In previous years visitors to Slabsides had enjoyed many hours hiking with Burroughs through the woods around Black Creek, but Miss Geithmann and her friends were hardly to spend more than two hours in the company of their host during their weekend at Slabsides. The girls arrived by train on a

Saturday in late April, about a week before Burroughs was to bury his wife at Tongore. They walked to Riverby from the station and found Burroughs in his study where he greeted them, gave them the key to Slabsides, and sent them on their way. Stopping first to buy provisions at the general store, the girls proceeded to the cabin and commenced exploring the hemlock woods that circled the place.

Burroughs had Julian drive him over to spend an hour with them in the late afternoon, during which he sat in a rocking chair on the porch and spoke forlornly of friends now gone who had tramped these woods with him—Whitman, Benton, and others. The girls spent a quiet night reading through the books scattered about the cabin. They were up early the next morning for a hike to Black Creek. After cleaning the cabin, they locked it behind them and started down the mountain to Riverby to return the key. Here they saw Burroughs once again. He gave each of them his autograph, and then walked with them a little part of the way toward the railway station. He was "joyous," reported Miss Geithmann, in the vicarious pleasure he took hearing of their experiences exploring Whitman Land on trails he no longer could negotiate.

The new widower spent his July and August, as usual, at Woodchuck Lodge with Barrus. Several of his friends had summer homes not far from him. The painter Orlando Rouland kept a cottage in the artist's colony at Onteora Park (Tannersville), as did Hamlin Garland. The friends made it their business to make sure Burroughs had company other than the strangers who dropped in to make demands on his time. The old man was included in the plans for every picnic and party. "August 15 a busy day!" wrote Garland in his journal. "At one we gave a luncheon with John Burroughs as guest of honor and at four Mrs. Rouland held a 'recipe party' at which Uncle John, wearing a long apron acted as cook and baked a huge pile of slapjacks."

At night Burroughs came over to Garland's house to sit while Garland played guitar and his two daughters sang folk songs. He made a grand picture dreaming in the light of Garland's fireplace. "I have on my mantel a photograph of him sitting in the firelight glow, craggily strong and weather-worn, his face wrinkled, his hands knotted," wrote Garland. "He was nearing the end of his path and I saw his fate in the ashes of the hearth. He loved the good old earth and was loath to leave it." [1] Later that same year, when Garland went to Rouland's Manhattan apartment for dinner on November 1, he found John Burroughs there. "I've been living alone at Riverby and cooking my own food all the fall," Burroughs told Garland, "and I'm tired of it. I shan't go back unless my son Julian comes to live with me. A house like that needs young life in it." Garland told Burroughs he thought him too old to live by himself. "I begin to feel that," he answered, nodding. [2]

Ursula's death had signaled the beginning of a new succession of losses for Burroughs. His life became a series of long hiatuses at Woodchuck Lodge or Riverby interrupted only by the occasional deaths of friends, the destruction of places he had known and loved, and public tributes that exhausted him. His nearest neighbor at West Park, John Jewell Smith, passed away just before Christmas of 1917. In the same week, Myron Benton's house at Troutbeck burned to the ground. Dr. Hull's place at Olive—where the young Burroughs had read medicine and written his poem "Waiting"—was torn down along with the rest of the town to make way for a lake created by a marvel of modern engineering: the Ashokan Dam. In the spring of 1918, he drove with Barrus to Tongore to look at his wife's grave and to see the new dam: ". . . walk down the road to the farm where wife was born," he wrote. "Much of it under water now." [3] One by one, the places, people, and things of his past vanished. One morning he came back from a walk beyond the railroad tracks in West Park, where he had been hunting a redwing's nest in the woods adjacent to the town dump. He was carrying a shabby black oilcloth bag. He had found the bag at the dump where someone—probably Julian—had thrown it after cleaning out the attic of the stone house. It was the bag he had carried in 1854 when he made his first journey from home.

That April, the old man went to Ohio for the unveiling of Pietro's heroic bronze statue of him. This was being presented to the city of Toledo by a wealthy resident of that town and cohort of Henry Ford's, W. E. Bock. By now, Burroughs was genuinely bored with such occasions. He had wanted to stay away, but Barrus insisted that he not risk insulting Ford's friend. "A great crowd," he informed his journal. "20,000 children pass in review before me, bringing flowers. Over one and one-half hours in passing. I stand there on the steps as smiling as a basket of chips . . . Pretty tired tonight. All is vanity and vexation of spirit." [4]

In the evening, as he sat dozing by the fireplace at Bock's house, Bock and Pietro returned from town to excitedly announce that they had just seen Douglas Fairbanks at a restaurant. "Who is Douglas Fairbanks?" asked Burroughs. The movies were something about which he was uninformed and skeptical. In a recent journal entry he had said that contemporary writers had a new problem to contend with, a problem that had not afflicted prose stylists of earlier decades. The contemporary writer had to learn how to address himself to "the moving-picture brain—the brain that does not want to read or think, but only to use its eager shallow eyes—eyes that prefer the shadows and ghosts of things to the things themselves." For his own part, he was sure he could not interest the moving-picture brain, and he did not want to. "How an audible dialogue would tire them—it might compel them to use their minds a little— horrible thought . . . What is to be the upshot of this craze over this mere wash of reality which the movies (horrible word!) offer our young people?" [5]

A FEW DAYS AFTER the death of Theodore Roosevelt on January 6, 1919, Garland heard that John Burroughs was at a doctor's office on the West Side of New York City. He decided to call on him there. "Although looking very old," recalled Garland, "[Burroughs] was hearty and sane and cheerful. He spoke of his growing infirmities in the straightforward way of a philosopher. He was deeply affected by Roosevelt's death, and talked of him for the most part." [6] On the 21st, Burroughs traveled to Oyster Bay to visit Roosevelt's grave. "Spend a half hour there," he wrote in the journal, "not all the time with dry eyes." The guard told him that William Howard Taft, Roosevelt's successor in office, had paid an unannounced visit the day before and had wept profusely. [7]

Garland next saw Burroughs at Riverby the following May. "Uncle John was out in the garden hoeing, or rather leaning on a hoe while watching a bird," recalled Garland. His hair and beard, white as wool, and the fixity of his pose gave him "the appearance of a statue." But as he turned to greet his guests the eighty-two-year-old seemed "frail and bloodless" to an extent that left Garland shocked. "He is able to leap up and kick his heels together, however, and did so just to show us that he still retained his agility." Taking Garland to the study, Burroughs showed the novelist sections of the manuscript of his current project for Houghton Mifflin, *Accepting the Universe.* "I write the drafts in longhand," he told Garland. "Then Dr. Barrus types them up for me and I revise on the typewriter sheets. I tried writing one chapter using the typewriter myself for the first draft, but the paragraphs came out sounding as though they'd been written by the machine instead of by me—and I believe they were." [8]

That July, when Garland returned to Onteora Park for the summer, he made a call at Woodchuck Lodge. In the month since they'd seen each other, Burroughs had suffered another loss. His brother Eden had died and been laid in the old glacial sand and gravel beside Hiram. "We found Burroughs in the process of being motion-pictured," wrote Garland. "He was a good subject for the camera with his shaggy head, brown shirt, and baggy trousers. How inescapably rustic he is." As soon as the Houghton Mifflin–financed camera was turned off and the crew sent away, Burroughs confessed to Garland that this was the type of thing he was getting very tired of. "I'm going on Sunday to join Edison and Ford on their annual outing" said Burroughs. "I am too old to go on such a trip, but I've promised to do it and I can't very well get out of it."

He told Garland of having dreamed of his dead brother Eden, and of Eden resting his hand on his shoulder and saying "John, time will fetch us." And he spoke of his brother Wilson, who had died as a young man so many years before, and who in his last delirium before succumbing to his fever said, "I must hurry, I have a long way to go over a hill and through a wood, and it is getting dark." The following October Garland would sit beside Burroughs in Orlando Rouland's darkened Manhattan apartment watching the Prizma color films made that sunny July day at the lodge. "John sat beside me," wrote Garland later, "and I wondered what was passing in his mind as he saw his shadow self upon the screen and realized how soon he must pass into history." [9] As is revealed by his writing at the time, the old man seems to have had a generally more positive view of his situation than did Garland.

The manuscript on which Burroughs was laboring, *Accepting the Universe*, was to be the last of his books to see print in his lifetime. *Accepting the Universe* is a work of radical optimism—a testament of faith in what Burroughs called "the universal beneficence" of manifold nature. The book tells the story of how Burroughs, now over eighty and certainly not far from the end of his life, had come to terms with his inability to believe in a personal God. He wrote that initially, as a young man, he had been unhappy with the conclusions he'd been forced to draw from his readings of Darwin, Huxley, and other scientists. He had not been content without God. "The words 'divine,' 'holy,' 'sacred,' 'heavenly,' are born of our reactions from this world," he wrote. "They are proof that we do not find this world divine or sacred and have no practical belief that we are in the heavens on this planet. Probably the main spring of all doctrinal religions is dissatisfaction with this world." He had needed, he wrote, to learn to insist upon religion without discounting the world. In the end, it was Emerson who had shown him how to do this.

God was incarnate in all nature, Emerson had argued. And man was uniquely blessed to perceive and relate to the Being in whose infinite bosom was all of endless time and space combined. The human mind was the only one in which God lived, for only humans were endowed with a moral nature. Man alone among other creatures had the ability to understand and appreciate the presence of the infinite. During the writing of *Accepting the Universe*, Burroughs borrowed a copy of Bishop Darcy's *God and Freedom in Human Experience* from his neighbor, Father O. H. Huntington, who had founded the Monastery of the Episcopal Order of the Holy Cross on property immediately to the north of Riverby. "Some parts of it go counter to my naturalism," he wrote Huntington in the note that accompanied the return of the book. "I can't stand any theological conception interjected into the scheme of Nature. Such a conception lies in my mind as a stone might in my stomach,—it will not digest and assimilate. I suppose I am an out and out pantheist. But I remember that Emerson says pantheism magnifies rather than be-littles God." [10]

He wrote of how God, as nature, had no moral consciousness. And he spoke of how the "Good Devils," in doling out personal tragedies to individuals, in the long run worked for the good of the evolution of all. Did not the forest fire, in addition to killing scores of innocent wildlife, also clear ground for new growth and thus keep the forest from strangling itself? Did not the bacteria of disease, though it kill and maim many in the short term, in the long work of generations serve to educate the body to resist illness? Was not the endless process of evolution full of little tragedies: weak species being annihilated to make room for the strong? Was not the human metabolism that ticked inexorably toward certain death also the same clock that enabled all physical and mental growth? "We select what we call the divine and stand confused and abashed before the residue," he wrote. It was foolish, he said, for one to expect nature, with its grand agenda, to have "scruples." He wrote that good and evil were strangely mixed in the world, and that both were a vital part of the cosmos that was God, Emerson's Over-Soul. "What is evil to one creature is often good to another . . . All parasites live at the expense of some other form of life and are to that extent evils to these forms; but Nature is just as much interested in one form as in the other; an ill wind to one blows good to another, and thus the balance is kept."

"You won't like my book at all," Burroughs wrote Julian shortly before the publication of *Accepting the Universe.* Julian, who was close friends with several monks from Holy Cross, had recently made a decision to be received into the Episcopal Church. "There are some days when I wish I could share your easy superstitions, but there are many more when I rejoice that I do not and wonder what has made you get married to such old prejudices and intolerances when you yourself are so young." [11] Burroughs made the point in *Accepting the Universe* that he would much rather have Huxley's religion than that of the bishops who sought to discredit him, or Bruno's than that of the church that burned him. He admired the Bible as a work of great beauty and wisdom. ("Have just been reading St. Paul," he wrote in his journal. "How eloquent, what good literature! These epistles

300 / JOHN BURROUGHS

would never have come down to us had they not been good literature. They are full of the wisdom of the soul—full of things that save
us in this world.") [12] However, he believed that the traditional view
of religion, which was based on a hope for the personal safety and
preservation of the spirit beyond the grave, was a theology burdened
with a "selfish" and "ignoble" foundation.

Nature had higher aims and aspirations than the preservation of
individual souls, wrote the man whose soul would surely soon
depart for parts unknown. Nature had the potential to create countless souls. Why should nature be concerned with preserving even
one? "Whoever is not in his coffin and the dark grave let him know
he has enough," Whitman had written in the *Leaves*. "It is all right,
John," Whitman had mumbled as the distraught Burroughs left the
poet's deathbed. "Of course it was all right," wrote Burroughs in
Accepting the Universe. "Our being here is all right, is it not?" If it
had been good to come, then it would be good to go—good in the
large, cosmic sense, good in that it was in keeping with the spirit and
purpose of the All. "I shall not be imprisoned in that grave where
you are to bury my body," wrote Burroughs elsewhere in the book.
"I shall be diffused in great Nature . . . My elements and my forces
go back into the original sources out of which they came, and these
sources are perennial in this vast, wonderful, divine cosmos." Burroughs sensed that, like a wave of the ocean, his momentary self was
a brief gathering of a unique blend of eternal forces. Like a wave, he
would rise and then subside. "We settle back into the deep, as a wave
settles back, or as it breaks and is spent upon the shore. The waves
run and run, the force or impulse that fills and makes them is co-
equal with the universe." [13]

As a replacement for ancient religions and rituals focused on the
hope for eternal life of the spirit, Burroughs once again, and for the
last time, argued for appreciation of the "high religious value" that
was inherent in a love of all elements of nature. The true creed was
written in the constantly changing leaves of the trees, the flowers of
the field, the sands of the shore, and, yes, the wholesome, natural
sexual instinct that Whitman had reveled in as the stuff of poetry.
For those with eyes to see, there was a new prayer every day—new
preachers and holy days all the week through. Every walk in the

woods was a religious rite just as was every child born, every bird sighted, every couple entwined, every trout lured and eaten. The communion service of nature's church could be had at all hours and in all seasons. Every man was a saint. None were sinners who did not condemn or despoil.

As HE AGED AND the state of his health became increasingly precarious, he reflected more and more on the importance of the fragile balance of ecological systems that combined to make the planet a healthy, vital island of life. "I am in love with this world," he wrote in his journal in 1919. "More and more I think of the globe as a whole . . . More and more I think of it as a huge organism pulsing with life, real and potential."

In "A Strenuous Holiday," Burroughs's account of his Smoky Mountain trip with Henry Ford and friends, he described the starting point of the sojourn, Pittsburgh, as a "Devil's laboratory" of smokestacks and smog—and he looked forward to what the alternative of solar power might do to clear the poison-filled skies of Pittsburgh and cities like it. He wrote that instead of burning the oil and coal of the earth, industries should come "above the surface, for the white coal, the smokeless oil, for the winds and the sunshine." Then, wrote Burroughs, "our very minds ought to be cleaner." In another late essay, "The Grist of the Gods," he penned a visionary portrait of the "thin pellicle of soil with which the granite framework of the globe is clothed." He wrote that until man realized, as he had not yet seemed to, that his fate was bound up with the fate of the planet, the race was like a child "playing with fire." Man routinely sought to manipulate nature for short-term results without a thought to long-term ramifications. "We are embosomed in nature," he wrote, "we are an apple on the bough, a babe at the breast . . . Our life depends upon the purity, the closeness, the vitality of this connection." [14]

He remained deeply skeptical of technology. When applied with forethought and vision, science could do splendid things. "Where there is no vision," he wrote, "science will not save us. In such a case our civilization is like an engine running without a headlight." Elsewhere he wrote that "We live in an age of iron, and have all we can do to keep the iron from entering our souls." He wondered whether the time had come when man's scientific knowledge and "the vast system of artificial things with which it has enabled him to surround himself" would cut short "history upon the planet." Envisioning a time when the earth's mineral and fossil fuel wealth would be depleted, the fertility of the soil used up, wild game extinct, and primitive forests vanished, Burroughs borrowed a phrase that Emerson had originated in describing Manhattan fifty years before. Burroughs spoke of what a "sucked orange" the earth would be if a sensitivity to ecological concerns was not fostered.

Burroughs spoke of the innate purity of nature in much the same tone as traditional theologians wrote of Adam's initial state of innocence. Nature untouched by man and machine was nature without sin or fault. Yet nature's innocent purity was all too easily corrupted by the sons of Adam, who had tasted the forbidden fruit of the tree of technology and now assaulted the world with their inventions. He wrote that he felt purified by a life led close to nature. He believed his life outdoors had brought him robust health through most of his days, and had made all his senses keen. He felt compelled to flee close rooms, and to leave the stench of cities behind him. "When I go to town," he wrote in the 1919 volume *Time and Change,* "my ear suffers as well as my nose: the impact of the city upon my senses is hard and dissonant; the ear is stunned, the nose is outraged, the eye is confused." Suffering from the original sin of being dissatisfied with God's creation, the sons of Adam had gone on to build cities with which to torment themselves.

AT CHRISTMASTIME IN 1919 Burroughs and Barrus were in southern California where they had taken a cottage at La Jolla that was to serve as their home for the winter. Burroughs had stayed at Riverby during much of the previous winter and had found the temperatures, ranging down to twenty below, too much for him to bear. He told a friend he had spent all his time complaining and trying to keep warm, and had no time left over for work. Here in the mild climate of La Jolla he felt well enough not just to do writing, but also some public speaking before the local Audubon chapter as well as other groups. The address he customarily gave at this time was not on nature appreciation or bird-watching, but rather on the great men he had known—first Whitman, Carlyle, and Emerson, then Roosevelt, Ford, and Edison. Barrus would often join him on speaking engagements now, and would follow up his talk with a short speech on the great man she had known: Burroughs.

In connection with the public lectures, Burroughs found himself socializing a great deal. At a house party near Pasadena he was an amazed onlooker as Will Rogers expertly swung his rope in magical loops and whipped off a barrage of jokes and stories. Burroughs had never seen or heard of Rogers before. He was impressed by the cowboy-comic's rope tricks, but even more so, he told his journal, by the "healthy cynicism" with which Rogers viewed politicians and all things political.

The house at La Jolla was situated on an ideal spot. From the parlor window he had a panoramic view of the Pacific. He wrote in his journal that it was the "greatest cradle on earth." Some days the cradle worked a little more gently than others, but the hand that nudged it was never idle. [15] Plovers foraged on the lawn of the cottage. Brown pelicans and black cormorants skimmed the waves. Seadogs barked above the blue waters, chasing unknown prey, sounding much like the foxhounds he'd heard in the Catskills when a boy. Sitting at his desk overlooking the ocean, he penned the essay "Under Genial Skies" in which he marveled at the homing instinct that allowed the seals to find the same unmarked trysting place here, at the edge of the Pacific, generation after generation. "What is the secret of it?" he asked. [16]

After a few weeks at La Jolla, he made an expedition to Imperial Valley, about a hundred and twenty miles away. Ford supplied a car and driver to take Barrus and Burroughs over the "great warty granite mountains." The high, narrow roads made him nervous; the desolate mountain scenery saddened him. "Rocky avalanches were hanging over you and waiting below you," he wrote. "Death and destruction seemed imminent on all sides." He was depressed by the lack of vegetation on the rocky mountainsides of the West. "The naked earth, the colored boulders, lay blistering in the sun," he wrote. "It was all like a nightmare." He had never seen mountain scenery further removed from the green, restful hills of the Catskills. "They tired me like a fever—a leprosy of stone." He wrote a nephew in the East that the barren slides and craters made him feel as though he were "on the moon, and just as lonely."

During much of her stay at La Jolla, Barrus labored on another book. This time she was focusing on Burroughs's childhood. Barrus used transcripts of interviews with Burroughs as well as his own written memoirs as the basis for *John Burroughs, Boy and Man*, which was to be published before the end of 1920. Burroughs was becoming impatient with Barrus's voracious appetite for every crumb and morsel from his past. He had decided he did not like much of *Our Friend John Burroughs*. In a letter to Hamlin Garland he complained that Barrus "is inclined to be too much of a hero-worshiper, and to lack a disinterested point of view." [17] Later in the year, when Burroughs helped Barrus review proof for *John Burroughs, Boy and Man*, he would complain that he was tired of reading about the same "old fellow" all the time, and thought surely there were more interesting subjects to write books about.

Early in the California sojourn, the forty-one-year-old Julian Burroughs was a third member of the party. Julian had long wanted to try painting with oils. He adopted the rocky landscape surrounding La Jolla as his first subject. Within days, Julian showed a surprising aptitude even though he had never before picked up a brush. While at work for Colonel Payne, he had demonstrated his ability as an architect when he designed and built many fine stone buildings for the colonel's estate, as well as a stone bridge over Black Creek. All these accomplishments fueled Burroughs's long-held conviction that his son was an artist at heart—an inspired creative force waiting to be unleashed. Now Burroughs renewed his fight to turn Julian into a full-time artist rather than full-time farmer and laborer.

"You are certainly a born artist and should have an artistic career,—architecture, or painting, or both," he wrote to Julian after the son's return to New York. "You have a genius for writing also, and a better style than mine, technically. I want to see you write a piece about Night. You can do it if you try. I want to see you have enough papers for a volume. Do it." Julian, for his part, though he did not enjoy writing to the extent Burroughs did, endeavored to submit a few pieces to magazines in order to placate his sometimes hard-to-please father. "I like to hear of your reading my books," wrote Burroughs to Julian, "but I wish you would read Darwin and Wallace, and the great masters of English literature, and of American literature, too. The better you know the great authors, the better your own work will be . . . You feed too much on the current magazines." He added that Julian should not be discouraged that his articles often came back rejected by editors. "I always rewrote my rejected articles. I could see their deficiencies when they came back with their tails between their legs."

When Julian sent a note to his father to announce that he'd found he could compose well on the typewriter, Burroughs was not optimistic. "I do not favor the typewriter," he told Julian. The machine would "get into" the writing if one wasn't careful. Type-writers, wrote Burroughs, "are a part of our mechanical age and I hate 'em." Julian's writing would lose its freshness and individuality if composed on a machine. Typewriters were "for business, and not for literature." In another note, Burroughs curtly thanked Julian for his "two type-written letters." He warned his son not to fancy that the typewriter would improve his style. "The style is in the man, and not in the ink-bottle, or in the machine . . . You have a style as distinctly as I have. My vessel draws more water than yours, but yours rides the waves more buoyantly." [18] In the end, Julian was to paint far more pictures than he would ever write essays. And he was never to publish a book comprised entirely of his own writings, nor to show any real interest in doing so.

Like father, not like son. Burroughs had regularly set aside the needs of his family in order to accommodate his writing. Julian, who had too often been neglected due to his father's self-centered dedi-cation to prose, refused to make the same mistake with his own family. "I've often thought how much more I had published than Thoreau did at the same age," wrote Julian in his unfinished mem-oirs. "But with me, writing was more and more crowded out by just the factors that Thoreau despised: material interests and duties—I inherited vineyards and buildings and I had a growing family with children to go to college. Perhaps if I had wanted to write badly enough I would have found a way to drive through the meshes of all the other interests and the duties that beset me on every side. I know that Father grieved that I let my 'pen rust out,' as he expressed it." [19]

ON MAY 23, 1920, Hamlin Garland stopped at Riverby on his way to Manhattan from Onteora Park. He found Burroughs sitting in an armchair by the fireplace in the Nest. Burroughs was wrapped in a thick gray blanket, and all about him was strewn evidence of literary labor. "It was a scholar's environment," wrote Garland. "His books looked like books in use. His table was a worktable. His papers, clippings, notebooks all indicated industry, as though we had interrupted him in the midst of a pressing task."

Burroughs had turned eighty-three the previous month, and was already entered upon the failing health that would kill him within a year. He suffered from almost daily bouts of irregular heart action. "A slight indiscretion now would carry him away," Barrus confided to Garland quietly. To Garland, Burroughs spoke movingly of the recently deceased William Dean Howells, his brother author and a man who had shared his same birth year, 1837. "Where is he now?" asked Burroughs. "Where has he gone? I can't think of him as nonexistent!" Then, suddenly, Burroughs's mind switched gears and he was jubilant and optimistic again. "I ran my car up to Slabsides the other day and expect to go again soon," he said. Barrus was not so certain. She looked Garland in the eye from behind Burroughs's back and shook her head no.

It was clear to Garland that his friend was never going to get any better. He made a point of dropping in at Woodchuck Lodge in late August to check on Burroughs, from whom he had not heard since May. "The lodge looked deserted," wrote Garland, "but at my knock, Clara Barrus came to the door." At the sight of Garland, her stern, forbidding expression was transformed into a smile. She called inside to Burroughs that he could come out from hiding. "It isn't a sightseer; it's someone you know." Following Barrus into a back room, Garland found Burroughs lying on a couch. A few days before, Burroughs had suddenly gotten dizzy and fallen in a heap on the floor. "Dr. Barrus thought I was dead," Burroughs confided to Garland, "but I remained conscious all the time." Barrus told Garland that Burroughs could not stand the flood of curious visitors. "They swarm on Sundays," she said. "They overflow the porch." Since the fainting spell, Barrus was not letting Burroughs drive his car. "I can still run my car, but Dr. Barrus is afraid to ride with me," said Burroughs. [20]

Garland noted in his diary that Woodchuck Lodge was a cheerless place on that rainy day. "It has no open fire, no pleasing colors, no glowing pictures, no ornaments," he wrote. "It has not even the picturesque poverty of a cabin. It displays the poverty of a poor farmhouse. It's couches are rickety and its chairs worn and cheap . . . No wonder he gets tired of it and is glad to get away." Thus it was that a few days later, on the 28th, Garland and a friend motored to Roxbury and brought Burroughs back to Onteora for a few days. "We found him ready and eager to come," recalled Garland. "His memory is failing and his thought is slightly inert, but he talks well and is interested in many things." Garland noted also that Burroughs no longer did much walking, and was subject to eccentric, often childish, behavior. "He makes rules for his diet and then breaks them on the impulse of the moment. He gets away from home with relief and then becomes childishly eager to return. All of which is amusing to some people, but of tragic import to me. These peculiarities are certain evidence of decline."

Burroughs himself was becoming preoccupied with the idea of death. On July 14 he and Barrus went into Roxbury so that he could visit the graves of his loved ones in the old Baptist burying ground. "I stood long and long at Father's and Mother's graves, and seemed very near them," he wrote. "I lingered about them all, and said goodbye to them all, and said I would come again if I lived." Barrus stayed behind in the car. She could see him wandering about the graves and hear him murmuring to himself in a low, sad tone. "We visit the graves of our friends and visualize them lying there in the utter silence and darkness," he wrote that night in his journal, "and know that we shall soon follow them, and yet we go home and are soon absorbed in a book or a paper, or are asleep in our chair! Blessed are we in not being able to realize the thought of death!" [21]

One evening, sitting on the veranda at Woodchuck Lodge, he startled Barrus by announcing abruptly: "This is a dreadful thought—there is never but one sound in the coffin—when the bones fall down." On a day when he felt strong, he engaged the help of a young nephew and worked hard at widening a section of road between the hay barn and the beech woods, opening it up where it had been a mere trench, breaking rocks, and filling in low places. "I never use that part of the road myself," he told Barrus, "but I have wanted to fix it for years, and I may not be around here another summer." A few days later he announced to Barrus that he did not want a black casket. He'd prefer a white one. When Barrus told him gray might be more suitable, that white was used for children, he rejoined, "I'm nothing but a child anyhow." [22]

IN THE FALL OF 1920, Burroughs's nephew John C. Burroughs decided to move to a place of his own. Julian, to whom Burroughs had deeded the homestead, would have to find a new tenant. In preparation for the move, John C. held an auction of some of the furnishings of the old home. Burroughs bid successfully on his mother's cherry dining table, but was outbid on his father's old saddle. Barrus would recall how he wandered sadly through the empty rooms of the house of his childhood, carrying a picture of Elder Hewitt (one of his father's favorite preachers) which he had found cast into the rubbish. On the 23rd he had Barrus drive him over to Hobart where he visited the graves of Hiram and Eden. Then, a few days later, he closed down the lodge for the last time. Before getting in the car he penciled a note on the gray siding of the porch: "October 26, 1920. Leave today."

A week later, at Riverby, he awoke from a nap with a start. He told Barrus he'd dreamed that Emerson had just been there, that he had been lecturing locally and dropped in for a visit. "I missed him and said, 'Has Emerson gone? Can't we keep him overnight?' But someone said, 'No, he wants to get home—he isn't very well—he has pain in the face.' Then I looked around and asked, 'Has he gone home?' and you said, 'Sh-h!' as though he were near. Someone sat there reading, a paper before his face. I don't know whether it was he or not, but I said to myself, 'I am going to sit down by him and tell him I think his poetry will be read as long as poetry is read.'"

When he and Barrus departed for California at the end of November, they brought with them Barrus's niece, sixteen-year-old Harriet Barrus, and Burroughs's granddaughter, fifteen-year-old Ursula. The trip west on the train was an easy one, with a stop at Dearborn to visit Ford and then another stop of several days at the Grand Canyon. When he arrived in La Jolla, he was in good spirits, but tired. He made no speeches and accepted but few invitations. "People must leave me alone now—I want nothing so much as to be left alone," he told Barrus. He spent most of his days in a comfortable chair before a big bay window that overlooked the sea, occasionally doing a little writing on a pad that he propped on the chair's wooden arm.

He wrote only sporadically now, and always briefly. The following year, when Barrus gathered up his writings from this last winter and edited them for publication, she would find herself grouping the brief pieces under broad general headings such as "Day by Day," "Gleanings," and "Sundown Papers." This was the only way to give some depth and cohesion to the short, random papers on such light topics as "Revisions," "The Daily Papers," and "The Alphabet."

One short essay written at La Jolla, "Notes on the Psychology of Old Age," gives a revealing glimpse of what Burroughs sensed was happening to his mental faculties. His mind, he wrote, was a vast storehouse of eighty years' worth of facts, incidents, and experiences. But the scattered memories did not hold together the way they had before; their relations were broken and uncertain. He might remember the name of some person from his past, but had lost the memory of his face or tone of voice. "It is a memory full of holes, like a net with many of the meshes broken." Some of the lapses were temporary. "Names and places with which one has been familiar all his life suddenly, for a few moments, mean nothing," he wrote. "It is as if the belt slipped, and the wheel did not go round. Then the next moment, away it goes again!" One day in December, sitting on the porch of the La Jolla cottage, he turned to Barrus, looking quite confused and helpless, and said, "I have forgotten where San Diego is." She explained that the city was sixteen miles to the south of where they were sitting. "Oh, yes, so it is," he replied. The slips became more regular. In conversation he revealed failings of memory: he believed Barrus had been with him on the Harriman Expedition when in fact he had not met her until two years after that trip, and he forgot that she had been with him in Hawaii. A woman from the staff of the American Museum of Natural History, whom he knew well and who had visited him at Slabsides less than three months before, came to see him in La Jolla and was met by him as a stranger. He had no recollection of her.

In a note to a friend he wrote that La Jolla was an "earthly paradise—all sun and sky and sea,—flowers blooming and birds singing and the Pacific beating its long roll one hundred yards below us." He wrote further that he felt well enough to do some work, and that he hoped to use the winter to "get another volume ready for press." [23] But the old man wearied of everything easily: company, the sea's beat, and even the warm sunshine that had presumably lured him to southern California in the first place. "The brilliant sunshine continues," he complained to his journal in December. "I begin to look for a day with the lid on. Oh, for the shut-in feeling of a storm! the privacy of a storm. I think I could get closer to myself on such a day. At any rate, it would be more like home." [24] To a friend in the East he wrote that the "desert of the Pacific" looked "forbidding and inhospitable." [25] He was getting tired of it.

Through December, more and more days were ones during which he searched for things to find fault with. His mood was increasingly petulant, unpredictable, negative. When Barrus suggested he add his name to a list of notables who were protesting the planned damming of the Colorado River and flooding of a section of the Grand Canyon, he astonished her by refusing. "You would let all that beauty be obliterated?" she asked. "Yes," he answered belligerently. "Beauty is the cheapest thing in the world. Why should that great hole in the ground be kept for people to gawp at?" He said he would gladly fill it up if necessary for the good of the masses. "I would abolish Niagara Falls. I would use all forces going to waste. Our coal is going to give out. We have got to get power from water." A few days later, when Barrus's niece Harriet commented on a beautiful sunset over the Pacific and called for Burroughs to come out on the porch to see it, he declined testily. "I have seen sunsets all my life," he growled. He was old, sick, and world-weary; his reactions and emotions were clouded.

In one of his very last papers, he returned to the theme of death. He titled his brief essay "Facing The Mystery," for that was indeed what he was doing: facing it head on. He was, in his most lucid moments, completely aware of how precarious his health was. He told Barrus not to try to fool him. He knew that the increasing pace and degree of his infirmities meant that he was failing generally, and that the end of his life could not be far off.

They moved to a cabin at Pasadena Glen, as planned, on February 3. It was here, on February 13, that he did his last literary work. In the morning he dictated a short paper to be read at the Howells memorial meeting of the American Academy of Arts and Letters. "When Mr. Howells died I think I felt much as a soldier must feel when a comrade falls by his side," Burroughs dictated to Barrus from where he lay on the couch of the cabin. "Although our tastes were so dissimilar, as well as our chosen fields of work, we were born in the same year, he being my senior by about a month; and we have been for more than fifty years before the reading public, he in his masterly portrayal of human nature, and I in my efforts to interpret outdoor nature."

On the same day, in the afternoon, he wrote the last paragraph he would ever compose. He had a paper he'd written several months before, a final reappraisal of Emerson entitled "Flies in Amber." When Barrus came to him and asked for a few closing sentences to round out the essay, he sat up in bed and obliged.

> Let us keep alive the Emersonian memories, that such a man has lived and wrought among us. Let us teach our children his brave and heroic words, and plant our lives upon as secure an ethical foundation as he did. Let us make pilgrimages to Concord, and stand with uncovered heads beneath the pine tree where his ashes rest. He left us an estate in the fair land of the Ideal. He bequeathed us treasures that thieves cannot break through and steal, nor time corrupt, nor rust nor moth destroy. [26]

At the brink of his demise, he turned one last time to do homage to the best of his first great teachers.

It was two days later, on the fifteenth, that Barrus discovered an abscess developing in the upper part of his chest, under the left pectoral. Within two days, he was in the local hospital where he would remain for four weeks. The abscess was quickly removed, but then problems of irregular heart action set in. Barrus stayed in his room with him, sleeping on a cot. Initially, in the first week, he seemed to improve. But after that, the course was one of steady decline. One night in March he awoke to tell Barrus that he felt as though his poem "Waiting" was etched in "frames of fire" on the wound from his surgery. Then he made her check to see if that were not the case. On an almost daily basis, Barrus found herself explaining to him why he was in the hospital and how they had happened to come to California in the first place. After three weeks in the hospital during which he showed no interest in reading or having anything read to him, he suddenly insisted upon having the latest *Atlantic Monthly*. He would not stop talking about his need for the magazine until it was fetched. Then, after it was brought, he did not bother to open it.

When Barrus checked him out of the hospital on March 17, she told him it was because he was doing better. In fact, she was taking him away because his rate of decline was accelerating and she thought she should get him home. The hospital had no cure for old age, only drugs for pain. The drugs could be dispensed by Barrus on a train just as easily as they could by a nurse in the hospital. They left California within days: Burroughs, Barrus, Harriet, and Ursula. Burroughs was placed in his bed before the train left the station. From his berth, he waved out the window to a few friends who had come to see him off.

As the train rolled across the country, Barrus and the two girls took turns tending to him. At night he was often feverish and disoriented. Through the days, he stared out the window from his bed as the landscape of America—first the desert, then the mountains, then the plains—hurried by. "The beautiful country," he murmured to Barrus. With each day, his condition became more grave. His heart and kidney functions were growing more and more irregular and inadequate. The train ran a losing race to get him home before the end came. At two in the morning on March 29, he awoke from his sleep and asked Barrus, "How far are we from home?" He was dead before she could answer. They were somewhere in Ohio—twelve hours from Riverby.

ARRIVING AT RIVERBY for the wake of John Burroughs on April 2, Hamlin Garland found many cars parked outside the Nest, where the service was to be held. Both Julian and Barrus stood by the door, greeting guests and jockeying for the position of chief mourner. Burroughs was laid out on a long wooden windowseat beneath two large windows facing the Hudson. He was dressed in a dark suit. His folded hands held a small bouquet of arbutus and hepaticas. At his feet was a large wreath sent by his publishers.

The company assembled was nonliterary: Julian's family and friends, Barrus's family, and a few of Burroughs's West Park neighbors. Garland, Dallas Lore Sharp, and Frank Chapman were the only writers in attendance. Edison sat nearby in an armchair, his deafness making conversation difficult. "He looked very old and white and sad," said Garland. Henry Ford was there as well—"a shy, ascetic figure." [27]

Garland thought the service shabby. It began with the playing of a phonograph record that was a favorite of Burroughs's. In deference to Julian's wishes, and in defiance of his father's, an Episcopal priest made a formal prayer. "This was followed by the reading of some verses which Burroughs is said to have valued for their philosophical content," wrote Garland. There were a few poems by Whitman, and one by Wordsworth. Garland took part, reading the Wordsworth from a handwritten index card that had been handed him.

> In common things that round us lie
> Some random truths he can impart, —
> The harvest of a quiet eye
> That broods and sleeps on his own heart.

The burial was to take place the next morning, April 3: John Burroughs's eighty-fourth birthday. The place of burial was to be the home farm. A number of the mourners planned on staying to join the cortege to the Catskills, but there was no room for guests at Riverby. Garland and a few other men, including Henry Ford, wound up sleeping next door at Holy Cross Monastery. "Rising at six . . . we ate our breakfast in silence, waited upon by silent monks," wrote Garland. "To find such an institution next door to the Burroughs home was an amazement to me." After breakfast, the men made the short hike through the trees to Riverby. At half-past eight the party started for Roxbury in seven cars provided by Ford.

At the home farm, the open grave in the pasture was surrounded by a throng that included more reporters than mourners. Sixty years later, Burroughs's granddaughter Elizabeth would still remember and be disturbed by the way in which the "merciless" newsreel cameras had ground out their footage of the grieving family.

The ceremony on the hillside was similar to that which had been presented at the Nest. The phonograph plaintively piped its little tune. A parson made a short prayer. Garland and a few others read some verses. And the mourners lined up to take a last look at Burroughs. Then the coffin was closed and lowered. A wreath made of ivy from Whitman's tomb was thrown down onto the casket.

"It was a glorious April day, Uncle John's eighty-fourth birthday, with a few birds piping," wrote Garland. He learned later that the old Devonian rock into which Burroughs was laid had been unyielding to the end. Twenty-four hours earlier, when it proved impossible to dig the grave into the hillside, local workers had resorted to dynamite. It wound up taking three earth-shaking blasts to gouge out the hole that was to be Burroughs's last resting place.

Despite the dynamiting of pasture and the irreverence of those whom Julian Burroughs would later call "the newsreel vultures," the place and the day in the end combined to create an eloquent coda to the life of John Burroughs. After the moguls and the camera crews left, and Barrus went off with a *Times* reporter for an interview, there was a brief moment of truth and peace before the work of filling the grave began. Only Julian and his family remained, along with the local cousins and neighbors who had not come to bury a famous writer, but rather to say goodbye to the man John Burroughs.

Julian, who had not spoken earlier in the service, now felt moved to do so. He rose and made a few impromptu remarks about how appropriate everything seemed. His father, born here on this hillside, had returned on his birthday, after eighty-four years of wandering, to be mixed with the soil of his home acres. "There were not many at this service today whom he would have cared to have attend. But you, his friends and kin, he would have wanted you to be here. I know he would want me to thank you for taking the time to be with him at this closing of his book, and more importantly for being a part of the life he knew and loved here." [28] At the end of it, Julian allowed how it would be appropriate for those gathered to take some of the flowers as keepsakes, if they'd care to. There was a moment of hesitation. Then one by one they approached, selected a blossom, and went away.

NOTES ON SOURCES

Manuscript Collections

The first stop for anyone doing serious research on John Burroughs must inevitably be the Berg Collection at the New York Public Library. Housed here are virtually all of the manuscripts, diaries, and letters that Burroughs entrusted to Clara Barrus. Dr. Barrus sold her complete archive to the Berg Collection in the 1930s. The most valuable of the Berg holdings are both sides of the Burroughs/Benton correspondence, and several manuscript drafts of *Notes on Walt Whitman as Poet and Person,* with Whitman's notes and emendations clearly legible. Here can also be found several of the little diaries John Burroughs kept during his various camping caravans with Henry Ford and friends. The Special Collections Division of the Vassar College Library houses many journals and manuscripts until recently held by the Burroughs family, together with hundreds of letters written to Burroughs through the years by his well-known friends and associates. The John Burroughs Collection in the Clifton Waller Barrett Library of the University of Virginia contains manuscripts and author's proofs for such early works as *Wake-Robin, Winter Sunshine,* and *Locusts and Wild Honey.* Much important material on Theodore Roosevelt's relationship with Burroughs is kept in the Theodore Roosevelt Collection at the Houghton Library of Harvard University. Extensive documentation on the Henry Ford/John Burroughs friendship is to be found in the Ford Archives of the Edison Institute, Dearborn, Michigan, where much on the Edison/Burroughs relationship can also be found. Another essential archive is the large cache of Whitman and Burroughs papers housed in the

Charles E. Feinberg Whitman Collection at the Manuscript Division, Library of Congress. This includes much correspondence between the two men, as well as many of Whitman's original manuscripts and notebook jottings. (Of special interest here are the original notebook entries from Whitman's three visits to Riverby, these having been later transcribed and edited for inclusion in *Specimen Days*, the original manuscript of which can also be found here along with that for Whitman's *Memoranda During the War*. Both these items are of immediate interest to the Burroughs researcher.) The Feinberg Collection also holds important diaries, letters, and manuscripts of William Sloane Kennedy.

Further important holdings of John Burroughs's manuscripts and letters can be found at the Yale, Columbia, and Princeton University libraries, while items relating to Myron Benton and his family are stored in the Poughkeepsie Room of the Adriance Memorial Library, Poughkeepsie, New York. Hamlin Garland's original diaries are housed at the Huntington Library, San Marino, California. The editorial archives and files of *Century Magazine* can be found at the New York Public Library on Fifth Avenue. Situated conveniently down the hall from the Berg Collection, this largely unsorted treasure trove holds originals of Burroughs's letters to the editors Richard Watson Gilder and Robert Underwood Johnson, as well as carbon copies of the *Century's* side of this correspondence. Also of use have been the private papers of Richard Watson Gilder, housed in the Berg Collection. Maury Klein's original research papers for his biography of Jay Gould contain much information on John Burroughs's youth. These papers are on deposit at the library of the University of Rhode Island, South Kingston, Rhode Island. Jay Gould's own personal library—including his set of the works of John Burroughs (complete through 1892, the year of Gould's death)—can still be found at his old mansion, Lyndhurst, located at Irvington-on-Hudson, in Westchester County. Lyndhurst is now a museum owned by the National Trust for Historic Preservation. The Jay Gould Papers housed at Lyndhurst hold valuable information on Gould's (and therefore Burroughs's) Roxbury boyhood. Additional documentation relating to the youth Burroughs and Gould shared can be found in the Helen Gould Shepard Papers of the New York Historical Society.

NOTES

Prologue: JOHN THE BAPTIST

1. Mumford, Lewis. *The Brown Decades*, 12.
2. Burroughs to Louis Untermeyer. 4 June 1919. The John Burroughs Collection, Vassar College Library Collection, Vassar College, Poughkeepsie, NY.
3. Twain to his brother, Orion Clemens. 27 March 1875. Twain Papers, Bancroft Library, University of California, Berkeley, CA.
4. Whitman, Walt. *Democratic Vistas*, 11.
5. Burroughs to Myron Benton. 11 October 1877. The Henry and Albert Berg Collection, New York Public Library, New York, NY.
6. Burroughs notebook entry. 17 January 1866. Berg Collection.
7. Burroughs. "The Poet and the Modern." *Atlantic Monthly,* (October, 1886).
8. Twain, Mark. "The Revised Catechism." *New York Tribune,* 27 September 1871.
9. Emerson. "On Nature." *Essays.*
10. Burroughs. "The Gospel of Nature." *Time and Change*, 212.
11. Burroughs journal entry. 2 March 1883. Berg Collection.
12. Burroughs journal entry. 12 May 1889. Vassar Library Collection.
13. Burroughs. *The Light of Day*, 137.
14. Burroughs. "Phases of Farm Life." *Signs and Seasons*, 219–20.
15. Burroughs to Julian Burroughs. 12 October 1920. Vassar Library Collection.

Chapter 1: PEPACTON

1. *Public Meeting of the American Academy and the National Institute of Arts and Letters in Honor of John Burroughs.* (New York, 1921), 1.
2. Article on John Burroughs's remarks at the American Museum of Natural History. *New York Times.* 5 April 1912.
3. Burroughs. *Pepacton and Other Sketches,* vi.
4. ————. *My Boyhood,* 2–5.
5. Burroughs to Walt Whitman. 12 February 1890. The Charles E. Feinberg Whitman Collection, Manuscript Division, Library of Congress, Washington, DC.
6. Burroughs journal entry. 3 April 1882. Vassar Library Collection.
7. Barrus, Clara. *Our Friend John Burroughs,* 69.
8. Ibid., 64–65.
9. Ibid., 55–56.
10. Burroughs. *The Light of Day,* 5.
11. Burroughs. *My Boyhood,* 34–35.
12. Burroughs. *Locusts and Wild Honey,* 111–12.
13. Barrus, Clara. *Our Friend John Burroughs,* 47.
14. Burroughs journal entry. 7 June 1913. Vassar Library Collection.
15. Barrus, Clara. Notes on Interview with Martin Caswell. 7 October 1907. Berg Collection.
16. Ibid.
17. Burroughs. *My Boyhood,* 7.

Chapter 2: STUDENT & TEACHER

1. Barrus, Clara. *Our Friend John Burroughs,* 17.
2. Barrus, Clara. *John Burroughs, Boy and Man,* 143.
3. Burroughs to Clara Barrus. 10 November 1912. Berg Collection.
4. Barrus, Clara. *Life and Letters of John Burroughs,* vol. 1, 32.
5. Burroughs notebook entry. "J. Burroughs — Olive, May 30, 1854." Berg Collection.

6. Burroughs notebook entry. 12 May 1855. Berg Collection.
7. Burroughs to Curtis Burroughs. Twelve letters dated 7 January 1856 through 12 April 1856. The Henry Huntington Library, San Marino, CA.
8. "Vagaries vs. Spiritualism." *Bloomville Mirror.* 13 May 1856. Berg Collection.
9. Jay Gould notebook in the possession of Kingdon Gould, Jr.
10. Ursula Burroughs to Amanda North. 22 August 1856. The John Burroughs Collection, Clifton Waller Barrett Library, University of Virginia, Charlottesville, VA.

Chapter 3: Myron Benton & Troutbeck

1. Ursula Burroughs to Amanda North. 18 November 1860. Clifton Waller Barrett Library Collection.
2. Burroughs heard the story of Lowell's checking the authorship of "Expression" from Lowell himself more than twenty years later when the two men shared a box at the Madison Square Garden Theater on April 15, 1887, to hear Whitman give his lecture on Lincoln. See Burroughs's journal for Spring, 1887. Berg Collection.
3. Burroughs to Julian Burroughs. 5 October 1901. Berg Collection.
4. Barrus, Clara. *Our Friend John Burroughs,* 129–30.
5. Kaplan, Justin. *Walt Whitman ,* 222.
6. Burroughs. "Analogy." *Knickerbocker Magazine.* (December, 1862).
7. Ursula Burroughs to Burroughs. 15 May 1862. Huntington Library Collection.
8. Burroughs to Ursula Burroughs. 16 June 1862. Huntington Library Collection.
9. Burroughs to Elijah Allen. 26 April 1862. Clifton Waller Barrett Library Collection.
10. Burroughs to Ursula Burroughs. 10 July 1862. Huntington Library Collection.
11. Burroughs to Myron Benton. 12 September 1862. Berg Collection.

12. Benton to Burroughs. 14 August 1862. Berg Collection.
13. Burroughs to Benton. 27 August 1862. Berg Collection.
14. Burroughs to Benton. 12 September 1862. Berg Collection.
15. Springarn, Joel, ed. *John Burroughs at Troutbeck*, 5.
16. Burroughs. "Springs." *Pepacton and Other Sketches*, 44.
17. Springarn, Joel, ed. *John Burroughs at Troutbeck*, 6.
18. Years later, after the turn of the century and the death of Myron Benton, Troutbeck became the home of the literary critic, editor, and NAACP board member Joel Springarn. Springarn's neighbor, the writer Lewis Mumford, remembered that Mulberry Rock remained a popular destination for picnics well into the 1930s. Springarn took to calling it "Burroughs Rock."
19. Burroughs. "The Adirondacks." *Wake-Robin*, 69.
20. Springarn, Joel, ed. *John Burroughs at Troutbeck*, 9–10.
21. Burroughs to Benton. 12 December 1862. Berg Collection.
22. Burroughs to Benton. 7 January 1863. Berg Collection.
23. Burroughs to Benton. 12 April 1863. Berg Collection.
24. Burroughs. "The Return of the Birds." *Wake-Robin*, 1–2.
25. Burroughs to Clara Barrus. 14 November 1916. Huntington Library Collection.
26. E. M. Allen to Burroughs. 5 May 1863. Feinberg Whitman Collection.
27. E. M. Allen to Burroughs. 23 May 1863. Feinberg Whitman Collection.
28. E. H. Allen to Burroughs. 12 September 1863. Feinberg Whitman Collection.
29. Ursula Burroughs to Amanda North. 2 June 1863. Clifton Waller Barrett Library Collection.

Chapter 4: WASHINGTON, WAR, & WHITMAN

1. Burroughs to Clara Barrus. 24 February 1912. Berg Collection.
2. Burroughs to Benton. 27 September 1863. Berg Collection.
3. Burroughs to Ursula Burroughs. 25 October 1863. Berg Collection.

Not used.

4. Burroughs to Ursula Burroughs. 14 November 1863. Berg Collection.
5. Burroughs to Ursula Burroughs. 24 November 1863. Berg Collection.
6. Burroughs to Ursula Burroughs. 6 December 1863. Berg Collection.
7. Burroughs to Ursula Burroughs. 8 January 1864. Berg Collection.
8. Burroughs to Ursula Burroughs. 20 January 1864. Berg Collection.
9. Burroughs to Ursula Burroughs. 31 January 1864. Berg Collection.
10. Burroughs to Ursula Burroughs. 18 February 1864. Berg Collection.
11. Burroughs to Ursula Burroughs. 8 November 1863. Berg Collection.
12. Whitman, Walt. *Specimen Days,* 102.
13. Burroughs to Benton. 19 December 1863. Berg Collection.
14. Burroughs to Benton. 9 January 1864. Berg Collection.
15. Burroughs notebook entry dated 14 December 1865. Berg Collection.
16. Whitman to Burroughs. 12 September 1874. Feinberg Whitman Collection.
17. Burroughs to Benton. 16 January 1864. Berg Collection.
18. Burroughs to Benton. 12 June 1865. Berg Collection.
19. Burroughs to Barrus. 3 September 1907. Berg Collection.
20. Burroughs to Benton. 1 August 1865. Berg Collection.
21. Burroughs to Ursula Burroughs. 10 August 1864. Vassar Library Collection.
22. Burroughs to Walt Whitman. 2 August 1864. Feinberg Whitman Collection.
23. Burroughs to Barrus. 17 December 1909. Berg Collection.
24. Burroughs to Barrus. 11 April 1911. Berg Collection.
25. Burroughs. *Winter Sunshine* ,18–21.

26. Burroughs to Benton. 15 September 1865. Berg Collection.
27. Kaplan, Justin. *Walt Whitman*, 307.
28. Burroughs to Thomas Wentworth Higginson. 12 May 1868. Higginson Papers, Houghton Library, Harvard College, Cambridge, MA.
29. Burroughs to Benton. 11 March 1868. Berg Collection.
30. Burroughs. "Before Genius." *Galaxy.* (April 1868).
31. Higginson to Burroughs. 28 March 1868. Vassar Library Collection.
32. Higginson to Burroughs. 24 April 1868. Vassar Library Collection.
33. Higginson to Burroughs. 10 June 1868. Vassar Library Collection.
34. Burroughs to Lucy Adams. 14 May 1865. Berg Collection.
35. Burroughs journal entry. 4 March 1865. Vassar Library Collection.
36. Burroughs. *Wake-Robin,* 126–56.

Chapter 5: ENGLAND & EMERSON

1. Burroughs to Myron Benton. 14 March 1867. Berg Collection.
2. William Douglas O'Connor to Burroughs. 7 April 1874. Vassar Library Collection.
3. Gurowski, Count Adam. *Diary* (Philadelphia, 1862), 147.
4. Whitman to Burroughs. 12 June 1870. Clifton Waller Barrett Library Collection.
5. Barrus, Clara. *Life and Letters of John Burroughs,* vol. 1., 145–46.
6. Ibid., 212.
7. Burroughs. Introduction to the 1895 edition of *Wake-Robin,* ix–xiv.
8. Burroughs. *Pepacton and Other Sketches,* 114.
9. Burroughs journal entry. 17 August 1863. Berg Collection.
10. Burroughs to Benton. 20 October 1871. Berg Collection.
11. Whitman, Walt. *Democratic Vistas,* 9.
12. Burroughs to John Thompson Trowbridge. 19 March 1868. Higginson Papers.
13. Burroughs to Walt Whitman. 22 October 1871. Feinberg Whitman Collection.

14. Burroughs to Walt Whitman. 3 October 1871. Feinberg Whitman Collection.
15. Burroughs. *Winter Sunshine,* 62.
16. Burroughs. *Winter Sunshine,* 33–50.
17. Burroughs. *Pepacton and Other Sketches,* 167–75.
18. Burroughs to Benton. 14 July 1875. Berg Collection.
19. Burroughs to Benton. 27 January 1872. Berg Collection. Note: All subsequent quotations relating to Emerson's visit to the Washington area come from this letter.
20. Burroughs journal entry. 22 December 1871. Vassar Library Collection.
21. Interview with Jay Gould. *New York Post.* 26 December 1869.
22. Klein, Maury. *The Life and Legend of Jay Gould,* 3.
23. Burroughs to Chauncey Burroughs. 4 November 1871. Berg Collection.
24. Burroughs. *Indoor Studies,* 215.

Chapter 6: RIVERBY

1. Burroughs to Walt Whitman. 12 January 1873. Clifton Waller Barrett Library Collection.
2. Ursula Burroughs to Burroughs. 23 February 1873. Berg Collection.
3. Whitman to Louisa Whitman (his mother). 26 February 1873. Feinberg Whitman Collection.
4. Burroughs to Ursula Burroughs. 2 March 1873. Berg Collection.
5. Burroughs to Edward Dowden. 4 May 1875. Edward Dowden Papers, Trinity College Library, Trinity College, Dublin.
6. Burroughs. *Signs and Seasons,* 183.
7. Burroughs. *Far and Near,* 131.
8. Whitman to Burroughs. 15 September 1873. Berg Collection.
9. Kelley, Elizabeth Burroughs. *John Burroughs, Naturalist,* 9.
10. Burroughs to Richard Watson Gilder. 10 September 1878. Berg Collection.
11. Burroughs. *Signs and Seasons,* 247–63.
12. Ibid., 190.

13. Burroughs to Whitman. 1 May 1874. Feinberg Whitman Collection.
14. Burroughs to Whitman. 7 July 1874. Feinberg Whitman Collection.
15. Burroughs to Myron Benton. 9 June 1874. Berg Collection.
16. Dowden to Burroughs. 12 November 1875. Vassar Library Collection.
17. Burroughs. *Winter Sunshine,* 131–48.
18. Burroughs to Benton. 4 August 1878. Berg Collection.
19. Burroughs to Whitman. 12 May 1874. Feinberg Whitman Collection.
20. Burroughs. *Locusts and Wild Honey,* 9–34.
21. Burroughs. Original manuscript for "The Pastoral Bees." Higginson Papers.
22. Burroughs. *Locusts and Wild Honey,* 66–76.

Chapter 7: IMMERSION IN THE LOCAL

1. Burroughs. *Birds and Poets,* 112.
2. Burroughs journal entry. 18 November 1877. Vassar Library Collection.
3. Burroughs journal entry. 4 December 1882. Vassar Library Collection.
4. Burroughs. *Signs and Seasons,* 1–33.
5. Burroughs to Myron Benton. 5 July 1876. Berg Collection.
6. Burroughs to Walt Whitman. 12 September 1876. Feinberg Whitman Collection.
7. Burroughs to Curtis Burroughs. 14 September 1876. Author's Collection.
8. Burroughs. *Locusts and Wild Honey,* 169–96.
9. Johns, Aaron. Holograph Manuscript. "Camping with John Burroughs." Library of Congress.
10. Burroughs. *Locusts and Wild Honey,* 169–96.
11. Burroughs journal entry. 7 August 1877. Vassar Library Collection.
12. Burroughs. *Riverby,* 32.
13. Edward Carpenter to Walt Whitman. 8 June 1877. Feinberg Whitman Collection.

14. Burroughs journal entry. 17 February 1877. Vassar Library Collection.
15. Whitman to Burroughs. 17 May 1877. Vassar Library Collection.
16. Burroughs to John Thompson Trowbridge. 4 October 1877. Trowbridge Papers, Houghton Library, Harvard College, Cambridge, MA.
17. Carpenter to Burroughs. Vassar Library Collection. 7 June 1877.
18. Benton to Burroughs. 1 June 1877. Berg Collection.
19. Thomas Wentworth Higginson to Burroughs. 12 June 1877. Vassar Library Collection.
20. James Russell Lowell to Burroughs. 10 June 1877. Vassar Library Collection.
21. Burroughs to Benton. 14 June 1877. Berg Collection.
22. Burroughs to Lowell. 18 June 1877. Higginson Papers.

Chapter 8: FATHERHOOD

1. Burroughs to Ursula Burroughs. 1 August 1876. Berg Collection.
2. Burroughs to Edward Dowden. 4 May 1875. Dowden Papers.
3. The story comes from the oral tradition as passed down within the Burroughs family. The direct source here is an interview with Burroughs's great-great-granddaughter (Julian's great-granddaughter) Joan Chamberlin, in 1979. See also the records of Ascension Church, West Park, where, in converting to Episcopalianism and being received into the Church, the mature Julian Burroughs listed a name other than Ursula's as that of his mother. There is no evidence that Julian ever met or corresponded with his natural mother.
4. Burroughs journal entry. 29 January 1878. Vassar Library Collection.
5. Whitman to O'Connor. 7 July 1878. Feinberg Whitman Collection.
6. Barrus, Clara. *Life and Letters of John Burroughs,* vol. 1, 200.
7. Clara Barrus to Julian Burroughs. 10 October 1923. Huntington Library Collection.

328 / JOHN BURROUGHS

8. Benton to Burroughs. 4 November 1878. Berg Collection.
9. Burroughs journal entry. 5 December 1886. Vassar Library Collection.
10. Burroughs to Benton. 12 November 1878. Berg Collection.
11. Burroughs to Benton. 14 November 1878. Berg Collection.
12. Burroughs to Whitman. 24 August 1879. Feinberg Whitman Collection.
13. Burroughs to James T. Fields. 11 October 1881. Higginson Papers.
14. Burroughs journal entry. 10 January 1881. Vassar Library Collection.
15. Burroughs to Julian Burroughs. 20 January 1921. Feinberg Whitman Collection.
16. Burroughs to Benton. 9 February 1879. Berg Collection.
17. Whitman to Burroughs. 19 September 1881. Berg Collection.
18. Whitman to Burroughs. 24 September 1881. Berg Collection.
19. Burroughs journal entry. 28 April–30 April 1882. Vassar Library Collection.
20. Burroughs to Benton. 3 August 1878. Berg Collection.
21. Burroughs to Benton. 6 January 1883. Berg Collection.
22. Burroughs to Eden Burroughs. 26 May 1882. Berg Collection.
23. Burroughs Notebook. 8 June 1882. Vassar Library Collection.
24. Burroughs. *Indoor Studies,* 176–77.
25. Burroughs Notebook. 14 June 1882. Vassar Library Collection.
26. Burroughs to Benton. 5 August 1882. Berg Collection.
27. Burroughs to Clara Barrus. 28 December 1906. Berg Collection.
28. Wilde to Oscar Houghton. 7 August 1882. Huntington Library Collection.
29. Burroughs journal entry. 7 August 1882. Vassar Library Collection.
30. Wilde to Oscar Houghton. 7 August 1882. Huntington Library Collection.
31. Ruskin, John. *The Crown of Wild Olive,* iii–iv.
32. Burroughs to Richard Watson Gilder. 10 August 1882. Feinberg Whitman Collection.

Chapter 9: A Plentiful Country

1. Burroughs journal entry. 27 September 1883. Vassar Library Collection.
2. Burroughs journal entry. 29 September 1883. Vassar Library Collection.
3. Whitman to Horace Traubel. 27 September 1883. Feinberg Whitman Collection.
4. Burroughs to Whitman. 10 October 1883. Feinberg Whitman Collection.
5. Burroughs to Dowden. 5 October 1883. Dowden Papers.
6. Burroughs journal entry. 6 August 1883. Vassar Library Collection.
7. Burroughs journal entry. 7 October 1883. Vassar Library Collection.
8. Burroughs to Whitman. 17 October 1883. Feinberg Whitman Collection.
9. Burroughs journal entry. 19 October 1883. Vassar Library Collection.
10. Burroughs to Benton. 15 December 1883. Berg Collection.
11. Burroughs to Whitman (postcard). 7 December 1883. Feinberg Whitman Collection.
12. Burroughs. *Indoor Studies*, 81–162.
13. Burroughs journal entry. 21 January 1884. Vassar Library Collection.
14. Burroughs journal entry. 24 January 1884. Vassar Library Collection.
15. Burroughs journal entry. 7 April 1884. Vassar Library Collection.
16. Burroughs journal entry. 21 January 1884. Vassar Library Collection.
17. Burroughs journal entry. 22 July 1884. Vassar Library Collection.
18. Burroughs journal entry. 19 December 1886. Vassar Library Collection.
19. Burroughs journal entry. 15 September 1885. Vassar Library Collection.
20. Burroughs to Julian Burroughs. 18 May 1899. Author's Collection.

21. Burroughs. *Riverby*, 33–60. All details of the Slide ascent come from here.

Chapter 10: BARRENNESS

1. Burroughs journal entry. 12 March 1887. Berg Collection.
2. Burroughs's copy of Whitman's round-robin letter to Burroughs, Bucke, Gilder, and others. 27 December 1886. Berg Collection.
3. William Sloane Kennedy journal entry. 17 November 1889. The Beinecke Collection, Yale University Library, New Haven, CT.
4. William Sloane Kennedy to Walt Whitman. 20 December 1890. Beinecke Collection.
5. Burroughs. *Literary Values*, 136.
6. Burroughs to Clara Barrus. 7 March 1906. Berg Collection.
7. Burroughs to Walt Whitman. 31 May 1889. Feinberg Whitman Collection.
8. Higginson to Burroughs. 14 January 1890. Vassar Library Collection.
9. Burroughs to Benton. 4 October 1891. Berg Collection.
10. Burroughs to Hamilton Wright Mabie. 4 April 1890. Beinecke Collection.
11. Burroughs to Myron Benton. 12 October 1888. Berg Collection
12. Burroughs to Ludella Peck. 16 May 1892. Vassar Library Collection.
13. Burroughs to Benton. 23 April 1888. Berg Collection.
14. Burroughs to Whitman. 25 April 1888. Clifton Waller Barrett Library Collection.
15. Burroughs journal entry. 24 July 1888. Berg Collection.
16. Burroughs to Benton. 7 September 1888. Berg Collection.
17. Burroughs journal entry. 27 March 1890. Berg Collection.
18. Burroughs journal entry. 29 April 1893. Vassar Library Collection.
19. Burroughs journal entry. 15 October 1891. Berg Collection.
20. Burroughs to Benton. 1 October 1891. Berg Collection.
21. Burroughs to Benton. 17 January 1893. Berg Collection.

22. Julian Burroughs's diary. 1888–1889. Vassar Library Collection. All Julian Burroughs's diary entries quoted are from this unpaged holograph.
23. Burroughs journal entry. 4 July 1889. Berg Collection.
24. Burroughs journal entry. 27 December 1888. Vassar Library Collection.
25. Kelley. *John Burroughs, Naturalist,* 87–89.
26. Burroughs. *Riverby,* 139–40.
27. Burroughs, Julian. *Memoirs.* Unpaged manuscript and audio tape. Vassar Library Collection.
28. Barrus, Clara. *Life and Letters of John Burroughs,* vol. 1, 330–31.
29. Garland, Hamlin. *Companions on the Trail,* 454–55.
30. Burroughs journal entry. 22 December 1888. Berg Collection.
31. Kelley. *John Burroughs, Naturalist,* 77.
32. Julian Burroughs to Clara Barrus. 12 September 1923. Huntington Library Collection.
33. Burroughs journal entry. 7 March 1889. Berg Collection.
34. Burroughs journal entry. 11 March 1889. Berg Collection.
35. Burroughs journal entry. 3 November 1889. Vassar Library Collection.
36. Burroughs journal entry. 7 December 1889. Vassar Library Collection.
37. Burroughs to Benton. 18 October 1891. Berg Collection.

Chapter 11: WHITMAN LAND

1. Burroughs. *Signs and Seasons,* 201–17.
2. Burroughs journal entry. 15 October 1895. Berg Collection.
3. Burroughs journal entry. 7 August 1877. Vassar Library Collection.
4. Burroughs journal entry. 6 November 1891. Berg Collection.
5. Burroughs journal entry. 24 December 1891. Berg Collection.
6. Burroughs journal entry. 15 January 1892. Berg Collection.
7. Burroughs journal entry. 29 March 1892. Berg Collection.
8. William Sloane Kennedy. Unpaged notebook entry. Spring 1892. Beinecke Collection.
9. Burroughs journal entry. 13 April 1892. Vassar Library Collection.

10. Burroughs. Undated holograph. Berg Collection.
11. Burroughs journal entry. 15 April 1892. Vassar Library Collection.
12. Burroughs journal entry. 7 April 1892. Vassar Library Collection.
13. Burroughs journal entry. 6 April 1892. Vassar Library Collection.
14. Bucke, Richard Maurice. *Man's Moral Nature*, 172.
15. Burroughs to Benton. 10 May 1892. Berg Collection.
16. Burroughs to Clara Barrus. 2 July 1901. Berg Collection.
17. Burroughs. "A Boston Criticism of Whitman." *Poet-Lore.* (August/September 1892).
18. Burroughs journal entry. 1 May 1895. Vassar Library Collection.
19. Burroughs to Mrs. Andrew Carnegie. 10 June 1895. Berg Collection.
20. Burroughs to Benton. 12 December 1897. Berg Collection.
21. Burroughs to Clifton Johnson. 10 December 1896. Berg Collection.
22. Burroughs to Hamlin Garland. 27 December 1896. Vassar Library Collection.
23. Burroughs to Benton. 14 July 1896. Berg Collection.
24. Burroughs to Gilder. 10 September 1896. Berg Collection.
25. Burroughs. "The Poet and the Modern." *Atlantic Monthly.* (October 1886).
26. Burroughs. *Whitman, A Study* , 47.
27. O'Connor to Burroughs. 13 December 1871. Vassar Library Collection.
28. Entry in Burroughs's unpaged journal for November 1896. Vassar Library Collection.
29. Kennedy to Burroughs. 7 December 1896. Vassar Library Collection.
30. Burroughs journal entry. 1 March 1893. Berg Collection.
31. Burroughs journal entry. 25 March 1893. Berg Collection.
32. Burroughs journal entry. 15 February 1896. Vassar Library Collection.
33. Burroughs journal entry. 17 February 1896. Vassar Library Collection.

34. Burroughs to Ludella Peck. 1 March 1896. Vassar Library Collection.
35. Burroughs journal entry. 2 March 1896. Vassar Library Collection.
36. Burroughs lecture notes. 27 November 1893. Beinecke Collection.
37. Burroughs to Gilder. 15 December 1896. Berg Collection.
38. Burroughs lecture notes. 17 December 1896. Beinecke Collection.
39. Burroughs. *Far and Near,* 131–56.
40. Burroughs. *Signs and Seasons,* 201–17.

Chapter 12: THE HARRIMAN EXPEDITION

1. Ward, Lyman. Holograph Manuscript. Author's Collection.
2. Dreiser, Theodore. "A Visit to John Burroughs." *Success Magazine* (September 1898).
3. Burroughs journal entry. 22 June 1896. Vassar Library Collection.
4. Ashton, Lenora Sill. "Visiting John Burroughs." *Audubon Magazine.* (April, 1921).
5. Averall Harriman to E. J. Renehan, Jr., 1 September 1977. Author's Collection.
6. Burroughs to Julian Burroughs. 25 May 1899. Huntington Library Collection.
7. Louis Agassiz to Clara Barrus. 4 September 1912. Berg Collection.
8. Burroughs journal entry. 1 June 1899. Vassar Library Collection.
9. Burroughs to Cordelia Harvey. 29 May 1899. The New York Historical Society, New York, NY.
10. Burroughs. *Far and Near,* 1–130. All Burroughs's descriptions of the Harriman Expedition are from this account.
11. Burroughs to John Muir. 12 September 1899. The John Muir Collection of the College Library, The University of California, Los Angeles, CA.
12. Burroughs to Julian Burroughs. 30 November 1899. Vassar Library Collection.

13. Burroughs to Clara Reed. 15 December 1899. Vassar Library Collection.
14. Burroughs journal entry. 31 December 1899. Vassar Library Collection.

Chapter 13: ENTER CLARA BARRUS

1. Clara Barrus to Burroughs. 4 May 1901. Berg Collection.
2. Burroughs to Clara Barrus. 12 May 1901. Berg Collection.
3. Barrus, Clara. *Life and Letters of John Burroughs*, vol. 2, 12–14.
4. Burroughs to Barrus. 5 December 1901. Berg Collection.
5. Burroughs to Barrus. 12 November 1901. Berg Collection.
6. Burroughs to Barrus. 7 December 1901. Berg Collection.
7. Burroughs journal entry. 2 October 1902. Vassar Library Collection.
8. Burroughs to Barrus. 15 September 1902. The American Literature Collection, Morgan Library, New York, NY.
9. Burroughs to Barrus. 3 April 1902. Berg Collection.
10. Burroughs journal entry. 9 May 1902. Berg Collection.
11. Burroughs journal entry. 12 May 1902. Berg Collection.
12. Burroughs journal entry. 14 May 1902. Berg Collection.
13. Burroughs journal entry. 25 September 1902. Vassar Library Collection.
14. Burroughs journal entry. 10 October 1902. Vassar Library Collection.
15. Burroughs journal entry. 25 November 1902. Vassar Library Collection.
16. Charles Benton to Richard Watson Gilder. 10 December 1902. Huntington Library Collection.
17. Burroughs to Barrus. 2 October 1902. Huntington Library Collection.

Chapter 14: THE NATURE FAKERS & ROOSEVELT

1. Garland, Hamlin. *Companions on the Trail*, 199–221.

2. Burroughs to Julian Burroughs. 31 March 1903. Vassar Library Collection.

3. Burroughs to Garland. 10 June 1903. Author's Collection.

4. Cutright, Paul Russell. *Theodore Roosevelt: The Naturalist,* 131.

5. Roosevelt to Burroughs. 5 March 1903. Vassar Library Collection.

6. Long, Rev. William J. "Animal Surgery." *Outlook.* (September, 1903).

7. Chapman, Frank. "Letter to the Editor." *Science.* (March 4, 1904).

8. Roosevelt to Burroughs. 15 October 1903. Vassar Library Collection.

9. Letter from Jack London. *Collier's Magazine.* (August 1907).

10. Long. "Open Letter to Theodore Roosevelt." *Philadelphia Public Ledger.* 2 June 1907.

11. *Everybody's Magazine.* (September 1907).

12. Upton Sinclair to Burroughs, 27 October 1909. Author's Collection.

13. Roosevelt to Frank Chapman. 4 February 1900. American Museum of Natural History.

14. Burroughs to Theodore Roosevelt. 2 April 1903. Higginson Papers.

15. Burroughs. *Camping and Tramping with Roosevelt* , 7.

16. Burroughs to Julian Burroughs. 15 May 1903. Vassar Library Collection.

17. Roosevelt to Burroughs. 27 February 1903. Huntington Library Collection.

18. Burroughs to Julian Burroughs. 31 March 1903. Vassar Library Collection.

19. Burroughs to Clara Barrus. 1 April 1903. Berg Collection.

20. Burroughs. *Camping and Tramping with Roosevelt,* 9–14.

21. Burroughs to Clara Barrus. 5 April 1903. Berg Collection.

22. Burroughs. *Camping and Tramping with Roosevelt,* 12.

23. Ibid, 28.

24. Burroughs to Julian Burroughs. 17 February 1906. Vassar Library Collection.

Chapter 15: THE GRANDFATHER

1. Burroughs to Clifton Johnson. 12 July 1903. The Morgan Library Collection.
2. Kelley, Elizabeth Burroughs. *John Burroughs's Slabsides*, 52.
3. Barrus, Clara. *Life and Letters of John Burroughs,* vol. 2, 68–70.
4. Burroughs. *Far and Near,* iv.
5. All the toasts, speeches, and poems of the evening were recorded in a 32-page special supplement to the Christmas Issue of *Harper's Weekly* (December 1905).
6. Burroughs journal entry. 6 December 1905. Berg Collection.
7. Burroughs to Clara Barrus. 19 November 1906. Berg Collection.
8. Burroughs to Gilder. 2 November 1906. Gilder Papers, New York Historical Society.
9. Burroughs to Clara Barrus. 19 November 1906. Berg Collection.
10. Whitman to Burroughs. 9 August 1877. Feinberg Whitman Collection.
11. Burroughs. Undated manuscript fragment, Author's Collection.
12. Burroughs to John Thompson Trowbridge. 12 May 1906. Trowbridge Papers.
13. Burroughs journal entry. 15 December 1903. Vassar Library Collection.
14. Burroughs journal entry. 9 January 1897. Vassar Library Collection.
15. Burroughs to Julian Burroughs. 9 August 1907. Vassar Library Collection.
16. Burroughs to Clara Barrus. 17 September 1905. Berg Collection.
17. Kelley. *John Burroughs, Naturalist,* 167.
18. Burroughs to Clara Barrus. 1 April 1903. Berg Collection.
19. Burroughs journal entry. 2 April 1904. Vassar Library Collection.
20. Burroughs to Ursula Burroughs. 10 March 1909. Huntington Library Collection.

21. Burroughs to John Muir. 20 August 1909. Huntington Library Collection.
22. Muir to Burroughs. 27 November 1909. Vassar Library Collection.
23. Burroughs to Muir. 7 December 1909. Huntington Library Collection.
24. Muir to Burroughs. 14 December 1909. Vassar Library Collection.
25. Burroughs to Muir. 31 March 1910. Huntington Library Collection.
26. Muir to Burroughs. 13 July 1910. Vassar Library Collection.

Chapter 16: THE WIDOWER

1. Burroughs journal entry. 3 May 1913. Vassar Library Collection.
2. Burroughs journal entry. 28 June 1913. Berg Collection.
3. Burroughs journal entry. 1 May 1913. Vassar Library Collection.
4. Burroughs to Clara Barrus. 5 June 1913. Berg Collection.
5. Barrus. *Life and Letters of John Burroughs,* vol 2., 280–81.
6. Burroughs journal entry. 12 February 1914. Berg Collection.
7. Barrus. *Our Friend John Burroughs,* 7.
8. Burroughs to Barrus. 25 March 1914. Berg Collection.
9. Barrus. *Our Friend John Burroughs,* 6.
10. Burroughs journal entry. 18 August 1916. Vassar Library Collection.
11. Burroughs journal entry. 11 August 1913. Vassar Library Collection.
12. Burroughs to Barrus. 13 December 1904. Berg Collection.
13. Burroughs. *The Summit of the Years,* 45.
14. Burroughs to Mrs. J. M. Patten. 16 July 1916. New York Historical Society Collection.
15. Furlow Lodge is now owned by Mr. Kingdon Gould, Jr., George Gould's grandson and Jay Gould's great-grandson.
16. Barrus, Clara. *Life and Letters of John Burroughs,* vol. 2, 181.
17. Burroughs. *The Last Harvest,* 3.
18. Burroughs journal entry. 12 November 1916. Vassar Library Collection.

19. Burroughs journal entry. 17 November 1916. Vassar Library Collection.
20. Burroughs journal entry. 18 February 1917. Vassar Library Collection.
21. Burroughs journal entry. 7 March 1917. Vassar Library Collection.
22. Burroughs to Barrus. 14 March 1917. Berg Collection.
23. Burroughs journal entry. 8 March 1917. Vassar Library Collection.
24. Burroughs journal entry. 10 March 1917. Vassar Library Collection.
25. Burroughs to Hamlin Garland. 10 April 1917. Columbia University Library, Columbia University, New York, NY.
26. Burroughs journal entry. 24 October 1917. Vassar Library Collection.
27. Burroughs journal entry. 17 May 1917. Vassar Library Collection.

Chapter 17: THE LAST HARVEST

1. Hamlin Garland journal entry. 15 August 1917. Huntington Library Collection.
2. Garland journal entry. 1 November 1917. Huntington Library Collection.
3. Burroughs journal entry. 14 March 1918. Berg Collection.
4. Burroughs journal entry. 12 April 1918. Berg Collection.
5. Burroughs journal entry. 9 November 1916. Vassar Library Collection.
6. Garland journal entry. 8 January 1919. Huntington.
7. Burroughs journal entry. 21 January 1919. Berg Collection.
8. Garland journal entry. 9 June 1919. Huntington.
9. Garland. *My Friendly Contemporaries,* 254–62.
10. The edition of Bishop Darcy's book still resides in the Library of Holy Cross Monastery. Burroughs's note of 10 June 1918 can be found in Father Huntington's papers, also at the Monastery.

11. Burroughs to Julian Burroughs. 20 September 1919. Berg Collection.
12. Burroughs journal entry. 27 December 1911. Vassar Library Collection.
13. Burroughs journal entry. 16 February 1878. Vassar Library Collection.
14. Burroughs. *Indoor Studies,* 64.
15. Burroughs journal entry. 12 December 1920. Vassar Library Collection.
16. Burroughs. "Under Genial Skies." *Scribner's Magazine.* (October 1920).
17. Burroughs to Hamlin Garland. 4 January 1918. Huntington Library Collection.
18. Burroughs to Julian Burroughs. 17 March 1920. Vassar Library Collection.
19. Kelley. *John Burroughs, Naturalist,* 180.
20. Garland, Hamlin. *My Friendly Contemporaries,* 304–12.
21. Burroughs journal entry. 9 July 1919. Berg Collection.
22. Barrus, Clara. *Life and Letters of John Burroughs,* vol. 2, 391–92.
23. Burroughs to H.S. Ardell. 26 December 1920. American Museum of Natural History.
24. Burroughs journal entry. 27 December 1920. Vassar Library Collection.
25. Burroughs to Judge Talbot. 22 January 1921. Clifton Waller Barrett Library Collection.
26. Burroughs. *The Last Harvest,* 102.
27. Garland. *My Friendly Contemporaries,* 347–50.
28. Garland. Diary. 4 April 1921. Huntington Library Collection.

LIST OF SOURCES

Books and Articles on John Burroughs

Barrus, Clara, ed. *The Heart of Burroughs's Journals.* Boston.
    1928.
Barrus, Clara. *Our Friend John Burroughs.* Boston. 1914.
————. *John Burroughs, Boy and Man.* Boston. 1921.
————. *The Life and Letters of John Burroughs (in two volumes).*
    Boston. 1925.
————. *Whitman and Burroughs, Comrades.* Boston. 1931.
Bergon, Frank. "Burroughs, Literature and Science in the Hudson
    Valley." *The John Burroughs Review,* Number One. April 3,
    1987.
Burroughs, Julian. "A Family Motorboat Cruise with John
    Burroughs." *Country Life in America.* June, 1910.
————. "A Race With the Ebb." *Forest and Stream.* April 10,
    1909.
————. "Boyhood Days with John Burroughs." *The Craftsman.*
    June, July, August, September, 1912.
————. "How I Built My Own Country House." *Country Life in
    America.* February, 1906.
————. "President's Visit to John Burroughs's Log Cabin."
    Leslie's Weekly. July 23, 1903.
Clark, Edward B. "John Burroughs." *Book-Lover.* July/August,
    1903.
Haring, H.A., ed. *The Slabsides Book of John Burroughs.*
    Boston. 1931.
Harte, Walter Blackburn. "Walt Whitman and the Younger

Writers." An interview with Burroughs. *Conservator.* July, 1896.

Hartmann, Sadakichi. "A Visit to John Burroughs." *Century Magazine.* March, 1921.

Johnston, Clifton, ed. *John Burroughs Talks.* Boston. 1922.

Kelley, Elizabeth Burroughs. *John Burroughs, Naturalist.* New York. 1959.

————. *John Burroughs's Slabsides.* West Park, NY: 1987.

Kennedy, William Sloane. *The Real John Burroughs.* New York. 1924.

Kilmer, Joyce. "Interview with John Burroughs." *New York Times.* May 21, 1916.

Mabie, Hamilton Wright. "John Burroughs." *Century Magazine.* August, 1897.

Markham, Edwin. "A Friend of the Fields." *Century Magazine.* May, 1902.

Renehan, E. J., Jr., ed. *A River View and Other Hudson Valley Essays by John Burroughs.* Croton-on-Hudson, NY. 1981.

Renehan, E. J., Jr. "John Burroughs and His River View." *Conservationist.* March/April, 1982.

————. "John Burroughs: Philosopher, Poet, Literary Naturalist." *Conservationist.* January/February, 1987.

————. "Remarks for Slabsides Day." *Wake-Robin, Newsletter of The John Burroughs Association.* November, 1987.

————. "Some Notes on a Native Son." *The Conservationist.* January/February, 1987.

Sharp, Dallas Lore. *The Boy's Life of John Burroughs.* New York. 1927.

Springarn, Joel E., ed. *John Burroughs at Troutbeck.* Troutbeck Leaflets No. 10. Amenia, NY: The Troutbeck Press (Private Printing). Pamphlet. Introduction by Vachel Lindsay.

Stoneback, H. R. "John Burroughs: Regionalist." *The Literature of the Mid-Hudson Valley.* New Paltz, NY. 1973.

————. "The Complete Quest: John Burroughs and Fishing." *The John Burroughs Review,* no. 1. April 3, 1987.

Westbook, Perry. *John Burroughs.* (A Twayne Series Biography). New York. 1974.

Books and Articles (General)

Allen, Gay Wilson. *The Solitary Singer: A Critical Biography of Walt Whitman.* New York. 1967.

Audubon, John James. *Ornithological Biography,* vol.1 Philadelphia. 1831.

———. *Ornithological Biography,* vol. 2. Boston. 1835.

———. *Ornithological Biography,* vols. 3–5. Edinburgh. 1835–1839.

Beebe, William, ed. *The Book of Naturalists.* New York. 1944.

Benton, Charles E. *Troutbeck, A Dutchess County Homestead.* Dutchess County Historical Society, Historical Monograph, no. 1. 1916. (With an introduction by John Burroughs.)

———. "John Burroughs." *Scribner's Monthly.* January, 1877.

Bergon, Frank, ed. *The Wilderness Reader.* New York. 1980.

Bishop, Joseph Bucklin, ed. *Theodore Roosevelt's Letters to His Children.* New York. 1919.

Brooks, Van Wyck. *The Confident Years.* New York. 1952.

———. *The Times of Melville and Whitman.* New York. 1947.

Bruce, Robert V. *The Launching of American Science, 1846–1876.* New York. 1987.

Bucke, Richard M. *Cosmic Consciousness, Revised Edition.* New York. 1969.

Chapman, Frank M. *Autobiography of a Bird-Lover.* New York. 1933.

Conway, Moncure. *Autobiography, Memories, and Experiences.* 2 vols. Boston. 1904.

Cutright, Paul Russell. *Theodore Roosevelt the Naturalist.* New York. 1956.

DeNatale, Douglas. *Two Stones for Every Dirt: The Story of Delaware County, New York.* Fleischmans, New York. 1987.

Doctorow, E. L. *Ragtime.* New York. 1974.

Ellmann, Richard. *Oscar Wilde.* New York. 1988.

Elman, Robert. *First in the Field: America's Pioneering Naturalists.* New York. 1977.

Emerson, Ralph Waldo. *Essays and Lectures.* New York. 1983.

Evers, Alf. *The Catskills, From Wilderness to Woodstock.* Garden City. 1972.

Flagg, Ernest. *Studies in Field and Forest.* Boston. 1857.

———. *The Woods and By-Ways of New England.* Boston. 1872.

Ford, James L. *Forty-Odd Years in the Literary Shop.* New York. 1921.

———. *The Literary Shop, New and Enlarged Edition.* New York. 1899.

Forester, Norman. *Nature in American Literature.* New York. 1923.

Garland, Hamlin. *Afternoon Neighbors.* New York. 1934.

———. *Companions on the Trail.* New York. 1931.

———. *My Friendly Contemporaries.* New York. 1932.

———. *Roadside Meetings.* New York. 1930.

Gilder, Richard Watson. *Authors at Home.* New York. 1902.

———. *The Poems of Richard Watson Gilder.* Boston. 1908.

Gilder, Rosamond, ed. *The Letters of Richard Watson Gilder.* Boston. 1916.

Goetzman, William H., and Kay Sloan. *Looking Far North: The Harriman Expedition to Alaska, 1899.* New York. 1982.

Gould, Jay. *A History of Delaware County.* Bloomville, NY: 1856.

Graham, Frank, Jr. *The Audubon Ark.* Boston. 1991.

Gregory, Henry King. *Biographical Memoir of Henry Fairfield Osborn.* Washington. 1938.

Hicks, Philip Marshall. *The Development of the Natural History Essay in American Literature.* Philadelphia. 1924.

Holloway, Emory. *Whitman: An Interpretation in Narrative.* New York. 1926.

Johnston, John. *Diary Notes of A Visit to Walt Whitman and Some of His Friends in 1890.* London. 1898.

Kaplan, Justin. *Walt Whitman, A Life.* New York. 1980.

Kasson, John F. *Civilizing the Machine: Technology and Republican Values in America, 1776–1900.* New York. 1977.

Kelley, Elizabeth Burroughs. *A History of West Park and Esopus.* Hannacroix, NY 1978.

Klein, Maury. *The Life and Legend of Jay Gould.* Baltimore. 1986.

Lacey, Robert. *Ford: The Man and the Machine.* Boston. 1986.

Lewis, Lloyd, and Henry Justin Smith. *Oscar Wilde Discovers America: 1882.* New York. 1936.

London, Jack. *The Call of the Wild.* New York. 1903.

————. *White Fang.* New York. 1906.

Marks, Alfred H. ed. *The Literature of the Mid-Hudson Valley.* New Paltz, NY 1973.

Marsh, George Perkins. *Man and Nature.* New York. 1864.

Matthiessen, Peter. *Wildlife in America, Revised & Updated Edition.* New York. 1987.

Morrison, Elting, ed. *The Letters of Theodore Roosevelt.* Cambridge. 1952.

Muir, John. *A Thousand Mile Walk to the Gulf.* Boston. 1916.

————. *The Mountains of California.* New York. 1894.

————. *My First Summer in the Sierra.* Boston. 1911.

————. *Our National Parks.* Boston. 1901.

————. *Steep Trails.* Boston. 1918.

————. *The Story of My Boyhood and Youth.* Boston. 1913.

————. *Travels in Alaska.* Boston. 1917.

————. *The Yosemite.* Boston. 1912.

Mumford, Lewis. *The Brown Decades.* New York. 1931.

————. *The Golden Day.* New York. 1926.

————. *Sketches from Life.* Boston. 1982.

Nash, Roderick. *Wilderness and the American Mind, Third Edition.* New Haven. 1982.

O'Connor, William Douglas. "The Carpenter." *Putnam's Magazine.* January, 1868.

Osborn, Henry Fairfield. *Impressions of Great Naturalists: Reminiscences of Darwin, Huxley, Balfour, Cope and Others.* New York. 1924.

————. *The American Museum of Natural History.* New York. 1911.

Packard, Winthrop. *Wild Pastures.* Boston. 1909.

————. *Wildwood Ways.* Boston. 1909.

————. *Wood Wanderings.* Boston. 1910.

Pizer, Donald, ed. *Hamlin Garland's Diaries.* Santa Monica. 1968.

Roosevelt, Theodore. *Hunting Trips of a Ranchman.* New York. 1882.

————. *Theodore Roosevelt, An Autobiography.* New York. 1913.

————. *The Wilderness Hunter.* New York. 1893.

Ruskin, John. *The Crown of Wild Olive.* New York. 1968.

Seton, Ernest Thompson. *Trail of an Artist-Naturalist.* New York. 1941.

Sharp, Dallas Lore. *The Face of the Fields.* Boston. 1911.

————. *The Lay of the Land.* Boston. 1908.

————. *A Watcher in the Woods.* New York. 1903.

————. *The Whole Year Round.* Boston. 1915.

Smith, Herbert. *Richard Watson Gilder.* New York. 1970.

Sylvester, Nathaniel Bartlett. *History of Ulster County, New York.* Kingston, NY 1880.

Torrey, Bradford. *Birds in the Bush.* Boston. 1885.

————. *The Foot-Path Way.* Boston. 1892.

Tracy, Henry Chester. *American Naturalists.* New York. 1930.

Trilling, Lionel. *Matthew Arnold.* New York. 1939.

Van Dyke, John Charles. *The Desert.* New York. 1901.

————. *The Grand Canyon of the Colorado.* New York. 1920.

————. *The Mountain.* New York. 1916.

————. *Nature For Its Own Sake.* New York. 1898.

Whitman, Walt. *Memoranda During the War [&] Death of Abraham Lincoln.* Camden, NJ 1875.

Whitman, Walt. *The Works of Walt Whitman, The Collected Prose,* vol. 2. With a Prefatory Note by Malcolm Cowley. New York. 1968.

Wilson, Alexander. *American Ornithology; or, the Natural History of the Birds of the United States.* Published in 9 volumes. Philadelphia. 1808–1814.

Books by John Burroughs (in order by date of publication)

Notes on Walt Whitman as Poet and Person. New York. 1867. (Second Revised Edition, with "Supplementary Notes" composed mostly by Whitman, 1871).

Wake-Robin. Boston. 1871.

Winter Sunshine. Boston. 1875.

Birds and Poets. Boston. 1877.

Locusts and Wild Honey. Boston. 1879.

Pepacton. Boston. 1881.
Fresh Fields. Boston. 1884.
Signs and Seasons. Boston. 1886.
Indoor Studies. Boston. 1889.
Riverby. Boston. 1894.
Whitman, A Study. Boston. 1896.
The Light of Day. Boston. 1900.
Literary Values. Boston. 1902.
The Life of Audubon. New York. 1902.
Far and Near. Boston. 1904.
Ways of Nature. Boston. 1905.
Bird and Bough. Boston. 1906.
Camping and Tramping with Roosevelt. Boston. 1907.
Leaf and Tendril. Boston. 1908.
Time and Change. Boston. 1912.
The Summit of the Years. Boston. 1913.
The Breath of Life. Boston. 1915.
Under the Apple Trees. Boston. 1916.
Field and Study. Boston. 1919.
Accepting the Universe. Boston. 1920.
Our Vacation Days of 1918. (Photo album and text). Privately
    printed. circa 1920.
Under the Maples. Boston. 1921.
The Last Harvest. Boston. 1922.
My Boyhood (*With a Conclusion by Julian Burroughs*). Garden City.
    1922.

**Important unreclaimed magazine essays/articles/poems by John
Burroughs (in order alphabetically by title)**

"American versus English Criticism." *New York Tribune.*
    April 12, 1876.
"Analogy." *Knickerbocker Magazine.* December, 1862.
"Before Genius." *Galaxy.* April, 1868.
"Boston Criticism of Whitman, A." *Poet-Lore.* August/September,
    1892.
"Broken Banks and Lax Directors." *Century Magazine.* March,
    1882.

"Emerson and Lowell's Views of Whitman." *Conservator.*
     June, 1895.
"Expression." *Atlantic Monthly.* November, 1860.
"Glance into Walt Whitman, A." *Lippincot's Monthly Magazine.*
     June 18, 1893.
"Indirections." *Leader.* July, 1861.
"Letter from John Burroughs." One of many tributes read at a
     public salute to Whitman at Camden, NJ in 1889. The
     proceedings were published as *Camden's Compliment To Walt
     Whitman—May 31, 1889—Notes, Addresses, Letters,
     Telegrams.* Horace Traubel, Editor. Philadelphia. 1889.
"London Adventure, A." *Scribner's Monthly.* May, 1877.
"Mere Egotism." *Lippincot's Monthly Magazine.* February, 1887.
"More About Nature and the Poets." *Appleton's Journal.*
     September 10, 1870.
"More Whitman Characteristics." *Conservator.* November, 1895.
"Mr. Howells's Agreement with Walt Whitman." *Critic.*
     February 6, 1892.
"Myron Benton." *Twentieth Century Review.* May, 1890.
"Nature in Literature." *Critic.* July 16, 1881.
"On a Dictum of Matthew Arnold's." *Atlantic Monthly.* May,
     1897.
"Poet and the Modern, The." *Atlantic Monthly.* October, 1896.
"Poet of Democracy, The." *North American Review.* May, 1892.
"Poet of Grand Physique, A." *Critic.* June 3, 1893.
"Real and Sham Natural History." *Atlantic Monthly.* May, 1903.
"Secret of Whitman's Following, The." *Critic.* March 19, 1898.
"Two Critics of Whitman." *Conservator.* August, 1895.
"Uniformity of Nature Again, The." *Popular Science Monthly.*
     January, 1886.
"Waiting." *Knickerbocker Magazine.* March, 1863.
"Walt Whitman." *Critic.* April 2, 1892.
"Walt Whitman After Death." *Critic.* April 9, 1892.
"Walt Whitman Again." *Conservator.* October, 1895.
"Walt Whitman and His Art." *Poet-Lore.* February, 1894.
"Walt Whitman and His Drum Taps." *Galaxy.* December 1,
     1866.

"Walt Whitman and His Recent Critics." One of two chapters by
Burroughs in the book *In Re Walt Whitman.* Philadelphia.
1893.

"Walt Whitman and the Common People." One of two
chapters by Burroughs in the book *In Re Walt Whitman.*
Philadelphia. 1893.

"Walt Whitman, Poet of Democracy." *Christian Union.* April 2,
1892.

"Walt Whitman's Poetry." *New York Tribune.* April 13, 1876.

"Whitman's Self-Reliance." *Conservator.* November, 1894.

INDEX